EDWARD BLAKE
Irish Nationalist

Edward Blake
Irish Nationalist

A CANADIAN STATESMAN
IN IRISH POLITICS

1892-1907

MARGARET A. BANKS

UNIVERSITY OF TORONTO PRESS

COPYRIGHT ©, CANADA, 1957
UNIVERSITY OF TORONTO PRESS
PRINTED IN CANADA
LONDON: OXFORD UNIVERSITY PRESS

To My

MOTHER AND FATHER

PREFACE

UP TO THE PRESENT time little attention has been given by either Canadian or Irish historians to the Irish career of Edward Blake. Canadian history books, on reaching the point at which Blake broke with the Liberal party in 1891, usually state simply that he entered the British House of Commons as an Irish Nationalist member in the following year, but that he achieved little in this new sphere of activity. Those of Blake's colleagues in the Irish party who were authors as well as politicians have referred in their books to Blake's valuable services to the Irish cause, but even their remarks are brief and give little idea of the full extent of Blake's work. The same is true of more recent writings on Irish history.

Perhaps the principal reason for this neglect has been the difficulty of obtaining access to all the material necessary to make a comprehensive study. It is true that Blake's private papers, which are in Toronto, have been available to scholars for many years. But as valuable as this collection is, it does not give a complete record of Blake's Irish political activities. To supplement it, a perusal of the private papers of Blake's principal colleagues in the Irish party is necessary, for among them are many letters written by Blake, of which there are no copies in the Blake Papers. Since it is only within recent years that the private papers of several of Blake's colleagues have become accessible, it is easy to understand why a complete study of Blake's Irish career could not have been made at an earlier date.

In preparing this book I have been fortunate enough to obtain access to most of the private collections in question, as well as to newspapers of the period during which Blake was an Irish member of the British House of Commons. This, together with such material as is provided in *Hansard* and elsewhere, has rendered it possible for me to make a detailed study of Blake's activities during the fifteen years he spent in Irish politics.

The object of this book is to describe and evaluate, in the light of all the available material, Blake's services to the Irish cause, and thereby to ascertain whether it is true, as is sometimes asserted, that he did not accomplish a great deal.

PREFACE

It is pleasant to record my indebtedness to the many people who have helped me in the preparation of this book. I am grateful to Dr. W. S. Wallace, former Librarian of the University of Toronto; Dr. W. K. Lamb, Dominion Archivist; Dr. G. W. Spragge, Archivist of Ontario; and to those members of the following Canadian libraries and archives who assisted me in any way: the University of Toronto Library; the Ontario Department of Public Records and Archives; the Legislative Library of the Province of Ontario; the Toronto Public Reference Library; the Public Archives of Canada; the Legislative Library of the Province of Quebec; and the Library of the Literary and Historical Society of Quebec.

For facilitating my research in the National Library of Ireland and for permission to quote from the John Redmond and the William O'Brien Papers, I wish to thank Dr. R. J. Hayes, Director of the National Library. My thanks are also due to members of his staff, especially Mr. T. P. O'Neill, who helped me in every possible way. During my visit to Ireland, arrangements were being made to transfer the Redmond Papers from University College, Cork, to the National Library in Dublin, and I owe a special debt of gratitude to Professor Denis Gwynn for sending on to the National Library that portion of the papers in which I was interested before the whole collection was moved. I had a very interesting conversation with the Misses O'Brien, daughters of J. F. X. O'Brien, in Dublin, and I am grateful to Miss A. O'Brien for adding some Blake letters to those of her father's papers which were already in the National Library. To Professor Myles Dillon of Dublin, who gave me access to his father's papers and permission to quote from letters written by his father and mother, I extend my thanks. Grateful acknowledgment is also due to the librarian and other members of the staff of the Royal Irish Academy who afforded me constant and ready help. Dr. F. S. L. Lyons of Trinity College, Dublin, who, in the course of writing the history of the Irish parliamentary party between 1890 and 1910, had examined much of the material which was of interest to me, was able to provide information regarding its location. For this and other assistance I wish to record my indebtedness to him.

For permission to quote from published works I am grateful to Messrs Chatto & Windus Ltd., London (Justin McCarthy and Mrs.

Campbell Praed, *Our Book of Memories*); Messrs Faber & Faber Ltd., London (F. S. L. Lyons, *The Irish Parliamentary Party 1890–1910*); Longmans Green & Company, Toronto, Canadian Agent for Constable & Co., Ltd., London (Algar Thorold, *The Life of Henry Labouchere*), and Macmillan & Company Ltd., London (John Morley, *Recollections*).

Mr. Verschoyle Blake of Toronto, grandson of Edward Blake, has been most kind in supplying information concerning personal and family history which was not available elsewhere. To him and to his sister, Mrs. F. H. Marani, who lent the photograph which is reproduced as the frontispiece of this book, I wish to express my sincere appreciation.

One of my greatest debts is to Professor F. H. Underhill, formerly of the University of Toronto, now Curator of Laurier House, Ottawa, who supervised my research on Blake and whose advice throughout has been invaluable. I am also grateful to Professor T. W. Moody of Trinity College, Dublin, who read the manuscript and offered encouragement and constructive criticism.

The cost of publishing this book is being borne by the University of Toronto Press and the Canadian Social Science Research Council. To both I extend my sincere thanks. I am also indebted to Miss Eleanor Harman, Assistant Director of the Press, for helpful advice, and to Miss Jean Houston and Miss E. Chalmers for their careful editing of the manuscript.

Finally, I wish to express my gratitude to my mother and father whose encouragement and aid in innumerable ways have helped to ensure the completion of this book.

MARGARET A. BANKS

Toronto, 1957

CONTENTS

PREFACE	vii
I. INTRODUCTION	3
II. BLAKE'S ENTRY INTO IRISH POLITICS	11
The Invitation	11
Member for South Longford	20
Early Activities	29
III. THE HOME RULE BILL OF 1893	44
Negotiations	44
First Reading	49
Second Reading	59
The Final Stages	63
IV. BLAKE AND PARTY FINANCE, 1893–4	69
Canadian and American Financial Missions	69
The Tweedmouth Incident	86
V. NATIONALIST DISSENSION AND THE GENERAL ELECTION OF 1895	109
The "Omagh Scandal"	112
VI. THE FINANCIAL RELATIONS COMMISSION	138
The Report	138
The Conference	147
The Debate in Parliament	156
VII. THE IRISH SITUATION AND BLAKE'S RELATIONSHIP TO IT, 1896–7	165
The Irish Race Convention	165
Party Resolutions	177
Blake and Canada	183

CONTENTS

VIII. NATIONALIST REUNION	197
The United Irish League	198
Negotiations for Reunion	206
A United Irish Party	229
The Party and the League	233
IX. IRISH NATIONALIST ACTIVITIES, 1900–2	243
Imperial Issues	243
Payment of Members	252
Protest Against Coercion	259
The League Delegation to America	263
X. BLAKE'S ACTIVITIES CURTAILED, 1903–6	270
The Land Question	275
The Cork Writ	290
Visits to Canada	302
XI. BLAKE'S CLOSING MONTHS IN IRISH POLITICS	309
The Irish Council Bill	309
Retirement	325
XII. CONCLUSION	333
BIBLIOGRAPHY	345
INDEX	355

EDWARD BLAKE
Irish Nationalist

I. INTRODUCTION

IN 1892 Edward Blake, ex-premier of Ontario and former leader of the Liberal party in the Canadian House of Commons, was invited by the Irish parliamentary party to stand for election to the British Parliament. This surprising invitation grew out of the conflicts and pressures of the Irish "home rule" controversy, then a major issue in British politics. The legislative union of 1801 between Great Britain and Ireland had been for a long time a cause of dissatisfaction in the latter country. Schemes for reform demanding anything from some sort of local self-government to complete independence from Great Britain had arisen from time to time, and in 1870, under the leadership of an Irish Protestant lawyer named Isaac Butt, the phase of the struggle known as the home rule movement began. Its avowed aim was to secure by constitutional means the establishment of an Irish legislature with full control over domestic affairs, but the vagueness of the term, home rule, attracted both moderates who sought only to secure Irish control over domestic policy, and radicals who regarded Butt's programme as a first step towards complete separation from Great Britain. Each group thought that its interpretation gave the full meaning of the term, home rule.

The political situation was aggravated by economic, social, and religious grievances. The land problem, in particular, was most serious, for among the landlords, who were for the most part Anglo-Irish or Scottish Protestants, were many who lived in Britain and took little or no interest in their Irish Roman Catholic tenants. Their only object was to draw as much rent as possible, and should they desire to put their property to other uses, it was easy for them to secure the eviction of their tenantry. The Irish land question had, of course, existed long before the legislative union of 1801, but another of Ireland's economic grievances had arisen directly from that union. It was claimed by many financial experts that Ireland, as compared with Great Britain, had to bear an undue share of taxation, an amount far beyond her capacity. Moreover, although the Irish people were predominantly Roman Catholic, adherents to that faith were at a disadvantage in many walks of life. For instance, from the

Catholic point of view the provisions for education, especially at the university level, were unsatisfactory.

While the attainment of home rule was of paramount importance to Butt and his followers, the securing of redress for these economic, social, and religious grievances also formed part of their programme.

Even before the advent of Butt's home rule movement, Britain's great Liberal statesman, William Ewart Gladstone, had recognized the urgency of the Irish question. In 1869, the year after the formation of his first ministry, he had secured the passage through Parliament of a bill providing for the disestablishment and partial disendowment of the Protestant Episcopal Church in Ireland. It was also under his leadership that in the following year an Irish land bill, the first of its kind to intervene between landlord and tenant in the interest of the latter, became law. Although this act fell far short of settling the land question, it was important as a first step towards that distant goal. In the field of educational reform Gladstone was less successful since his Irish university bill of 1873, having failed to satisfy the Irish Catholic clergy, was defeated by a small majority in the House of Commons.

Meanwhile, the home rule movement was making considerable progress. After winning three by-elections in 1871, its adherents went on to establish themselves as a third party in the British House of Commons, electing fifty-seven members in the general election of 1874. For a time, under Butt's leadership, the Irish parliamentary party pursued a moderate course of action, seeking only to persuade the House to inquire into the nature and extent of the Irish demand for home rule. But when the House refused to make such inquiries, some of Butt's followers began to advocate obstructionist tactics. By talking against time they hoped to impede the progress of British legislation until they secured serious consideration for their demand for a legislature of their own. By 1878 this more active policy had gained the support of the majority of the party members, and, two years later, Charles Stewart Parnell, its leading spokesman, was elected chairman of the party.[1]

By this time agrarian distress in Ireland, increased by a series of

[1]After the death of Butt, who opposed obstruction, in 1879, the party was led for a short time by another anti-obstructionist, William Shaw.

bad harvests, had fostered a project known as the "New Departure," which was especially associated with the name of Michael Davitt.[2] Davitt, a member of the violent Irish Republican Brotherhood, generally known as the Fenians, had become convinced by 1878 that what Ireland needed most was an agrarian revolution. It was largely as a result of his efforts and those of certain American Fenians that, in the following year, an Irish National Land League of tenants' interests was formed. Although at first the Irish party had been inclined to oppose Davitt's policy, the fact that Parnell became President of the Land League indicated that there was to be some co-operation between the party and the new organization. Many leading members of the Land League were Fenians; and, indeed, the essence of the "New Departure" was the linking up of the physical force men with the constitutionalists. To achieve this it had been necessary to convince extremists that success might be attained by a vigorous constitutional policy, based upon a land reform campaign.

When the general election of 1880 resulted in the defeat of the Conservative government which had been in office since 1874, the new Liberal ministry, recognizing the urgency of the Irish land question, sought to pass a bill requiring landlords who evicted tenants to pay them "compensation for disturbance." But this bill, having passed the Commons, was overwhelmingly rejected by the House of Lords, and there were immediate outbreaks of violence in Ireland. Property was damaged, cattle maimed, and men murdered. Any person who took land from which its former occupier had been evicted was "boycotted"; tenants refused to deal with or work for him. While the leaders of the Land League appear to have encouraged boycotting, they were opposed to the terrible outrages which were occurring daily.

This agrarian situation led the Liberal government, which re-

[2]Michael Davitt (1846–1906), born Co. Mayo; aged 5 when family evicted and moved to England; aged 11 when as child-worker in Lancashire cotton mill he lost right arm in accident with machinery; joined I.R.B., 1865; sentenced to 15 years penal servitude, 1867; released on ticket-of-leave, 1877; sent back to prison for Land League activities, 1882; M.P. at various times between 1882 and 1899; anti-Parnellite, 1890–1900; helped the Boers, 1900–2; advocate of land nationalization.

mained in power until 1885, to alternate between conciliation and coercion in its policy towards Ireland. One important measure of these years was the Land Act of 1881 which provided for the long demanded "three F's"—fair rent, fixity of tenure, and free sale. Yet this Land Act was greeted with little enthusiasm by Parnell and the majority of his followers, for they feared that the benefits yielded to the tenants would not be very substantial ones.

Indeed, neither conciliation nor coercion proved to be an effective policy in dealing with Ireland, and by 1885 several prominent British politicians were beginning to realize that some attention would have to be paid to the Irish demand for home rule. In that year, Joseph Chamberlain, President of the Board of Trade in the Gladstone cabinet, proposed the establishment of a system of local government in Ireland with a central board in Dublin. While Gladstone supported this proposal, most of his cabinet colleagues opposed it, and before the matter could be carried further, the Liberal government fell from power.

For a time it appeared that the Conservative ministry which now took office would be willing to grant some form of home rule, for Lord Carnarvon, who was known to be friendly to the idea, was appointed Viceroy of Ireland. But it turned out that Carnarvon's colleagues were not as well disposed to the Irish cause as he was, and by 1886 it was abundantly clear that the Liberals (or at least a majority of them) were to be the champions of home rule, while the Conservatives were to oppose it. This came about as a result of Gladstone's conversion, late in 1885, to the principle of home rule— he had now become convinced that even Chamberlain's scheme would be insufficient, and that a form of self-government similar to that demanded by the Irish parliamentary party ought to be established.

By the end of January, 1886, a Liberal government was again in office, and a Home Rule Bill granting Ireland a legislature and executive of its own to deal with local affairs was introduced in the Commons in April. Though the bill met stiff opposition from the Conservatives, and especially from the Ulster Unionists, it was the dissentients in Gladstone's own party who were chiefly responsible for its defeat. Strangely enough, one of the most influential of these dissentients was Joseph Chamberlain, who had long been regarded as a friend of Ireland, but who objected to the type of home rule now proposed. When the bill was defeated on second reading by a majority of thirty votes, Gladstone sought a dissolution and a general election followed. But once again, as in the Commons, the dissentient Liberals, or the Liberal Unionists as they became known, were responsible for Gladstone's defeat. He resigned from office and a Conservative ministry was once more formed.

The Irish situation was now becoming more critical than ever, for not only were the people disappointed at the fate of the Home Rule Bill, but they were also approaching another period of economic distress. As a result of a general fall in the price of agricultural produce, many tenants were unable to pay their rents, and consequently large-scale evictions occurred. As a result a "Plan of Campaign," especially associated with John Dillon[3] and William O'Brien,[4] was adopted. This Plan of Campaign proposed the organization of the tenants of each estate for the protection of their own interests. They were to negotiate as a united body with their landlord, and if he would not agree to a reasonable reduction in their rents, they would decide on what they considered a fair reduction, and pay their rents less this amount to an Irish Nationalist member of Parliament who would hold the money in trust for the landlord until he came to terms. If the landlord, instead of submitting, resorted to eviction, the money paid to the member of Parliament would be used in the defence of the tenants. The many agrarian disturbances which resulted from the Plan of Campaign led the government to adopt a most drastic policy of coercion. Under a Crimes Act passed in 1887, extraordinary powers of arrest and imprisonment were granted the authorities in Ireland. At the same time, however, a bill which was intended to relieve the burdens on Irish tenants by providing for a revision in rents also became law.

Towards the end of 1890, there occurred an event which had far-

[3]John Dillon (1851–1927), qualified as medical doctor and surgeon, but did not practise; M.P., 1880–3, 1885–1918; chairman of anti-Parnellites, 1896–9, and of Irish parliamentary party, 1918.
[4]William O'Brien (1852–1928), born Co. Cork; journalist; M.P. at various times between 1883 and 1918; anti-Parnellite, 1890–1900; founder of United Irish League, 1898.

reaching consequences for Ireland. Parnell, who for ten years had led the Irish party, was named as co-respondent in a divorce suit. At first it appeared that this exposure of his private life would not interfere with his political leadership. Indeed, at the beginning of the parliamentary session in November, 1890, shortly after the uncontested divorce proceedings had taken place, he was re-elected as chairman of the Irish party. But when it was revealed that many British Liberals who had been advocates of home rule would no longer support that cause if Parnell remained its leader, the Irish party felt compelled to reconsider its decision. Pressure from Gladstone, who realized the strength of the Liberal non-conformist demand, brought about the split which now divided the ranks of the Irish party.

After several meetings had been held to consider the question of Parnell's leadership, it was abundantly clear that he was unwilling to resign and that no immediate agreement could be reached between his supporters and opponents. So, on December 6, 1890, Justin McCarthy,[5] the party's vice-chairman, together with forty-five of his colleagues, withdrew from a party meeting, leaving only twenty-eight members to support Parnell. Then, at a gathering of their own, the anti-Parnellites, as the larger group became known, formally deposed Parnell from the leadership and elected Justin McCarthy in his place. The unfortunate divorce action had proved disastrous both to Parnell's career and to the Irish cause, for when Parnell's popularity in Ireland was tested in a by-election held in Kilkenny in December, 1890, his candidate was defeated by an anti-Parnellite by a majority of almost two to one. In two further by-elections in the following year, Parnellite candidates were again defeated. The party was divided against itself.

The real purpose of most of the anti-Parnellites in electing a new chairman had not been to split the party in two, but rather, by their decisive action, to show Parnell that he could not hope to remain leader. It was thought that when he saw this, he might retire voluntarily, at least for a time, and that the party might be reunited

---

[5]Justin McCarthy (1830–1912), born Cork; journalist, novelist, short story writer, historian; M.P., 1879–1900; vice-chairman of Irish parliamentary party, 1880–90; chairman of anti-Parnellites, 1890–6.

under McCarthy or another prominent Nationalist. The accomplishment of this object was, however, rendered very difficult by the Kilkenny by-election and the fierce and vigorous campaign which was being waged against Parnell by a large section of the Irish press and a number of anti-Parnellites, notably Timothy M. Healy,[6] who felt that no compromise with the Parnellites should be attempted.

In spite of these difficulties, two prominent Irish Nationalists, John Dillon and William O'Brien, hoped that a settlement might be reached with Parnell. These men, although they felt that Parnell ought to retire from the leadership at least temporarily, were well fitted to conduct negotiations with him, for, having been in the United States at the time of the split, they had not yet become involved in the factional quarrels which were going on in Ireland. Their meetings with Parnell, held in France a few weeks after the division of the party and known as the Boulogne negotiations, appear to have come very close to success. In the end, however, they had to be abandoned; and Dillon and O'Brien soon became active though moderate members of the anti-Parnellite party.

During the months which followed the Boulogne negotiations, the breach between the two groups of Nationalists widened. Since the National League, founded to replace the Land League which had been suppressed by the government in 1882, remained Parnellite, the anti-Parnellites organized the Irish National Federation in March, 1891. Dublin's *Freeman's Journal*, a leading Nationalist newspaper, also continued to support Parnell, so the *National Press* was started in opposition to it. But, in the summer of 1891, the *Freeman's Journal* changed sides in the political controversy and the *Irish Independent* later became the chief organ of the Parnellite party.

Although, by the summer of 1891, it was clear that the struggle was going very much against Parnell, he continued to fight desperately in an effort to regain his popularity. In doing so, however, he seriously impaired his health, contracting rheumatism which quickly affected his heart. He died on October 6, 1891, at the age of forty-five.

[6]Timothy Michael Healy (1855–1931), born Co. Cork; lawyer, Q.C.; M.P., 1880–1918; anti-Parnellite, 1890–1900; Governor-General of Irish Free State, 1922–7.

The antagonism between the two groups of Irish Nationalists proved too great for a reconciliation even after Parnell's death. On November 7, 1891, John Redmond[7] was elected leader of the party which had remained loyal to Parnell. Some months before the general election of 1892, the anti-Parnellites attempted to bring about an arrangement whereby each party would agree not to run candidates in certain seats likely to be won by the other. But nothing came of this plan or of negotiations with the Parnellites which took place shortly before the opening of the election campaign.

With the Irish Nationalists thus divided, the cause for which they had long been striving seemed lost. Yet each faction continued to seek what even the united party had, up to that time, been unable to obtain, and it was in this situation that the anti-Parnellites invited Edward Blake to join them in their attempt to secure home rule.

[7]John Redmond (1856–1918), born Dublin; lawyer; M.P., 1881–1918; chairman of Parnellites, 1891–1900, and of reunited party, 1900–18.

II. BLAKE'S ENTRY INTO IRISH POLITICS

The Invitation

THE DECISION to invite Edward Blake to enter Irish politics was made at a meeting of the Irish parliamentary party's electoral committee[1] held in Dublin on June 13, 1892. The committee's minute book records it briefly thus: "Hon. Edward Blake, Toronto, to be cabled to and asked to become member of next Parliamentary Party. He could be put forward for South Down."[2] A cable reading, "Irish party unanimously invite you accept Irish seat at general election,"[3] was immediately sent to Blake; he received it in Toronto the same day and cabled the following reply: "Deeply sensible high honor. Fear too old and unfamiliar for service. But if thought anyway useful to great cause would accept safe seat. Could not attempt doubtful or costly contest. Rather difficult start forthwith. Please cable essential points time place character expense."[4]

It was perhaps not surprising that Blake feared himself "too old and unfamiliar for service." He was fifty-eight, not in the best of health, and the distinguished career which lay behind him had been in Canadian, not Irish, politics. Yet he was deeply interested in the Irish cause, for, although an Anglican, he was of southern Irish descent, and his study of history had convinced him that the home

[1]This committee was elected by the party and associated with the chairman in the conduct of the election campaign of 1892. For the resolution setting it up, see John Dillon Papers, Minutes of the Irish parliamentary party, May 26, 1892.
[2]J. F. X. O'Brien Papers, Minutes of the committee conducting the election of 1892. The minutes of the meeting are misdated Monday, June 14; the meeting must have been held on Monday, June 13, since Blake received the invitation on that day.
[3]The cable, dated June 13, 1892, is among the Blake Papers. It is signed by Justin McCarthy, the chairman of the party, and four of the members of the electoral committee: Michael Davitt, John Dillon, Timothy Healy, and William O'Brien.
[4]The copy of this cable in the Blake Papers is undated. It was read, however, at a meeting of the electoral committee held in Dublin on June 15, 1892. See J. F. X. O'Brien Papers, Minutes of the committee conducting the election of 1892.

rule party was justified in its demands. He considered the question of vital importance not only to Ireland, but also to the Empire, and to Canada as a part of the Empire, and for this reason he had more than once encouraged the Canadian Parliament to express sympathy with the Irish cause. In 1882, he had vigorously supported a motion in the Canadian House of Commons in favour of Home Rule for Ireland[5] and, in 1886, when the first Home Rule Bill was before the British Parliament, he had moved an address expressing satisfaction that such a measure had been introduced.[6] At the same time, however, he had declared himself unable to accept certain provisions of this bill, being especially opposed to the exclusion of Irish members from Westminster. But he felt Irish Nationalists should vote for second reading in the hope that satisfactory amendments might be secured in committee.

Blake's convictions as to the justice of the Irish cause had been strengthened by travels in the land of his origin and by meetings with prominent members of the Irish parliamentary party. He had been host to Justin McCarthy during the latter's visit to Toronto in 1886, and in Ireland a year or so later, having gone with some of the Irish Nationalist leaders to witness an eviction, he had expressed sympathy with the sufferings of the tenants. Then, in May, 1888, at a dinner at the Eighty Club, a prominent Liberal organization in London, he had sat beside Parnell who, as guest speaker, delivered an important address on the Irish situation.

Yet another factor tended towards Blake's acceptance of the Irish offer. When he received it, the differences of opinion dividing him from the majority of the members of Canada's Liberal party undoubtedly had made him fear that his usefulness in Canadian public life was over, at least for the time being. So, feeling that, despite his age and unfamiliarity with Irish politics, he might now be of greater

[5]For Blake's speech on this occasion, see *Canada, House of Commons Debates*, XII, 1034–46. It is also printed in a pamphlet entitled "The Irish Question, Hon. Edward Blake's Speech in the House of Commons—1882."

[6]For Blake's proposed address see *Canada, House of Commons Debates*, XXII, 1024. Blake's address was considerably amended and it was only in a weakened form that it passed the House of Commons by a vote of 140 to 6. *Ibid.*, 1143. For the wording of the amended form see *ibid.*, 1097.

service to Ireland than to Canada, it was natural that he should cable his cautious and conditional acceptance of the offer which came to him from Dublin. However, although he knew that it was only the anti-Parnellite or majority group of the Irish party which had "unanimously invited" him to accept a seat, he did not realize that even within this group dissension would soon become acute.

In view of Blake's outstanding ability, the desire of the Irish party to secure his services was indeed natural. Born near Katesville, in the township of Metcalfe,[7] County Middlesex, Upper Canada, on October 13, 1833, Edward Blake was the elder son of William Hume Blake and Catherine Hume, both members of distinguished Irish families, who, following their marriage in 1832, had emigrated to Canada. William Hume Blake had joined the Canadian Bar and had become prominent as a lawyer, reform politician, and judge, attaining the positions of Solicitor-General and Chancellor of Upper Canada. His son, Edward Blake, proved himself a brilliant student both at Upper Canada College, where he was a Governor-General's prizeman, and at the University of Toronto, where he obtained his B.A. with the silver medal in Classics in 1854 and his M.A. in 1858. Throughout his life, he retained a profound interest in his university, becoming its Chancellor in 1876 and an honorary member of its law faculty in 1888. He also contributed largely to the finances of the university, beginning with a small sum in 1876, and founding scholarship funds in 1878, 1888, and 1891.

In 1856 Blake was called to the Bar and in partnership with S. M. Jarvis entered into legal practice in Toronto. Later, with his younger brother, Samuel Hume Blake, he founded a legal firm of which he became the head. As an equity lawyer, he rose rapidly to prominence, and in 1864 he was created a Q.C. by the Governor-General, Viscount Monck. Following Confederation, Blake came to be regarded as one of the foremost authorities on the Canadian constitution. In 1869 he was offered the chancellorship of Ontario and in 1875 the chief justiceship of Canada, but he declined both appointments. In 1858 Blake married Margaret Cronyn, second daughter of the Rt.

[7]Most published accounts state that he was born in the township of Adelaide, but research by his grandson, Mr. Verschoyle Blake, has proved this incorrect.

Rev. Benjamin Cronyn, first Anglican Bishop of Huron. They had seven children, of whom three died in early childhood. Three sons and one daughter survived.

It was only after Confederation that Blake entered political life. In 1867, having been elected as a Liberal to both the Ontario legislature and the federal House of Commons, he was offered the leadership of the opposition in the Ontario legislature, but did not accept the position until 1869. Then, on the defeat of the government in December, 1871, he became Premier of Ontario. When, however, in the following year, the Ontario House of Assembly passed an act prohibiting its members from holding seats in the federal and provincial legislatures at the same time, Blake was compelled to choose between a federal and a provincial career. He decided on the former and consequently had to resign the premiership of the province.

A Liberal administration headed by Alexander Mackenzie was in office at Ottawa from November, 1873, until October, 1878. It was with reluctance that Blake agreed to join it, even as a minister without portfolio. He resigned from the cabinet early in the following year, but returned as Minister of Justice in May, 1875. In this capacity, he was instrumental in establishing a number of important constitutional practices regarding the powers of the Governor-General, about which a controversy with the Colonial Office had arisen. Blake insisted that the prerogative of pardon, as well as the power of disallowing provincial legislation, must not be exercised by the Governor-General independently of his Canadian advisers; these powers, like his others, must be exercised on ministerial advice. He also persuaded the Colonial Office to stop instructing the Governor-General to reserve for the consideration of the British government bills on certain subjects enacted by the Canadian Parliament. In May, 1877, Blake declined a knighthood in recognition of his public services, and, the following month, he resigned the portfolio of justice and took the nominal post of President of the Council. In January, 1878, he once more resigned altogether from the cabinet.

Legal responsibilities and ill health were the reasons which Blake gave for his frequent resignations and general reluctance to hold cabinet office during these years. It was clear, however, that there was another reason, for, when he was out of office between February, 1874, and May, 1875, he advocated reforms which the cabinet and a large part of the Liberal party did not support. These included compulsory voting, extension of the suffrage, representation of minorities, and reform of the Senate. For a time there was a split in Liberal ranks, Blake leading what was known as the Blake or progressive wing of the party, and even after Blake returned to the cabinet, it was clear that he held more radical views than did the majority of his colleagues.

Despite these differences of opinion, Blake's outstanding ability was widely recognized. As early as 1872, he had been offered the leadership of the national Liberal party. It was only after he declined it that Alexander Mackenzie became leader. Following the defeat of the Liberals at the polls in 1878, there was growing discontent with Mackenzie's leadership, and in April, 1880, he was persuaded to resign. Blake was chosen to succeed him and this time did not refuse.

For seven years and through two general elections, Blake led the Liberal party. Since throughout that period the Conservatives were in power, his role was restricted to criticizing the government. One of the principal issues of those years was the government's railway policy, particularly with regard to the Canadian Pacific Railway then under construction. The intricacies of financing the railway appealed to Blake and he made himself master of them, brilliantly criticizing the terms of the government's contract. His financial genius was to be demonstrated again after he became an Irish Nationalist member of the British House of Commons.

In 1887, following the second defeat under his leadership, Blake, discouraged and in ill health, resigned his position as head of the Liberal party and recommended Wilfrid Laurier as his successor. The party caucus accepted Blake's advice and elected Laurier. For two sessions, Blake was absent from Parliament, but in 1889 he returned. However, rumours that he would soon resume the leadership of the party proved to be false and, in the general election of 1891, because he was opposed to one of the principal planks in the Liberal platform, that of unrestricted reciprocity with the United States, he did not even contest a seat. Although he was persuaded to withhold his denunciation of his party's proposed policy until the election was over, it was not surprising that he had little further connection with the Liberal party. In the months which followed the election, an attempt was made within the inner circle of the Liberal party leaders to bring him back to the Liberal ranks, but it was not successful. Thus the offer of an Irish seat in the British House of Commons came to Blake at a time when there seemed to be no immediate prospect of his return to Canadian politics.

Many of Blake's Canadian admirers felt that his outstanding ability might, at this time, be used to better advantage in Ireland than in Canada. Blake was, above all, a constitutional expert, while Canadians in the decades following Confederation were primarily interested in national economic development rather than in constitutional questions. Ireland, on the other hand, was seeking from the British Parliament a home rule measure, the drafting of which would, in fact, be the making of a constitution. On such a matter, Blake, with his detailed first-hand knowledge of the working of self-government in Canada, might give advice of inestimable value. It was for this reason that many Canadians, in newspaper reports or in letters to Blake, expressed the opinion that he should accept the Irish offer. Though stating that his services would be sadly missed in Canada, the majority felt that he would find much greater scope for his talents in the imperial House of Commons. J. S. Willison, editor of the Toronto *Globe*, expressed this opinion in the following words: "Of course I am more anxious to see you return to Canadian politics, but this country is too small for the full play of your abilities."[8]

Others of Blake's correspondents pointed out that his purity of purpose and aspirations towards a higher morality in the conduct of public affairs were simply not appreciated in Canada. This was the opinion of W. T. R. Preston, the general secretary of the Ontario Liberal Association. "The failure of the people of this, your native country, to appreciate your self-sacrificing efforts to stem the torrent of corruption and wrong-doing in high places," he wrote to Blake, "caused you no greater disappointment than it did me."[9] Seeing little likelihood of improvement in the near future, he advised the

[8]Blake Papers, J. S. Willison to Blake, June 14, 1892.
[9]*Ibid.*, W. T. R. Preston to Blake, June 13, 1892.

former Liberal leader to let Canada drift and to go to the assistance of the English Liberals and the Irish Nationalists.

The opinions expressed by Canadians at this time are interesting in showing what was expected of Blake if he agreed to go to Ireland; clearly, it was believed that his role in the struggle for home rule would be no minor one. Many thought that he would reunite and perhaps lead the party which had been split over the question of Parnell's leadership. "Certainly his presence in Ireland at the present crisis of affairs would go far in healing the unfortunate differences of opinion which now prevail in Ireland,"[10] said Mr. P. Boyle, editor of the *Irish Canadian,* when interviewed by a reporter from the *Toronto World.* An Irish Protestant resident of Toronto wrote: "I will say that I feel that you are eminently qualified to . . . step into the breach at the present juncture and lead the Irish party to victory in the establishment of a parliament of their own."[11] And the Hon. David Mills, a prominent Canadian Liberal, well qualified to evaluate Blake's ability, declared, "That he will within a short time become leader of the Irish party is a certainty."[12]

There seems to have been considerable misunderstanding as to the part which an Irish Nationalist could be expected to play in the British House of Commons. Although to remain in power a British government might have to depend on Irish support, it was unlikely that a member of the Irish party would hold a cabinet post, for even if it were offered him, he would undoubtedly reject it. Many Canadians, apparently unaware of this, expected Blake to enter Gladstone's cabinet if the Liberals were victorious in the forthcoming general election. Even David Mills thought that Blake might become not only leader of the home rule party, but also Secretary of State (i.e., Chief Secretary) for Ireland.[13] More than one person interviewed by the *Toronto World* expressed the opinion that Blake would lead not only the Irish party, but also, when Gladstone retired, the British Liberals as well.[14] J. G. A. Creighton, law clerk of the Canadian Senate, sought the position of private

[10]*Toronto World,* June 15, 1892.
[11]Blake Papers, T. E. Robertson to Blake, June 15, 1892.
[12]*Toronto World,* June 16, 1892.
[13]*Ibid.*
[14]*Ibid.,* June 15–16, 1892.

secretary to Blake, assuming that, as a member of Gladstone's cabinet, he would require the services of such a man.[15]

More reasonable was the assumption that Blake, with his wide knowledge of the working of self-government in Canada, would aid Gladstone in the framing of a home rule measure. To do so, he would not have to be a member of the government, for a Liberal cabinet would certainly consult with leading Irish Nationalists about the details of their proposed Home Rule Bill. As a representative of the Irish party, Blake might then offer valuable suggestions based on his practical experience in Canadian politics.

There were, however, some Canadians who recognized the limitations of an Irish Nationalist's role in imperial politics and felt that, if Blake were going to enter the British House of Commons, he should do so as a Liberal. This was the opinion which G. W. Ross, Ontario's Minister of Education, expressed to Blake in the following words: "While it would be quite an honour no doubt to be a representative Home Ruler, I think it would be a greater honour to be a representative Liberal, and as no one can tell what the future may bring forth, in the latter capacity you would have a wider scope and be freer from alliances which might curtail your liberty of action."[16] And the *Toronto World*'s Ottawa correspondent reported that the general opinion in Canada's capital was that Blake would wait until Gladstone requested him to join his ranks before making any decision.[17]

Even some Canadians who were opposed to Gladstone's home rule policy favoured Blake's entry into Irish politics since they felt that his advice might have a moderating effect on it which would save Ireland for the British Empire. One Canadian of Unionist sympathies wrote to Blake as follows: "While unable to accept Mr. Gladstone's policy on the 'Home Rule' question, it is to me no little consolation that a man of your ability and high sense of right will be his coadjutor in determining the course of his party, on, if it be possible, lines that will not endanger the integrity of the Empire. . . ."[18]

[15]Blake Papers, J. G. A. Creighton to Z. Lash, June 20, 1892. Lash was a partner in Blake's law firm.
[16]*Ibid.*, G. W. Ross to Blake, June 18, 1892.
[17]*Toronto World*, June 15, 1892.
[18]Blake Papers, M. Rowan to Blake, June 21, 1892.

More cautious in its predictions was Toronto's Liberal journal, the *Globe*, which pointed out that the acceptance of the Irish offer would mean for the former Liberal leader an enormous sacrifice for the sake of a cause whose immediate success was, to say the least, doubtful. It would entail for Blake a great reduction of his income (for he would have to relinquish his very lucrative law practice in Toronto) together with a serious increase in his expenditure. Furthermore, if the Liberals lost the election, home rule might be indefinitely postponed, and if Gladstone died without achieving what he desired for Ireland, it was not clear what the Liberal attitude would then be to home rule. Even if the Liberals won and Gladstone succeeded in piloting his bill through the House of Commons, it was almost certain to be rejected by the Lords. But if, in spite of this situation, Blake decided to make the necessary sacrifice, his advice would, the *Globe* concluded, be of immense value in the event of a Home Rule Bill's being framed.[19]

While many were sorry that Blake might leave Canada and expressed the hope that, after accomplishing his task in Ireland, he would return to Canadian public life, there were only a few who advised him definitely not to enter imperial politics. One of these wrote to him as follows: "I submit Canada has first claims on you and she is in more need of your services than Ireland."[20] Another of Blake's correspondents, while considering the Irish offer a compliment, was angered at the eagerness with which so many Canadian Liberals were urging him to accept it. Their real object, this gentleman suspected, was to prevent the former Liberal leader's return to Canadian politics, where Blake's best friends considered there was still great and important work for him to do.[21]

But whatever their opinions as to the advisability of Blake's accepting the Irish invitation, his Canadian admirers were united in considering it a great honour both to the man and to his country. Those in sympathy with the Irish cause showed, of course, a special interest. "Home Rulers of all shades of opinion were in transports of delight, this feeling being shared as well by Conservatives as by

[19]*Globe*, Toronto, June 17, 1892.
[20]Blake Papers, William Norris to Blake, June 15, 1892.
[21]*Ibid.*, James Young to Blake, June 18, 1892.

Reformers," reported the *Toronto World*.²² All eagerly awaited the result of Blake's further negotiations with the leaders of the Irish party.

Member for South Longford

Upon receiving Blake's conditional acceptance, the Irish party's electoral committee decided that he should contest South Longford, undoubtedly because it was a safer seat than South Down. But instead of informing him of this decision and replying to his request for particulars, the committee, at a meeting held on June 18, resolved to cable him for a definite reply. Blake's response to this was a further cablegram, accepting once more the invitation provided that a safe seat was found, but also requesting answers to his previous questions.²³ It was not until June 21 that a reply to some of these questions arrived in Toronto; the message, "Longford perfectly safe. Expenses under 300 pounds" was immediately telegraphed to Blake, who had, by this time, gone to his summer home, "Maison Rouge," at Murray Bay, Quebec. The details apparently proved satisfactory, for he replied: "Agreed. Cannot leave forthwith. Cable latest possible date for arrival." On the twenty-second came word that Blake should arrive in Ireland by July 6, whereupon he cabled the Irish leaders, "Sailing Parisian Sunday. Expecting full advice Derry."²⁴

Thus it happened that, less than two weeks after receiving the anti-Parnellite offer, Blake was on his way to Ireland. His decision to accept the invitation had been made with scarcely any hesitation and without consulting either friends or former colleagues in Canada, though, as has been seen, many had written offering advice. Indeed, Blake remarked in a letter to David Mills: "I decided to reach a conclusion on the subject of the Irish telegram without troubling any Toronto friends, only ascertaining the views of my wife on such a heart-wrenching question. . . ."²⁵ Apparently he did not con-

²²For this excerpt, dated June 16, 1892, see the Blake Scrap Books.
²³There is no record of these cablegrams in the Blake Papers, but see J. F. X. O'Brien Papers, Minutes of the committee conducting the election of 1892, meetings held on June 18 and 21, 1892.
²⁴For these cables see the Blake Papers.
²⁵Blake Papers, Blake to David Mills, June 16, 1892.

sult other members of his family, most of whom, according to one of his descendants,²⁶ would have preferred to see him remain in Canada to carry on his law practice, if not to re-enter Canadian politics. But if they were opposed to his going to Ireland, they did not allow their personal feelings to prevent them, in the years which followed, from helping Blake in the home rule struggle. It will be seen in the course of this book that his second son, Edward Francis, and his brother, Samuel Hume, gave much needed assistance in raising funds in Canada for the Irish cause.

When Blake sailed from Quebec for Ireland on Sunday, June 26, he was accompanied by his youngest son, Samuel. Moreover, the *Toronto World*, showing much interest in the former Liberal leader's entrance upon his new career, sent a correspondent to Ireland by the same boat to report on Blake's reception there. This correspondent, H. T. Howard, remained in Ireland until after the South Longford election and his accounts of Blake's speeches and the receptions accorded him by the various factions in Irish politics are of considerable interest and value. These are contained in cables and letters sent from Ireland and in a series of articles entitled "Rambles around Longford" written after Howard's return to Canada.

According to Canadian historians one of Blake's failings as a public man was his aloofness of manner, his inability or want of desire to mix easily with people who were not his intimate friends or fellow-workers. The *World* correspondent's description of Blake's life on shipboard seems to support this contention. Daily life on the "Parisian" was too monotonous to afford scope for much description, Howard reported; he gave the following brief, though enlightening, account of Blake's activities:

> Suffice it to say that Mr. Blake is a regular early riser, that he daily takes his "constitutionals" on the cabin deck, that he has never been known to visit any other part of the ship, that except on rare occasions he "keeps himself to himself," that the affairs of Ireland and the lighter affairs of poetry and the heart, as set forth in the limited Parisian library, occupy much of the statesman's attention. He is abstemious at the table, he does not smoke, nor doth he apply strong waters to his blood.²⁷

---

²⁶His grandson, Mr. Verschoyle Blake, who mentioned the attitude of the family in a conversation with the author.
²⁷*Toronto World*, July 18, 1892.

Nor was Blake anxious, during the voyage, to discuss his views regarding Irish home rule. In the course of Dominion Day celebrations on shipboard he did give a brief address, but it contained no detailed statement of his opinions. He expressed his belief that the Irish cause was one, not of disruption, but of true and cordial union, and declared that he was going to Ireland because he felt it was his duty to answer the call of his fellow-countrymen to assist in a high, glorious, and holy work.[28] Following this speech, the *World* correspondent and several other passengers apparently sought in vain for a more definite statement of his views.[29] In an earlier report, however, Howard claimed that Blake, despite his reticence, had finally given him an outline of his scheme for a settlement of the differences between the two groups of Irish Nationalists.[30]

Blake landed in Ireland in the predominantly Protestant, Unionist north. As he left the "Parisian" at Moville, near Londonderry, "cheer after cheer was raised by the hon. gentleman's fellow-passengers, and these were taken up and emphasized by the Irish compatriots on the tender, which took off the passengers and mails."[31] Blake was met by several prominent priests and by a delegation of Home Rulers, but not by the leaders of the party, who were busy with their election campaigns.[32]

A great deal of activity was crowded into Blake's first few days in Ireland. On July 4, the day of his arrival, he addressed a meeting in Derry, after which he left immediately for Belfast. There, at a conference with some of the Irish leaders, he arranged his Longford platform and the next day returned to Derry to speak in support of Justin McCarthy who was seeking election there. Then he went to Dublin to make further plans for his election campaign.[33]

Blake's first few days were not only active, but also suggestive of his future role in Irish politics. His conception of home rule, together with the contribution he hoped to make towards its achievement, was well expressed in his first speeches; the receptions he was

[28]*Ibid.*, July 19, 1892. See Blake Scrap Books.
[29]*Ibid.*, July 18, 1892.
[30]*Ibid.*, July 5, 1892. See Blake Scrap Books.
[31]*Ibid.*, July 18, 1892. See Blake Scrap Books.
[32]*Ibid.*, July 5, 1892. See Blake Scrap Books.
[33]*Ibid.*, July 22, 1892.

given showed that Irishmen, as well as Canadians, expected his part to be an important one, and finally, the criticism he received from some quarters indicated that the difficulties which had faced him as a public man in Canada might be present to an even greater extent in his new career in Ireland.

At the first meeting which Blake attended in Derry, the Nationalists gave him an address of welcome in which they referred to his glorious career in Canada and thanked him for coming to aid the Irish cause.[34] In the course of his reply, Blake made a statement which he was to repeat many times, both in his speeches and in his private correspondence; he said that he was glad to come to help Ireland in the rank and file of the party. Obviously he expected to play a role quite different from that hoped for by his Canadian admirers, and, as will be seen presently, by many of the Irish leaders. One reason which he gave for his decision to accept the Irish invitation does not seem to have occurred to his admirers. He hoped that his coming might result in a revival of interest in the Irish cause on the other side of the Atlantic where it "had somewhat flagged of late." Like his admirers, he felt that his experience with the working of home rule in Canada might be of some assistance. His speech closed with a warm tribute to Justin McCarthy, the leader of his party, in support of whose candidature in Derry, he was, as already mentioned, to speak at a later meeting.[35] Blake's first speech was widely praised. Even the anti–home rule *Londonderry Sentinel* declared that it was "unquestionably eloquent and powerful," although it went on to say that Blake was advocating "a purely idealistic Home Rule for an idealistic Ireland." Because home rule worked fairly well in Canada was, it claimed, no reason why it should be adopted or would work well in Ireland.[36]

It was thought, at first, that Blake might be elected by acclamation for South Longford, but very soon after his arrival in Ireland it became known that he would have a Unionist opponent. This, however, was not looked upon as a serious obstacle to his election.

[34]Blake Papers, Address of the Nationalists of Derry to Hon. E. Blake.
[35]Blake's first speech at Derry is reported in the *Toronto World*, July 22, 1892.
[36]Quoted *ibid.*

J. P. Farrell, secretary of the Longford branch of the Irish National Federation, reported in a letter to Blake that a Parnellite candidate was also threatened, but that this threat was not taken seriously.[37] This opinion was shared by the *World* correspondent who declared in a cable dispatch of July 5 that he considered the appearance of a Parnellite candidate unlikely since Blake had so far received a warm welcome from both sides.[38]

Howard's account of the plans made for Blake during the election campaign give some idea of what the Irish leaders expected of their new recruit. He was to spend very little time in his own constituency where his election was considered certain, but instead was to make a rapid tour through several doubtful constituencies to speak for home rule without any reference to individuals whether anti-Parnellite or Parnellite. It was deemed best, the *World* correspondent reported, to keep him apart from the differences which divided the Irish Nationalists.[39] If the Irish leaders took this attitude, they, like so many Canadians, must have had the idea that Blake would be able to reunite the warring factions. It would appear that they expected him to be a leader, rather than a rank-and-file member, of the party.

The custom of holding elections throughout the entire country on one day had not yet been adopted in Great Britain and Ireland; in 1892, polling took place in some constituencies as early as July 4, in others as much as three weeks later. Polling day in South Longford was set for July 13, nomination day for July 7. Blake did not arrive there until the ninth, but at the suggestion of J. P. Farrell[40] he sent from Dublin on July 7 an address to the electors, which was immediately printed and published in the constituency. In this address, Blake gave very clear expression to his views on home rule; his ideal was a federal system, similar to Canada's, with provincial legislatures for each of the divisions of the United Kingdom and a central parliament to deal with matters common to all. He expressed his views thus:

[37]Blake Papers, J. P. Farrell to Blake, July 6, 1892.
[38]*Toronto World*, July 6, 1892. See Blake Scrap Books.
[39]*Ibid.*
[40]Blake Papers, J. P. Farrell to Blake, July 6, 1892.

I wish for Ireland a local Legislature with efficient powers for the regulation of her local affairs; and for the United Kingdom a supreme Parliament for the management of Common and Imperial concerns.

I think that in the Imperial Parliament Ireland should be duly represented; and that the great divisions of Britain should receive, as early as they will accept them, the same benefits as Ireland will derive from Home Rule, by the remission of local concerns to local bodies, and the relief of the Imperial Parliament from its intolerable burden.

Pending the realization of these hopes, provision may be made, which, though open to obvious objections and failing to satisfy all the conditions of completeness and efficiency, shall yet improve the present position, and assure without delay the thing imperatively needful, the Irish settlement.

Among the common concerns of the United Kingdom I place legislation on Trade and Commerce, including duties of customs and excise.

Among local affairs I place legislation on the land.

Elaborating his views on the land question, Blake expressed the opinion that most of the tenant occupiers of Irish farms should obtain the right, on fair terms, to become their proprietors. He also favoured moving the surplus population in the congested districts to other parts of Ireland. To bring about these ends, he felt that compulsory powers of purchase and the credit of the state should, so far as necessary, be employed, and that these questions should be considered when a Home Rule Bill was being prepared.[41]

It was clear that the type of home rule advocated by Blake for Ireland was not identical with that which existed in Canada. The latter had no representatives in the Imperial Parliament, while Ireland, under Blake's scheme, would have such representation. That Blake should favour the inclusion of Irish representatives at Westminster was not surprising, for he had once been strongly attracted by the idea of an imperial parliamentary federation of all the self-governing countries in the British Empire. It was only because he felt that such a scheme was impracticable that he had come to oppose it. Since, however, he realized that the federation of the British Isles would not involve the difficulties which would be encountered in establishing imperial federation, he favoured the former plan. There were, therefore, two aspects of Canadian government which provided Blake with examples for the Irish scheme. First, although Canadian home rule was not identical with what Blake desired for Ireland, it

[41]For the full text of Blake's address to the electors of South Longford see the Blake Papers.

provided a useful example since Canada was free to govern herself in all but imperial matters. Secondly, Canada's seven provinces, each with a local legislature to deal with local affairs, but united by the federal Parliament at Ottawa which legislated in matters of concern to all, provided a model for the federation of the British Isles.

When Blake arrived in Longford on July 9, he received an enthusiastic welcome. Quite a royal procession, H. T. Howard reported, accompanied him to the Stafford Hotel, where he was given an address of welcome. The Blake who that day spoke at Longford appears, from Howard's account, to have been a different person from the quiet, reserved gentleman on shipboard. "Perched on a chair, with his head and shoulders projecting from the upraised window, Mr. Blake made his first speech to the electors of South Longford."[42] "I am for Home Rule in Canada and I am for Home Rule in Ireland," he declared, "and I have come across the broad Atlantic to lend what aid I can to your glorious cause and to achieve this Home Rule."

It has been seen that many people expected Blake to reunite the two sections of the Irish Nationalist party. That he ardently desired such a reunion was also certain; yet some of his remarks on the subject in the course of this first speech in Longford were not calculated to please the Parnellite members of his audience. Here is what Blake said, together with the reaction of his audience, as reported by the *World* correspondent:

> I will not say a word to increase the bitterness of faction which unfortunately exists, for I grieve over the occasion of this breach; for I can sympathize to a great extent with those who have such a personal devotion to the great man, Charles Stewart Parnell, who had been their courageous leader, but who had fallen. (Parnellite dissent and Nationalist cheers.) I will only say that I think their devotion to Mr. Parnell has misled them, and I say it decidedly, yet impassionately, that the voice of the majority of the Irish members ought to be respected. (Renewed cheers and dissent.)

Blake followed these words with a dramatic appeal for union: "Let us be united—Ireland ! our cry; Home Rule our purpose. . . . "Therefore I appeal to you all to shake hands, to bridge the bloody chasm, to remember that it is not any one man's cause, but the cause of

[42]*Toronto World*, July 22, 1892.

old Ireland we are advocating. Let us therefore sink minor differences, work together as one man, and may God save Ireland."[43]

The next day, Sunday, July 10, a huge open-air meeting was held at Kenagh, one of the chief polling places in South Longford. Blake went there, it was believed, because many of its residents were Parnellites, who were thought to be hostile to him not only because he was a McCarthyite candidate, but also because he was an imported Protestant "foreigner."[44] Yet the meeting was a great success. "It was admitted," declared H. T. Howard, "that Longford had never seen such a gathering."[45] As Blake's carriage came into sight, "the bands played their loudest, cheer followed cheer, and many went forth to meet the hero of the day. No royal conqueror could have had a better or more hearty reception."[46]

Many of Blake's remarks were similar to those made on previous occasions, but, in addition, he sought to prove that he was not a foreigner. Declaring himself an Irishman first and last, he told the people of his ancestry. His father came from Galway, his mother from County Wicklow. The Humes of Wicklow had represented the district for three generations. Moreover, Blake's wife was connected with the constituency in which he was offering himself as a candidate, for, while her father was a native of Kilkenny, her mother came from County Longford in the neighbourhood of Kenagh.[47]

Meanwhile, on July 7, voting in Derry had resulted in the defeat of Justin McCarthy. Therefore, Timothy Healy, who had already been elected for North Longford, resigned his seat so that McCarthy could contest it. Healy was subsequently elected for North Louth. On July 12, the day after Blake's Kenagh meeting, McCarthy was to be nominated for North Longford. Because of illness, the Nationalist leader could not attend the meeting, but Healy and Blake went to Granard to speak in support of his candidature. In the course of his address Healy referred to Blake as "the Gladstone of Canada,"[48]

[43] *Ibid.*
[44] *Ibid.*, Aug. 8, 1892.
[45] *Ibid.*, July 11, 1892. See Blake Scrap Books.
[46] *Ibid.*, Aug. 8, 1892.
[47] *Ibid.*
[48] *Ibid.*, Aug. 11, 1892.

and the *World* correspondent reported that the ovation Blake received exceeded that accorded him in South Longford. Some people even expressed the wish that North instead of South Longford had been chosen as the Canadian stateman's safe seat. One old Irish farmer told the reporter that Blake reminded him of Daniel O'Connell, the leader of the repeal movement in the 1840's.[49]

Blake's popularity among the Parnellites of South Longford was not increased, however, by his taking part in McCarthy's nomination meeting. While continuing to assert that a native of the county should represent South Longford, they also began to complain that Blake was altogether too sure of his election and was spending too little time in the constituency. There was also criticism from another quarter, for Blake had offended the Protestants of the county by taking part in the Sunday political meeting at Kenagh.[50] Such discontent increased when Blake spent polling day not in Longford, but in Dublin. Howard reported that there was undoubtedly a cooler feeling arising towards the candidate. He went on:

> The people are somewhat unreasonable. They expected Mr. Blake to spend his whole time here, although to have done so would have been pure waste when his services are so much needed elsewhere.... The general comment is that he is too stiff for the boys. They would like a man hail-fellow-well-met. That Mr. Blake can never bring himself to be.[51]

In spite of this, Blake defeated G. H. Millar, his Unionist opponent in South Longford by a large majority, receiving 2,544 votes to the latter's 347. The Parnellites, having no candidate of their own, abstained from voting. Howard reported that even Blake's supporters were a little annoyed that their newly elected member was still in Dublin when the poll was declared. He mentioned this when he met Blake in Dublin, but found that "it did not seem to have occurred to him." The Canadian statesman was, however, quite jubilant over the result of the polling.[52]

Irish Nationalists showed considerable interest in Blake's election. One Longford man wrote to him, presumably about this time, saying

---

[49]*Ibid.*, Aug. 12, 1892.
[50]*Ibid.*, July 13, 1892. See Blake Scrap Books.
[51]*Ibid.*, July 14, 1892.
[52]*Ibid.*, July 15, 1892. See Blake Scrap Books.

that he expected Blake to be Ireland's first Prime Minister under home rule.[53] From Canada too letters and cablegrams of congratulation poured in upon the former Liberal leader. There were also messages from Canadians then living in England and from Englishmen who had previously spent some time in Canada. British Liberals were evidently also interested in the Canadian statesman's entrance into imperial politics, for in addition to letters of congratulation Blake received several requests for photographs and interviews from British newspapers and was soon to be showered with requests to address meetings in Britain.

So, with the election over and Blake the member for South Longford, it remained to be seen how the role he played would compare with that predicted for him by many of his admirers.

Early Activities

The general election of 1892 gave no one party a clear majority of seats in the House of Commons. Liberals won 273; Conservatives, 269; Liberal Unionists, 46; anti-Parnellites, 72; Parnellites, 9; and Independent Labour, 1. Of these members, 355 supported the Irish demand for home rule while 315 opposed it. Gladstone would, therefore, with the aid of the Irish members, have a majority of 40 seats.

The Salisbury government did not resign when the election results became known, but instead decided to meet the new House of Commons when Parliament assembled on August 4. Thus it was not until the government's defeat on an amendment to the address that Salisbury resigned and Gladstone once more became Prime Minister. And since Parliament adjourned on August 19 to enable the newly appointed cabinet ministers to seek re-election and no autumn session was held, it was not until early in 1893 that a Home Rule Bill was introduced.

Though Blake did not speak in Parliament during the short session of August, 1892, he was kept fully occupied. At the time of the split in Irish Nationalist ranks, the anti-Parnellites had decided that a committee should be associated with the chairman in the

[53]Blake Papers, Peter Monahan to Blake, n.d.

management of their party to prevent him from exercising the autocratic powers that Parnell had enjoyed. The chairman and committee were elected at the beginning of each parliamentary session. On August 4, 1892, at its sessional meeting in London, the anti-Parnellite party elected Blake to this committee,[54] thereby showing its confidence in his ability and its desire that he should take a place among its leaders.

Even before the opening of Parliament, leading British Liberals were showing considerable interest in the newly elected member for South Longford. On July 27, James Bryce, who was to become Chancellor of the Duchy of Lancaster in the Gladstone cabinet, wrote inviting Blake to discuss the Irish situation with him privately. At the same time he expressed the desire that Gladstone should have the opportunity of talking with Blake about Ireland and thereby learning his views. To afford such an opportunity, Bryce invited Blake to dinner with Gladstone.[55] The member for South Longford apparently agreed to both these proposals, for, in a letter of July 28, Bryce acknowledged Blake's acceptance of the invitations.[56]

Then the day Parliament opened, Blake was guest speaker at a dinner at the Eighty Club. On this occasion he spoke of the Irish question with special reference to home rule in Canada, but began by insisting once more that his role in Irish politics must be a minor one. He described himself as "a mere private in the ranks, a raw recruit—nay worse, a soldier who has learned the drill of another manual, who has been trained to a different service, and whose first work must be to unlearn much in order that he may be able to learn more."

In describing the stages of development in establishing home rule in Canada, Blake explained that first representative government without a responsible executive had been granted. Following this, the demand that the executive should be responsible to the elected branch of the legislature was satisfied, but only after a second mistake had been made, that of creating a legislative union between Upper and Lower Canada. This legislative union, like the existing

[54]Dillon Papers, Minutes of the Irish parliamentary party, Aug. 4, 1892.
[55]Blake Papers, James Bryce to Blake, July 27, 1892.
[56]*Ibid.*, Bryce to Blake, July 28, 1892.

one between Britain and Ireland, had not worked well; it had therefore been abandoned in favour of a federal system. Blake described this change and the results which followed, pointing out the benefits of federation which he hoped would some day be enjoyed in the British Isles.

> In the end, after twenty-five years' trial, we decided to abandon it, substituting Federal for Legislative Union; in a word we restored Home Rule in local matters to each province, and formed a Union limited to their common concerns. The results, though they have not in all respects answered some high expectations, have yet fully justified the advocates of the principle of Home Rule. . . .
>
> The relations of hostility and suspicion, jealousy and opposition, which were most conspicuous as between the two provinces, ill-joined in a legislative union, have now largely disappeared. Each feels secure in the possession of its conceded local freedoms and powers. Each agrees that the great principle of domestic control over local affairs and joint regulation of common concerns has been the true solvent of our cardinal difficulty; each, being allowed to manage its own, is content to be united with the other for the disposition of joint affairs. . . .[57]

This address attracted much attention in political circles, and was warmly praised by the Liberal and Nationalist press. The *Pall Mall Gazette* declared that Blake's statement of Canada's experiences in the working of home rule was a most important contribution to the subject,[58] while the *Eastern Daily Press*, Norwich, felt that if a slight allowance were made for transatlantic differences of manner, the speech was worthy in every way of the orator and the theme.[59] The *Freeman's Journal*, in its issue of August 5, described the address as "moderate, forcible and eloquent—an appeal to the reason and good sense of all classes of Irishmen," and added that it "cannot but influence very materially the public opinion of England on the Irish question."

There was, of course, some criticism from the Unionist press. *The Times* declared that Blake had no real acquaintance with the problem which he purported to treat, while the *Irish Times* claimed that he betrayed the utmost ignorance of Irish parties, social distinctions,

---

[57]Blake's speech is published in a pamphlet entitled "The Irish Question with special reference to Home Rule in Canada" (London, 1892). The foregoing quotations are from pp. 13 and 21–2.
[58]Quoted in *Toronto World*, Aug. 6, 1892.
[59]For this excerpt, dated Aug. 6, 1892, see the Blake Scrap Books.

religious differences, and of the Irish problem in general.⁶⁰ Nor was Dublin's Parnellite journal, the *Irish Independent*, complimentary in its comments. In an editorial published on August 5, it declared that Blake had told of the evils which had sprung from piecemeal concessions of autonomous rights in Canada, but was willing to accept any inadequate scheme of home rule Gladstone might offer.

Some surprise was also felt that Blake, in delivering his address, had followed his manuscript so closely.⁶¹ More than one newspaper which praised the subject matter of the speech remarked that Blake had read a carefully prepared essay.⁶² In a letter to Laurier, his successor in the leadership of Canada's Liberal party, Blake explained why he had done so and also gave his opinion regarding the press comments on his speech. "My speech at the Eighty Club was far the most difficult job I ever attempted, and I thought it better to weigh every word. I was conscious of the adverse criticism that would be evoked by such close reference to manuscript. But I believed this the lesser of two evils, and that it was better to give up form to the critics than substance. I have seen but little attempt to find fault with the substance, and the speech has given very general satisfaction in many quarters...."⁶³

Blake's activities in England in the days following his address at the Eighty Club were varied; his services appear to have been in constant demand. On August 11, he addressed a meeting of the Home Rule Union in London. Then, on the fifteenth, he went to Newcastle to speak in support of John Morley, the Chief Secretary for Ireland, who was seeking election there.⁶⁴ Morley, the only member of the newly appointed cabinet who was not re-elected without opposition, won this by-election on August 25.

By this time dissension within the anti-Parnellite party was becoming acute. An attempt was being made to amalgamate two of its newspapers, the *Freeman's Journal* and the *National Press*, but no

⁶⁰For these excerpts, dated Aug. 5 and 6, 1892, respectively, see *ibid*.
⁶¹*Toronto World*, Aug. 6, 1892. See Blake Scrap Books.
⁶²Two newspapers which took this attitude were the *Whitehall Review*, Aug. 6, 1892, and the *Bradford Observer*, Aug. 6, 1892. For their comments see the Blake Scrap Books.
⁶³Sir Wilfrid Laurier Papers, Blake to Laurier, Aug. 31, 1892.
⁶⁴For press reports of the foregoing meetings see the Blake Scrap Books.

agreement could be reached about the composition of the newspaper's board of directors. Another dispute concerned the Paris funds, a sum of money which, in the days when Parnell still led a united Irish party, had been lodged with an American firm of bankers in Paris as a precautionary measure in case of the National League's being declared illegal and its money confiscated by the British government. Some arrangement had now to be reached as to whether these funds were to be divided between the Parnellites and anti-Parnellites. McCarthy, Dillon, and some of their followers desired a peaceful settlement with the Parnellites, while other members of the party, notably Healy, wished to fight it out to the bitter end. In December, 1892, this dispute almost caused an open split in anti-Parnellite ranks.

That Blake, very early in his Irish career, was becoming discouraged with this situation can be seen from a report of a conversation which took place on August 23 between Justin McCarthy and his literary colleague, Mrs. Campbell Praed. Speaking of the wranglings among the members of his party, McCarthy appeared especially low-spirited about the effects they would have upon their Canadian ally, who had told him that, had he realized the constant internecine warfare among prominent Nationalists, he would not have left his home in Canada to come over to serve Ireland. McCarthy told Mrs. Praed that he feared Blake "might throw up the whole business in open dissatisfaction." The anti-Parnellite leader felt that, at a time when Gladstone was ready to prepare a new Home Rule Bill, this would be one of the worst things that could possibly befall the Irish cause.[65] From Blake's correspondence it appears, however, that although he did not plan a long career in Irish politics, he had no intention of withdrawing at this time. Writing to Laurier of the struggle for home rule he declared: "There are many drawbacks, difficulties, and doubts; and there is much to dishearten; indeed I fear that I shall be kept a year longer than I expected, or say three years, before getting free of my commission and returning to home and friends."[66]

[65] Justin McCarthy and Mrs. Campbell Praed, *Our Book of Memories* (London, 1912), 328.
[66] Laurier Papers, Blake to Laurier, Aug. 31, 1892.

Meanwhile, on August 18, Blake had sailed for Canada on a trip which was to be more than a family visit. Hoping as he did that his entry into Irish politics might help revive interest in the home rule cause on the other side of the Atlantic, he did all in his power, in the weeks which followed, to secure from Canadians financial aid towards it. He also tried, on visits to the United States, to promote better understanding between Irish-Americans and the leaders of the parliamentary party in Ireland.

On the evening of September 19, a huge reception was tendered Blake at the Horticultural Pavilion in Toronto.[67] Other Canadian cities, including Montreal and Ottawa, requested the former Liberal leader to address meetings, but the brevity of his visit to Canada forced him to decline these invitations. That the public appeal to Canadians which he made at the Toronto meeting met with considerable response can be seen from a letter which he wrote three weeks later to Justin McCarthy, telling him that a subscription had been started with his brother, the Hon. S. H. Blake, and Senator Frank Smith, a Roman Catholic Conservative, as joint honorary treasurers. Five names, Blake reported to McCarthy, were down for a total of $6,000.

In the same letter, Blake explained to the leader of his party, the Canadian attitude towards home rule: "You are probably aware that a very large proportion of the English speaking and Protestant supporters of the Canadian Conservative party is Orange, and even where not Orange, anti-Home Rule. It is only by means of the almost unanimous support accorded by the Roman Catholic English speaking Conservatives and the French Conservatives that I am able to claim a majority of Conservatives for the cause. On the other hand, the Liberals of all origins and creeds are practically unanimous for Home Rule." Blake was happy to be able to report that since his entry into Irish politics, many Canadians who had previously sympathized with the Parnellites were now willing to support the majority party: "One most gratifying circumstance is, that since I accepted your invitation, and more particularly since the people here

---

[67]Blake's speech is published in a pamphlet entitled "The Blake Demonstration, Pavilion, September 19, 1892." For a copy of the pamphlet, together with press reports of the meeting, see the Blake Scrap Books.

observed the line I took with reference to the schism, it has almost disappeared in Canada. So at least it is reported to me, and amongst others by men who had previously been strong Parnellites. I do not say that all everywhere have changed; but I am sure the great majority have; and I entertain a strong hope that time will complete the cure. . . ."[68]

Blake was also invited to address meetings in the United States under the auspices of the Irish National Federation of America, an organization founded to aid the home rule movement in Ireland. In the end, he spoke only at Boston where the mayor, in the course of introducing him, declared that Blake had been "paid the compliment, unprecedented in the history of politics, of being called from one country to represent another in the parliament of a third."[69] Before sailing for England on November 2, Blake also met privately in New York with prominent members of the Irish National Federation of America, including its president, Dr. T. A. Emmet. With them he discussed the work of their organization in aiding the Irish cause.

A meeting of the parliamentary committee of the Irish party was held on November 13, followed by a general meeting of the party on the fourteenth. Since Blake was scheduled to speak at Bristol on the latter date[70] he was unable to attend either of these meetings, but he sent to McCarthy an interesting and detailed account of his work in the United States, explaining in particular the attitude of the National Federation of America to the Irish parliamentary party. He stated that at the Boston meeting he had attempted to vindicate the position of the Nationalist party firmly, yet without giving offence to any honest man of Parnellite sympathies. He was assured

[68]Blake Papers, Blake to Justin McCarthy, Oct. 11, 1892.
[69]Quoted in *Globe*, Toronto, Oct. 29, 1892, from the *Boston Post*. Many reports of the meeting from Boston newspapers are included in the Blake Scrap Books.
[70]After his return from Canada Blake was invited to speak in favour of home rule in many English cities under the auspices of either local Liberal associations or the Irish National League of Great Britain. Although so much public speaking must have been a severe strain upon him, he agreed, for he realized the importance of popularizing the Irish cause in England. For press clippings regarding Blake's meetings in England between Nov., 1892, and Jan., 1893, see the Blake Scrap Books.

that in Boston there were now comparatively few Parnellites and that the general impression produced by his speech was very favourable.

Regarding his interview with Dr. Emmet and his friends in New York, Blake reported their annoyance that the National Federation of America had received no official acknowledgment of funds sent to the Irish parliamentary party. Blake strongly advised the party to give due recognition to the American organization: "The National Federation of America is the only available organization by which you can raise funds or work the movement. It should be acknowledged, recognized, *magnified*, by the people at home." He therefore suggested that the Irish National Federation should pass a resolution of warm thanks for the National Federation of America and appeal to it to renew its efforts to aid the Irish cause. He also recommended that some person or persons should be appointed as a corresponding committee to keep the executive of the National Federation of America in touch with the policy of the party.[71]

Illness prevented McCarthy from going to Dublin for the committee meeting on the thirteenth, but Dillon assured Blake that if the meeting were held in McCarthy's absence he himself would see that Blake's advice on American affairs was carried out.[72] It is clear that at least one of Blake's suggestions was accepted, for in a letter to Dillon on November 26, 1892, Blake referred to the fact that he and Dillon had been appointed a corresponding committee. This committee was evidently expected to correspond with Canadians interested in home rule as well as with the National Federation of America, for Blake suggested that he should take the chief part in the Canadian correspondence and Dillon in the American.[73]

A speech given by Blake at a convention held in Longford on November 17 to inaugurate a collection on behalf of the evicted tenants led to the publication of a report, which gained wide circulation, that Blake was attempting to unite the Parnellites and anti-

[71]Blake Papers, Blake to McCarthy, Nov. 11, 1892.
[72]*Ibid.*, Dillon to Blake, Nov. 12, 1892.
[73]*Ibid.*, Blake to Dillon, Nov. 26, 1892. In a letter dated June 3, 1893, to J. F. X. O'Brien, Blake resigned from the committee, but agreed to continue to conduct unofficially the correspondence with Canada. See J. F. X. O'Brien Papers.

Parnellites under his leadership. Speaking of the schism in Irish ranks, Blake said that he had never hesitated in the conclusion that the action of the majority was right, although many honest and sensible men had differed from the majority at the time of the split. He believed that the present duty of the anti-Parnellites was to do all in their power to bring about a reunion of the Irish people, and he appealed to them to deal with the Parnellites in a conciliatory, kindly, and forbearing manner which might induce them to take their places once more in Nationalist ranks. Blake then told his audience what he had already related to McCarthy about the situation in Canada, how many of the Irishmen there who had previously been Parnellites were now united in support of the Irish parliamentary party. In the United States too, he declared, while there were still some Parnellites, men who had been apathetic or despondent after the split were again working for the national movement.

Next, Blake attempted to prove that he himself was a Parnellite in the true sense of the term; he was, he said, a Parnellite as Mr. Parnell had been when they had all believed and trusted in him. In the autumn of 1892, one of the chief differences of opinion between the majority party and the Parnellites concerned the question of the evicted tenants, in whose interests this Longford meeting had been called. The Parnellites had wanted an autumn session of Parliament to deal with the question, while the majority party, feeling that this would thrust home rule, the more important question, into the background, had not favoured such a move. Blake now quoted from a manifesto issued by Parnell in 1890, in which the then Irish leader had declared that he had pledged himself to stand by the evicted tenants. At the same time, however, he had said that this question was a limited one and should not be allowed to interfere with the interests of the country. Thus, Blake explained, he was a true Parnellite in insisting that home rule, the big question, must not be sacrificed for the more limited question of the evicted tenants; he was sure that the Irish people throughout the world would see that they did not suffer. The Irish party, he said, had not asked for an autumn session of Parliament because it did not believe that it would benefit the tenants; the Parnellites, in wanting an autumn session to throw home rule into the background and to discuss only the case of the evicted tenants, had adopted a policy opposed to that of their late leader whom they professed to be following.[74]

As we know, the idea that Blake might reunite under his leadership the two groups of Irish Nationalists was not new. Many Canadians had believed he would accomplish this task and as early as August, 1892, reports had appeared in the English press that Blake was the coming leader of the Irish party. It was, in fact, suggested then and later that it was the Liberals who were promoting him for the Irish leadership. One newspaper declared that Blake's reception at the Eighty Club was "an outward and visible sign of a powerful movement for putting him over the heads of many of his less worthy colleagues,"[75] while another went so far as to suggest that he had been provided with a seat in the Imperial Parliament as a member for an Irish constituency expressly at Gladstone's request.[76]

It would, of course, have been to the advantage of both Liberals and Irish Nationalists if the Parnell split could have been healed before the introduction of a new Home Rule Bill. The controversy over the Paris funds was in progress at this time, and it appears that in November, 1892, an effort to effect a reunion on the basis of a speedy release of these funds in aid of the evicted tenants was being made by Archbishop Croke of Cashel. Blake was also reported to be taking a leading part in this effort at reunion.[77] Furthermore, he had made it clear in many of his speeches that everything possible should be done to bring about a reconciliation. It was not surprising, therefore, that his speech at Longford, in which he had made a special effort to show that the majority party was following Parnell's policy, should give rise to the assumption that reunion might be achieved under his leadership.

This rumour about Blake appears to have gained especially wide publicity in the American press. One Chicago journal reported:

[74]A report of the meeting including Blake's speech is given in the *Freeman's Journal*, Dublin, Nov. 18, 1892. See Blake Scrap Books.
[75]*St. Stephen's Review*, Aug. 4, 1892. See Blake Scrap Books.
[76]*Gazette*, Giverton, Aug. 9, 1892. See Blake Scrap Books.
[77]*Herald*, Chicago, n.d. The dispatch from Dublin is, however, dated Nov. 17, 1892. See Blake Scrap Books.

Edward Blake, who is working daily to reconcile the factions, is hopeful of ultimate success. It is stated that some of the Parnellite leaders are willing to join hands with the opposition under his leadership. . . . Mr. Blake's speech is thought likely to have more effect towards creating harmony between the factions than any previous efforts in that direction. He has the leadership bee in his bonnet, and, although neither faction admires him, he would have a better chance of securing the prize, in case of reunion than any other man, as he has not made himself obnoxious to either party.[78]

Another American newspaper, which apparently had more admiration for Blake, published an interesting editorial, of which the following is an excerpt:

. . . Edward Blake, Nationalist member for South Longford, is the Moses who may lead the McCarthy and Parnellite factions out of the darkness of disagreement into the light of common good. By a stroke of diplomacy he has accomplished a probable union of policy. The grave matter of difference has been over the issue of the evicted tenants. By showing that Mr. Parnell, before his death, had pledged not to desert their interests but still believed the home rule question to be the main one and to be gained first, he has appeased the Parnellites; and now he may be recognized as the leader of both wings and hold them in line when they are assembled in the house of commons. By making the single issue of home rule the chief object and subordinating all others to it, Mr. Blake is endorsed by the Irish people all over the world.[79]

The suggestion which had been made by some English newspapers in August that the Liberals, and especially Gladstone, were eager for Blake to lead the Irish party, was now revived with added vigour. It was reported that a prominent Irish-American visitor to Britain, desiring to know who was the real leader of opinion in Irish politics, had asked Gladstone "whom we were to follow among the Irish leaders to inform ourselves as to the true condition." To this query Gladstone was said to have replied: "Read everything that Edward Blake says. Possess yourself of his wishes and plans. He seems by far the strongest man whom they [the Irish party] have put forward."[80]

[78]*Ibid.*
[79]*Evening Telegram*, Portland, Oregon, n.d. This is, however, obviously a commentary on Blake's Longford speech of Nov. 17, 1892. See Blake Scrap Books.
[80]*Evening Mail*, Dublin, n.d.; and *Evening Echo*, Nov. 24, 1892. See Blake Scrap Books.

Before the end of November, reports of Archbishop Croke's failure to reunite the two groups of Irish Nationalists appeared in the press, but a rumour regarding the leadership of the anti-Parnellites next arose. It was reported that Justin McCarthy was planning to resign this position at the beginning of the next parliamentary session, because he feared that ill health and the pressure of literary engagements would prevent him from giving constant attendance at Westminster during the passage of the Home Rule Bill through the House of Commons. So, even if Blake did not become leader of a reunited party, it was now thought that he might at least succeed McCarthy as chairman of the anti-Parnellites. In its issue of November 29, the *Irish Times*, Dublin's principal Unionist journal, mentioned Blake, Davitt, and Dillon as three possible candidates for the position and added that, although Davitt and Dillon each had a following, it was not large enough to ensure success to either of them. Blake, it stated, "is favourite with Mr. Gladstone . . . and the Premier's wishes will of course have considerable weight in the counsels of the Irish parliamentary party, especially as they are certain to be backed by Mr. T. M. Healy." It went on to explain that since Healy was content "to pull the strings behind the scenes" he would support Blake rather than either of the others.

That Blake, in spite of so many rumours, continued to regard himself as a new recruit, a mere rank and file member of the party, can be seen from his correspondence at this time with David Sheehy, secretary of the Irish National Federation. Explaining that it was customary for a prominent member of the party to preside at the regular fortnightly public meetings of the central branch of the Federation in Dublin, Sheehy asked Blake to preside on November 30.[81] Blake's reply was typical. At such a critical period, he felt that the duty of presiding and of saying what might be deemed appropriate should be discharged by someone of greater weight, larger experience, and wider knowledge than he possessed. He would very much prefer not to act but would do so if Sheehy could find no one else.[82] Thereupon, Sheehy replied:

[81]Blake Papers, David Sheehy to Blake, Nov. 24, 1892.
[82]*Ibid.*, Blake to Sheehy, Nov. 27, 1892.

Having every confidence that whatever subjects you may elect to speak on will be treated in a masterly manner and draw a wide attention, I would therefore feel gratified if you could say that I can announce in to-morrow's paper that you will preside. As I can get no better man I need not look for one while I have you.[83]

In view of Sheehy's persistence, Blake agreed to preside,[84] and the fact that he did so was taken as another indication of his coming leadership.[85]

By the beginning of December, McCarthy's health had improved and it was denied that he intended to resign the leadership of the party. Some newspapers continued, however, to speculate on the possibility of Blake's eventually becoming leader. One Scottish journal, while admitting that he was an able man, nevertheless declared: "The spectacle of his stepping over from Canada and forthwith entering on the leadership of the Irish Party would involve a dangerous admission of the difficulty of the party in selecting a leader from the two or three men who, for a dozen or fifteen years, have borne the heat and burden of the day."[86] This view had already been expressed by an Irish Unionist paper which, when commenting on Gladstone's statement about Blake, had remarked: "This is surely another argument in favour of Home Rule, when it is admitted that a competent Parliamentarian cannot be found among the Irish members who support Mr. Gladstone, and that one must be dug out of a colonial legislature in order to satisfy the requirements of the author of the Home Rule Bill."[87]

Rumours continued to be circulated in December, several Canadian and American newspapers reporting that the Liberals were training Blake for leadership.[88] But his denial of any aspirations to such a position also appeared in the Irish press.[89] For although he

[83] *Ibid.*, Sheehy to Blake, Nov. 28, 1892.
[84] *Ibid.*, Blake to Sheehy, Nov. 28, 1892.
[85] The *Express* (probably the *Daily Express*, Dublin), Dec. 1, 1892, reported: "Hon. E. Blake, M.P., the expected future leader of the party, presided." See Blake Scrap Books.
[86] *Scottish Leader*, Dec. 2, 1892. See Blake Scrap Books.
[87] *Evening Mail*, Dublin, n.d. See Blake Scrap Books.
[88] For their comments see the Blake Scrap Books.
[89] *Irish Independent*, Dublin, Dec. 17, 1892. See Blake Scrap Books.

sincerely desired to see a reunion of the Irish factions and was doing his best to bring it about, he appears to have had no desire for the leadership of the party which some newspapers claimed that he was seeking.

The argument might be advanced that the apparent desire of the Liberals and possibly of Healy to see Blake attain the leadership of the Irish party was not an unmixed compliment. The Unionist press certainly implied that the Liberals wished him to secure the position because they believed he would support their policies without question. Likewise it was suggested that Healy would not object to Blake's leadership because he thought he would be able to control him behind the scenes.

It is true, of course, that Blake had a profound admiration for the principles of British Liberalism, and the esteem in which he held Gladstone and many of his colleagues was probably greater than that felt for them by most of the Irish members. With this in mind, some Liberals may have thought that Blake, if he became Irish leader, would prove a most tractable ally, ready to obey their every command. Similarly, Healy, noting Blake's repeated assertions that he was but a new recruit in the Irish ranks, may have believed that so modest a gentleman, if he became leader, would gladly accept the advice of a man as experienced as he was in Irish politics.

Anyone who could hold such views must, however, have been entirely ignorant of Blake's career in Canadian politics. It is impossible to imagine the man who led the progressive wing of Canada's Liberal party or who later left his party altogether because he could not accept one aspect of its policy becoming the tool of any man, however much he might admire him. In fact, it seems very unlikely that Gladstone or any of his more prominent colleagues had any thought of controlling Blake. Their respect for his views was undoubtedly sincere, as will be seen from their frequent consultations with him in connection with the Home Rule Bill. Furthermore, if they really wished him to lead the Irish party,[90] it was probably

[90]There is considerable evidence that they did. The fact that Bryce and apparently Gladstone were so anxious to learn Blake's views on home rule, that Blake was invited to address the Eighty Club and to assist in Morley's campaign at Newcastle, and that the Liberal leaders, especially Morley, as will be seen in the next chapter, considered Blake's advice on the Home Rule

because they felt that, with Blake in this position, the English people would be more likely to accept Gladstone's home rule policy. In the election of 1892, England, as distinct from the United Kingdom of Great Britain and Ireland, had returned a majority opposed to home rule, and both Liberals and Irish Nationalists recognized the importance of winning additional English support for their cause. Blake was the type of man likely to appeal to English electors who tended to think of the Irish politician as a fiery agitator, unfitted for the task of self-government. Hearing Blake, an Irish member, but also a calm and logical constitutionalist, advocate home rule for Ireland, they were likely to reconsider their views, realizing that a man like him would not favour such a scheme if it were impracticable. This was undoubtedly one of the reasons why Blake received so many invitations to address meetings in England; it probably also explains why many Liberals would have liked to see him become leader of the Irish party.

Bill of great value, certainly suggest that promiment Liberals would have liked to see Blake in a position of leadership. Nevertheless, some newspaper reports were undoubtedly exaggerated; it seems unlikely that Gladstone and his colleagues were actually training Blake for the Irish leadership.

III. THE HOME RULE BILL OF 1893

Negotiations

TO FRAME a Home Rule Bill which would satisfy Irish Nationalists without antagonizing the more moderate British Liberals was not an easy task. Yet since their majority depended on the Irish vote, Gladstone and his colleagues would have to accomplish it if they were to avoid a defeat in the Commons. The bill was drafted by a committee of the cabinet consisting of W. E. Gladstone, John Morley, Lord Spencer, Lord Herschell, Henry Campbell-Bannerman, and James Bryce. To ensure its acceptability among Irish Nationalists, these cabinet representatives discussed its details with the leading members of the Irish majority party.

Since the negotiations were secret, information regarding them is comparatively meagre. Letters of the period do, however, indicate the frequency with which meetings were held among the Irish leaders themselves and between them and the representatives of the British cabinet, and references are made to differences of opinion between the two groups of negotiators. The principal meetings were those held between Morley and the Irish leaders in the Shelbourne Hotel in Dublin during the winter of 1892-3. They were apparently open to all members of the committee of the Irish majority party, but since several of them were away from Dublin only the leading members participated. Writing of the meetings in his *Recollections*, Morley states that he "worked over the frame of a measure with three or four of the Irish leaders, including the important assistance of Blake, a prominent lawyer and politician from Canada, who had come over and held an Irish seat, as an expert in the making and working of subordinate parliamentary constitutions."[1]

Before Blake's return from Canada, his advice on the framing of the Home Rule Bill had already been sought by James Bryce, one of the members of the cabinet committee. The question at issue was whether the Irish legislature should consist of one or two houses.

[1] John Morley, *Recollections* (Toronto, 1917), I, 358.

THE HOME RULE BILL OF 1893

Ontario had a unicameral legislature, while the Dominion and most of the other provinces had two-chambered houses, and Bryce asked whether Blake had formed a decided view as to the advantages of one or the other system.[2] Blake replied that the one-chambered legislature had worked fairly well in Ontario because of certain conditions favourable to it: it had been led by first ministers of moderate and cautious views; the constituency was very largely still composed of agricultural freeholders, a fine class of yeomanry; and the province had enjoyed municipal government for half a century. But he realized that in such a system there was a serious danger of which he had seen symptoms in his native province—that of precipitate legislation under influences of party or of passion, rushed through without proper time for second thought by the assembly or for any expression of opinion by the people at large. Thus the fear already existing in some quarters of unjust and confiscatory proceedings by an Irish legislature might be intensified by the abandonment of the principle of a second chamber. Ontario's experience, therefore, could hardly be said to be a safe guide for Ireland. Blake also reminded Bryce of the formal adhesion not only of Parnell, but also of the proposers and supporters of the Home Rule Bill of 1886, to the plan of two "orders."

Blake went on to explain, however, that he did not favour all the details of that plan. According to it, the Irish legislature was to consist of two "orders," one of 103 members representing the nobility and propertied class, and the other of 204 members. Both "orders" were to sit together, but they could vote separately if they desired, and each was to have a suspensory veto over measures brought in by the other. Blake objected to the two "orders" sitting together; he was inclined to follow the ancient paths and let them sit separately. But in order to prevent the Upper House from assuming a position of co-ordinate power with the Lower, the former's numbers should be smaller than those proposed in the bill of 1886. There should also be a general definition of the nature of its functions as a second chamber and some express provision to meet the case of deadlock.

Finally, realizing that no Home Rule Bill could establish for

[2]Blake Papers, James Bryce to Blake, Oct. 10, 1892.

Ireland a perfect constitution which would never require amendment, Blake emphasized the importance of distinguishing between its permanent and temporary provisions:

> In framing the Home Rule Bill, you should, in my opinion, make cardinal distinctions between the consideration you give to the permanent, and that which you accord to the transient or temporary provisions. We may be disposed to submit to and work under defective stipulations, of which we see that a reasonably short time will make an end; but, to such provisions, to be imposed on us by the British people, and to be unalterable by the Irish people, it will be very difficult to command our assent. I should care little about the form of your second Order, if, even after a certain interval of years, its provisions became practically open to amendment by the Irish Legislature; but, I feel great difficulty in assenting to their perpetual existence, as propounded by the Bill of 1886.[3]

Some negotiations took place while Blake was still in Canada, for on November 2, the day Blake sailed from New York, McCarthy wrote to Mrs. Praed:

> . . . I had terribly hard work in Dublin.—We met in committee every day at eleven o'clock, and we sat until about midnight or later . . . John Morley came every day at four and we talked matters over. He gave us his views on each point—his views and those of Gladstone. We gave him *our* views—then he telegraphed to London and brought us a new interchange of ideas next day, on which we took further counsel. Nothing could be more satisfactory so far as things have gone, and I think we shall be in perfect understanding.[4]

Despite these lengthy negotiations, the Irish leaders were not acquainted with the details of the bill several days later, for on the seventh, Dillon wrote to Blake, who was to arrive in Liverpool on the tenth: "With reference to your question about the details of the Home Rule Bill—I have heard nothing yet—but it is possible you may hear something from McCarthy on this subject as the Cabinet has been meeting frequently during the last ten days and I fancy they have been engaged on the details of the Bill." But on November 8 McCarthy cabled Blake on shipboard: "Nothing new. Bill in preparation but have not details."[5]

Blake crossed to Dublin on November 15 to attend a committee meeting there the following day. Then, during the remainder of the

[3]*Ibid.*, Blake to Bryce, Oct. 24, 1892.
[4]Justin McCarthy and Mrs. Campbell Praed, *Our Book of Memories* (London, 1912), 332.
[5]For these two communications see the Blake Papers.

month, he met frequently with Dillon and Thomas Sexton[6] to discuss the question of a satisfactory home rule measure, and on December 1 the Irish leaders conferred with Morley at the Shelbourne Hotel. On the following day they still lacked full knowledge of the details of the proposed bill, and Blake wrote to the Irish secretary complaining that it was extremely difficult to deal with the measure as a whole when they knew only some of its parts. He did not hesitate to say that certain points not yet discussed might cause dissension, though he seemed hopeful of ultimate agreement: "The settlement of the Land and the Financial and other questions yet to be disclosed may perhaps give a different complexion to the whole. But looking as far as I now can upon the whole, I seem to perceive an effort to attenuate the provisions of the Bill of '86 so far as may render it unacceptable to Ireland...."[7]

In the period between Morley's return to London to confer with his colleagues in the cabinet committee and with the cabinet as a whole and his next meeting with the Irish leaders in Dublin, scheduled for December 20, there were many moments of hope and despair. Morley wrote Dillon that all had gone as desired[8] but McCarthy, writing to Mrs. Praed,[9] feared that Gladstone would be unable to carry certain members of the cabinet with him in preparing a bill which the Irish party would accept. However, the meeting with Morley, postponed to the twenty-second, was evidently quite successful, for McCarthy received from Dublin a telegram with one word, "Satisfactory."[10]

Even in the midst of these important negotiations, it appears that the dissension within the Irish party continued. It was about this time that the dispute over the Paris funds almost caused a split in anti-Parnellite ranks. Blake, distressed that such a situation should exist on the eve of the introduction of a Home Rule Bill, apparently

[6]Thomas Sexton (1848–1932), M.P., 1880–96; High Sheriff of Dublin, 1887; Lord Mayor of Dublin, 1888–9; chairman, Freeman's Journal Limited, 1892–1912.
[7]Blake Papers, Blake to Morley, Dec. 2, 1892.
[8]See Blake Papers, Dillon to Blake, Dec. 18, 1892.
[9]McCarthy and Praed, *Our Book of Memories*, 339.
[10]McCarthy and Praed, *Our Book of Memories*, 341. The receipt of the telegram is reported in a letter from McCarthy to Mrs. Praed, dated Dec. 22, 1892.

expressed a desire to resign from the parliamentary committee of the party. Although his role in the negotiations regarding the Home Rule Bill was obviously one of leadership, he once more declared that he could serve the party better in a subordinate position. That McCarthy did not agree with this opinion can be seen from the following excerpt from a letter which he wrote to Mrs. Praed:

> I have had a long letter from Edward Blake to-day expressing a wish to be allowed to resign—not his seat, which at first I thought with much alarm he proposed to do—but his place as a member of our committee. He argues that he could serve us better by simply being one of the rank and file. Our internal quarrels distress him. He does not understand them and dreads the responsibility of being a leader where he finds it hard to grasp the whole situation. I will ask him not to make up his mind finally until he and I have talked it over when he comes to London. Apart from the splendid services he can render us in the details of the Home Rule Bill, I think his presence as an entirely impartial newcomer might in our committee have a moderating and a salutary influence. As to serving in the rank and file—he *could not* be one of the rank and file. As I think I told you before, he has, after Gladstone himself, no superior in the House of Commons. Such a man cannot reduce himself to the rank and file. . . . [11]

In spite of his dissatisfaction, Blake was prevailed upon not to resign from the committee, and he continued to give assistance in the preparation of the Home Rule Bill. Although he was in London when some of the later meetings were held in Dublin, he was kept informed of the progress of the negotiations by Dillon, who reported that serious difficulties had arisen over the financial question. Not only was Sexton sending his proposed amendments to the cabinet, but he and Dillon had requested Morley not to let his colleagues come to any conclusion until the Irish leaders had a further opportunity of discussing the matter.[12]

By January 20, most of the Irish leaders were in London for the opening of Parliament which was scheduled to meet on the thirty-first, and negotiations on the Home Rule Bill were continued there. The cabinet and the Irish Nationalists were evidently by then closer to agreement, for on January 20 McCarthy wrote to Mrs. Praed:

[11] *Ibid.*, 343. The letter is dated Dec. 27, 1892.
[12] Blake Papers, Dillon to Blake, Jan. 11, 1893.

I have only time to write you a few lines. I have been kept very busy over the Home Rule Bill. Blake, Sexton, and I spent several hours to-day with Morley going over the clauses, and we are to meet him again at nine to-night, and shall probably sit up till somewhat of a late hour. There are, of course, some difficulties of detail, but I see nothing of serious difficulty ahead. To-day we are engaged mainly with the financial clauses—to-night we shall go into the general question. I expect some days of pretty hard work over the measure.[13]

But with the approach of the day on which the bill was to be introduced in the House of Commons, it became clear that complete agreement would not be reached and that the Irish members would have to rely on the possibility of securing certain amendments when the bill was in committee. On February 4, five days after Parliament had opened, McCarthy reported to Mrs. Praed that no final agreement had yet been reached on the details, and on the twelfth, the day before the bill was to be brought in, he wrote: "I think the Bill will be satisfactory on the whole, but there are still some points in dispute."[14] But time did not remain to settle these points before the outline of the bill became public.

First Reading

On February 13, 1893, Gladstone outlined in the House of Commons the main provisions of the new Home Rule Bill.[15] Like the bill of 1886, it constituted an Irish legislature with power to make laws for the peace, order, and good government of Ireland in matters of an exclusively domestic nature; all matters relating to the Crown, regency, and viceroy, peace and war, defence, treaties and foreign relations, dignities and titles, the law of treason, the law of alienage, external trade, coinage and some other subsidiary subjects were to be reserved to the Imperial Parliament, and certain other restrictions were to be imposed upon the new legislature. The Queen was to be represented by a viceroy, whose position was to be free from all religious disabilities, and whose appointment would usually run for

[13]McCarthy and Praed, *Our Book of Memories*, 348–9.
[14]For both these letters see *ibid.*, 352.
[15]Gladstone's speech is recorded in *Hansard*, 4th Series, VIII, 1241–75.

six years, subject to the revoking power of the Crown. On the advice of an executive committee of the Privy Council in Ireland, the Viceroy would give or withhold his assent to bills, subject to the instructions of the sovereign in respect to any given bill.[16]

Instead of the two "orders" planned in 1886, the new legislature was to have two chambers. The legislative council would consist of 48 members, elected for an eight-year term by new constituencies made up of voters who had a rating qualification of twenty pounds. The legislative assembly's 103 members were to be elected for a five-year term by the existing constituencies, but electors and constituencies of the assembly were to be alterable after a term of six years so long as there was due regard to the distribution of population. In case of a deadlock between the two houses, when a bill had been adopted by the assembly for a second time after an interval of two years or after a dissolution of the legislature, the two houses might be required to meet together to decide the fate of the bill.

One of the most controversial issues in 1886 had been the provision that Ireland should cease to be represented in the Imperial Parliament after the establishment of its own legislature. This provision was now reversed, and Ireland was to send 80 members to Westminster. In his speech introducing the bill, Gladstone went fully into the government's difficulties in deciding on the voting power of these members. Should they vote on all matters or only on those of Irish or imperial concern? There were, Gladstone believed, strong arguments on both sides. In favour of allowing them to vote on all questions was the fact that it was sometimes difficult to distinguish between matters which were purely British and those which were imperial. In any event, Irish members could not be excluded from their part in determining the composition of the executive power, for their votes might be decisive in sustaining or defeating a British ministry on a motion of confidence. Moreover, unless they voted on all questions a great parliamentary tradition, that of the absolute equality of all members of the house, would be broken. On the other hand, it did not seem right that Irish members should be allowed to vote on purely British matters, when British members would not be permitted to vote on Irish internal affairs,

[16] This veto question caused much controversy in the debates which followed.

these being decided by the legislature in Dublin. And there was the danger that the retention of Irish members for all purposes might lead to political intrigue if the two great parties were divided on a purely British question and the members knew that whichever could bring over the 80 Irish representatives, or a large contingent of them, would carry the day. The government had concluded that the arguments in favour of limiting the voting powers of the Irish representatives were stronger than those against it and had decided on the former course. Irish members were not to vote on any motion or bill expressly confined to Great Britain, on any tax not levied in Ireland, on any vote or appropriation of money not for imperial services, or on any motion or resolution exclusively affecting Great Britain.

Another problem was the financial question which had also caused great difficulty in 1886. The new bill provided for one system of legislating for all the kingdom on commercial affairs, and Ireland was to bear her fair share in imperial expenditure. Instead of the method of the lump sum which had been a feature of the earlier bill, a particular fund would be appropriated by the imperial government to stand in fulfilment of all the obligations of Ireland for imperial purposes. This fund would consist of the proceeds of the customs duties, a field of taxation which would continue to be controlled by the Parliament at Westminster. The Irish government would levy and collect most other taxes and would take over the whole of the civil government charges of the country, except the constabulary charges of which it would bear two-thirds. It was provided that the financial arrangements of the bill might be reconsidered after fifteen years on an address either from the House of Commons or from the Irish legislative assembly.

A measure for buying out the Irish landlords was to have followed the passage of the Home Rule Bill of 1886, but the new bill did not deal with this matter. In reply to a question from Sir Edward Clarke, who had been Solicitor-General in the Conservative government, the Prime Minister stated that "the Land Question is reserved to the imperial parliament for a period of three years."[17]

Following Gladstone's address in the Commons, the Irish parliamentary party met to consider the provisions of the bill. At this

[17]*Hansard*, 4th Series, VIII, 1276.

meeting, Blake, T. P. O'Connor,[18] T. M. Healy, and others appealed to the members of the party not to criticize too sharply the details of the bill and urged them to support heartily and cordially its main provisions. It was admitted unanimously that the measure was a better one than the bill of 1886, although the financial clauses as they stood could not be accepted by the Irish party.[19]

Blake made his maiden speech in the British House of Commons on February 17, 1893, in the course of the five-day debate on the first reading of the bill. It was a long and skilful speech which received wide acclaim, but it was made under circumstances of great difficulty. Blake had been prepared to reply the day before to Lord Randolph Churchill's attack on the bill, but plans had been changed and he was scheduled instead to refute Joseph Chamberlain's address. In his speech, generally admitted to have been the best one against the bill delivered during the debate, Chamberlain had brilliantly and vigorously attacked the constitutional defects of the bill.[20] He was, he insisted, in favour of granting to Ireland the widest possible extension of local government consistent with the unity of the Empire, the supremacy of Parliament, and the protection of minorities. But he was convinced that the present measure satisfied none of these conditions. On the one hand, because of Ireland's geographical position, the granting to her of an independent legislature weakened imperial unity. On the other, although encouraging the growth of Irish nationality at the expense of the Empire, the bill denied Ireland certain rights of nations and could not, therefore, provide a permanent settlement of the Irish question.

Again, in establishing a separate legislature with a separate executive responsible to it, the bill was virtually giving up all pretence of the maintenance of any sovereignty by the Imperial Parliament. Neither the mere statement of supremacy[21] nor the veto of the Crown would be effective against a large majority in the Irish legis-

[18]Thomas Power O'Connor (1848–1929), born Athlone; journalist; historian; M.P., 1880–1929; became Privy Councillor, 1924. Though a member of the Irish parliamentary party, he represented the Scotland division of Liverpool during most of his parliamentary career.
[19]Dillon Papers, Minutes of the Irish parliamentary party, Feb. 13, 1893.
[20]Chamberlain's speech is recorded in *Hansard*, 4th Series, VIII, 1717–44.
[21]There was a statement of the supremacy of the Imperial Parliament in the preamble to the bill.

lature. Even the retention of Irish members at Westminster, a policy which Chamberlain favoured, presented insurmountable difficulties under the system proposed by the bill. There were only two practicable and logical ways of carrying it out: the Irish legislative body might be a wholly subordinate one, something like an enlarged edition of the London County Council; or a federal system might be adopted with a provincial legislature for each of the four divisions of the United Kingdom and a central one for legislating on matters common to all. But under the system which the present bill proposed to set up, with the Irish members voting only on imperial matters, the government might be sometimes in a majority, at other times in a minority. Without Irish help the present government would, for instance, be in a minority of forty on purely British affairs.

Finally, Chamberlain asserted that the bill provided no adequate protection for minorities. The establishment of a church was declared unlawful and there was some provision with respect to education, but these could be evaded. Moreover, the second chamber in the legislature provided no protection, for, even if it were composed entirely of the minority, its numbers were so small that it could be outvoted when the two houses met together, as provided in case of deadlock.

The task of replying to this powerful speech was indeed difficult. To a constitutional expert of Blake's calibre, the defects of the bill must have been only too obvious, and to refute Chamberlain's brilliant presentation of them required all the parliamentary skill he possessed. Chamberlain had mentioned federalism as one possible solution of the problem, and it was well known that this plan was strongly favoured by Blake. While Chamberlain refused to say whether he actually favoured the federal system, he felt that, if it were to be adopted, the change should not be gradual, but should be fully adopted at one time. Blake, on the other hand, while realizing the defects of the present scheme and looking to federalism as the ultimate solution of the problem, saw too that the Irish question demanded an immediate settlement which could not await the time when the other divisions of the United Kingdom would be ready to accept local self-government. He was therefore willing to agree to the present imperfect proposal as a step towards the federation of the British Isles. Blake understood what H. A. L. Fisher had said in his biography of James Bryce, that the real case for the Home Rulers lay not in the adequacy of their experiment, but in the contention that the Irish had not been reconciled to the union and that therefore some other way had to be found.[22]

On this theme, the role of the Home Rule Bill as an immediate, if not perfect, solution to the Irish question, Blake spoke for an hour and a half, forcibly dealing with point after point raised by the leader of the Liberal Unionists and holding the close attention of a full house.[23] He began by remarking upon the difficulty of dealing with a measure whose text was not yet before the House. Another difficulty arose from the fact that the two groups of people who opposed the bill approached it from different standpoints. There was the old Tory view that "resolute government" would cure all Ireland's ills; Arthur J. Balfour had argued that the current state of tranquillity in that country was a good reason against home rule. But it was not the Conservatives' "resolute government," but the attempt of the Liberals in 1886 to grant home rule, and the hope it engendered for the future, that had brought temporary quiet to Ireland. Then there was the view held by Joseph Chamberlain and his followers that some form of home rule was desirable, but that the scheme presently proposed was unsatisfactory. It was strange that each suggested scheme of home rule turned out to be absolutely impracticable from Chamberlain's point of view, especially since he had been one of the first persons of prominence in Britain to assert that Irishmen had a right to govern themselves. His great objection to the bill of 1886 had been the non-inclusion of Irish members in the Imperial Parliament, but now that provision was made for their retention he found fault with the method of carrying it out.

But the great virtue of the bill, in Blake's view, was that it would improve relations between Britain and Ireland; he pointed to its general acceptance by the Irish all over the world as proof of this assertion. Ireland would have her just share of control, no more and no less, in matters of imperial concern. The bill did not provide for the repeal of the union, but sought to continue it in matters which were of common interest. It did not sow the seeds of future demands,

[22]H. A. L. Fisher, *James Bryce* (New York, 1927), I, 286–7.
[23]The speech is recorded in *Hansard*, 4th Series, VIII, 1744–61.

as Chamberlain claimed, but removed the great cause of complaint which had existed up to that time. Blake insisted that the danger to Britain from Ireland was much greater before 1886 and would be lessened, not increased, by the passage of a Home Rule Bill. The leader of the Liberal Unionists had claimed that the supremacy of Parliament, despite the good intentions of the government, was being impaired by this bill. But, Blake replied, Chamberlain had repeatedly declared that the retention of the Irish representatives in the British Parliament would effectively produce the supremacy which he now questioned. This had been his cardinal point and his reason for voting against second reading in 1886. He had complained, too, that the mere statement of the supremacy of Parliament was insufficient; Blake, on the other hand, felt that it was unnecessary to mention it at all since it was admitted on all sides. But it should not be enforced "by means of a constant, continuous operative review and re-consideration of all Irish legislation and administration"; that would make Irish self-government a sham. Blake's opinion was that the Imperial Parliament's policy in respect to the veto should be one of non-interference unless the spirit or letter of the act creating the Irish legislature was violated. Chamberlain had suggested that the use of the veto might involve the resignation of the Irish ministers, but Blake believed that it would plant them more firmly in their offices if the power were unwisely used, since they could not be called on to resign for an act for which they did not accept the responsibility.

Blake admitted that there were difficulties and complications involved in the bill, but their ultimate solution, he thought,

was to be found in the shape of local institutions for other parts of the Kingdom, with an Imperial Parliament for all. He was an advocate of that policy, though he knew the time for it had not yet arrived. He believed that the passing of this bill, the experience that Parliament would derive from it, the enormous relief it would have from a mass of Irish business, the new spirit that would attend their deliberations, and the beneficial results of Home Rule in Ireland, would go far to advance and bring into the region of practical politics the adoption of this plan in reference to other portions of the United Kingdom.[24]

---

[24]*Ibid.*, 1757.

In the meantime there remained the problem that, with the Irish members voting on some questions and not on others, the government might at some times be in a majority, at others in a minority. Chamberlain had complained that, under these circumstances, it might be impossible to legislate on local matters. While Blake admitted that this theoretical objection was great, he felt that a practical solution would be found by adopting home rule in substance if not in form for each of the divisions of the United Kingdom. The local opinion of Scotland would be deferred to by England and Wales, that of Wales by England and Scotland, and that of England by Wales and Scotland.

Blake spoke in favour of the second chamber which he considered much better than the one provided by the bill of 1886. Based on the principle of election, though the franchise was a restrictive one, it was designed to give what protection could reasonably be given to minorities. It provided for full debate and discussion by an elected body of any proposition of the more popular chamber, together with the power of rejection twice. That was a great security against injustice; it gave time for full inquiry and second thought. If, after all that, the popular chamber insisted on the measure, it could insist upon it absolutely, for there was the joint vote, and, therefore, the power of the second chamber would influence the decision of the popular one with results tending to equality. In that way there would be ample security against rash and unjust legislation.

Finally, Blake dealt with the problem of Ulster. It was his opinion that the Protestants of that province would be quite able to take care of their own interests in an Irish legislature. He believed that they would scorn the suggestion that they be separated from their fellow-countrymen in the remainder of the island. Some wished to provide special treatment for Ulster because they thought she was not safe, but if this were true, in what position were the scattered men of Blake's own faith in the south and west of Ireland? Blake did not think, as Chamberlain evidently did, that the two populations of Ireland were to be divided for ever by hate and distrust; he believed in a better future for the country. Concluding his address with a fervent plea for goodwill among the peoples of Great Britain

THE HOME RULE BILL OF 1893 57

and Ireland, he recommended the adoption of the Home Rule Bill as a first and most effectual step towards a happier relationship between the two countries. As Blake resumed his seat, he was loudly cheered by both Liberals and Irish Nationalists, the latter standing and waving their hats.[25] Leonard Courtney, the Liberal Unionist member who followed him in the debate, welcomed Blake to the British Parliament and expressed the admiration of "every hon. Member present" for the character and ability displayed in his speech.[26] Shortly afterwards, Sir William Harcourt, Chancellor of the Exchequer, declared in an interview that Blake's speech was the best ever uttered in Parliament on the subject of home rule.[27] There was also much favourable comment in the Liberal and Irish Nationalist press. One English journal remarked that Blake's answer to Chamberlain was that of a practical statesman to a political theorist,[28] another that it was a bold thing for Blake to attempt an impromptu reply to Chamberlain, but that he had acquitted himself very well.[29] It was natural that the *Freeman's Journal*, the organ of the Irish majority party, should praise the speech, declaring that Blake had vindicated the principle of home rule with the eloquence of a great orator and the fervour of a great Irishman.[30] More noteworthy, however, was the fact that the Parnellite *Irish Independent*, so often critical of anti-Parnellite members, also praised Blake in its report of his address. "It was no light effort," it declared, "for the Canadian statesman to follow a debater of the deadly skill of Mr. Chamberlain, and to follow him not alone successfully, but triumphantly, is a feat which, performed by a new man, marks him as one destined to achieve high success in the Councils of Parliament."[31] Blake's maiden speech also revived the rumour that he would become leader of a reunited Irish party. The Toronto *Globe*, in its issue of February 21, reported: "The Cana-

[25]*Globe*, Toronto, Feb. 20, 1893.
[26]*Hansard*, 4th Series, VIII, 1761–2.
[27]*Globe*, Toronto, Feb. 20, 1893.
[28]*Daily News*, London, Feb. 18, 1893. See Blake Scrap Books.
[29]Quoted from *Westminster Gazette* in *Globe*, Toronto, Feb. 20, 1893.
[30]*Freeman's Journal*, Dublin, Feb. 18, 1893. See Blake Scrap Books.
[31]*Irish Independent*, Dublin, Feb. 18, 1893. See Blake Scrap Books.

dian's speech is expected to herald Mr. Blake's selection as the man to lead the Irish party. In this way it is hoped that the Parnellites and the anti-Parnellites will be united."

Blake received letters of congratulation from many admirers on both sides of the Atlantic, including Lord Aberdeen, who was soon to become Canada's Governor-General.[32] The Canadian attitude was admirably expressed by John Cameron, president and manager of the *London* (Ontario) *Advertiser*: "Your friends are very much satisfied with the splendid impression you have already made. . . . Some of the anti–Home Rule Tories hardly know which feeling to indulge —that of satisfaction that a Canadian should hold his own among the best of them at Westminster, or that natural to opponents of Home Rule."[33]

Unfavourable comment upon Blake's maiden effort at Westminster came from the Unionist press, which not only condemned his advocacy of the principle of home rule, but also found other grounds for complaint. Blake's speeches in the Canadian House of Commons had frequently been criticized for their length; it was felt by some that their wealth of detail lessened their effectiveness. The opposition press now levelled at Blake the type of criticism he had sometimes received in Canada. While admitting that his speech was a good one, the London *Evening News* complained that Blake was "excessively Sextonian—another way of saying that he was wordy and windy," and that "the length of his speech and its affectation of elocutionary perfection tired out his hearers."[34] Elsewhere it was reported that Henry Labouchere, the radical newspaper proprietor and editor, had complained of the length of Blake's sentences and declared that he was "too diffuse and plied word on word with needless redundancy."[35] And (Sir) Henry Lucy, in his book on the home rule Parliament, called Blake's address "a compendious effort with

[32]Blake Papers, Lord Aberdeen to Blake, Feb. 17, 1893.
[33]*Ibid.*, John Cameron to Blake, March 18, 1893.
[34]*Evening News*, London, Feb. 18, 1893. See Blake Scrap Books.
[35]*British Daily Mail*, n.d. See Blake Scrap Books. Labouchere was M.P. for Northampton, editor of *Truth*, and chief proprietor of the *Daily News*. He had been in favour of Chamberlain's local government scheme for Ireland and, like him, had opposed coercion. In 1886 he had tried unsuccessfully to reconcile Chamberlain to Gladstone's Home Rule Bill.

something subtly colonial in its character."³⁶ *The* (London) *Times* restricted its criticism to the subject matter of Blake's address:

> Mr. Blake, who is evidently going to run as the big man of the Nationalist party, assured the House that this invertebrate measure is accepted by Irishmen all over the globe as a settlement—a continuing settlement, we presume—of the long standing feud. Mr. Blake evidently does not want for audacity in prediction, for it only needs a reference to the criticism upon the financial and other portions of the Bill by Irishmen to see that it is no more a settlement from their standpoint than from ours. . . .³⁷

But although there was criticism as well as praise of Blake's maiden speech at Westminster, it is clear that it attracted much attention in all political circles. The fact that press comments on the address fill fifty-two pages in one of Blake's scrap books is an indication of the significance attached to his entry into the Imperial Parliament.

Second Reading

The Home Rule Bill was read a first time on the night of Blake's maiden speech, and the government hoped that it would pass second reading before Easter. The opposition, however, by resorting to obstruction, attempted to prevent this, and Gladstone was forced to postpone the beginning of the debate from March 13 to 16. But it soon became clear that this date was also too early, and, to the disappointment of the Irish leaders, Gladstone and his colleagues decided to put off the second reading until after Easter. The debate finally began on April 6.

Blake took part in this debate on April 14. In some respects his address on this occasion was abler than the one he had made during the debate on first reading, for it was not impromptu. It followed a speech against the bill by Admiral Field, who as a naval man had complained that it would weaken the Empire's power of offence and defence in time of war.³⁸ Although Blake's speech dwelt on the greater content and loyalty that would be produced in Ireland once

³⁶(Sir) Henry Lucy, *A Diary of the Home Rule Parliament, 1892–5* (London, 1896), 58.
³⁷*The Times*, London, Feb. 18, 1893. See Blake Scrap Books.
³⁸Field's speech is recorded in *Hansard*, 4th Series, XI, 397–408.

the measure was in effect,[39] the greater part of it was a reply not to Admiral Field but to statements made three days earlier by T. W. Russell, Liberal Unionist member for South Tyrone.[40] Towards the close of 1892, Russell had paid a visit to Canada with the express object of studying the system of government there, so that he might "authoritatively refute" the arguments of Blake who supported the Irish demand for home rule by analogies drawn from his experience of Canadian institutions.[41] In his address in the Commons on April 11, Russell dealt at some length with the Canadian situation. He said that it was claimed by Home Rulers who referred to Canada in support of their cause that that country was rebellious and discontented up to 1839, but that Britain then sent out Lord Durham who gave home rule, after which discontent and rebellion wholly vanished. Russell agreed that Canada had been rebellious and that Durham had made a satisfactory settlement, but he claimed that Durham's policy had been one not of disruption, but of consolidation. The two provinces of Upper and Lower Canada had been united, and the English-speaking Protestant one, although it had a smaller population, was given equal representation with the other.

In choosing to speak on these aspects of Canadian history, Russell had given Blake an ideal opportunity to explain to the House the working of home rule in Canada and to draw certain parallels between the situation in Canada and that in Ireland. With his knowledge of Canadian and Irish history he was able to make a most impressive speech, demonstrating the fallacy of Russell's views on the effectiveness of the Durham settlement, and showing how the granting of home rule to British North America had brought a large degree of contentment to once rebellious colonies.

Rebellion, he explained, had occurred in Canada because England had granted to each province an imperfect form of self-government, a legislative assembly with power to make laws, but without an executive responsible to it. Durham had recognized the need for responsible government and had recommended it, but, influenced

[39]Blake's speech is recorded in *ibid.*, 408–23.
[40]Russell's speech is recorded in *ibid.*, 62–81.
[41]*Freeman's Journal*, Dublin, Nov. 26, 1892. For this and other British, Irish, and Canadian press reports on Russell's visit to Canada see the Blake Scrap Books.

by the English-speaking minority of Lower Canada, he had also proposed the reunion of the two provinces. "In other words," said Blake, "he proposed the Anglicising of the two provinces; the making of them into one harmonious whole, in which the French lamb would be inside the British lion." But, though Russell had not mentioned it, that part of the settlement had wholly failed. After twenty-five years union had been replaced by federalism, with each province being granted a legislature for the control of its own local affairs, while a central parliament dealt with those of common concern.

Blake dealt too with Russell's reference to Quebec's Protestant minority as the Ulster of Quebec. Quebec had its own legislature, and the Protestants there, Russell claimed, were oppressed by the Roman Catholic majority; the same situation would, he believed, occur in Ireland if home rule were granted. Blake, on the other hand, denied that the Protestants of Quebec were oppressed; the minority there had always had its share, and generally more than a proportionate share, in the government of the province. There were always one or more English Protestant ministers in the provincial government, and, so far as he could learn, there had been an extraordinary degree of liberality with reference to representation in Parliament of those who were not merely of an absolutely different race, but of another tongue and creed. As to the possible position of the Protestants in Ulster under home rule, Blake wondered why the minority, which its supporters claimed was so infinitely superior in all attributes excepting the counting of heads, would not be able to hold its own in the Irish legislature. It had been suggested that this legislature would be divided into two parts—Roman Catholic Nationalists and loyal Protestants. But did anyone suppose that if the Irish legislature met to discuss questions of common interest, such, for instance, as municipal institutions, its members would not discuss them apart from such considerations? Among the good qualities of Catholic Nationalists was a tendency towards a very considerable difference of opinion which sometimes arose at inconvenient times. They would continue to disagree on many points after home rule was granted, and some would be found on one side of the legislature and some on the other. Moreover, if, as the opposition claimed, eighty Irish members were going to be so powerful in the British House of Commons, why could not the Protestant members, making one-third or even one-quarter of the Irish legislature, assume the same position there?

Then after effectively refuting specific assertions made by Russell about the Province of Quebec, Blake stated that Canada, considering all conditions and circumstances, was wonderfully contented. That she was not completely contented was the result of one shortcoming —it was because those national attributes which Ireland agreed to share in common with Great Britain could not be offered to Canada by the United Kingdom. This difficulty did not, however, arise with regard to Ireland, for that country now had a national share in imperial and national affairs. Let Parliament give her that local control she asked for, leave her that share in national concerns which she rightly demanded, and a settlement in substantial terms of finality would be obtained.[42]

Finally, Blake pointed out that the essence and substance of the whole controversy depended on whether Parliament was going to adopt a policy of trust and belief or a policy of incredulity and despair. The suggestions put forward that the Roman Catholics were unworthy of confidence belied the Catholic emancipation. By granting Roman Catholics the franchise, they had acknowledged them as capable citizens. They should now entrust these men with the duties of capable citizenship; they should trust them and believe them to be equal to that trust.

The importance of Blake's speech was fully recognized by the *Freeman's Journal* which presented his case clearly in an editorial on April 17: "Mr. Blake's resumé of Canadian history has recalled the fact, carefully obscured by Mr. T. W. Russell, and almost forgotten by the advocates of home rule, that not only does the constitu-

[42]Thus Blake supported the retention of Irish representation at Westminster, an aspect of the bill of 1893 which he, unlike some leading British advocates of home rule, strongly favoured. Gladstone, in his speech introducing the bill, declared that he considered the matter of secondary importance. Morley, writing years afterwards, admitted that he thought exclusion of the Irish members from Westminster would have been best, but that he was content to accept provisional inclusion if that was the indispensable condition of home rule. Morley, *Recollections*, I, 363.

tional history of Canada afford ample proof of the wisdom of the principle of local autonomy, but that it also contains an important object lesson in the folly of the policy of which the Irish Act of Union was the offspring. . . ." This parallel between Canadian and Irish history was exactly what Blake had tried to illustrate in this and many of his other speeches. In his knowledge and understanding of the constitutional issues at stake he made an important contribution to the Irish cause.

The Final Stages

On April 21, 1893, the second reading of the Home Rule Bill was carried by 347 to 304 votes, and on May 8 the House of Commons resolved itself into committee of the whole to discuss the bill clause by clause. Amendments were proposed chiefly by the Unionists who wished to weaken the bill and by the Parnellites who hoped to strengthen it.

At the beginning of the parliamentary session, just before the Home Rule Bill was introduced, the government had requested the parliamentary committee of the Irish majority party to name a subcommittee of three to confer with the government from time to time upon the details of the bill. Sexton, Dillon, and Blake were named to this sub-committee, which now, during the committee stage of the bill, had its most important work to do. But apart from a few references to meetings with Morley in the correspondence of the period there is little information about its work.

About the middle of June, Blake sought to be relieved of some of his responsibilities. Writing at that time to J. F. X. O'Brien,[43] secretary of the party's committee, he expressed a desire to resign from the sub-committee. He did not explain why he wanted to resign, saying only that he found himself for various reasons unable to continue a member. At the same time he declared that there had been "entire unanimity of opinion on the part of the sub-committee

[43] James Francis Xavier O'Brien (–1905), tea and wine merchant, Dublin; M.P., 1885–1905; for many years one of the treasurers of the Irish parliamentary party.

about the matters on which they had been so far called to consult and act. . . ."[44] No reply to Blake's letter has been found, so the committee's action with regard to his request can only be surmised from the events which followed.

On June 21 Blake sent McCarthy his resignation from the parliamentary committee of the party, this time giving a definite reason for his action. If there was entire unanimity on the part of the subcommittee, the same was evidently not true of the larger committee. Blake's letter explains the situation:

> I have always felt that we should, as originally arranged, hold frequent and regular meetings to consult on the approaching sections and amendments and the line to be taken in debate on them.
> This not seeming to be the general view of the Committee, I have for some time ceased to mention the subject to any of my colleagues, quite recognizing as I do that under such circumstances conferences are worse than useless.
> I have tried hard to reconcile myself to the continuance under existing conditions of my special responsibilities as a member of the Committee.
> But I find myself unable to do so longer, and therefore I am constrained to anticipate the step which, as you know, I had intended to take on the recess, and to resign my seat on the Committee.[45]

Further correspondence makes it clear that on the following day both McCarthy and William O'Brien spoke to Blake about the action he proposed to take. Explaining to him that his resignation at this time would increase the already great troubles with which the committee was beset, they urged him at least to postpone his action for the time being.[46] On the twenty-third, Blake wrote again to the leader of his party stating: "I have spent a sleepless night upon the business; and, intolerable tho' the position seems to me, I have decided to try to endure it for a little longer, rather than appear to my friends to aggravate their troubles. . . ."[47]

Although Blake's desire to resign from the committee was communicated to only a few leading members of the party, reports of his dissatisfaction did reach the press. Among the Blake papers is

[44] Blake Papers, Blake to J. F. X. O'Brien, June 15, 1893.
[45] *Ibid.*, Blake to McCarthy, June 21, 1893.
[46] This information is contained in the letters which Blake wrote agreeing to postpone his resignation. See Blake Papers, Blake to McCarthy, June 23, 1893; Blake to William O'Brien, June 23, 1893.
[47] *Ibid.*, Blake to McCarthy, June 23, 1893.

a clipping from the *Scotsman* of June 24, 1893, which reports that Blake had expressed the strongest dissatisfaction with the state of affairs in the Irish party and had intimated to McCarthy his desire to resign his seat. Since the report does not say, "his seat on the committee," its readers must have assumed that it meant his seat in Parliament. Another press report, referring to Blake's rumoured resignation, asserted that he had had "a severe difference" with Arthur O'Connor, a member of the party committee, regarding the Paris funds question.[48] Arthur O'Connor supported Healy in demanding that there should be no peaceful settlement of this question with the Parnellites.

Blake's too frequent resort to resignation in the face of difficulties must be regarded as one of his shortcomings. It would be wrong, however, to judge him too severely for this failing, for he never enjoyed very good health, and on almost every occasion when he threatened to resign he was not only discouraged but also very ill. This was true in the case presently under discussion, for, in his letter of June 23 to McCarthy, Blake reported that he was too ill to go down (presumably to the House of Commons) that afternoon. In these circumstances, his decision, however reluctantly made, to remain a little longer on the committee, must surely be considered a courageous one. Indeed, both McCarthy and William O'Brien, while urging Blake to remain on the committee, felt that he was justified in being discouraged with the situation. McCarthy, writing shortly before to Mrs. Praed, declared: "I am sorry from my heart for Blake—the gallant and gifted friend who gave up his home and his well earned ease to come over and fight this hopeless battle—which is to be lost by our own fault! He says he feels heartbroken—and his conviction is that the present Bill is lost. I am not quite so unhopeful—but I feel terribly depressed. . . ."[49] William O'Brien, writing on the same subject, expressed his sympathy with Blake who, he remarked, "could but lay his head on the table covered by his clasped hands while he listened to the mean disputations in which he found himself immersed."[50]

[48]*Globe*, Toronto, June 26, 1893.
[49]McCarthy and Praed, *Our Book of Memories*, 362. The letter is dated June 10, 1893.
[50]William O'Brien, *An Olive Branch in Ireland and Its History* (London, 1910), 72-3.

There remains the question whether Blake continued as a member of the sub-committee. Two letters written at this time seem to suggest that his resignation from that body was accepted. On June 27, Morley wrote to Blake asking him to attend a meeting at the Irish office the following day since a part of the bill where his aid would be invaluable was to be discussed. Morley added that he had told Sexton, who warmly concurred, of his intention to invite Blake. If the latter had still been on the sub-committee, it seems unlikely that he would have received a special invitation to this meeting or that Morley would have made a point of telling Sexton about it. In a letter of the same date, McCarthy told Blake of the meeting and of Morley's desire that Blake should be present. McCarthy was anxious that Blake should attend the meeting because the veto question was to be discussed and he was the only member of the party who could really claim to have any practical knowledge of this subject.[51]

The much disputed veto formed only part of the bill's fifth clause which dealt with the executive branch of the government, defining the powers of the Lord-Lieutenant or Viceroy and of the Executive Committee of the Privy Council in Ireland. What it said was, in effect, that the Lord-Lieutenant would be responsible to the British Parliament through the British cabinet in matters of imperial concern and to the Irish legislature through his Irish advisers, subject, however, to the veto of the British government, in domestic affairs. Several aspects of this clause were controversial; it was not the veto power alone which caused difficulty. Objection was taken by some people to the dual responsibility of the Lord-Lieutenant, and when this subject was discussed in the House of Commons, Blake, who from his experience in Canadian politics understood the working of the system, was able to speak with authority upon it. There was no cause for friction, he explained, for the Lord-Lieutenant would act upon the advice of the Irish government in reference to so much of the executive power as was connected with Irish affairs and upon the instructions of a Secretary of State responsible to the British House of Commons in matters of imperial concern: "The officer in one case, in Irish concerns, acts as a Constitutional Monarch upon the advice of the Cabinet responsible to his Legislature. The officer, in the

[51] For both these letters see the Blake Papers.

other case in which he acts as the Imperial delegate, carrying out the will of the Imperial government, acts upon the instructions of a Minister of this Government responsible to this Parliament."[52]

The final provision of the fifth clause was that the Lord-Lieutenant should "on the advice of the executive committee, give or withhold the assent of Her Majesty to bills passed by the two Houses of the Irish legislature, subject to any instructions given by Her Majesty in respect to such bill." To this provision was proposed an amendment that the words, "on the advice of the said executive committee," be omitted.[53]

In speaking against this amendment,[54] Blake explained that to propose that in all matters the Lord-Lieutenant should exercise his own independent discretion upon the question of assent would tend to give life to the veto in the normal condition of affairs. This, he declared, was contrary to the recognized practice, not only in Britain, but in all subordinate legislatures with which he was acquainted. As an illustration, he spoke of Canada and its provinces between 1867 and 1891, claiming that in no case in which imperial considerations did not arise was there any suggestion that the action of the Governor-General or the Lieutenant-Governor, with regard to bills passed by the legislature, should be otherwise than according to the advice of his council. The normal action upon the question of assent to a bill should, Blake believed, be action on the advice of those responsible to the legislature which passed it. This was provided by the clause as it stood; it was expected that assent to the great mass of legislation in Ireland would be given or withheld by the Lord-Lieutenant on the advice of his Executive Committee. Coupled with the provision for normal action was the power of veto which the Irish members understood would be exercised only if their legislature attempted to pass an act believed to be injurious to imperial interests, or one which, although local, was a grave abuse of the powers entrusted to it. In such a case, if it ever occurred, the veto would be exercised by the Lord-Lieutenant on instructions

[52]*Hansard*, 4th Series, XIV, 741. The amendment which proposed the abolition of dual responsibility and against which Blake had spoken was defeated by a vote of 274 to 247. See *ibid.*, 767.
[53]*Ibid.*, 979.
[54]The speech is recorded in *ibid.*, 986-9.

from the imperial executive. Thus, in Blake's opinion, clause 5 of the bill, without the proposed amendment, adequately provided for the giving or withholding of assent to bills in both ordinary and exceptional cases.

The amendment was defeated by a vote of 290 to 248.[55]

After July 6, the date on which Blake's last mentioned speech was delivered, the bill proceeded much more quickly through committee, due to the application of the closure. The committee stage was completed on July 27, and the third reading was finally carried in the early morning of September 2 by a vote of 301 to 267.

In several important respects the bill now differed from the form in which it had been introduced by Gladstone on February 13. An important change had been made in the clause dealing with Irish representation at Westminster. In view of the difficulties involved in restricting the voting power of the Irish members, it had been decided that they should be permitted to vote on all matters. Moreover, the discovery of an error made in computing Ireland's contribution to the spirit duty had led to a revision of the financial clauses of the bill. It had been decided to reduce the term for which the financial arrangements would endure from fifteen to six years, during which period no change would be made in managing or collecting existing taxes. The Irish legislature would, however, be empowered to establish new taxes; and Ireland's contribution to the imperial exchequer would be one-third of her ascertained revenue, in addition to the whole yield of any imperial tax imposed upon her by the Parliament at Westminster expressly for war or special defence. At the end of six years the whole arrangement was to be revised; and Ireland would then collect and manage her own taxes with the exception of those connected with customs, excise, and the post office.

As had been expected, the Home Rule Bill was rejected by the House of Lords. On September 10 it was defeated on second reading by a vote of 419 to 41. Nevertheless, its acceptance by the House of Commons was generally regarded as a triumph for the Nationalist cause, for it was thought to be an important step towards its eventually becoming law.

[55]*Ibid.*, 1006.

IV. BLAKE AND PARTY FINANCE, 1893–4

Canadian and American Financial Missions

RAISING FUNDS to carry on the home rule movement was a vital task throughout the eighteen-nineties. After the Parnell split, Irishmen at home and abroad were less hopeful of the success of the cause and therefore hesitated to give it financial aid. And for a number of reasons the situation became even worse towards the close of 1893 and in the years which followed.

After the rejection of the Home Rule Bill by the House of Lords there was a slackening of interest in the cause. Many who contributed when the bill was actually in preparation or before the Commons were less willing to do so when the achievement of their goal seemed to be in the very indefinite future. This situation was not improved by Lord Rosebery's succession to the premiership upon Gladstone's retirement from that post in March, 1894. The new Prime Minister, in a speech on the twelfth of that month, made very clear his position with regard to Irish home rule. Before it could be granted, he declared, "England, as the predominant member of the partnership of the Three Kingdoms, will have to be convinced of its justice and equity."[1] In fact no important Irish legislation was passed during his government's tenure of office.

But by far the greatest obstacle in the way of fund raising was the growing dissension within the Irish majority party. The Parnell split had been bad enough, but discord among the anti-Parnellites was to cause even more trouble. The chief antagonists in the struggle were John Dillon and T. M. Healy. Each had considerable support from the rank and file of the party, but most of the leading men, including Blake, were on Dillon's side. The party's nominal chairman, Justin McCarthy, although not a leader in this contest, sympathized with Dillon's views. At first these internal quarrels did not reach the public, but soon rumours began to appear in the press.

While the struggle between Dillon and Healy was partly one of

[1] Lord Crewe, *Life of Lord Rosebery* (London, 1931), II, 444–5.

personal rivalry, there were also differences of principle between the two men regarding the composition and direction of the Irish party. Dillon believed that home rule would never be achieved except by a highly unified and centralized organization; he felt that strong leadership was necessary and that decisions as to policy should be made by the leader, with the aid of his principal followers, rather than by the party as a whole. Accordingly, he wished to limit the freedom of constituencies and of individual members of the party in the interests of unity and discipline. In short, he wished for the type of party which had existed before the Parnell split. Healy, on the other hand, was opposed to this principle of centralization. He felt, partly no doubt for personal reasons, that too much power should not be given to the chairman of the party, but that it should be divided more or less equally among the members of the committee. Moreover, he insisted that the constituencies should be absolutely free to choose their own candidates without interference from any central authority in the party.

The two men also differed in their attitude towards Britain's political parties. Dillon was a strong supporter of the Liberal alliance, for he believed that through it home rule would eventually be obtained. Healy, however, distrusted both Liberals and Conservatives, and felt, especially after Lord Rosebery's pronouncement of March, 1894, that the Irish party ought to be completely independent of British political parties. He thought that Irish Nationalists should be prepared to accept beneficial social legislation from either of them, but should also be free to attack them if they adopted policies contrary to Ireland's interests. Dillon, on the other hand, was not at all anxious that Ireland should secure measures of social reform from the Imperial Parliament, for he feared that such legislation might lessen the Irish desire for self-government. Home rule, he felt, should come first; other reforms could be obtained later from the Irish legislature. It was not surprising that, holding such widely divergent opinions, these two men often disagreed;[2] it was, however, unfortu-

[2] For a fuller account of the differences in outlook and policy between Dillon and Healy, see F. S. L. Lyons, *The Irish Parliamentary Party, 1890–1910* (London, 1951), 40–4, 48–9.

nate that their quarrels and those of their followers should so undermine the Irish cause.

Under these circumstances it was naturally difficult to secure financial aid. Yet, if the movement were to be kept alive, funds had to be secured, for in addition to the ordinary expenses of any political party the Irish party had to pay many of its members in order to retain their services at Westminster. At this time, no salary was attached to membership in the House of Commons, and since many Irish Nationalists, unlike most members of the British parties, were not self-supporting, they could not afford to attend Parliament regularly unless they received allowances from the party funds.[3] It was in the raising of funds during these discouraging years that one of Blake's greatest contributions to the Irish cause was given. Not only did he subscribe generously himself, but he did his best to encourage sympathizers with home rule in Canada and the United States to do likewise.

On September 2, 1893, just after the Home Rule Bill had passed third reading in the Commons, Blake sailed for Canada. One of his principal speaking engagements during this visit was to be at an Irish Day celebration on September 30 at the Chicago World's Fair, where he was to represent the Irish party. It seemed likely to be an important occasion, and the Irish leaders hoped that it might result in considerable financial aid for the cause.

But for a time it appeared that here too dissension might mar the proceedings. On the Chicago committee which was arranging the celebration there were several Parnellites who wished to have no speaking on political topics, and therefore tried to persuade Blake to change the subject of his address from "Home Rule" to "The Irishman in Statesmanship."[4] The situation was further complicated by the arrival in the United States of Arthur O'Connor and Florence O'Driscoll, two Healyite members of the Irish party. O'Driscoll had come out as British Commissioner to the World's Fair, but O'Connor's decision to accompany him had been unexpected. With Blake's

[3]For a fuller discussion of this matter, see *ibid.*, chap. 6.
[4]For Blake's correspondence with members of the Chicago committee, see Blake Papers, General Irish Political Correspondence, Sept., 1893.

approval O'Connor was invited to speak at Chicago, but he caused some embarrassment to the committee by protesting his right, as the senior member of Parliament, to precede Blake in speaking. Blake was personally indifferent, but the committee wished him to speak first, and O'Connor finally agreed to this arrangement.[5] The dispute with the Parnellites was also cleared up, and Blake spoke on home rule.

His speech was well received. After paying tribute to Parnell's work and showing that the majority party was following his policy, Blake stressed the significance of the fact that the Home Rule Bill had been passed by "the people's House in Parliament." He then read a letter which Gladstone had sent him expressing pleasure that he was attending the Irish Day celebration. Gladstone, like Blake, considered the passage of the bill through the Commons as a great triumph and felt that even its rejection by the Lords could not long delay its becoming law.[6]

Blake's Chicago friends, pleased with the effect of his speech and feeling that it would encourage fund raising, immediately invited a number of prominent Irish residents of Chicago to a private meeting with Blake to consider plans for beginning a subscription fund.[7] The meeting proved satisfactory, a small committee being appointed to study the situation and to summon a larger private meeting if a basis for action could be agreed upon.[8] Later in October, Blake was informed that money could probably be raised in Chicago if it were specified that it was for political purposes and not for the evicted tenants' fund.[9] While agreeing that this might be done, Blake added that money was also needed for the latter purpose.[10]

[5]For details of the dispute with O'Connor and O'Driscoll, see *ibid.*, Blake to Dillon, Oct. 1, 1893.
[6]An account of Blake's speech, including the text of Gladstone's letter, is published in the *Globe*, Toronto, Oct. 2, 1893.
[7]This is reported in Dillon Papers, Blake to Dillon, Oct. 1, 1893.
[8]The situation is described in *ibid.*, Blake to Dillon, Oct. 3, 1893.
[9]Blake Papers, James Sullivan to Blake, Oct. 23, 1893.
[10]*Ibid.*, Blake to Sullivan, Oct. 25, 1893. About $5,000 was raised in Chicago following the Irish Day celebration. Blake reported this in a speech at New York on Oct. 17, 1894. See *Home Rule Bulletin* (New York, Nov., 1894).

Tentative arrangements had been made for Blake, O'Connor, and O'Driscoll to address meetings at New York, Philadelphia, and Boston, but in view of the difficulties caused by the two Healyites before the Chicago celebration, Blake decided that it would be unwise to accept a joint invitation with these men. The officers of the Irish National Federation of America therefore cancelled the meetings.[11] However, Blake went to New York to confer with the officers of the Federation, arriving there on October 26, two days before his sailing date, and a most important conference took place with leaders of the organization from Boston and Philadelphia as well as New York. In a very long letter which he wrote while on shipboard, Blake gave McCarthy a detailed account of this private meeting.[12]

Before the conference was long under way, Blake was informed of the principal reason for holding it. The officers of the Federation felt that they had a right to receive information on certain points regarding the administration and disposition of funds collected through their efforts. They had received a disturbing report on the financial administration of the party, and unless they were assured of its falseness, they feared they could no longer continue to aid the Irish cause. This report had been given by O'Connor and O'Driscoll in an interview with the officers of the Federation, who now invited Blake to give his version of the matters on which the other two men had spoken. On those relating to finance, the officers of the Federation claimed a right to be informed, while, on the others, they would be glad to hear from Blake if he thought fit to speak.

O'Connor and O'Driscoll had claimed that certain members of the party were seeking to control it and as a result a highly unsatisfactory situation had arisen. There had been no regular meetings of the party for months; no statement of finances had been made, and no satisfactory information regarding them could be obtained, for the finance committee of the party "was practically controlled by a clique,

---

[11] See Blake Papers, J. P. Ryan (Secretary, Irish National Federation of America) to Blake, Oct. 8, 1893, and Daniel P. Sullivan (Boston) to J. P. Ryan, Oct. 18, 1893.
[12] *Ibid.*, Blake to McCarthy, Nov. 2, 1893.

who were treasurers, paymasters and auditors all in one, without any disposition to give any satisfaction to anyone for the irregularity." They also alleged that a large proportion of all money received, including that which came from the United States, was arbitrarily transferred from the political fund to the evicted tenants' fund without consultation with the party. Consequently, there was a serious shortage of money for political purposes and, although the members who supported the party clique had no difficulty in obtaining funds to cover their election expenses or to carry on their parliamentary duties, the pressing needs of those members who questioned the wisdom of the foregoing proceedings were wholly disregarded.

Blake did his best to answer the specific allegations of O'Connor and O'Driscoll. He declared that there was no stated time for holding party meetings, which were called by the chairman, with or without the request of the committee or of any of its members, or on a requisition from members of the party. Nevertheless, several meetings had been held within the last few months; there was, therefore, no foundation for any statement to the contrary.

To prove that information regarding the financial administration of the party was available to its members, Blake explained the working of the system. All the money which reached the party was paid into the trust accounts of the national trustees. During the past year there had been three funds: the evicted tenants' fund, raised from Irish and a few colonial subscriptions; the parliamentary fund, which was composed almost entirely of collections made in the United States through the Federation; and the home rule fund, the result of subscriptions from the colonies and from Ireland, which was used for the general purposes of the cause. The national trustees drew no cheques on any of these funds unless they were authorized to do so by a specific resolution of the committee of the party. In 1892 the accounts of the various funds had been audited independently, submitted to the committee, and, under its order, laid before the party. Blake added that the "finance committee" to which O'Connor and O'Driscoll had referred did not exist; there was no separate committee to deal with financial questions.

Speaking of the evicted tenants' fund, Blake admitted that in August, 1893, when it was almost exhausted, the committee had authorized the advance of the sum of £3,000 to it from the other funds. But the whole question had first been discussed at a party meeting, where a resolution had been unanimously adopted, recommending such a step. This resolution had been heartily supported by Healy and Arthur O'Connor. Blake realized, however, that the cause of the evicted tenants was no longer very popular in the United States and there was considerable demand from American sympathizers that money which they contributed should be used exclusively for political purposes. He therefore assured the officers of the Federation that if American subscribers imposed such limitations they would be sacredly observed.

Blake did not believe that there was any basis for the charge that certain members of the party had no difficulty in obtaining funds, while the needs of others were disregarded. The administration of the parliamentary fund had been entrusted to an independent committee, which did not disclose the names of members who received allowances from it. When the independent committee required money to pay the allowances, a requisition was made on behalf of its treasurers for the entire sum. The parliamentary committee then authorized the issue of a cheque for this sum to the independent committee, which distributed the money in the form of separate cheques to the individual members concerned. Occasionally, however, a fresh case came before the parliamentary committee for consideration, but Blake had never seen the slightest disposition to deal unfairly with any of the few proposals for payment which had come up.

As far as election expenses were concerned, these were managed through the office of the Irish National Federation in Dublin. A general report, pointing out the most urgent needs and giving a list of the grants considered absolutely necessary, was sent to the parliamentary committee, which, after discussion, ordered them to be made. From time to time, special cases also came before the committee which disposed of them on their merits. Blake had never heard the charge that any grant made had been unnecessary, and, within his recollection, no grant proposed by any member of the committee had been rejected.

At the conclusion of his statement, Blake reported, there was a unanimous expression of satisfaction with his explanations, and a vote of thanks was adopted by acclamation. But the officers of the Federation told him that an appeal for funds could not be made before January.

Because of the importance of Blake's letter giving the report of the New York conference, copies of it were printed and circulated confidentially among members of the Irish party. A copy was also sent to Dr. Emmet, president of the Irish National Federation of America, to whom Blake wrote after his return to Britain estimating the amount of money which would be required by the Irish party during 1894. In listing the items for which money was needed, he omitted the evicted tenants' fund, since American sympathizers did not wish to subscribe to it. But, in addition to such items as payment of members, by-elections, and British propaganda, he included a general election, which many believed would take place towards the end of 1894. His estimate of the total requirements for the year was £31,280, of which £4,000 would be needed on January 1, 1894.[13] It has, however, been asserted by one historian that Blake's estimate was a generous one, and that he was probably pitching his claims very high, knowing that he would obtain only a fraction of what he sought.[14]

The task of raising such a sum of money was neither an easy nor an enviable one, but Blake agreed without hesitation to do what he could to help. He had intended to spend the Christmas recess in Italy, but after consultation with McCarthy, he willingly abandoned this plan in order to make another trip to America in the interests of the Irish cause.[15] Shortly before his departure, the committee of the Irish party passed a resolution requesting him "to confer with the Executive of the Federation in New York as to the best means of providing for the urgent present needs of the National Movement, and also to attend meetings in furtherance of this object, if the Executive shall so desire." Healy, who had not been present at the

[13]*Ibid.*, Blake to Emmet, Nov. 14, 1893.
[14]Lyons, *Irish Parliamentary Party*, 206n.
[15]This decision is announced in Blake Papers, Blake to Emmet, Nov. 14, 1893.

beginning of this meeting, arrived later and was the only member of the committee to oppose the resolution.[16]

The financial situation was indeed so serious that McCarthy requested several members of the party to become responsible for specific amounts of money to make provision for members' allowances which had to be paid on January 1, 1894. In a memorandum dated December 15, 1893, J. F. X. O'Brien listed the names of ten members who had already complied with McCarthy's request. Nine of these men were to be responsible for £100 each, while Blake had agreed to the sum of £300. Application was being made to ten other members in the hope of securing the necessary £2,000. The money was to be obtained in the following manner. Each man who had agreed to assume responsibility was to give a bill for his amount, to be discounted at a London bank, under the arrangement that the earliest party remittances were to be used for the retirement of the bills, which were at three months from December 28, 1893. This meant that if the Irish party had not secured sufficient funds by the end of March, 1894, the men responsible would have to meet the bills.[17]

Blake arrived in New York from Britain on the evening of December 24, 1893, and went immediately to Dr. Emmet's home, where he met several members of the executive of the Federation. They told him that they had sent a circular to the heads of their more important branches asking whether meetings could be arranged in January or early February for the purpose of launching an appeal for funds. But since most American cities were suffering from a very severe depression and local calls for charity seemed more pressing than did the Irish cause, the replies to this circular were not at all encouraging. Boston was the only city which appeared enthusiastic about a meeting; so Blake went there two days later to discuss the advisability of holding one. Despite the situation and attitude elsewhere, the leaders in Boston decided to proceed with their plans, but Blake was not very hopeful that much money would be raised. He told McCarthy that if

[16] J. F. X. O'Brien Papers, Minutes of the party committee, Dec. 14, 1893.
[17] See Blake Papers, Blake to McCarthy, Dec. 28, 1893. The text of O'Brien's memorandum is included in this letter.

the depression in America continued and the resources of the party failed, he would, towards the end of March, try to borrow $5,000 to keep the party going until conditions improved.[18]

To Blake's distress the financial situation became urgent long before March. Prior to his departure from Britain, he had arranged with Sir Thomas Esmonde, one of the party whips, to send him a cable which would meet him on his arrival in New York if there were any hitch in the arrangements for discounting the bills in order to pay members' allowances on January 1, 1894. Having received no cable, Blake had assumed that everything was all right and at his New York conference had told his friends of this plan to meet current expenditures.[19] But on January 1 Blake received a cable dated December 30, which Emmet had sent on to Toronto and which told him that the London bank had declined to discount the bills.[20] Blake was very much irritated at not having been informed earlier of this situation and wrote to McCarthy: "I must say it occurs to me very extraordinary that matters should have been left to 30 December in this state. Why was I not advised?" But, in spite of his irritation, Blake was ready with a plan to help: "I am sorry to say that, having given up my practice, I no longer have an income which would enable me to stand in the breach. But I cannot allow the cause to fail at this moment, even for lack of supplies which I might have secured from others had the emergency been disclosed. I am therefore going to make private enquiries (which is all I can do this holiday) and, if I can manage it, I will raise a call loan on the security of some stock which I still own, and cable you a remittance to-morrow."[21] The next day, January 2, Blake secured a loan of £1,500. He calculated that, together with the amount which the Irish party had on hand, this would be enough to meet the immediate requirements.[22]

Meanwhile Blake had begun his campaign for funds in Canada

---

[18]*Ibid.* Blake gave an account of his conferences in New York and Boston in this letter.
[19]For a description of Blake's arrangement with Esmonde regarding the cable, see *ibid.*, Blake to McCarthy, Jan. 1, 1894.
[20]The cable, though presumably from Esmonde, is not signed. It is in the Blake Papers.
[21]*Ibid.*, Blake to McCarthy, Jan. 1, 1894.
[22]See *ibid.*, Blake to McCarthy, Jan. 3, 1894.

and the United States. Before his departure from England, he had written to the Most Rev. John Walsh, Roman Catholic Archbishop of Toronto, asking if anything could be done in his diocese. The Archbishop, a staunch supporter of home rule, was anxious to help and a few days after Blake's arrival in Toronto on December 28, he wrote inviting him to a small meeting at his residence to discuss the situation.[23] In a letter accepting this invitation, Blake proposed that before making an appeal to the masses, wealthy Irishmen should be approached for subscriptions. He added: "A quarter of a century of public life has left me far from rich, and possessed of but a very modest competence, while my acceptance of an Irish seat has almost destroyed my sources of professional income. I cannot therefore do what I would wish. But I will gladly meet the largest subscription which any other Irish Canadian may give."[24]

The meeting, which took place on January 5, was attended not only by Blake and Archbishop Walsh but also by Archbishop Cleary of Kingston, several of the clergy, and a number of young and active laymen connected with various Irish societies. Both the Archbishops, as well as a number of other men, spoke to the gathering of the need for funds, and two wealthy Torontonians—Senator Frank Smith and G. W. Kiely—offered to contribute $1,000 each; Blake then put his name down for the same amount. It was agreed to hold a meeting of the heads of Irish societies and other workers with a view to organizing a canvass for collections throughout the city; at the same time it was decided that church collections should be taken up in the rural parts of the diocese. Archbishop Cleary intimated his intention to raise $2,000 in his diocese, but, with due regard to the farming season, this collection as well as the rural ones in the diocese of Toronto would be postponed until May or June.[25] Two days after this meeting Blake was able to tell McCarthy that two other wealthy Torontonians had been successfully approached; Hugh Ryan had promised to give $1,000, and Thomas Long, $500.[26]

Meanwhile, the Hon. John Costigan, a prominent Roman Catholic

[23]This information is contained in *ibid*.
[24]*Ibid*., Blake to the Archbishop of Toronto, Jan. 2, 1894.
[25]For Blake's report of this meeting, see *ibid*., Blake to McCarthy, Jan. 6, 1894.
[26]*Ibid*., Blake to McCarthy, Jan. 8, 1894.

Conservative, had written to members of the Episcopate all over Canada asking if they would be willing "to countenance and aid in arranging for a collection in each parish of the Archdiocese (or Diocese) by the respective Parish Priests."[27] Blake told both Costigan and McCarthy that he doubted the expediency of appealing to the Roman Catholic clergy all over the country, irrespective of the nationality of their people,[28] and, in fact, the appeal met with little response. In Quebec, where the majority of the Roman Catholic population was French, rather than Irish, most of the bishops, while expressing sympathy with the Irish cause, showed little enthusiasm for organizing a collection. Most of them declared that the population was poor, crops had been bad, and winter was not a suitable time for attempting to raise money. Nor were the replies from other parts of Canada much more encouraging, although the Archbishop of Halifax said he would arrange for a collection in January.[29] On Blake's advice, and in view of the attitude elsewhere, Costigan suggested to the Archbishop that he postpone the collection until the spring.[30]

In spite of this situation, Blake continued his efforts to stimulate collections, either then or in the spring, whenever it seemed possible to make them. His correspondence during the remaining weeks of his stay in Canada shows that he devoted much of his time to communicating with people in many parts of the country who might be able to help in the campaign for funds.

Apparently it was decided not to adhere to the decision, made at the meeting at Archbishop Walsh's, to postpone the collections in the rural parts of the diocese of Toronto until May or June, for on January 24 the Archbishop wrote a circular letter to the clergy of the diocese asking that collections be taken up for the Irish cause on February 4. In this letter the Archbishop paid a warm tribute to Blake:

> This appeal is not only sanctioned, but is urged as a matter of the last importance, by the Hon. Edward Blake, who, with all the earnestness, zeal and

---

[27]Blake quoted one of the letters, a copy of which had been sent to him by Costigan, in a report to McCarthy dated Jan. 4, 1894. See Blake Papers.
[28]*Ibid.*, Blake to McCarthy, Jan. 4, 1894; Blake to Costigan, Jan. 6, 1894.
[29]The replies of many of the bishops are quoted in *ibid.*, Blake to McCarthy, Jan. 4, 1894.
[30]See *ibid.*, Blake to McCarthy, Jan. 15, 1894.

enthusiasm of a Knight of old, has devoted his time and talents to the cause of Home Rule for Ireland.

The sacrifices of time and money and of personal ease and comfort made by this distinguished gentleman for the liberty, prosperity and happiness of Ireland are certainly stimulating and encouraging, and loudly call, not alone for our admiration, but primarily and specially for our imitation. . . . [31]

Despite the difficulties involved, Blake's efforts to secure funds before returning to Britain in February met with considerable success. The subscriptions from wealthy Torontonians, together with a few smaller ones, amounting in all to almost $5,000, were transmitted to him about the middle of January by the treasurers of the Toronto committee. He at once applied them towards the payment of the loan which he had raised at the beginning of the month.[32] Considerable amounts were also raised in Ottawa and Montreal, where Blake addressed meetings on January 25 and 29 respectively.[33] But most encouraging of all was the Boston meeting held on January 31, which Blake described to McCarthy as "an immense success."[34] Subscriptions amounting to more than $4,000 were announced and a great many others promised.[35]

At the Hoffman House, New York, on the evening of February 9, Blake was given a reception by the trustees and city council of the Irish National Federation of America. In an address presented to Blake by the council, the Irishmen of New York pledged themselves to do all in their power to aid the Irish cause. Prominent Irishmen from other American cities also declared that in their section of the country Irish-Americans would do their part.[36]

On the whole the situation in Canada and the United States appeared more encouraging when Blake sailed from New York on

[31]There is a copy of this circular letter in the Blake Papers.

[32]Blake reported this to McCarthy in a letter of Jan. 19, 1894, which has not come to light. He repeated it in a letter to McCarthy, dated Feb. 21, 1894. See Dillon Papers.

[33]See Blake Papers, Blake to McCarthy, Jan. 26 and Feb. 5 and 6, 1894.

[34]*Ibid.*, Blake to McCarthy, Feb. 2, 1894.

[35]The meeting is reported in the *Freeman's Journal*, Dublin, Feb. 14, 1894. Blake's speech is also published by the Municipal Council of the Irish National Federation of Boston and vicinity in a pamphlet entitled "Address in aid of Home Rule in Ireland."

[36]There is an account of the reception in the *Freeman's Journal*, Dublin, Feb. 20, 1894.

February 10 than it had on his arrival there in December and on his return to Britain, he was warmly praised for his work. McCarthy, to whom he had sent lengthy reports of his progress, declared: "No man ever served a political cause better, under conditions only too difficult and discouraging, than he served our national cause by his recent visit to Canada and the United States."³⁷ And Davitt wrote:

> A thousand welcomes back and heartiest congratulations upon the splendid work which you performed during your "holiday"! I have had the advantage of reading the interesting letters you sent to McCarthy and I have learned in this way of your sleepless efforts to obtain the sinews of war under the frightfully adverse circumstances which prevailed in the States and in Canada. Nobody else could have done what you accomplished.³⁸

In an editorial published on February 24, 1894, the *Freeman's Journal* gave Blake the highest praise. Commenting on his work, the appeal issued by the Archbishop of Toronto, and the Canadian contributions, it remarked:

> There is one Irish representative to whom no small share of the credit of this Canadian demonstration on behalf of Ireland and its cause belongs. Mr. Blake, M.P., has been made the intermediary between the chosen treasurers of the Canadian Nationalists and the National trustees. That his personal example has borne good fruit in Canada the Archbishop of Toronto's letter indicates. Such fruit is only part of the happy result that has followed from Mr. Blake's enlistment as a worker for the emancipation of the land of his forefathers. His services are prized and treasured in the memory of a not ungrateful nation. We commend his efforts and the efforts of his compatriots to the example of Irishmen at home and abroad.

But the Parnellite *Irish Independent* did not consider Blake's work at all admirable. Having heard the report that he had raised money in Canada on his personal security, it remarked, in its issue of March 20, that if this were true, "the imported Canadian is running the Irish party with Canadian money." "It may," it went on, "be pure generosity on the part of Mr. Blake in raising loans in Canada for the support of the Whigs [anti-Parnellites]; but it is a very dangerous form of generosity, as it places him in a position of power which no untried and imported politician should be allowed to occupy in the Home Rule struggle. . . ." Although it is clear from a study of Blake's career that he made no attempt to run the Irish party on

---

³⁷Blake Papers, McCarthy to J. J. Curran (Solicitor-General of Canada), Feb. 22, 1894.
³⁸*Ibid.*, Michael Davitt to Blake, Feb. 19, 1894.

the strength of his large financial contributions to it, this charge was probably, under the circumstances, a natural one for an opposition journal to make.

Shortly after Blake's return to Britain, further trouble arose regarding Arthur O'Connor and Florence O'Driscoll. Having become convinced that Blake's report of his meeting with the Irish National Federation of America, which had been circulated among members of the Irish parliamentary party, was in reality a campaign document, Arthur O'Connor decided, more than three months later, that a reply to it was necessary. So, on February 25, 1894, he wrote two letters, one to his colleagues of the Irish parliamentary party, the other to the secretary and members of the executive of the Irish National Federation of America.[39] In both these letters he declared that he had intended his visit to the United States to be a private one, but that cables sent to Irish-Americans in New York, warning them of the supposed intentions of O'Connor and O'Driscoll, had made this impossible. They had been met at the docks by reporters who questioned them about dissension in the party and had afterwards been invited to a meeting of the executive of the National Federation of America, where they were requested to answer questions about this dissension. Furthermore, they had not been informed of the purpose of the meeting until they arrived, but when they were urged to express their views and were practically subjected to cross-examination by the officials of the Federation, they felt it impossible to deny them the expression of their opinions. What O'Connor wished to prove by this explanation was that he and O'Driscoll had not sought out the officials of the Federation in New York with the deliberate intention of assailing certain members of their party.

In the letter to the executive of the National Federation of America, O'Connor also repeated certain of the charges which he had made at New York, that the committee of the party exercised too much power and that the administration of party finance was unsatisfactory. Among other things, he complained that the treasurers who administered the parliamentary fund were not completely independent of the party committee since one of the treasurers, J. F. X. O'Brien, had also become secretary of the committee. O'Connor's

[39]The text of both these letters is published in the *Irish Independent*, Dublin, March 23, 1894.

principal charges were against Dillon and William O'Brien who, he felt, from the time of the Boulogne negotiations, had done nothing but harm to the party; he criticized especially what he considered the too powerful position of Dillon, who was not only a trustee and a member of the party committee, but also a member of the evicted tenants' committee. He also denied Blake's assertion that in 1892 the accounts of the various funds had been laid before the party by order of the committee.

Doubtless these letters were at least partly responsible for the action taken against O'Connor and O'Driscoll by the Irish party at its sessional meeting in March, 1894. O'Connor was not re-elected to the party committee or to the position of honorary secretary which he had held for fourteen years, while O'Driscoll failed to secure re-election as one of the party whips.[40]

It was not until some time after the sessional meeting of the party, namely on March 23, that the text of O'Connor's two letters appeared in the press. Blake, who already knew their contents, was deeply distressed at their publication. He had not wished to be re-elected to the committee of the party at the beginning of the 1894 session, but had been persuaded by McCarthy and Dillon to carry on.[41] A few days after the publication of the letters, Blake wrote to McCarthy intimating his intention of withdrawing from the committee at the earliest opportunity. Declaring that "the public has before it the injurious aspersions and erroneous statements of Mr. O'Connor, while it remains ignorant of the other side," he went on to say that the publication of papers and facts to disprove O'Connor's charges would, at the present time, feed the fuel of controversy; he did not, therefore, ask that this should be done. He explained, however, that his own position, under these circumstances, was intolerable:

> I have no such roots, no such character or standing based on long service, among the people with whom I have cast my lot as would enable me without a vindication to retain that leading place into which I was unexpectedly thrust, and in which I have been against my will retained.

---

[40]Dillon Papers, Minutes of the Irish parliamentary party, March 12 and 14, 1894.

[41]See Blake Papers, Blake to McCarthy, Jan. 3 and Feb. 5, 1894.

I feel that I am so discredited that my usefulness is gone; and indeed I do not think I could endure to show my face in a leading position under such circumstances.[42]

No definite decision was reached at this time, and in a letter dated April 12, Blake had to explain to Davitt, who had written urging him to remain on the committee,[43] why he wished to resign from it. He was somewhat more frank with Davitt than he had been with McCarthy, for while giving the same reason for his desire to withdraw from the committee, he told Davitt his true opinion of current party policy. This policy seemed to be to ignore O'Connor's accusations, and although it was Blake's opinion that such a course would be injurious to the party, he felt a delicacy in stating that view. But during the past two or three days there seemed to be a growing feeling that in the general interests of the party, the charges would have to be answered. If this opinion prevailed, Blake would, for the time being, remain on the committee.[44]

It appears, however, that no attempt was made at this time to answer O'Connor's charges,[45] for twice within the next month Blake again intimated his intention of resigning from the committee.[46] A disagreement within the committee over a proposed financial arrangement had added to his dissatisfaction, and was at least partly responsible for the first of these proposed resignations. Therefore, although Blake finally agreed to remain on the committee at McCarthy's request,[47] he was far from happy about the situation. To William O'Brien who, like McCarthy, had evidently told him that his resignation would be harmful to the cause, he wrote: "I must take it as another proof of my incapacity for the position that I am quite unable to comprehend the possibility of the consequences you predict from my retirement on my special grounds from the com-

[42]*Ibid.*, Blake to McCarthy, March 29, 1894.
[43]*Ibid.*, Davitt to Blake, April 10, 1894.
[44]*Ibid.*, Blake to Davitt, April 12, 1894.
[45]It was not until August 6, 1894, that McCarthy wrote to Emmet enclosing a confidential memorandum answering the charges. For a copy of McCarthy's letter and a typewritten copy of the memorandum see the Blake Papers. There is a draft of the memorandum partly in Dillon's and partly in Blake's handwriting among the J. F. X. O'Brien Papers.
[46]Blake Papers, Blake to McCarthy, April 25 and May 8, 1894.
[47]*Ibid.*, Blake to McCarthy, May 10, 1894.

mittee. I can understand the injurious effects to myself, but I alone am able to balance the account in this personal aspect. For the public and the cause the matter seems to me absolutely trivial."[48] It was undoubtedly to this letter that Dillon referred when he wrote to O'Brien: "Blake's mood is deplorable and to me inexplainable. It is impossible to understand how a man with so much that is noble in his nature could write such a letter as that you sent me. He is a very great danger so long as he remains in that temper. . . ."[49] Dillon's attitude is understandable in view of the fact that O'Connor, although replying to Blake's report, had really been much more severe on Dillon than on Blake. The attack apparently left Dillon unmoved and he could not understand why Blake should regard it in such a manner. In fact, although Dillon was Blake's most intimate friend and admirer, he never came to understand his frequent desire to resign.

It must be urged in defence of Blake's frequent threats to resign that, in May, 1894, not only were both he and his wife ill, but they had had very unsatisfactory reports of the health of their youngest son, Samuel, who was then in Canada. Seriously worried about his health, they felt they should be with him and were trying to arrange for him to come to England. On May 10, the day that Blake agreed to remain on the committee, they had not yet succeeded in their attempt.[50] It seems likely that these private troubles were partly responsible for Blake's disturbed state of mind at this time.

The Tweedmouth Incident

When Blake returned to Britain in February, 1894, the finances of the Irish party were still at a very low ebb. A considerable portion of the loan which he had raised in Canada remained to be repaid, and money was needed for the next instalment of members' allowances, due on April 1. Yet it seemed inexpedient at this time to make an appeal to Ireland for political subscriptions, because a campaign to secure money for the evicted tenants' fund was then in

---

[48]*Ibid.*, Blake to W. O'Brien, May 17, 1894.
[49]Dillon Papers, Dillon to W. O'Brien, May 22, 1894.
[50]See Blake Papers, Blake to McCarthy, May 10, 1894.

progress. The financial prospects of the party were rendered still worse by the publication of Arthur O'Connor's letters on March 23, and, in fact, only a portion of the quarterly allowances to members was paid in April.[51] By the beginning of May the situation had become desperate, and on the third of that month a meeting of the party was held to consider the advisability of making an appeal to Ireland for funds to sustain the party at Westminster. The meeting was adjourned without a decision's being reached.[52]

It was probably shortly before this meeting that Lord Tweedmouth, a prominent British Liberal, offered, in a private conversation with Blake, to give to the Irish party, either in his own name or anonymously, the sum of £2,000. Lord Tweedmouth, who had succeeded to this title on the death of his father on March 4, 1894, had, as Edward Marjoribanks, been Financial Secretary of the Treasury in the Gladstone ministry and chief whip of the Liberal party in the House of Commons. On succeeding to the title, he had, of course, entered the House of Lords and ceased to have any control of Liberal party funds or management of party affairs in the House of Commons, though he had entered the cabinet as Lord Privy Seal and Chancellor of the Duchy of Lancaster. Blake told Lord Tweedmouth that he did not think it would be possible to accept his very generous offer, but, not wishing to take upon himself the responsibility of refusing it, he said that he would consult some of his colleagues. Consequently, without revealing Lord Tweedmouth's name, Blake told McCarthy and a few members of the committee about the offer. He evidently also mentioned it to the party at the meeting of May 3.[53] The fact that he wrote to Lord Tweedmouth three days later, telling him that no action had yet been taken on his proposal,[54] suggests that there was considerable discussion of it, though very soon after this it was decided that the money could not

[51]See *ibid.*, Blake to McCarthy, April 11, 1894.
[52]Dillon Papers, Minutes of the Irish parliamentary party, May 3, 1894.
[53]There is no mention of the offer in the party minutes, but Blake stated in two letters that he had told the party about it. See Blake Papers, Blake to Lord Tweedmouth, May 6, 1894; Blake to McCarthy, Sept. 4, 1894.
[54]*Ibid.*, Blake to Tweedmouth, May 6, 1894. Blake mentioned in this letter that "there were three meetings on finance, the last one yesterday." There is, however, no record in the party minutes of any meeting between those of the third and seventh. The second and third meetings to which Blake referred were probably private ones with the colleagues he consulted.

be accepted. Doubtless it was felt that, although there were no conditions attached to the offer, its acceptance might endanger the independence of the Irish party. Nothing more was heard of the offer at this time, even Blake's closest colleagues knowing only that it had been made by a British politician, while Blake alone was aware of his identity. On May 7 the party voted in favour of an appeal to Ireland,[55] and a month later McCarthy announced that up to that date the response to this appeal had been very satisfactory.[56] So, for the time being at least, the financial crisis seemed over.

The task of raising sufficient funds to carry on the movement was, however, a continuous one, and on August 8, 1894, a meeting was held at the Westminster Palace Hotel, London, to consider one method of obtaining money.[57] This meeting, held under the auspices of the Metropolitan Branch of the Irish National League of Great Britain with T. P. O'Connor, the president of that organization, as its chairman, was attended not only by London Irishmen and several prominent members of the Irish party, including both McCarthy and Dillon, but also by a number of British sympathizers with the cause of Irish home rule. In the course of his address, the chairman declared that the meeting had been called for the purpose of giving the Irishmen of London and British sympathizers with the Irish cause an opportunity of helping to support it. In furtherance of this object, it was decided to launch an appeal for funds in England. No objection to accepting money from Englishmen as well as from Irishmen resident in England appears to have been raised, for subscriptions were received from men of both nationalities at the meeting. It is not, however, entirely clear whether appeals to prominent British Liberals, including past and present members of the government, were intended. This question afterwards became a serious matter of dispute.

The appeal was issued in a circular letter dated August 22, 1894, and signed by J. F. X. O'Brien, who had been named treasurer of the committee in charge of the appeal. Subscriptions were requested for the Irish parliamentary fund and cheques were to be made payable

[55]Dillon Papers, Minutes of the Irish parliamentary party, May 7, 1894.
[56]*Ibid.*, June 7, 1894.
[57]There is an account of the meeting in the *Freeman's Journal*, Dublin, Aug. 9, 1894.

to Justin McCarthy, T. P. O'Connor, or J. F. X. O'Brien. With each circular was enclosed a list of those who had subscribed at the meeting of August 8.[58] Whatever the original intention regarding the appeal, it is clear that copies of the circular were sent to many well-known British Liberals, including some who were or had been members of the government. Within a few days, replies began to come in, among them a letter from Lord Tweedmouth to McCarthy, which read as follows: "I have a note from Mr. Gladstone enclosing a cheque for £100 to aid your new Parliamentary Fund, which I have great pleasure in sending on to you, together with one of like amount from myself. I hope contributions will come freely in response to your circular of the 22nd. I dare say you will acknowledge Mr. G's cheque direct to himself at Hawarden."[59]

It was customary to acknowledge publicly the receipt of subscriptions to any of the Irish party's funds by printing the letters accompanying them in the *Freeman's Journal*. Consequently, the subscriptions sent in reply to the circular were acknowledged in this way, and Tweedmouth's letter appeared in that journal on September 1. Immediately a storm of protest against the appeal to British Liberals arose from the Healyite wing of the Irish party. Letters from many of the Irish members appeared in the *Freeman's Journal* between September 3 and 14, most of them written by Healy and his supporters in condemnation of the appeal. Their argument was that the independence of the Irish party was being seriously endangered by this appeal to British Liberals for funds to help support Irish members of Parliament. Some of the letters suggested that the subscriptions from British Liberals should be returned with thanks and an explanation to the donors,[60] while one proposed, as an alternative to this, that, with the donors' permission, the money should be transferred to the evicted tenants' fund.[61] It is clear, however, that Healy, while condemning the appeal, did not think that his supporters should press for the return of the subscriptions. Discussing this

---

[58]For a copy of the circular letter and of the list of subscribers which was enclosed with it, see the J. F. X. O'Brien Papers.
[59]*Freeman's Journal*, Dublin, Sept. 1, 1894. The letter is dated Aug. 27, 1894.
[60]*Ibid.*, Sept. 3 and 4, 1894.
[61]*Ibid.*, Sept. 7, 1894.

aspect of the question in a letter to Bernard Malloy, one of his supporters, he declared: "What practical men have to remember is that the party must be carried on, and, therefore, that it is better to submit to be pelted for the rest of this Parliament with an incident for which our responsibility is disengaged than to risk the bringing about of a crisis like that precipitated in the last three years by mere reckless men."[62]

It is not surprising that Healy and his supporters were joined in their attack on the appeal by the Parnellite *Independent* and the Unionist *Irish Times*. On May 3 the *Independent* declared that the Irish whig party (as it always called the anti-Parnellites) was not only in receipt of British money, but had asked for it through its nominated leader, Justin McCarthy. The *Irish Times*, on the same day, went even further, stating that the appeal proved that the Irish parliamentary party was no longer an independent organization, but that it was subservient to the British Liberals.

Several leading members of the Irish parliamentary party hastened to answer the attack of the Healyites, Parnellites, and Unionists. Already, on September 3, the *Freeman's Journal* had attempted to refute the charges in an editorial, an excerpt from which follows: "As a matter of fact no appeal has been made for subscriptions by the Committee or by the Party to any Minister or ex-Minister. No such appeal was authorized. No such appeal was made. . . . These subscriptions reached the National Trustees as the voluntary offerings of two of the staunchest friends of Home Rule within the United Kingdom. . . ." The next day the *Freeman's Journal* published a letter from Dillon which made a somewhat similar claim. Dillon, writing on September 3, declared that no appeal had been made to any Englishman—much less to any member of the government—by the committee of the party, or with its knowledge or approval. He added that he expressed no opinion as to whether Lord Tweedmouth's subscription ought or ought not to be accepted. Published with this letter was a telegram from McCarthy to Dillon which the latter had sent to the *Freeman's Journal*. It read: "No appeal ever made as far as I know to Gladstone or Tweedmouth, or any English public man. Tweedmouth's letter quite unexpected by me. It would be stupid rudeness to refuse the subscriptions. Do not understand allusion to the circular

[62]*Ibid.*, Sept. 5, 1894. The letter is dated Sept. 4, 1894.

of the 22nd. Assumed at time must have meant one of circulars published in my name by Metropolitan Branch. I take entire responsibility for accepting subscriptions and publishing names and letter."

The publication of these communications only made matters worse, for the *Irish Catholic and Nation*, a weekly newspaper which was a strong supporter of Healy, sent a telegram to Lord Tweedmouth asking him the nature of the circular to which he had referred in his letter to McCarthy. To this Tweedmouth replied: "Circular sent out as consequence of Conference at Westminster Palace Hotel, held on August 8th, signed by J. F. X. O'Brien. Cheques payable to him, Justin McCarthy, or T. P. O'Connor."[63] Needless to say, some further explanation was now required from those who denied that any appeal had been made to members or ex-members of the government. But the explanation given by J. F. X. O'Brien proved far from satisfactory. O'Brien had already made one statement regarding the appeal before the publication of Tweedmouth's telegram in the *Irish Catholic and Nation*. When, on September 4, the London correspondent of the *Freeman's Journal* had communicated with him on the subject of the circular, he had replied that he knew nothing about it. Then, in a telegram which appeared on the tenth in the same newspaper, he declared that, although the circular was issued in his name, neither he nor any other member of the Irish party had anything to do with drafting, signing, or distributing it. But on September 14 the *Freeman's Journal* published a letter dated September 11, which its editor had received from O'Brien and which read as follows:

> On arriving at the office to-day I find to my surprise that I was in error in saying in my telegram—which appeared in Monday's *Freeman*—that I did not *sign* the circular. It seems that the draft of it was submitted to me, and not only did I sign it but I made some alteration in the wording.
> Clearly it was also in error that I wired to your London correspondent in reply to his inquiry, "I know nothing of circular."
> In fact I had forgotten all about it until the circumstances were brought to my recollection to-day.
> With the distribution of the circular I had nothing to do.
> I desire to make this correction as early as possible.

---

[63]*Irish Catholic and Nation*, Dublin, Sept. 8, 1894.

This repudiation of his former statements did nothing to improve the position of O'Brien and his colleagues. Meanwhile, on September 5, the committee of delegates from the London branches of the Irish National League of Great Britain, which had issued the circular, passed a resolution declaring that it had "never invited, or contemplated inviting," subscriptions from any member or ex-member of a British cabinet, and that if any had received circulars, they must have been dispatched "either through clerical inadvertence or through the unauthorised action of some person or persons into whose hands copies had fallen." Some time later, the leaders of the Irish party decided that subscriptions received from any Englishman, not only from members or former members of the government, should be returned to the donors. Thereupon, J. F. X. O'Brien sent to each of them a copy of the resolution of September 5, together with a letter explaining that the donor's contribution was being returned to him because the circular in response to which he sent it had been addressed to him in error and without authority.[64]

The only two British subscriptions which were not returned at this time were those of Gladstone and Tweedmouth, the two which had caused the most controversy. This was because McCarthy, as will be seen presently from his correspondence with Blake, continued to feel that they should be accepted. Not very long afterwards, however, McCarthy reluctantly agreed that Tweedmouth's subscription should be returned to him. Gladstone's cheque, on the other hand, was retained.

Blake, who was in Canada while these events were taking place, was both confused and troubled by the reports which were reaching him of British political subscriptions to the parliamentary fund. Arrangements were being made for him to address meetings in several American cities, where he would undoubtedly be expected to give some explanation of the acceptance of these contributions. Even before he was aware that any circular had been issued, he felt that the acceptance of these subscriptions, which he assumed to be voluntary, constituted a reversal of party policy.

[64]For the text of the resolution, together with a copy of the letter, dated Sept. 21, 1894, see the J. F. X. O'Brien Papers.

Writing to McCarthy, Blake expressed surprise that, having rejected the earlier offer of £2,000, the party could now accept subscriptions from Gladstone, Tweedmouth, and other British Liberals. Feeling that the party's attitude should be consistent, he would, he declared, have been inclined to suggest the propriety of acknowledging the kindness involved in the offers, while courteously declining the money. But since it was probably now too late to adopt this course, he would try to justify the party's action before his American audiences. He described his plan thus:

> My own idea is to deal with the matter when the occasion arises, by saying that we have always preserved our independence, and in proof of that assertion telling the story of the proposed subscription of £2,000 and our refusal, but adding that when it had been made clear that the Irish at home and abroad had saved and were prepared to save the situation, we did not feel that we could with propriety refuse to receive as tangible evidences of goodwill the moderate sums which had been accepted, whose aggregate did not seriously affect the total of our resources, but the offer of which was a precious testimony of sincere and continued interest in our cause.[65]

Shortly after sending this letter Blake obtained further information which indicated that the situation was even worse than he had realized. Writing to McCarthy again the next day he told him that cable reports now seemed to intimate that the subscriptions from Gladstone and Tweedmouth were "in pursuance of some application made more or less generally for that purpose." Blake went on to say that he could hardly suppose that any such application had been made, but he asked McCarthy to give him any information he would need to explain the situation to his American audiences.[66]

After seeing still later cable reports in the Canadian press about the appeal to British Liberals, Blake became really alarmed. He described his attitude and subsequent action in a further letter to McCarthy:

> Later cables say that the recent subscriptions have been the result either of a forged circular, or of an unauthorized circular, or of a circular not authorized to be transmitted to certain parties. I think you will agree that it is a very different thing to do what you seem to have done, viz., not to decline subscriptions sent, as you understood, spontaneously and without application; and

[65]Blake Papers, Blake to McCarthy, Sept. 4, 1894.
[66]*Ibid.*, Blake to McCarthy, Sept. 5, 1894.

to ask for subscriptions in such quarters. As you know, from my former letter, my own opinion would have been to decline, even under the former hypothesis; but my wish is to help, if I can at all, to make the best of the existing situation; and it seems to me that the best thing that can be done is to return the money which was obtained by means of this unauthorized application. I feel great hesitation in even making a suggestion without the opportunity of consultation, but you will make allowances for my anxiety, circumstanced as I am. I have thought it right accordingly to cable you this morning as follows:— "Suggest return fruits erroneous circular. Best escape."[67]

Although no immediate action appears to have been taken upon the receipt of Blake's cable, it was undoubtedly one of the factors which led eventually to the decision to return the British subscriptions to their donors.

On September 21, McCarthy wrote to Blake telling him that all subscriptions obtained from Englishmen as a result of the unfortunate circular were being returned. No one in office or authority of any kind, he declared, knew that the circular had been sent to any but Irishmen. But since McCarthy had assumed the subscriptions from Gladstone and Tweedmouth to be voluntary, or the result of their having seen a published circular somewhere, and had received and acknowledged them himself, he felt that the responsibility of accepting them was his alone. He considered Gladstone's contribution as the graceful gesture of a great statesman now out of public life, and he did not think he could distinguish between the two offerings which had come together. The cheques from Gladstone and Tweedmouth were, therefore, not being returned.[68]

Many of the men who usually supported McCarthy did not, however, agree with him on this matter. Moreover, Dr. Emmet, president of the Irish National Federation of America, who like Blake realized that American sympathizers with Irish home rule would insist on some explanation of the appeal to British Liberals before giving further support to the cause, made a hurried trip to England to try to ascertain the true state of affairs. Like many of McCarthy's colleagues, he favoured returning Tweedmouth's contribution. McCarthy finally agreed, in deference to the views of Emmet, Blake, Dillon, T. P. O'Connor, and others, to send back Tweedmouth's

[67]*Ibid.*, Blake to McCarthy, Sept. 6, 1894.
[68]*Ibid.*, McCarthy to Blake, Sept. 21, 1894.

cheque, but he told Blake that, in doing so, he was submitting his own judgment and inclinations to the better judgment of others. He still would not agree to the return of Gladstone's cheque which, he asserted, stood upon a somewhat different footing.[69]

Blake was pleased when he heard that it had been decided to return the British subscriptions, though he felt that the delay in adopting this course had been dangerous. Moreover, he was still in favour of returning not only Tweedmouth's, but also Gladstone's cheque. In a letter to T. P. O'Connor, he remarked that it would, in his judgment, "have been better had the remedial steps, which have been taken at last, been taken at once, and had they been even more thorough. . . ."[70]

Meanwhile, Blake had received the issues of the *Freeman's Journal* which contained the letters, written by various members of the party, regarding the appeal. He was very critical of Healy's action in publicly condemning his colleagues, especially since he knew that Healy had previously suggested the adoption of the policy which he now accused them of putting into effect. In a letter to McCarthy, Blake remarked that in the *Newry Standard* of May 11, 1894, there was a quotation from a then recent article of Healy's in which he had declared that if adequate subscriptions were not received from America, it would be necessary to depend upon English political funds for Irish parliamentary purposes. Blake also reminded McCarthy that during their committee discussions in the spring Healy had actually suggested an appeal to members of the government, asserting that, since these men were really dependent on Irish votes for the continuance of their salaries, it would be perfectly reasonable to ask them for contributions. This proposal had received no encouragement from any other member of the committee, and it seemed to Blake "an extraordinary streak of bad luck that the situation should now be so completely reversed."[71]

But while condemning Healy for his action, Blake also censured those who had provided him with so excellent an opportunity for making an attack. Writing to Davitt, he asserted that, though the

[69]*Ibid.*, McCarthy to Blake, Sept. 27, 1894.
[70]*Ibid.*, Blake to T. P. O'Connor, Oct. 3, 1894.
[71]*Ibid.*, Blake to McCarthy, Sept. 25, 1894.

mistakes which had been made rendered "the disloyalty and conduct of Healy none the less odious," they nevertheless gave him "an advantage in a controversy having its root in the circular and the Gladstone and Tweedmouth subscriptions, etc."[72] And, in his letter of October 3 to T. P. O'Connor, Blake remarked: "The proceedings of the meeting of August, the despatch of the circular, the acceptance of the subscriptions, the mistake of J. F. X. O'Brien, altogether make a most unfortunate and damaging catena; and, had Healy used his opportunity wisely, the results would have been most serious. As it is they are serious enough. . . ." Nevertheless, though disagreeing with much that had been done, Blake told T. P. O'Connor that he was "prepared to take any feasible course which might be necessary to render his (McCarthy's) position tenable," and intended to shape his public utterances accordingly. "It would," he went on, "be a poor return for his services and sacrifices to his country, that his friends should think for a moment of any other line of conduct."[73] Moreover, Blake realized that unless he could justify McCarthy's action, his chances of securing funds in the United States would be seriously impaired.

In October, 1894, Blake addressed meetings under the auspices of the Irish National Federation of America in four American cities: New York; Philadelphia; Atlanta, Georgia; and Brooklyn, New York. It was at New York that he spoke of the Tweedmouth incident.

In accordance with his desire to do what he could to make McCarthy's position tenable, Blake explained to his New York audience what the chairman of the party had already told him about the acceptance of the Gladstone and Tweedmouth cheques. When McCarthy received the subscriptions, he believed them to be spontaneous, supposing that Tweedmouth's reference to a circular applied to some notice which he might have seen in a newspaper. McCarthy felt it impossible to refuse Gladstone's testimonial of goodwill, and difficult to return Tweedmouth's cheque which had been sent with it. Moreover, Blake explained, these subscriptions of £100 each were "but a drop in the bucket." Ireland, in response to the appeal for funds, had by this time given about £5,000 and was still subscribing,

[72]*Ibid.*, Blake to Davitt, Sept. 27, 1894.
[73]*Ibid.*, Blake to T. P. O'Connor, Oct. 3, 1894.

so the contributions from Gladstone and Tweedmouth did not alter the national character of the parliamentary fund.

Nevertheless, when it became clear that these and some other subscriptions had been sent in response to a circular erroneously addressed, McCarthy, after full consideration, decided that all such subscriptions, with the exception of Gladstone's, should be returned, and this had been done. "In truth," Blake declared, ". . . there never could have been any idea in the mind of Mr. McCarthy, or, for that matter, as I know and as I shall prove to you, in the mind of Messrs Sexton, Dillon, O'Brien, or O'Connor, of asking for subscriptions from those quarters for the Parliamentary Party fund." He then proceeded to give his audience the evidence for this statement:

I give you my proof. Last spring, in our very darkest hour, when the session was going on, when the fate of the Home Rule government and the Home Rule cause depended upon the Irish vote being kept at Westminster, when the Canadian subscriptions were exhausted, when there was nothing from the States, when it was absolutely impossible, for reasons connected with the evicted tenants' fund, which I have described, to make any appeal to Ireland, when we did not know where to turn, when we were within measurable distance of collapse for want of funds, I myself, as a person who was known to have had some little success in collecting funds on this continent, was approached by a generous friend, by a British Liberal, who was a staunch ally of our cause, who had done much for us politically, and who did not want to see it fail in this miserable way. I was approached by him, and he said to me, "I have done a little for this cause, I have labored for it. I don't want it to fail in this way. It ought not so to fail." And being a very wealthy man, he said to me, "I am willing, and I offer as a testimony of my continued interest in the cause, to give you in my own name or anonymously, or any way you please, two thousand pounds sterling,"—$10,000—"as a subscription to the Irish Parliamentary Fund." That, gentlemen, was Lord Tweedmouth. The offer was made in the handsomest spirit. It was made in a spirit of respect for those to whom it was made. I told Lord Tweedmouth that I did not believe it would be possible to accept that offer; but that I was not going, in the circumstances under which we stood, to take on my own shoulders the responsibility of decision. I had some private conversation, not mentioning the name—for this is the first time I have mentioned the name; I have thought it due to Lord Tweedmouth, under the circumstances, that it should now become known, and I make it known to the world to-night. Without mentioning the name I told the offer to some friends, to the gentlemen I have named —Messrs McCarthy, Sexton, T. P. O'Connor, Dillon and O'Brien. They one and all declared to me their opinion that the money could not be accepted, even although a collapse of the movement were inevitable. They said, "Better the movement should fail than that we should put ourselves in the position of accepting such a subscription from a member of the British Government."

I felt that the party must have the opportunity of dealing with the offer because the situation was too serious for the assumption of individual responsibility; and I named it at a meeting of the party at which we were considering our financial condition. We had three meetings before we decided to make an appeal to Ireland. I conveyed the offer to the party at the first of these meetings. But the party did not accept the offer; they determined instead to appeal to Ireland; and I communicated to Lord Tweedmouth that the Irish Parliamentary Party had decided on that course, not availing itself even in that crisis and that emergency, of his handsome proposal. Now, gentlemen, there is only one single man of the Irish Parliamentary Party, whose name if I should give it, you would hear with great amazement—there is only one single man whom I have at any time heard propose an appeal to members of the British Government for aid.[74]

Though nothing said by Blake or anyone else could entirely remedy the situation created by the appeal and the acceptance of the British subscriptions, the revelation of the rejection of Lord Tweedmouth's £2,000 offer undoubtedly improved the Irish party's position. Moreover, it was generally recognized that Healy was the man to whom Blake had referred as the only person in the party who had ever proposed an appeal to members of the British government; and this naturally lessened the effectiveness of Healy's attacks upon his colleagues. In some quarters, however, Blake was severely criticized for publicly revealing Lord Tweedmouth's £2,000 offer. One newspaper referred to his action as a "blazing indiscretion," while others argued that, since the money was not accepted, Blake should have said nothing about it.[75]

Lord Tweedmouth himself was not at all pleased at the course which Blake had taken. A few days after the text of his New York speech appeared in the Irish press, Blake, who had by then returned to Britain, wrote to Tweedmouth,[76] saying that he had been very much worried about the cheque controversy and had thought it due to Tweedmouth and others to give a brief statement at New York

[74]The full text of this speech, which was delivered on Oct. 17, 1894, is printed in the *Home Rule Bulletin* (New York, Nov., 1894), 5–13. The foregoing quotations are from page 13.
[75]Among the Blake Papers are several clippings from Canadian newspapers in which are quoted remarks, mainly from British journals, about Blake's revelation of Tweedmouth's offer. The clipping in which Blake's action is called a "blazing indiscretion" is, however, from the *Irish Times*.
[76]Blake Papers, Blake to Tweedmouth, Nov. 5, 1894.

about the offer made in the spring. In his reply, Tweedmouth expressed sorrow that Blake had found it necessary to take his New York audience and the world into confidence regarding their conversation. He did not think his name at any rate should have been mentioned without first consulting him. Because he was being severely criticized for making the original offer, he asked Blake, if he were pressed for further information regarding it, to make the following points clear: that at the time of their conversation he had for some weeks ceased to be parliamentary secretary; that the money was to come from no party fund but from his own pocket; and that no stipulation with regard to support of the government was made.[77]

Blake's reply reveals his distress:

> Knowing that you had offered to give the money under your name and that you had since forwarded another subscription to the fund, it never entered my head to conceive that there could be any possible objection to the earlier offer any more than the later subscription becoming public. . . .
> I need not say that I most deeply regret that, under mistaken impressions and with the best intentions, I took the step of which you disapprove. . . .

If Tweedmouth desired it, he would write a letter to the *Freeman's Journal* in which he would include the three points mentioned by Tweedmouth. Blake's own opinion was, however, that it would be better to let the matter drop.[78]

In a second letter Tweedmouth explained that he did not wish Blake to initiate any further discussion of the matter, but had only suggested the points which he wished to be made plain in case Blake should be forced into a fuller explanation. He added that there was no reason whatever for an apology and that he was sure the New York speech had been "actuated by the best and most friendly motives."[79] Blake was greatly relieved by the contents of this letter and told Tweedmouth that his part in the incident had been so creditable that he (Blake) had perhaps been blinded to the possibility of misinterpretation.[80]

To consider the situation arising out of the appeal and the events which followed it, several private consultations were held in London

[77]*Ibid.*, Tweedmouth to Blake, Nov. 6, 1894.
[78]*Ibid.*, Blake to Tweedmouth, Nov. 6, 1894.
[79]*Ibid.*, Tweedmouth to Blake, Nov. 6, 1894.
[80]*Ibid.*, Blake to Tweedmouth, Nov. 7, 1894.

early in November. These were attended by McCarthy, Blake, and a few of their colleagues. Then on November 12 a meeting of the Irish party was held in Dublin. Blake's views were well expressed in the "Confidential Note on the Affairs of the Irish party with reference to the meeting called for 12th November" which he prepared at this time.[81] While he had already recorded most of these views in his correspondence of September and October, this memorandum provides a useful summary of them.

In his opinion the line of policy to which the party was committed had been more or less departed from at the August London meeting and by the issue of the circular and the acceptance of the British Liberal subscriptions. If Healy had opened his campaign better, "it might have gone hard with those concerned," Blake stated. "It would be folly to ignore the line he and his friends will now take, namely, that their views were right, and that they have been, by rough methods it may be, but still that they have been the saviours of the Party independence."

Blake then made a number of suggestions as to the policy which he believed ought to be adopted at the party meeting. It should be explained that any remonstrance against the appeal or the acceptance of British subscriptions should have been made privately. Next, the dishonesty, disloyalty, and impropriety of Healy's course should be demonstrated by proving that he himself had proposed an appeal to members of the government for aid. In his New York speech, Blake had opened the way for the revelation of this incident. A verdict of censure on the disloyalty of Healy's course might well be expected to follow.

It may be implied from Blake's memorandum, even more than from his earlier correspondence, that, when he learned all the facts of the situation, he did not believe that the actions of McCarthy and his supporters could be fully justified. Blake did not approve of the proceedings of the August meeting, which had been attended and supported not only by T. P. O'Connor, who presided, but also by McCarthy and Dillon. He believed that the issue of the circular and the acceptance of subscriptions from British Liberals, even had they been voluntary, constituted a reversal of party policy. Though he

[81]There is a copy of this "Confidential Note" among the Blake Papers.

does not appear to have stated it in writing, he must have thought it very peculiar that both McCarthy and Dillon denied any knowledge of an appeal to Englishmen and declared their opposition to it, when, at the August meeting, both London Irishmen and British sympathizers with Irish home rule had been invited to support the cause. McCarthy and Dillon were, of course, quite correct in saying that no appeal to Englishmen had been made by the committee or the party, for the circular had been issued by a committee appointed by the London branches of the Irish National League of Great Britain. It is difficult, however, to believe that an appeal to Englishmen, though perhaps not to members of the government, did not have their approval, for the issue of the circular seemed a very natural sequence to the meeting at the Westminster Palace Hotel. And even if they did not know that the circular had been sent to Englishmen, it is clear that they had no objection to accepting subscriptions from them. Furthermore, the contradictory statements of J. F. X. O'Brien indicated that he knew more about the appeal than he had at first acknowledged.

At the meeting of November 12, however, McCarthy's line of defence was similar to that which he had used previously. While he condemned the Healyites for their public attack, the point which he emphasized most strongly was that both he and the committee of the party had known nothing about the circular and were free from the responsibility of issuing it.[82] In view of the statements made by Blake in his memorandum, it appears unlikely that he was in favour of placing such emphasis on this point, though he undoubtedly realized that, after so many mistakes had been made, it was difficult for McCarthy to take up a new line of defence. But it is interesting to speculate whether the course of events would have been different if Blake had been present at the August meeting in the Westminster Palace Hotel, or if he had been in Britain during the controversy which arose after the circular had been issued. Certainly he would not have advised the adoption of the policy which was carried out by his closest colleagues.

It was hoped that the party meeting of November 12 would close

[82]Dillon Papers, Minutes of the Irish parliamentary party, Nov. 12, 1894. See also T. M. Healy, *Why Ireland Is Not Free* (Dublin, 1898), 106.

the controversy regarding the appeal and the acceptance of the British subscriptions. In an attempt to accomplish this, the party resolved to publish McCarthy's statement regarding his own position and that of the committee and to have no further discussion of the matter. But in January, 1895, the controversy was revived as a result of the publication of a new version of Tweedmouth's original £2,000 offer.

In London, on January 13, 1895, J. F. X. O'Brien addressed a meeting of the St. Pancras branch of the Irish National League of Great Britain. The London *Times*, which published an account of the speech the next day, reported O'Brien as having said that about a year previously Lord Tweedmouth, then Mr. Marjoribanks, had sent him (O'Brien) a cheque for £2,000 for the purposes of the National League. That body had, however, declined the gift except for the specific purpose of relieving the evicted tenants.[83] Although O'Brien, in a letter to *The Times*, denied that he had made such an assertion, adding that "the offer of £2,000 was not made to me nor for the National League, and it was declined absolutely,"[84] his explanation was regarded by many as unsatisfactory. Editorials and letters appeared in *The Times* demanding further details regarding the controversy, which became still more confused by the statement of another Irish member, Charles Diamond, that it was quite true that Tweedmouth's £2,000 cheque had been accepted for the evicted tenants' fund.[85] O'Brien was reported to have said that Tweedmouth had sent the £2,000 cheque while he was still Mr. Marjoribanks. It was, therefore, suggested that since at that time he was patronage secretary of the Treasury, the money might have come from Liberal party funds or even from the secret service money of the government. *The Times* declared that Lord Tweedmouth, who must know the facts better than anyone else, ought, without further delay, to reveal them to the public.[86]

It seems reasonable to suppose that Tweedmouth made only one offer of £2,000 to the Irish party, for if, early in 1894, his cheque

[83] *The Times*, London, Jan. 14, 1895.
[84] *Ibid.*, Jan. 17, 1895. The letter is dated Jan. 16.
[85] For comments on O'Brien's speech and letter, see *ibid.*, Jan. 18–22, 1895.
[86] *Ibid.*, Jan. 22, 1895.

was accepted for the evicted tenants' fund, it is unlikely that he would have offered another £2,000 only a few months later. But there is ample evidence, especially in the correspondence between Blake and Tweedmouth, to prove that an offer was made to Blake and that it was rejected. Furthermore, it is clear that it was not made while Tweedmouth was still Mr. Marjoribanks, for he succeeded to the title on March 4, 1894, and the money was not offered until shortly before the Irish party's meeting of May 3, or, at any rate, not earlier than the month of April. As already noted, Tweedmouth had no control of Liberal party funds at this time. So whether or not O'Brien made the statements imputed to him by *The Times*, it seems reasonable to conclude that there is no basis for his reported version of the incident.

All the accounts of Tweedmouth's offer seem, however, to contradict each other in some respect. Healy, commenting on the report of J. F. X. O'Brien's speech, described in the following words how Blake had told the party of Tweedmouth's offer: "Mr. Edward Blake mentioned that an offer of £2,000 had been made to him by "a friend of the Irish cause" whose name he could not disclose and he urged his colleagues to accept the gift. Several members pressed for his name, but this Mr. Blake refused to give, nor would he state if he was an Irishman, an Englishman, a Canadian or an American. In view of this reticence, the Party declined to accept the offer, and Mr. McCarthy intimated that he was not consulted, and was not told the proposed donor's name. . . ."[87]

Blake's accounts of the incident, both in his correspondence and in his New York speech, do not suggest that he urged the party to accept the gift or that he refused to disclose the nationality of the "friend of the Irish cause" who offered it. On the other hand, there is no definite statement in Blake's speech or letters of what he told the party. His accounts state simply that, without revealing Tweedmouth's name, he mentioned the offer to the party, and that the party rejected it. It appears unlikely, however, that Healy's assertion that Blake refused to disclose the nationality of the donor is correct, for Healy's own statements in this regard are contradictory. Dealing with the Tweedmouth incident in a letter written in 1895, he de-

[87]Healy, *Why Ireland Is Not Free*, 109.

clared that Blake had tempted the party, "in a long and urgent speech, to accept a 'gift' of £2,000 from an anonymous *British* friend."[88] Moreover, not only is it clear from Blake's correspondence[89] and his speech at New York that he revealed the nationality of the donor to those whom he consulted privately, but it can also be implied from Blake's accounts that the party rejected the offer not because it was ignorant of the nationality of the proposed donor, but because it knew that he was a British politician. The question of whether there is any possibility that Blake urged the party to accept Tweedmouth's offer will be considered presently.

It was not until January 18, 1899, in an address to his former constituents of Berwickshire, that Lord Tweedmouth gave his version of the £2,000 offer. The following is a press report of the portion of his speech which dealt with this incident:

Dealing with the facts on which the history of what he termed the apocryphal £2,000 cheque had been founded for the benefit of an incredulous public, Lord Tweedmouth said that early in June, 1894, three months after he had left the House of Commons, and had ceased to have any management of the affairs of a party in that House or control of its funds, he was asked by Mr. Blake, the treasurer of the Irish Parliamentary Party, if he might have a conversation with him (Lord Tweedmouth) with regard to the position of the Irish Parliamentary Party, especially with regard to the question of funds. Mr. Blake accordingly had an interview with him. He explained the then position of the Irish party fund in great detail, and undoubtedly at that moment their exchequer was at a very low ebb, and there did not seem much likelihood of its being replenished, at any rate, for two or three months. His advice having been invited, Lord Tweedmouth said he asked for two or three days for consideration. Two days later he said to Mr. Blake that the only thing he could suggest was to offer to put at his disposal, out of his own private purse, a sum of £2,000. He made that offer without any condition whatever. He did not care whether it was taken as a gift in his own name or an anonymous gift, or whether Mr. Blake took it, and advanced it as from himself without any question of his (Lord Tweedmouth's) intervention, in a manner that he had been accustomed to do on former occasions. As treasurer of the fund, Mr. Blake, without a moment's hesitation, said the offer was a very kindly and generous one, but one impossible for them to accept. Eventu-

---

[88] The letter, dated Aug. 6, 1895, was written to the editor of the *Freeman's Journal.* It appeared in that newspaper on Aug. 8, 1895. As the letter dealt mainly with the "Omagh scandal," which will be described in the next chapter, more will be said of it there.

[89] In his letter of Sept. 4 to McCarthy, Blake spoke of the £2,000 offer of "a British politician."

ally Mr. Blake said he did not like himself to take the responsibility of refusing such an offer, and suggested a consultation with some of his colleagues. Mr. Blake did consult his colleagues, and they absolutely and entirely agreed that it was impossible for them to accept such an offer. That was the whole history of the £2,000 cheque, a cheque that was never written, and the offer of which was absolutely declined by the Irish party without even consideration. . . .[90]

While this account bears no resemblance to the one reported by *The Times* in January, 1895, it is substantially the same as that given by Blake in his New York speech. There are a few factual errors in Tweedmouth's account, but this is not surprising since he was speaking of events which had taken place more than four and a half years previously. He said, for instance, that his interviews with Blake were held in June, 1894, when it is clear that they took place before the Irish party's meeting of May 3. This does not, however, alter the important fact that Tweedmouth made the offer after he succeeded to his title. The statement that, at the time of their conversations, Blake had been treasurer of the Irish party is also incorrect.

The only important difference between the accounts of Blake and Tweedmouth concerns the question of which of the two men took the initiative in the matter. In his New York speech Blake reported that he had been approached by a British Liberal, whereas Tweedmouth now said that Blake had requested an interview with him about the affairs of the Irish party, and had asked his advice on its financial position. There is one piece of evidence which suggests that Tweedmouth's version is correct—a letter from Tweedmouth to Blake dated April 11, 1894, which reads as follows: "I am called out of town to-day and fear I shall not be back before the house rises. If I am I will look in about 5.15 and ask for you. If it is of pressing necessity for you to see me to-day 7 o'clock at 134 Piccadilly would find me."[91] Although the date of this letter is rather early for it to have anything to do with the £2,000 offer, it is possible that it refers to the interview in question. Tweedmouth's conversations with Blake may have taken place in April even though his offer was not mentioned to the party until May 3.

[90] *Daily Nation*, Dublin, Jan. 20, 1899.
[91] Blake Papers, Tweedmouth to Blake, April 11, 1894.

When the matter is fully considered, it seems very probable that some discussion with Tweedmouth regarding the financial position of the Irish party did precede his £2,000 offer. For, while it was generally known that the Irish party was in need of funds, it appears unlikely that Tweedmouth would have made such an offer without a definite statement from some leading member of the party about its immediate requirements. Yet, assuming that Blake sought an interview, it is difficult to conjecture his object in doing so if he did not hope that Tweedmouth would offer a large subscription to the Irish party. If, however, Blake believed that the party would not accept money from a British politician, it appears unlikely that he would have requested an interview for this purpose. Perhaps he approached Tweedmouth as a man who had had considerable experience in the management of party funds, hoping that he might offer some suggestion as to how to raise them; this, at any rate, could be implied from Tweedmouth's account of the incident. Whatever the explanation, if Blake did request an interview, he probably thought it unwise to tell his New York audience about it, in case it would be thought that he had asked Tweedmouth for a subscription. If any such suspicion had been aroused, Blake's revelation of the incident, instead of serving to vindicate the Irish party, would have strengthened the case of those who accused it of seeking support from British Liberals. With this in mind, Blake probably decided to omit mentioning his first interview with Tweedmouth, and to begin his account with the second conversation, when Tweedmouth did approach him to make the £2,000 offer.

But in view of Tweedmouth's assertion that Blake had requested an interview, it is necessary to consider whether Healy's claim that Blake urged the party to accept Tweedmouth's offer may be correct. It must be remembered that Blake, in his New York address, did not give his personal opinion as to how the offer should have been treated; he reported only his statement to Lord Tweedmouth that he did not believe the party would accept it. Since this is the case, it might be argued that Blake, knowing that there were no conditions attached to Tweedmouth's offer, felt that there was no reason to reject it. In support of this view it should be noted that Blake's principal reason for opposing the acceptance of the later subscriptions from Tweedmouth, Gladstone, and other British Liberals, was that it was inconsistent with the action taken regarding Tweedmouth's original offer. So, even here, there is no proof that Blake had been personally opposed to the acceptance of the £2,000 gift.

Nevertheless, the argument in favour of Healy's assertion is not very convincing, for the whole tone, not only of Blake's New York address, but also of his private correspondence, strongly suggests that he was opposed to the acceptance of Tweedmouth's original offer. Furthermore, there is one statement in the memorandum which Blake prepared for the party meeting of November 12, 1894, which proves his conviction that even before the rejection of the £2,000 gift, the party was committed to the policy of refusing to accept money from British Liberals. For he stated in this memorandum that the party was committed to this course by the parliamentary proceedings on Lord Wolmer's speech.[92] Here Blake referred to an incident which had occurred in 1893, so if he believed that from that date the party was pledged to the line of policy under discussion, it seems most unlikely that he would have urged the party to accept Tweedmouth's gift of £2,000.

A statement made by William O'Brien supports the conclusion that Healy's charge was false. In August, 1895, O'Brien wrote to the editor of the *Freeman's Journal* denying, among other things, Healy's assertion that Blake had urged the party to accept the £2,000 offer. O'Brien declared:

> Mr. Blake was himself the first to avow publicly the circumstances under which a wealthy Liberal Minister offered a subscription of £2,000 to the funds of the Irish party. . . . That Mr. Blake "tempted the Party to accept it in a long and urgent speech" is, to the knowledge of every member of the Party who was present, slanderous and untrue. Mr. Blake set forth, as he was bound to do, the offer he was requested to make, the Party agreed without discussion that the offer could not be entertained, and there the matter ended. . . .[93]

---

[92]Lord Wolmer's statement that the Irish party was kept by Liberal moneys had been declared a scandalous breach of the privilege of Parliament. Sexton had at that time declared: "Whatever help we may require we shall seek from our own countrymen, and certainly if that help is not sufficient, we shall never seek it anywhere else." Healy quoted this statement of Sexton's in a letter of Sept. 9, 1894 to the editor of the *Freeman's Journal*. It is published in that newspaper on Sept. 10, 1894.

[93]The letter, dated Aug. 8, 1895, is published in the *Freeman's Journal*, Dublin, Aug. 10, 1895. It is a reply to various charges made in Healy's letter which appeared in the same newspaper on Aug. 8, 1895.

There is so much contradictory evidence regarding the whole question of the acceptance of money from British Liberals that it is difficult to draw any definite conclusions about it. Certainly the reputation of many leading Irish Nationalists was not enhanced by the controversy. If it were not for the question of whether Blake requested an interview with Tweedmouth, and, if so, with what object in mind, his part in the incident could be entirely justified. But in the absence of further evidence on this matter, it can only be said that Blake at least emerged from the controversy in a more favourable light than did many of his colleagues.

V. NATIONALIST DISSENSION AND THE GENERAL ELECTION OF 1895

DURING the general election campaign of 1895 the seriousness of the dissension within the ranks of the anti-Parnellite party was revealed most clearly to the public.[1] This was the result of the disputes which occurred in the course of choosing anti-Parnellite candidates. The candidates were selected at county conventions which met in most of the constituencies at any time from a number of weeks to only a few days before the holding of a general election. These conventions, which were attended by the clergy and by delegates from the local branches of the Irish National Federation, usually met in private, the press not being admitted, and were followed by a public meeting at which an official report of the convention was given to the press.

In practice, however, the conventions seldom had absolute freedom in their choice of candidates. When Parnell had been leader of a united Irish party, he had held informal caucuses to influence the conventions. But in 1892 the anti-Parnellites had discontinued this practice and chosen an election committee, consisting mainly, though not exclusively, of members of Parliament in the party,[2] to conduct the campaign. In the campaign of 1895 the special committee was replaced by the chairman and the ordinary party committee. Both the election committee in 1892 and the party committee in 1895 exercised considerable influence over the conventions' choice of candidates.

Healy had been a member not only of the election committee of 1892, but also of subsequent party committees. When, however, he was elected to the committee chosen at the party's sessional meeting of February 5, 1895, which afterwards conducted the election campaign of that year, he announced his intention not to serve.[3] During

[1] In connection with this chapter, see F. S. L. Lyons, "The Irish Parliamentary Party and the General Election of 1895" (*Irish Historical Studies*, Sept., 1952).
[2] For the resolution setting up this committee see Dillon Papers, Minutes of the Irish parliamentary party, May 26, 1892.
[3] *Ibid.*, Feb. 5, 1895.

the campaign which followed a few months later, he chose instead to attack the committee in every conceivable way.

Although a general election had been considered likely for some time, it came rather suddenly and unexpectedly in the early summer of 1895. The Liberal government, following its defeat on a minor issue in the House of Commons on June 21, 1895, decided to resign at once. Thereupon, the Conservatives, supported by the Liberal Unionists, returned to office, a dissolution followed, and the general election took place in July.

The principal feature of the election campaign in Ireland was the struggle, not between opposing parties, but within the ranks of the anti-Parnellites. This dissension was, of course, made the basis for attack on the anti-Parnellite party by the Parnellites and Unionists. Healy opened his campaign against his colleagues on June 28, 1895, at a meeting of one of the Dublin branches of the Irish National Federation. Pointing out that the election committee of 1892 had not been composed exclusively of party members,[4] he claimed that there was no precedent for the party committee's assuming control of the elections. The meeting was evidently in sympathy with Healy's views, for it passed resolutions condemning the delegation of the management of the elections to the party committee, demanding that a national convention be summoned to choose an impartial election committee, and that there should be perfect freedom of selection and election of representatives, and finally, expressing dissatisfaction with the policy of the party during the previous three years.[5] The fact that these resolutions were also passed by the executive committee of the Irish National Federation by eleven votes to three showed that in the Federation's inner circles Healyites were for the moment in control.

Healy had a fairly large following in the party, and, if candidates favourable to him were chosen in many constituencies, he would have a chance of controlling the party after the election. It was certain, therefore, that the party committee, where the

[4]It was true that two of the members of the 1892 electoral committee, W. M. Murphy and Michael Davitt, were not, at that time, members of Parliament. Murphy, however, had only recently retired from Parliament and Davitt was elected to it that year. See Lyons, "Irish Parliamentary Party and General Election of 1895."

[5]The meeting is reported in the *Freeman's Journal,* Dublin, June 29, 1895.

Healyites had always been in a minority, would do its best to prevent the county conventions from selecting Healyite candidates. This was undoubtedly the principal reason why Healy opposed the management of the election by the committee, although, in doing so, he was able to pose as the champion of the independence of the constituencies. The fact that he and his followers demanded the summoning of a national convention suggests that they believed they were stronger in the country than in the party, and indeed, in many parts of the country, Healy had a large following, especially among the Roman Catholic clergy. It was natural that this should be so, for, since many of the delegates to the county conventions were priests, they of course wished the conventions to be free to choose their own candidates. One of Healy's objections to the electoral arrangements was that some of the conventions were to be held at a time when the priests were on retreat. Their absence would lessen the chances of Healyite candidates being selected.

Following the publication of the resolutions, McCarthy, as chairman of the party, wrote a letter to the press condemning the Federation for its action in passing them. While expressing regret that the notice given in summoning the conventions was short, he declared that the reason for this was the suddenness of the dissolution of Parliament, over which the Irish party had no control. He refused to allow any alteration in the arrangements for the conventions, saying that the Federation must not control or overrule the work of the party.[6]

There were now two ways in which Healy might interfere with the work of the committee. The first, that of summoning rival conventions, he attempted without success, but by means of the second, that of using the existing conventions to appeal to the constituencies for a decision between him and his opponents, he was able to do a great deal of damage. Disputes arose at many of the conventions, the most serious occurring at Leitrim, Tipperary, and Mayo.

The member for Mayo in the previous Parliament had been Daniel Crilly, a follower of Healy. At the county convention trouble began when the committee tried to substitute for him a man more

[6] For the text of McCarthy's letter, see *ibid.*, July 4, 1895.

likely to support the Dillonite wing of the party. "The numbers were running so close," William O'Brien explained later, "that for all we knew to let Mr. Crilly pass unchallenged might mean putting Mr. Healy in a majority in the new party."[7] In view of this situation, O'Brien and Blake had been sent to Mayo to try to persuade the convention to accept the candidature of John Roche. The two men realized that their task would be a difficult one, for the clergy were known to be strong supporters of Crilly.

Following the committee's instructions, O'Brien proposed Roche's name to the convention, over which Blake presided. According to Healy's account of the proceedings, Crilly demanded a hearing, but "this, in the interests of national unity, was refused."[8] At any rate, the clergy from North Mayo withdrew in protest against the rejection of Crilly, and in their absence Roche was selected. The committee, however, on learning the extent of clerical opposition to its candidate, grew alarmed and asked Roche to withdraw. So Crilly, after all, became the Nationalist candidate and was re-elected to the House of Commons as member for Mayo.

Although the committee ultimately failed in its attempt to prevent the re-election of a Healyite in Mayo, the incident shows the method which the committee was prepared to use to secure the selection of Dillonite candidates.

Blake had only a minor part in the Mayo quarrel, but by an unfortunate chance he was the central figure in the most serious of the disagreements between Dillonites and Healyites at this time, a disagreement which became known as the "Omagh scandal."

The "Omagh Scandal"

On July 8, 1895, the Tyrone County convention met in the town of Omagh. It was attended by both Dillon and Healy, each of whom apparently had the support of a large number of delegates. Although the press was usually excluded from county conventions, on this

[7] William O'Brien, *An Olive Branch in Ireland and Its History* (London, 1910), 84–5.
[8] T. M. Healy, *Why Ireland Is Not Free* (Dublin, 1898), 117.

occasion several reporters were inadvertently admitted. As a result of this oversight, detailed reports of the proceedings at the convention appeared the next day in the Parnellite and Unionist press, describing the events which they said occurred.[9]

Although Dillon presided at the meeting, there was much opposition to his chairmanship. Disorder followed the proposal of a resolution that he should not be allowed to interfere with the meeting in any way, and that the convention should choose its own chairman. Amid the uproar, Dillon attempted to explain that he had been authorized by the Irish parliamentary party to preside, while Healy angrily retorted that he was there with as much authority as Dillon, although the party had not asked him to attend. It was, however, after the withdrawal of the resolution of protest against Dillon's chairmanship and the temporary restoration of order that the climax of the proceedings was reached.

In spite of the fact that the convention had been summoned to choose candidates for only two of the divisions of the county, East and Mid Tyrone, the chairman was asked whether a candidate for North Tyrone would be selected that day.[10] Dillon replied that he understood the Nationalists of that division had already taken upon themselves to select Serjeant C. H. Hemphill and that he did not think their action could be questioned.[11] Since Serjeant Hemphill was a Liberal Home Ruler and not a member of the Irish party, this announcement was greeted with cries of "Why select a Liberal placehunter?" and a scene of great confusion followed. Healy jumped upon the platform, and, waving a letter which he held in his hand in the direction of the chairman, he told the gathering that Dillon and his followers were guilty of selling Tyrone seats to an English party.

[9]For these accounts, see the *Irish Times* and the *Irish Independent*, Dublin, July 9, 1895. The two reports correspond very closely.

[10]Both the *Irish Times* and the *Irish Independent* reported that the question about North Tyrone had been asked by a delegate. Dillon, however, as will be seen presently, declared that Healy had asked the question, and Healy himself supported this version. See Healy, *Why Ireland Is Not Free*, 124–5.

[11]Hemphill had been selected at a convention for North Tyrone which had been held at Strabane a few days previously. In view of this, North Tyrone delegates had not been invited to Omagh. Delegates from South Tyrone were invited, but no candidate for that division of the county was chosen. See *Irish Independent*, Dublin, July 9, 1895.

"Here," he shouted, "is a letter from Mr. Blake, the ex-Canadian statesman, to Mr. Thomas Dickson, one of her Majesty's Privy Councillors."[12]

The press reports of the letter which Healy then read were indeed startling. According to the *Irish Times,* Blake had been instructed to state that the executive of the Irish National Federation could not in future subsidize North Tyrone, South Tyrone, North Derry, or South Derry, and that they must in future be considered Liberal home rule seats. He was further requested by the Irish party to consult Mr. Ellis, the chief Liberal whip, to find out whether the Liberals would be willing to give £200 a year for each of the seats. The letter was also reported to state that Mr. Ellis had consented to this only on the understanding that the seats should be considered Liberal and not home rule, and that the Irish party had agreed to this arrangement.

According to the press reports, the reading of this letter caused further disorder, and Healy, speaking above the din, accused Dillon of being the man chiefly responsible for what he termed this compact with the Liberals. In the course of his remarks he referred to Dillon as a traitor and a Parnellite, and, according to the *Irish Independent*, declared that Liberal placehunters were going to be sent down by "Mr. Dillon, Mr. William O'Brien and this ex-Canadian statesman, Blake."

Dillon, when he found an opportunity to speak, denied Healy's charges and condemned him for reading a private letter at the convention. To show that Healy had not been kept in ignorance of the contents of the letter, he added that it had been read at a meeting of the committee of the Federation at which Healy and one of his supporters, T. D. Sullivan, had been present. The *Irish Times* reported that Healy denied any knowledge of the letter until "a couple of months after it was written."

The reports of the Tyrone convention were used to good advantage by the opponents of the Irish party. The Unionist press in both Britain and Ireland joined the Parnellites in interpreting the letter as meaning that the Irish party had handed over four northern

[12]*Irish Times*, Dublin, July 9, 1895.

seats to the Liberals in return for an annual subscription of £800 to the party funds. The Irish party could hardly ignore so serious a charge, especially in the middle of an election campaign.

On the day the proceedings at Omagh were described by the *Irish Times* and the *Irish Independent*, no mention of them was made by the *Freeman's Journal*. But, on July 11, that newspaper devoted much space to an examination of the charges which had been made against the committee of the party. Since the meeting at Omagh had been private, the *Freeman's Journal* had been unable to give the public any account of what had taken place, and it did not know, therefore, how far the reports given by "the coercionist and Parnellite newspapers" were accurate. But it quoted a telegram which McCarthy had sent to Charles Diamond, a member of the Irish parliamentary party: "Charge made of selling four Northern seats to Liberal Party absolutely untrue. Full statement will be published. I cannot too strongly condemn the making of baseless charges against the party at a crisis like the present. Such proceedings can only result in strengthening the hands of faction and disorganizing the National ranks."

In the same issue of the *Freeman's Journal* appeared a letter of July 10 from Healy, in which he remarked that since the press was excluded from the convention at Omagh—he evidently refused to admit that some newspaper men were present—the reports which had been published on the subject were "chiefly works of the imagination." He explained that he had gone to Omagh "to watch what explanation would be tendered for the extraordinary action about North Tyrone," where the committee of the Irish party had "allowed the people the unusual luxury of making their own arrangements." Healy had considered Dillon's explanation unsatisfactory, and, to throw more light upon the subject, had read an extract from Blake's letter.

While claiming that the press reports of the proceedings at Omagh were largely fanciful, Healy made no attempt, in this letter, to correct them by revealing exactly what charges he had made against his colleagues. For this he was severely criticized by the *Freeman's Journal*, which pointed out that his charges, as reported by the Parnellite and Unionist press, were doing serious harm to the Irish party, and that if the published accounts of what he said were inaccurate it was Healy's duty to correct them.

The principal public denial of Healy's charges was made by Blake on July 10 when he presided at the Cork convention. Speaking at the public meeting which followed the private proceedings, he declared that it was "absolutely without a particle of foundation in fact that the Irish Parliamentary Committee ever proposed, ever agreed to, ever asked for, or ever accepted any arrangement under which they were to receive £200 a year or a sixpence in respect of any seat. . . ." Up to 1891 the Irish party had spent large sums of money for registration in North and South Derry and North and South Tyrone, he explained, and in making arrangements for the general election of 1892, the party's electoral committee, of which both Healy and W. M. Murphy (a Healyite) were members, had wisely decided to entrust the candidature in these divisions to Gladstonian Liberal Home Rulers. This had been done because it was felt that a greater chance of returning Home Rulers would be obtained by adopting such a course. Gladstonian Liberals had, therefore, contested three of the seats. In North Derry, however, the Unionists were so powerful that the Liberals had considered it useless to attempt a contest.

Blake related how, in 1893, Thomas A. Dickson, the principal organizer of the Liberal home rule vote in Ulster, had suggested to the committee of the Irish party that the Nationalists should continue to pay the cost of registration and that a joint committee of Liberals and Nationalists should be formed to deal with the Ulster seats, including the four in question. The committee, however, had decided not to agree to any conjunction with the Liberals in seats which were going to be contested by Nationalists. It had also concluded that the party could no longer contribute, out of funds which had become too scanty, to the registration of divisions in which the home rule candidates were going to be Liberals rather than Nationalists. When Dickson, on being told of the committee's decision, complained that he had no money for registration, the committee decided that it had the right to represent to the Liberal whip that he ought to see that money was provided for the work in the divisions in the north of Ireland where Liberal home rule candidates had to be run. There was, Blake asserted, absolutely no suggestion that the Irish party should receive subsidies to hand over the seats. The members of the committee simply pointed out that if the candidates were to be Liberals, then the Liberal party should pay the expenses incurred by their own agents. To this the Nationalists would add the voluntary labour of their own organization without fee or reward.

Blake then spoke of the occasions on which the matter had been discussed by the committee. On October 3, 1893, at a meeting attended by McCarthy, William O'Brien, Blake, T. P. O'Connor, and Sexton, Dickson's letter about registration in North and South Tyrone and North and South Derry was read and confirmed. The secretary was instructed to inform Dickson that the committee had agreed to give Canon McCartan £25 for South Tyrone in addition to the £50 already granted, but that the Nationalists would have to leave the other three divisions to the attention of their Liberal friends. On October 10, 1893, the foregoing minute was read and confirmed in the presence of McCarthy, William O'Brien, Blake, and T. M. Healy. The subject came up again on June 18, 1894, when it appeared that the registration was in an unsatisfactory condition. It was at this meeting, attended by McCarthy, T. D. Sullivan (a Healyite), Dillon, William O'Brien, Blake, Sexton, and T. P. O'Connor, that Blake was authorized to write the letter which had been said to contain the shameful proposal to sell four seats for £200 apiece. On June 21, 1894, the foregoing minutes, authorizing Blake to write to Dickson and communicate with the Liberal whip, were confirmed, their being present at the meeting McCarthy, Blake, Dillon, William O'Brien, Sexton, and T. D. Sullivan. "I defend these gentlemen, including myself," Blake told his audience, "for we are all equally responsible under this shameful misstatement which is said to have been made. . . ."

From Blake's closing remarks, it can be seen that he believed the most effective way of disproving the Omagh charges would be to publish the text of his letter to Dickson. He said:

I have not got my letter; I believe a copy of it is locked up in London. I challenge its production. There are letters which we write, which we do not want made public, not because they are shameful, not because they contain anything we are ashamed of, but of course, confidential concerns must be confidentially described. You to-day conducted your business in private up to a certain stage; you were not ashamed of anything you were going to do or say, but convenience required it. I deeply regret, indeed, that such a statement is alleged to have been made that a course of action, innocent, laudable, praiseworthy, of which honourable men have no cause to be ashamed, should have been distorted into a shameful transaction with which the press of both these islands is now ringing, to the loss and hurt of the National interest and the National cause.[13]

There were, in fact, demands from all sides that the Blake letter should be published. McCarthy's telegram, it will be remembered, had promised that a full statement would be made. Blake's explanation at Cork was considered insufficient; he himself had felt it should be followed by the publication of his letter. Both Healy and W. M. Murphy wrote to the *Freeman's Journal* denying that the electoral committee of 1892 had entrusted the candidature of the four seats in question to Gladstonian Liberal Home Rulers; it had, they asserted, simply decided not to run Nationalist candidates because there was no possibility of winning the seats.[14] Healy stated that he withdrew nothing which he had said at Omagh, and demanded the publication of Blake's letter and the minutes of the meeting at which he had been authorized to write it:

Let the Blake document and the "minute" be printed side by side to show what each discloses. Mr. Blake does not cite the "minute" which he had under his hand. He did not read the letter which he says is locked up. Why is it not on the records also? . . .
In the full statement which Mr. McCarthy is preparing let minute and letter be published, and then the public can pronounce on the whole transaction.

Even the statements of Thomas Ellis, former chief whip of the Liberal party, did not satisfy the critics of the Irish party's committee. In an address delivered on July 11, Ellis denied that he had ever spoken or written to Blake with regard to any Irish seat—he must have meant "with regard to the sale of any Irish seat," for there seems to be little doubt that Blake communicated with him about the registration. Ellis went on to say that he had "never offered to buy nor at any time received an offer to sell any Irish

[13] The speech is reported in *Freeman's Journal*, Dublin, July 11, 1895.
[14] Both letters appeared in *ibid.*, July 12, 1895. They are dated July 11.

seat," and that he had "never promised to pay two hundred pounds a year or any other sum whatsoever for any seat."[15] But in spite of this denial, the demand for the production of the Blake letter continued.

The publication of the letter, together with other related documents, would, in fact, have proved that Blake's version of the situation was substantially correct. The minutes of the party committee confirm his statements about the meetings mentioned in his address at Cork, the facts being taken directly from the minute book. Blake's only error here was in the dates of the 1893 meetings, which, according to the minutes, were held on August 3 and 10, not October 3 and 10.[16]

Having been authorized by the committee of the party at its meeting in London on June 18, 1894, to write to Dickson and to communicate with the Liberal whip regarding registration in North and South Derry and North and South Tyrone, Blake had lost no time in carrying out his assignment. He must have seen Ellis immediately, for he reported his conversation with him in the letter which he wrote to Dickson the next day. A careful study of this controversial letter shows considerable difference between it and the press reports of the one read by Healy at the Tyrone convention. Blake's letter contains no request that the Liberals should buy seats from the Nationalists, nor does it mention any agreement or even suggestion that the seats should be considered Liberal and not home rule.

Blake told Dickson that it was necessary for the committee to limit in every possible way its contributions to the Irish National Federation's expenditure in connection with registration. It would, therefore, he went on, be impossible this year to recommend a subvention towards registration expenses in North and South Tyrone and North and South Derry, divisions in which Liberal Home Rulers were to be candidates. The local branches of the Federation, which had done much of the preliminary work of registration in 1893, could, however, he expected to continue their voluntary

---

[15] Ellis's speech is reported in *ibid*.
[16] The relevant extracts from the minutes of the 1893 and 1894 meetings mentioned by Blake are among the Dillon Papers. See also J. F. X. O'Brien Papers, Minutes of the committee of the Irish parliamentary party.

efforts. Then, after telling Dickson that the Federation officers estimated the subventions required by the branches for disbursement in North Tyrone, South Tyrone, and South Derry at £190 each, Blake wrote as follows:

> The committee being unable to recommend funds for this purpose requested me to see Mr. Ellis, the chief Liberal Whip; to explain the situation to him; and to point out the importance to the Liberals, as well as to ourselves, of their fighting the four seats, and the propriety of his making provision for the payment of say £200—in addition to any other provision contemplated in this regard—so as to fill up the deficit occasioned by our inability to contribute in money to the registration work in these divisions.
> I saw Mr. Ellis accordingly and stated the case to him. He expressed his good will, and his anxiety to meet as far as possible our views; and promised to consider the matter fully; and he asked me, when writing to you, to say that he would be glad to hear from you fully as to the registration expenses in these four divisions; and that he would await your letter before further consultation. May I therefore express the hope that you will write to him without delay.
> If the suggested arrangement is carried out, then, apart from the volunteer work to be done by the local branches, the expenses of the registration in these four divisions will be borne by the Liberals; and the divisions would of course be treated as Liberal Home Rule, but not Nationalist divisions; the Nationalists doing all in their power to second the efforts of the Liberals to secure the seats.

Blake added that any committees or organizations for the management of affairs in these divisions would naturally be formed locally, under the direction of Dickson and leading local Liberals "with due regard to the importance of keeping all elements united." In this connection, he reported the Irish parliamentary committee's decision not to support the suggested formation of a northern local committee to deal conjointly with the affairs of the four divisions in question and with those of one or two other divisions, such as Derry City, in which Nationalist candidates were to be run. For many reasons, it was thought best "to maintain in all the Nationalist divisions, the existing system, without attempting to introduce exceptional machinery, or new local authority, dealing in combination with Liberal and Nationalist divisions."[17]

[17] The full text of Blake's letter has been published by F. S. L. Lyons as a select document under the title "The Irish Parliamentary Party and the Liberals in Mid-Ulster, 1894" (*Irish Historical Studies*, March, 1951). The original letter and the copy sent by Blake to J. F. X. O'Brien are in the Dillon Papers. There is also a copy in the Blake Papers.

It can be seen that the subjects discussed here were the same as those dealt with by Blake in his address at Cork, and that the publication of the letter would have shown his statements on that occasion to be substantially correct. The only apparent discrepancy is that some of the proposals mentioned by Blake in his Cork address as being made in 1893 do not seem to have been put forward until 1894.

The wide variation between the original and the press versions of Blake's letter is difficult to understand. It is possible that the letter which Healy read at Omagh was an incorrect reproduction of the original, but a more likely explanation is that the reporters at the convention either did not hear or did not grasp the details of the letter and thus misinterpreted its real sense.[18] This is suggested not only by Healy's assertion that the press reports of the convention were inaccurate, but also by Dillon's apparent reaction to the reading of the letter. For while he denied Healy's charges against the committe of the party, he did not suggest that the letter read by Healy was not genuine.[19] Instead, he condemned him for disclosing the contents of a private letter. It is possible that Healy, by the reckless charges which he made both before and after reading the letter, led the reporters to misinterpret its contents, for, whatever he read, it appears certain that he accused the party committee of selling seats to the Liberals.

Certain other documents throw additional light on the situation. In a letter dated June 19, 1894, Blake told J. F. X. O'Brien that he had submitted his letter to Dickson "to such of the committee as I could find, viz., Messrs. McCarthy, Sexton, and Dillon" and that, as they approved of it, he had sent it on. Since O'Brien was secretary of the party committee, Blake enclosed a copy of the letter for his files "in case of subsequent correspondence or suggestion arising."[20] Dickson's reply to Blake's letter indicated his general agreement with the proposed arrangement, though he added that "the

[18] This hypothesis is suggested by Lyons in "Irish Party and General Election of 1895."
[19] This is clear from the reports in both the *Irish Times* and the *Irish Independent*, as well as from Dillon's statement to the party on Aug. 16, 1895. For notes of his statement see the Dillon Papers.
[20] Dillon Papers, Blake to J. F. X. O'Brien, June 19, 1894.

withholding of the usual contribution of £200 or more" would entail extra work for himself and his friends.[21] Blake sent this letter and a copy of his reply to it[22] to O'Brien asking him to lay them before the committee.[23]

Blake was naturally eager to have the letters published. He was deeply distressed at his personal position in relation to the controversy and believed that the delay in producing his letter was harmful both to himself and to the party. His attitude is clearly illustrated in the opening paragraphs of a letter which he wrote to McCarthy on July 12:

> It would be impossible for me, and so I shall not attempt, to express the depth of my distress at the accusations levelled mainly against me, who am for the second time the scapegoat of the Irish party.[24] I am sorry indeed to trouble you at this time. But as a stranger in England I am too weak and isolated to allow this attack on my honor to proceed unanswered. I must however approach you with some words on practical points.
>
> You telegraphed to Diamond, about the time at which with the approval of the committee I was speaking at Cork, that a full statement would be published. Your telegram has not unnaturally been interpreted, as well by Healy as by the general public, as promising something from yourself and something fuller than my speech; and the publication of your full statement is being called for. I don't know whether you meant by your telegram to refer to my speech. If so, I think it would have been better to have said so. But whatever you meant the result is such as I have stated. I have experienced a natural delicacy in pressing on the attention of my colleagues the necessity, or at any rate the propriety, of considering to some extent my personal position, in which unhappily the cause is more or less involved. I feel that delicacy still. But I cannot forbear to point out that the whole controversy has been made, by the mode of treatment, to centre on the letter which, unfortunately for me, I wrote as their organ and under their instructions, of which they approved, and a copy of which is now on the fyles of the committee; that the publication of that letter has been demanded; and that every day of delayed action is in my judgment damaging if not disastrous.

In the same letter Blake expressed his annoyance at not being invited to attend a private conference which McCarthy and Dillon

[21] *Ibid.*, T. A. Dickson to Blake, June 23, 1894.
[22] *Ibid.*, Blake to Dickson, June 25, 1894.
[23] *Ibid.*, Blake to J. F. X. O'Brien, June 25, 1894.
[24] Undoubtedly he considered the controversy arising from his letter about the O'Connor and O'Driscoll charges as the first time. The two situations were somewhat similar and the attitude taken by Blake was the same in both cases.

had had with Dickson the previous day. He was also displeased that McCarthy had declined Dickson's offer to get the letter for him. It appears that the committee's copy of the controversial letter had been mislaid, for Blake informed McCarthy that he had written to J. F. X. O'Brien to see if he could give him any clue as to its whereabouts, and that he himself was going to London the following Tuesday (July 16) and would at once try to find the copy of the letter and any helpful records of the election committee of 1892. "If nothing more has been meantime done by you or others I will publish the letter, since references infinitely more damaging than anything which it can possibly contain (being as it is the letter of an honorable man) will be drawn from its non-production. I know that it will be quite too late for the general public, that it will be said to be extorted, and that it may only serve to revive the flame; but for these consequences I cannot hold myself responsible."[25]

Although McCarthy had declined Dickson's offer to produce the original letter, he evidently decided, on learning Blake's attitude, to reverse his policy. Replying very promptly to his colleague's letter, he told him that a telegram had been sent to Dickson asking him to come to Dublin at once—that night, if possible—and to bring the controversial letter with him. "Do not," he added, "imagine for a moment that we could be indifferent to the public maintenance of your honour. Your honour is as our own." But he told Blake that he thought his speech at Cork "ought to have satisfied every honest man."

Later the same day, July 12, McCarthy told Blake that Dickson was unable to come to Dublin that night, but would arrive the next day when he would see McCarthy at the Shelbourne, and Blake was invited to join them there.[26] Dickson had wished Blake to attend the previous conference, and the failure to invite him had been simply the result of a misunderstanding.[27]

There is no record of what occurred at the meeting with Dickson on July 13, but it was not followed by the publication of Blake's letter. Instead, McCarthy wrote a letter to the editor of the *Freeman's*

[25] Blake Papers, Blake to McCarthy, July 12, 1895.
[26] For both McCarthy's letters of July 12, see the Blake Papers.
[27] This is explained in *ibid.*, Dillon to Blake, July 12, 1895.

Journal in which he declared that Healy had never defined nor repudiated the charges attributed to him, and that he was perfectly at liberty to publish any disclosures or documents which he might think fit to make public. McCarthy repeated his earlier denial of the charge that the committee of the Irish party had corruptly sold four northern seats for £800 a year, and added that Healy had long been aware of the arrangements made in connection with those seats. Referring to his promise in the telegram to Diamond to publish a full statement, he declared, "That statement was made by Mr. Blake at Cork on Wednesday. And I and my colleagues on the Committee adopt Mr. Blake's statement, and accept to the fullest extent responsibility for everything contained in it. . . ." Finally, McCarthy asserted that the country expected and would demand from Healy some explanation of the grounds on which he had made false charges against his colleagues, especially at a time when they were certain to inflict enormous injury on the Nationalist cause.[28] But in his reply, which appeared a day later in the *Freeman's Journal*, Healy still made no attempt to repudiate or define his charges. He simply told McCarthy to publish the Blake letter if he was not ashamed of it.[29]

Although Blake never ceased to believe that his letter to Dickson should have been made public, he eventually decided against publishing it without the approval of the committee. To McCarthy he explained his reason for this decision:

> Had I been about to continue on the committee I should have felt it inconsistent with that position to abstain from publishing. But as it is my intention not to serve on the committee in the new Parliament, and to withdraw as soon as at all possible from Parliament, I am disposed to say that, retaining my own opinion, I can defer to the judgment of my colleagues, not merely as to their own action, but also as to mine. I could have wished to leave public life under other circumstances. But that wish, like others, I will forego. . . .
> I write this as it enables the committee to deal with a much freer hand with the question, since they have the assurance that if they decide I ought not to publish, I shall, while dissenting, act on their view.[30]

---

[28]*Freeman's Journal*, Dublin, July 15, 1895. The letter is dated July 13.
[29]*Ibid.*, July 16, 1895. The letter is dated July 15.
[30]Blake Papers, Blake to McCarthy, n.d. This was probably written towards the end of July.

It must have been towards the end of July that the committee decided against publishing the letter,[31] and Blake, in accordance with his decision, did not act contrary to its wishes.

The decision of the committee did not, however, close the incident. When the general election resulted in a sweeping victory for Lord Salisbury's new government, it was said that the Omagh charges had contributed to the defeat of the Liberals, who, of course, had been condemned for buying the seats which the Nationalists were accused of selling. In view of this situation, many leading Nationalists felt that, so long as dissension within their own ranks continued, there would be little likelihood that a House of Commons favourable to home rule would again be elected. Some of them believed, therefore, that McCarthy, as chairman of the Irish party, should issue a manifesto pointing out the dangers of dissension, condemning Healy once more for his conduct at Omagh, and appealing for unity in Nationalist ranks.

At the end of July, Dillon told Blake that unless McCarthy issued such an address at once, the party would "go to pieces."[32] Blake, however, expressed some doubt as to the expediency of such a move, and in a long letter to Dillon on August 1, he pointed out that McCarthy had already published both a telegram and a letter regarding the Omagh incident. Furthermore, Healy had repudiated the report of his speech at Omagh, had made no new or definite charge, and had called for the publication of Blake's letter to Dickson. This letter had not been published, and Blake felt that if Healy were to be condemned on some new ground, it was difficult to know what it was to be. In this connection, he mentioned that both he and McCarthy had been trying to frame a vote of censure against Healy to be proposed at the sessional meeting of the party, but since Healy had never defined his charge, they had been faced with much difficulty. Blake could only suggest that, in the manifesto or the vote of censure, it might be pointed out that Healy's duty was not merely to deny the truth of the report of his Omagh speech, but to state what he did say, and that since he had not done this, he must be held to

[31]In a letter of Aug. 1, Blake remarked that the committee had decided against publishing the letter. See Dillon Papers, Blake to Dillon, Aug. 1, 1895.
[32]Blake Papers, Dillon to Blake, July 31, 1895.

the report, the truth of which he had denied. Still convinced that a serious error had been made in not publishing his letter to Dickson immediately after the Omagh convention, he added, "I fear that the psychological moment for giving the truth of our side in this case, as in that of A. O'Connor, has been let slip and that the mischief is irremediable."[33]

But in spite of his views on this matter, Blake told McCarthy that for the present he would reserve his opinion as to the manifesto.[34] When it was finally decided that one should be issued, Blake and McCarthy, who were then in London, revised the draft which Dillon and William O'Brien[35] had prepared and sent over from Dublin. Writing to Dillon about the manifesto on the day on which it was sent to the press, Blake remarked that, in both its original and revised forms, it contained "radical defects of a serious and inevitable nature," which provided Healy with openings for an attack. Since, however, these defects arose from the existing situation, he felt that nothing could be done about them. Although he believed that the manifesto would do little good, he remarked to Dillon: "I daresay you are right that without something of this kind the game is up, and therefore this thing may as well be tried before throwing down the cards."[36]

The manifesto, dated August 6, signed by Justin McCarthy, and addressed to his fellow-countrymen, appeared in the *Freeman's Journal* on August 7. It began by stating that the election of a great anti–home rule majority to the House of Commons proved that dissension in Irish ranks was ruinous to the Nationalist cause, and that a thorough restoration of discipline, together with a genuine observance of the party pledge, was necessary to repair the disaster. The election results might not, it asserted, have been so adverse to the cause of home rule "had it not been for the action of the so-

[33]Dillon Papers, Blake to Dillon, Aug. 1, 1895.
[34]*Ibid.* Blake told Dillon in this letter of his statement to McCarthy.
[35]O'Brien was no longer a member of Parliament, having retired two weeks before the defeat of the Rosebery government and not having sought re-election. See O'Brien, *Olive Branch*, 76–7. But he continued, on occasion, to take part in deliberations with leading Irish Nationalists.
[36]Dillon Papers, Blake to Dillon, Aug. 6, 1895.

called Irish Nationalists who had been endeavouring openly to bring back the Coercionists to power, and the still more lamentable blows aimed at the Irish Party and the Irish National cause by one of our own colleagues at the most critical moment of the election." A condemnation of Healy's action at Omagh followed this statement. According to his own statement, the information on which he professed to base his charges had been in his hands months before the Tyrone convention.[37] Thus, even if the charges had been founded, it would have been an act of treason for Healy to make them, without a word of inquiry to his colleagues, in the middle of an election campaign. Since, however, they were wholly untrue, Healy's action in making them was even more deserving of reproach.

McCarthy closed his manifesto with an appeal that the "Omagh scandal" should be the last of the series of attacks which had been levelled against the unity and efficiency of the Irish party. He felt bound, before the opening of Parliament, to inform his colleagues and his fellow-countrymen of the views which he held and which, if he were re-elected to the chairmanship of the party, it would be his duty to attempt to enforce.

Healy answered this manifesto in a long letter to McCarthy which appeared in the *Freeman's Journal* on August 8.[38] In this letter Healy repeated his assertion that the press reports of his Omagh speech were inaccurate, and added: "The writing of the Blake letter and the making of the compact it discloses is the sole charge brought by me against any colleague. Your refusal to publish this document demonstrates its discredit, for, of course, the independence of our party is gone the moment such arrangements can be entered into." He afterwards mentioned that the chief Liberal whip had been asked "to fill up the deficit in our funds by providing £200 a year for registration work in North Tyrone." Apparently, then, Healy had not charged the committee with ac-

[37]While the *Irish Times*, July 9, 1895, reported Healy as having said that he had heard of it two months after it was written, Healy, in his letter of July 11, which appeared in the *Freeman's Journal* on July 12, declared that he had known nothing about the transaction for months afterwards.

[38]This letter is dated Aug. 6, but if this is correct he must have read the manifesto before it was published.

cepting from the Liberals £800 a year for the Irish party funds in return for the seats; rather, it was the true arrangements made about the northern seats which he regarded as dishonourable.[39]

In this letter to McCarthy, Healy also attempted to justify his action in making his attack during the election campaign rather than at an earlier date by explaining that, until he learned from Dillon at Omagh that there was to be no Nationalist candidate in North Tyrone, he had been prepared not to disclose the contents of the Blake letter. He also repudiated what he called the insinuation that he had ever failed in his pledge to sit, act, and vote with the Irish party. Accusing McCarthy and a few of his colleagues of seeking to "hold themselves out as 'the party,'" he went on to attack Blake in a most offensive manner:

> The pledge we take is one to act with the Irish Party, and not with individuals like Mr. Edward Blake. I owe no "loyalty" to Mr. Blake, and I yield none. Our honest party before now, in its greatest hour of need, spurned with indignation the temptation he set before it, in a long and urgent speech, to accept a "gift" of £2,000 from an anonymous British friend—who turned out to be a Cabinet Minister. With men who are strangers to nationalist traditions in our ranks it is necessary to be on the alert, and after the breakdown of his attempt upon the integrity of the party, that he should be made the emissary for the shady transaction in North Tyrone is significant and deplorable. . . .

In making these statements and in referring repeatedly to the arrangement which he condemned as "the Blake compact," Healy made it clear that he regarded Blake as the man primarily responsible for it. At Omagh, however, he was reported to have placed the chief blame on Dillon.

In a letter dated August 8, which appeared in the *Freeman's Journal* on the tenth, Healy was severely criticized by William O'Brien for making such an attack upon Blake. O'Brien declared that it was time "to make some protest against the unbridled blackguardism with which Mr. Blake's name is dealt with in Mr. Healy's letter." Healy, he asserted, was perfectly aware that the decision to abandon the four northern seats had been made by "Messrs. Healy, Murphy, and Co., who dominated the Election Committee of 1892,"

[39]This is clear too from Healy's statements in his memoirs about the Omagh scandal. See T. M. Healy, *Letters and Leaders of My Day* (London, 1928), II, 420-2.

before Blake had even become a member of the party. "Mr. Blake's letter," he went on, "was a mere secretarial act undertaken at the request of his colleagues for the purpose of obliging the Liberal Party to assume the expense along with the advantages of an arrangement for which Mr. Healy himself is more responsible than any other living man, and for which Mr. Blake had no more responsibility than he had for the Norman invasion."

The suggestion that it was the Healyite members of the election committee of 1892 who actually promoted the arrangements which they now condemned does not seem to have been made by anyone except O'Brien. It appears unlikely that McCarthy and Dillon would have ignored it if it had been true. But even if some of O'Brien's statements are not quite accurate, this does not lessen the effectiveness of his vindication of Blake's conduct. The fact remains that Blake was not a member of the election committee of 1892 which made the original arrangements regarding the four northern seats.

After denying Healy's version of Blake's part in the Tweedmouth incident,[40] O'Brien went on to say that this attack "upon a 'stranger,' who has so many claims upon our tenderness and respect," was all the more blameworthy since Blake had had "nothing but loss of power and purse to face in embracing the Irish cause." Healy's assault on Blake was the latest phase of a policy to drive every man of delicate feeling from the service of Ireland.

The sessional meeting of the Irish party began on August 13, and Justin McCarthy was re-elected to the chairmanship on that day.[41] It had been expected that the Omagh incident would also be discussed on this occasion, but time did not permit, and the meeting was adjourned until the sixteenth. Blake was greatly disturbed at this arrangement, for his departure for Canada would prevent his attendance at any meeting after the fourteenth, and he feared that his absence when the Omagh incident was discussed would be construed by the Healyites as an admission of guilt on his part.

Blake's views regarding this situation are recorded in two letters which he wrote to McCarthy at this time.[42] In one dated August 13,

[40]For the text of this portion of O'Brien's letter, see above p. 107.
[41]Dillon Papers, Minutes of the Irish parliamentary party, Aug. 13, 1895.
[42]For both these letters, see the Blake Papers.

he expressed his regret as "the throwing of the business over tomorrow, which will result in the Omagh affair being discussed in my absence." It was not, however, until the next day, when he had become much more distressed about the matter, that he related his views in detail:

> The falseness of the position in which I have been placed by the adjournment of the meeting over the only day possible before my departure has been painfully accentuated in interviews to-day.
> Having been first exposed to the implication of concealing my letter when I was most anxious that it should be produced, I am now plausibly accused of fleeing from a discussion at which I fully expected and was most anxious to vindicate myself.

Blake wished his letter to Dickson to be read to the party, but he was afraid that this would not be done in his absence. He was, however, determined to take a firm stand on this matter, and expressed his position forcibly to McCarthy:

> My wish to be present was latterly increased, because, although T. P. O'Connor told me the letter was to be read, I have since observed indications which lead me to think he is mistaken.
> I request that the letter may be read and I wish to say that in case it is not read I hold myself free at the first party meeting I attend to read it (all too late tho' that may be) and also as much of this letter as is necessary to show that I made this request.

It will be remembered that Blake had previously stated his intention not to serve on the party committee in the new Parliament. At his colleagues' request, he had evidently reversed his decision, but now that his inability to attend the adjourned sessional meeting placed him in an awkward position, he renewed his request that he might be allowed to retire from the committee. "I am quite aware," he added, "that this course may be taken as an admission of conscious wrong doing; but even at this hazard I prefer to give up a struggle in which I have been prevented from defending myself in the only way which seems to me essential and worthy."[43]

In reply McCarthy expressed his regret that the sessional meeting had had to be adjourned to a date when Blake could not attend. He explained that he had fully expected the Omagh incident to be discussed on the thirteenth and had set aside the fourteenth for

[43] *Ibid.*, Blake to McCarthy, Aug. 14, 1895.

journalistic work which absolutely had to be completed and sent away that night. For this reason the meeting could not be resumed that day, but McCarthy assured Blake he would give the fullest and closest consideration to every suggestion made by him in his letter of August 14.[44]

At the party meeting on the sixteenth, Dillon was to make a statement regarding the Omagh incident. Prior to leaving London, Blake wrote to him offering some advice upon this subject. As an aid in preparing the statement, he proposed that Dillon should read over carefully Healy's published letters, since they contained his plan of campaign. Prominent among Healy's points, Blake declared, was the privacy of the convention. He advised Dillon to meet this boldly, stating that even party meetings were not always private, and that such charges as Healy made in the presence of two or three hundred men were certain to reach the public. Furthermore, while Healy asserted that the press had not been present at the convention, the *Independent* claimed that five reporters had been in attendance. Blake suggested that, in considering Healy's statement that the press reports were imaginative, Dillon should remember the similarity between the accounts in the *Irish Times* and the *Independent*. Finally, Blake gave Dillon the following well-reasoned advice: "Don't declare yourself, in the start, unable to have heard or to recollect the bulk. You put yourself at his [Healy's] mercy thus. State what you do remember, the salient points, but keep yourself free as to other points which he may later allege. If you have said in advance you recall no more, you will have given free scope to his fancy for the rest." Blake also expressed to Dillon, as he had to McCarthy, the hope that his letter to Dickson would be read at the party meeting.[45]

In answer to this letter, Dillon told Blake that he would do his best at the meeting, where it was his intention to read in full Blake's letter to Dickson, together with Dickson's reply.[46]

It is stated in the minutes of the meeting held on August 16 that Dillon gave "a lengthened account" of the proceedings at Omagh

[44]*Ibid.*, McCarthy to Blake, Aug. 14, 1895.
[45]Dillon Papers, Blake to Dillon, Aug. 15, 1895.
[46]Blake Papers, Dillon to Blake, Aug. 15, 1895.

and read Blake's letter to Dickson. Whether he read Dickson's reply is not altogether clear, though the wording of a resolution proposed by Healy at the close of Dillon's remarks suggests that it was read. The notes of Dillon's statement before the party, which have been preserved among his private papers, show that his account of the incident corresponded very closely with the press reports which Healy had described as imaginative.

Dillon told the party that the election committee had deputized him to attend the Omagh convention. At the opening of the proceedings, during a somewhat disorderly discussion on the question of the chairmanship, he understood that some reporters had entered the hall. As soon as Dillon had taken the chair, Healy asked whether it would be in order to nominate a candidate for North Tyrone. Dillon replied that he was bound to receive nominations for any of the divisions of the county, but that, since the North Tyrone men had already held a conference and selected a candidate, he did not expect a nomination to be made for that division. Thereupon, Healy made a violent attack on the committee of the party, charging it with having sold four northern seats to the Liberal party for an annual sum of £200 apiece. In support of his charges, he read some passages from Blake's letter to Dickson. Thus, Dillon's account of the Omagh incident confirmed the assertion of the Parnellite and Unionist press that Healy had accused the party committee of selling four seats to the Liberals. It appears, therefore, that the only serious error made by the press was in its summary of the contents of the Blake letter.

Referring to Healy's assertion that the charges had been made at a private meeting, Dillon—obviously acting on Blake's advice—reminded his colleagues that the meeting had been attended by about 240 delegates and, as it turned out, by a number of newspaper reporters. Adding that even meetings of the party were not always private, he declared that the Omagh convention had not been the proper place to bring forward such charges, even if they had been true.

The remainder of the notes on Dillon's statement deals with the arrangements regarding registration which Blake had described in his speech at Cork. To verify his account, Dillon read excerpts from the minutes of the party, as well as from those of the executive committee of the Irish National Federation. On reading Blake's letter, Dillon explained to the party that Blake had had "much less responsibility in these transactions than any other member of the Committee," and he added that "in writing the letter about which so much scandal has been made, he simply acted by order of the Committee."

At the close of Dillon's statement, Healy moved and one of his supporters seconded that the correspondence between Blake and Dickson, which had now been disclosed to the party, should be given to the press. In opposition to this, an amendment expressing approval of McCarthy's manifesto of August 6, denying Healy's charges, and condemning him for thus attacking his colleagues, was proposed and seconded. But it was evidently considered inexpedient to attempt to carry so strong a resolution of censure against Healy, for after a discussion the amendment was negatived without a division. Another amendment, reading as follows, was proposed in its place: "That having heard the statement of Mr. Dillon as to the incident at the Omagh Convention, and having read to us Mr. Blake's letter and other documents in connection with the registration in and the representation of North and South Derry and North and South Tyrone, we hereby express our entire approval of the action of the Chairman and Committee in connection with these seats."[47] This amendment, which was carried by a vote of 33 to 26, was something of a compromise, for, while vindicating the committee, it made no actual mention of Healy's charges. But, as was later pointed out to Blake, its express reference to the reading of his letter at the meeting gave it one advantage over the stronger amendment.[48]

Blake's colleagues did not agree to his request that he should be permitted to retire from the committee. Together with Davitt, Dillon, Healy, Knox, Arthur O'Connor, T. P. O'Connor, and Sexton, Blake

[47] The text of the various resolutions and the action taken upon them are recorded in Dillon Papers, Minutes of the Irish parliamentary party, Aug. 16, 1895.

[48] This advantage was mentioned by Captain A. Donelan in a letter to Blake, misdated Aug. 16, 1895. As will be seen presently, it was obviously written on Aug. 17. For the letter see the Blake Papers.

was elected to the committee just before the close of the sessional meeting. Some of the Dillonites were not very well pleased with the result of this election, which gave seats on the committe to three Healyites, namely, Healy himself, Knox, and Arthur O'Connor. Since Blake had now left for Canada and Davitt was in Australia, this meant that, until their return, the Dillonites and Healyites would be equally represented on the committee; it was indeed fortunate for the Dillonites that the chairman of the party was on their side. The number of votes received by each man elected to the committee was also significant. The figures were as follows:[49]

E. Blake	31	votes	T. Sexton	29 votes
J. Dillon	31	"	M. Davitt	28 "
T. M. Healy	31	"	E. F. V. Knox	28 "
A. O'Connor	29	"	T. P. O'Connor	28 "

Since the three Healyites each received more than 26 votes, it is clear that some members who voted in favour of the amendment vindicating Blake and his colleagues nevertheless felt that the Healyites should have some representation on the committee of the party. Thus it would probably have been inexpedient to attempt to expel Healy from the party, as some members desired to do at this time.

Following the meeting of August 16, Captain A. Donelan, a supporter of the Dillonite wing of the party, wrote to Blake assuring him that his absence was not being misinterpreted, since care had been taken to make known that it was absolutely unavoidable. Indeed, Donelan expressed the belief that the resolution vindicating Blake's action would "carry far more weight and be far more effective" since the latter had not been present to influence opinion in his favour. Donelan closed his letter by telling Blake that if he knew the trust, confidence, and affection in which he was held by the Irish people, it would reward him for all the sacrifices he had made on their behalf.[50]

Somewhat similar sentiments regarding the respect felt for Blake were expressed in a letter to him by T. P. O'Connor. After remark-

[49]This list is given in F. S. L. Lyons, *The Irish Parliamentary Party, 1890–1910* (London, 1951), 53.

[50]Blake Papers, A. Donelan to Blake. This letter is dated Aug. 16, 1895, but certain remarks, including a reference to "yesterday's meeting," indicate that it was written on Aug. 17.

ing that, at this time, it was the duty of Blake's warm friends to assure him how deeply they appreciated his services to the Irish cause, he added:

> If these attacks by unworthy men upon you have wounded you—as they must have done—find some consolation in the fact that these attacks have increased the warmth of the affection and respect of honest men for you. Many little unpleasantnesses and some deplorable "contretemps" may occasionally have made you think that this was not so, but knowing how men feel about you and speak about you, I can assure you that I rightly describe their feelings.[51]

At least one Dillonite member of the Irish party felt that Blake had not been adequately defended by his colleagues against Healy's charges. Alfred Webb, one of the party treasurers, wrote to McCarthy on August 20, 1895, announcing his intention of retiring from Parliament. He gave a number of reasons for his decision, among which was the following: "It [the party] has not effectually denounced baseless attacks upon the character and patriotism of Mr. Blake and other members of the committee, made at a moment and in a manner most calculated to injure National interests...."[52]

Thus closed the public dissension regarding the "Omagh scandal," but it was to have far-reaching effects, for it led to a decline in the prestige and popularity of the Irish party.[53] As far as Blake was concerned, he had, through no fault of his own, been placed in a most awkward position, his distress at which is entirely understandable. The failure of his colleagues to produce the letter, in spite of his advice, needlessly strengthened the charge that it contained the details of some shameful compact with the Liberals. Though the proposals regarding registration which it revealed might have excited some criticism, especially from Healy, publication would have shown that press versions of the letter were very inaccurate, that the Irish party had not handed over any seats to the Liberals in return for an annual subscription to the party funds, and that Blake's part in the whole incident was entirely honourable.

[51] *Ibid.*, T. P. O'Connor to Blake, Aug. 16, 1895.
[52] Webb's letter is published in the *Freeman's Journal*, Dublin, Aug. 21, 1895.
[53] For an account of the results, see Lyons, "Irish Parliamentary Party and General Election of 1895."

In the campaign which occasioned these disputes Blake told the electors of his own constituency, that, if returned to the House of Commons, he would not be able to be in constant attendance and might not retain his seat for the whole of the next Parliament.[54] In spite of this, he was re-elected by acclamation as member for South Longford.

Blake was away from Britain for several months following the general election, and this was one of the reasons why he had told his constituents that he would be unable to maintain constant attendance in Parliament. After spending about two months in Canada, he left for New Zealand to serve as arbitrator in a dispute between the New Zealand government and the New Zealand Midland Railway Company. During his stay in that country and in Australia, which he visited from January to February, 1896, he also addressed meetings in support of the Irish cause. He arrived back in Britain in March, 1896.

By that time the Irish party had a new chairman. Justin McCarthy had told his colleagues at the end of 1895 that he must be allowed to retire from that post owing to ill health and the pressure of literary work. His resignation was announced on February 3, 1896. There was considerable discussion behind the scenes as to who should succeed him, for it was difficult, if not impossible, to find a man who would be acceptable to both Dillonites and Healyites. Thomas Sexton was suggested as a suitable candidate, but he was anxious to leave public life, and, after some consideration, decided not only to refuse the chairmanship, but also to retire from Parliament.[55] The *Annual Register* for the year, 1896, states that "unofficial overtures were made by a section of the party to induce Mr. Blake to allow his name to be put forward, but they came to nothing."[56] There is no mention of any such overtures in the Irish leaders' correspondence during this period, but letters between

[54]He mentioned this declaration to his constituents in an undated letter to McCarthy. It is among the 1895 correspondence with McCarthy in the Blake Papers.
[55]He had originally intended not to seek re-election in the general election of 1895.
[56]*The Annual Register, A Review of Public Events at Home and Abroad for the Year 1896* (London, 1897), 218.

Dillon and Blake in 1899 indicate that the latter's name was suggested, but that the matter was not actually brought to the attention of Blake, who was in Australia at the time. Towards the close of 1899, Blake wrote to Dillon that he had been given to understand that his name had been mentioned by Healy as a chairman he would be willing to accept, on three occasions, the first of which was during Blake's absence prior to Dillon's first election in 1896.[57] In reply to this assertion, Dillon wrote:

> On the first occasion—before my first election and when you were, I think, on your way to Australia—to the best of my recollection—Dr. McDonnell spoke to me on the subject and stated—amongst other things—that Healy had assured him that if Blake were proposed for the Chair he (H) would accept the nomination and cordially support you. I have not a very distinct recollection of what passed between us—but to the best of my memory—what I said was that I was not in a position to enter into any negotiations with him as to the election of a Chairman and that in any case I could not consider any communication from Mr. Healy as a basis for discussion unless it was in Mr. H's own writing. I cannot recall now having heard anything more on the subject at that time though on this latter point I can't pretend that I can absolutely rely on my memory. I consulted the friends with whom I was then acting and who were within reach and acted to the best of my judgment and upon their advice.[58]

At any rate, a party meeting was held on February 18, 1896, and Dillon was elected to the chairmanship by a vote of 38 to 21.[59] In an effort to achieve the unity and centralization which he desired, Dillon secured the abolition of the party committee,[60] and, in directing the policy of the party, sought the advice of only his most intimate colleagues, among whom was Blake.

[57] Blake Papers, Blake to Dillon, Dec. 24, 1899. For references to the two other occasions on which Healy suggested Blake for the chairmanship, see below chap. VIII.
[58] Ibid., Dillon to Blake, Dec. 26, 1899.
[59] For a fuller account of the negotiations regarding the chairmanship, see Lyons, Irish Parliamentary Party, 57–62.
[60] Ibid., 62. When Dillon secured its abolition, Healy and Arthur O'Connor had already been expelled from it. For their expulsion, of which more will be said in chap. VII, see Dillon Papers, Minutes of the Irish parliamentary party, Nov. 14, 1895.

VI. THE FINANCIAL RELATIONS COMMISSION

The Report

SINCE THE PASSAGE of the act of legislative union between Great Britain and Ireland, complaints had been made repeatedly that the financial arrangements between the two countries were not satisfactory, or in accordance with the principles of the act, and that the resources of Ireland had had to bear an undue pressure of taxation. There had been frequent demands for inquiries into the financial relations between Great Britain and Ireland, and, in 1811, 1812, 1815, and again in 1864, committees of the House of Commons had been appointed to investigate the situation. In spite of the fact that the committee appointed in 1864 collected much valuable evidence and reported upon it the next year, no practical measures followed. In 1890, G. J. Goschen, the Chancellor of the Exchequer in Lord Salisbury's government, consented that another committee should be appointed to make a further inquiry. But this committee was named too late in the session for it to make much progress. For a number of reasons, it was not reappointed, and nothing further was done about the matter before the change of government in 1892.

It will be remembered that, before the Home Rule Bill of 1893 passed the House of Commons, important changes were made in its financial clauses. After Gladstone had explained the revised scheme to the House, a debate arose over the proposal of a Scottish member that Goschen's select committee should be reappointed. During this discussion, John Redmond, leader of the Parnellites, suggested that, since the new financial scheme was of a provisional character, Gladstone should consider the advisability of appointing some tribunal such as a Royal Commission to investigate the financial relations between the two countries, so that at the end of the provisional period the House would be in a position to know with some degree of accuracy what the proper contribution of Ireland to the imperial expenses should be. Not long afterwards, Gladstone announced that a Royal Commission would be appointed, since this was considered the best way of obtaining the information necessary to fix definitely the financial relations betwen the two countries. The matter came up several times during the session of 1893, and it was understood that the rejection of the Home Rule Bill by the House of Lords would not interfere with the plans for a commission. In reply to questions on September 1 and December 1, Gladstone announced that it would be appointed early in the next year and on March 24, 1894, the royal warrant for the commission was finally issued.[1]

A month before this, John Morley had written to Blake expressing the hope that he would consent to serve on the commission. Morley believed that Blake's political friends would warmly approve of his appointment, and that his presence on the commission would be "a great advantage in many ways."[2]

Since the committee of the Irish party had expressed a desire that Nationalists invited to serve on the commission should consult it before accepting, Blake was unable to give Morley a definite reply. He could only tell him that he would, "at the earliest moment," confer with his colleagues, but he added: "I feel honored by your proposal, and I will have great pleasure in accepting it if that step should meet with the approbation of my colleagues."[3]

The committee evidently approved Blake's appointment, for, when the names of the commissioners were announced in the spring of 1894, his was among them. The commissioners, representing various shades of political opinion, were: The Right Hon. Hugh C. E. Childers; Lord Farrer; Lord Welby; The Right Hon. the O'Conor Don; Sir Robert Hamilton; Sir Thomas Sutherland, K.C.M.G., M.P.; Sir David Barbour, K.C.S.I.; The Hon. Edward Blake, M.P.; Bertram W. Currie; W. A. Hunter, M.P.; C. E. Martin; John E. Redmond, M.P.; Thomas Sexton, M.P.; Henry F. Slattery; G. W. Wolff, M.P. All these men were distinguished in the field of finance, several having held important posts with the British treasury. Childers, for instance, had been both Financial

---

[1] For a fuller account of the financial situation, see Thomas Kennedy, *A History of the Irish Protest Against Over-Taxation, from 1853–1897* (Dublin, 1897).
[2] Blake Papers, John Morley to Blake, Feb. 24, 1894.
[3] *Ibid.*, Blake to Morley, Feb. 27, 1894.

Secretary of the Treasury and Chancellor of the Exchequer, while Lord Welby, before his elevation to the peerage, had been Permanent Secretary of the Treasury. Sir David Barbour was a recognized authority on Indian finance, and Sir Robert Hamilton had been head of the financial branch of the Board of Trade.[4]

The terms of reference to the commission were:

> To inquire into the Financial Relations between Great Britain and Ireland, and their relative taxable capacity, and to report:—(1) Upon what principles of comparison, and by the application of what specific standards, the relative capacity of Great Britain and Ireland to bear taxation may be most equitably determined. (2) What, so far as can be ascertained, is the true proportion, under the principles and specific standards so determined, between the taxable capacity of Great Britain and Ireland. (3) The history of the Financial Relations between Great Britain and Ireland at and after the Legislative Union, the charge for Irish purposes on the Imperial Exchequer during that period, and the amount of Irish Taxation remaining available for contribution to Imperial expenditure; also the Imperial expenditure to which it is considered equitable that Ireland should contribute.[5]

The work of the commission extended over a period of two years, in the course of which many witnesses were examined and much valuable evidence collected. Before its labours were completed, the commission lost the services of two of its members. Sir Robert Hamilton died early in 1895, and Hugh C. E. Childers, the chairman of the commission, in January, 1896. All the evidence had been collected before Childers' death, but much important work remained to be done in the preparation of reports. Proceedings were suspended until instructions came from the Secretary of State that the commission should elect a new chairman. In April, 1896, the O'Conor Don was chosen for the post.

On June 24, 1896, deliberations of the commission were brought to a close. A joint or majority report, signed by eleven of the thirteen surviving commissioners, was afterwards issued,[6] listing the conclusions on which these men were agreed. They were:

[4]For details regarding the careers of all the commissioners, see Kennedy, *Irish Protest Against Over-Taxation*, 118–25.

[5]*Final Report of the Royal Commission on the Financial Relations between Great Britain and Ireland* (London, 1896), 1.

[6]The majority report and all the separate reports were not issued officially until Aug., 1896, but the *Freeman's Journal* obtained the text of the majority report and Sexton's report immediately after the deliberations ended. On

I. That Great Britain and Ireland must, for the purpose of this inquiry, be considered as separate entities.
II. That the Act of Union imposed upon Ireland a burden which, as events showed, she was unable to bear.
III. That the increase of taxation laid upon Ireland between 1853 and 1860 was not justified by the then existing circumstances.
IV. That identity of rates of taxation does not necessarily involve equality of burden.
V. That whilst the actual tax revenue of Ireland is about one-eleventh of that of Great Britain the relative taxable capacity of Ireland is very much smaller, and is not estimated by any of us as exceeding one-twentieth.[7]

Blake's contribution to the work of the commission was praised by the O'Conor Don in the course of an address delivered in December, 1896. After remarking that "the clearness with which Ireland's case was educed from the mass of evidence is largely due to the ability of Mr. Sexton's examination and cross-examination of the witnesses," he added:

It may, perhaps, be invidious to mention any other name, but I feel so strongly that we are much indebted to another member of the Commission that I cannot refrain from mentioning him. I refer to the Hon. Edward Blake, M.P. To Mr. Blake's wise foresight, to his conciliatory address, to his large-minded views, and his clearness and precision in enunciating them, we are much indebted for having secured practical unanimity in what is called the Joint Report; and as Chairman of the Commission I feel bound to notice the important assistance he has rendered in bringing about that agreement which has proved of so much value.[8]

In a private letter to Blake, who had evidently written to thank him for his kind remarks, the O'Conor Don expressed the same opinion even more forcibly: "I am pleased that you were gratified with my references to you. They were fully deserved and due to you. I do not think we should have had the joint report only for your persuasive remarks. Sexton would not have signed and then no one would have joined. We should have had a jumble of separate reports that would have been valueless."[9]

June 25, it published the conclusions contained in the majority report, and, in two instalments, on June 27 and 29, it printed the text of Sexton's report.
[7]*Report of Royal Commission on Financial Relations*, 2.
[8]The O'Conor Don's words are quoted in Alfred Webb's introduction to Edward Blake, *The Over-Taxation of Ireland* (Dublin, 1897), viii.
[9]Blake Papers, the O'Conor Don to Blake, Jan. 2, 1897.

But the majority report, after listing the points on which eleven of the commissioners were agreed, added that there were points on which they differed. Separate reports on these points of difference were made: jointly by the O'Conor Don, John Redmond, C. E. Martin, W. A. Hunter, and G. W. Wolff; jointly by Lord Farrer, Lord Welby, and B. W. Currie (with a memorandum by Lord Welby); jointly by Thomas Sexton, Edward Blake, and H. F. Slattery (with a memorandum by Blake); by Sir David Barbour, one of the dissentient commissioners; and by Sir Thomas Sutherland, the other dissentient commissioner. There was also a draft report by the deceased chairman, Hugh C. E. Childers.[10]

The report issued in the names of Sexton, Blake, and Slattery, was the work primarily of Sexton,[11] but Blake, by affixing his signature, expressed substantial agreement with it. Differences of opinion among the commissioners had made it impossible, in the majority report, to give detailed statements regarding the terms of reference to the commission. Sexton, however, in his report, outlined the conclusions which he had reached on these matters.

The report dealt with the terms of reference in the order in which they were given. Beginning with the first section of term one, it stated that the relative capacity of Great Britain and Ireland to bear taxation might be most equitably determined by a comparison of their resources. The existing system of levying equal rates of taxes on both countries would have been equitable only if the resources of the two countries had been alike. In principle, the best foundation for comparison of their resources appeared to be "the aggregate annual income possessed by the people." But, since the ratio of income to population was so much more favourable in Great Britain than in Ireland, taxation in proportion to gross incomes would apply

---

[10]For all these reports, see *Report of Royal Commission on Financial Relations*. The majority report and the separate reports are published as a parliamentary return (C8262, 1896). There are also two volumes of evidence (C7720, 1895, I & II).

[11]Sexton drafted it, but reports are issued in the names of all who sign them. See Blake Papers, Sexton to Blake, July 19, 1896. For the report, see *Report of Royal Commission on Financial Relations*, 61–106. After listing conclusions (61–6), it deals with the evidence on which they are based.

unequal pressure to the resources of the two countries, pressing more heavily on Ireland, the poorer, since a large proportion of its more limited income had to be expended in providing the necessities of life. The true measure of resources was not, therefore, the gross income, which included the cost of subsistence, but the surplus left after the cost of subsistence had been deducted. Taxation should therefore be measured by comparison of the surplus incomes of the two countries. Furthermore, in view of the slender means of Ireland and the possibility of large increases in the expenditure of the United Kingdom, provision should be made to limit Irish taxation to a specified maximum annual sum or to a certain defined proportion of the estimated Irish surplus.

Regarding the application of specific standards, the other point mentioned in term one, Sexton's report stated that the only general record of income was the income tax assessment. It therefore suggested that the net assessment, or the produce of the tax, afforded the most appropriate standard then available for estimating the proportion between the respective incomes of Great Britain and Ireland.

Concerning the second term of reference to the commission, Sexton's report concluded that the true proportion of Irish to British taxable capacity was as one to thirty-six. The majority report, it will be recalled, had stated that none of the eleven commissioners who signed it believed that the relative taxable capacity of Ireland to Great Britain exceeded one-twentieth.

In considering the third and last of the terms of reference, Sexton's report dealt first with the general history of the financial relations between Great Britain and Ireland at and after the legislative union. It declared that, between 1794 and 1801, the Irish Parliament had been unable to exercise any real control over the expenditure imposed on Ireland by the policy of the British government. There was nothing in the financial provisions of the Act of Union to suggest that the resources of Ireland had been measured at that time when her expenditure was so immense, including as it did the whole military outlay in Ireland arising from the war which was then in progress between Great Britain and France, the cost of suppressing the insurrection which had occurred in Ireland in 1798, and the cost of maintaining a large army in Ireland during the progress of the project of union.

In the union scheme of finance, it was unfair, Sexton's report asserted, to fix Ireland's future contribution "on the basis of the proportion of the swollen expenditure charged against Ireland in the previous seven years, to the British expenditure in that period." The report continued:

> The calculation on which the proportion of 2 to 15 was founded was manifestly fallacious, for three reasons—(1) because it reckoned as permanent annual Irish expenditure, the temporary military charges connected with the insurrection and the Union; (2) because it left out of the expenditure the great annual charge for debt, although, to the extent of the proportion to be fixed by the calculation, Ireland was to be liable for all new debt incurred and the proportion of charges for existing debt was the obvious measure of this liability; and (3) because a false average was struck between the higher proportion of Irish expenditure to the moderate British expenditure in peace, and the lower proportion of it to the inflated British expenditure in war.

Sexton next pointed out that, in adopting the proportion of 2 to 15, excessive though it was, the framers of the Act of Union had at least admitted that the taxable capacity of Ireland was much lower than that of Great Britain. But later in the same act, by making "the strange provision . . . that when the charge for pre-Union debts came into the same proportion as the relative capacity, indiscriminate taxation might be imposed," they had entirely ignored this fact. Such a provision, Sexton's report declared, "was repugnant to equity, and irreconcilable with reason."

The financial terms of the Act of Union were bad enough, but some of the arrangements carried out in opposition to its principles were, Sexton asserted, even worse. The provisions of the act concerning debt incurred after the union had been absolutely disregarded. The great bulk of post-union debt should have been dealt with as joint debt of the United Kingdom, but instead it was all divided into separate debts of Great Britain and of Ireland in contravention of the Act of Union. The division of the joint debt and the addition of the separate ones to the pre-union debts of each country were breaches of the treaty of union, and, as is was by means of them that the condition as to the proportion of debt which authorized indiscriminate taxation was satisfied, "the proceedings of the Imperial Parliament in 1816—abolishing the separate exchequers, discontinuing the quota system, discarding revision,[12] and opening up a way to indiscriminate taxation—were contrary to the express covenants of the Treaty of Union." In the years which followed, Ireland, already taxed far beyond her capacity, had to bear much additional taxation, although her circumstances were very different from those of Great Britain, whose capital, income, and population were rapidly increasing, while Ireland's steadily declined.

Concerning the next two questions, the charge for Irish purposes on the imperial exchequer and the amount of Irish taxation remaining available for contribution to imperial expenditure, Sexton's report explained that, under the union, Ireland's whole revenue was contributed to "the expenditure of the United Kingdom." The Act of Union did not indicate any mode of subdividing that expenditure into charges for Irish and for non-Irish purposes, nor did it authorize or even contemplate any such division. It appeared to Sexton that the cost of imperial government in Ireland was more likely to be augmented than reduced until it was made subject to domestic control.

Finally, the report dealt with what imperial expenditure it was considered equitable that Ireland should share. Sexton assumed that what was contemplated by this question must be "the transfer of control over Irish Finance to an Irish Legislature, and a specified contribution to certain Imperial expenditure from the Irish Exchequer." He pointed out that imperial expenditure was incurred, as a general rule, in the interest of Great Britain, especially for the promotion of her trade and commerce, and that it would be the same if Ireland did not exist or had no connection with Great Britain. Since Ireland obtained no substantial advantage from it, and in view of "the over-taxation of Ireland since the Union, and the effect of Imperial administration on future public charges in Ireland," Sexton concluded that "it would be no more than merely equitable, if Ireland became responsible for her own financial affairs, that she should be exempt from contribution to Imperial expenditure for a time,

[12]The Act of Union had provided for periodical revision of the proportion of taxation between the two countries.

and that such contribution should afterwards be limited according to the measure of the benefit derived from such expenditure by Ireland."

Sexton's report was followed by Blake's memorandum[13] which began with the following words: "I express by my signature my general assent to the Report of Mr. Sexton, without committing myself to every phrase of that report. I desire to append the draft which I submitted at the meeting of 22nd June, as an attempt to embody, largely in language taken from the draft report prepared by Lord Farrer, what I conceive to be conclusions on the two first branches of the inquiry, to which the great majority of the Commissioners might have given joint assent, subject, of course, to the reservations noted." What followed was not, therefore, a commentary on Sexton's report, but rather Blake's suggestion for a majority report, somewhat more detailed than that which was actually issued. It bore much resemblance both to the majority report and to Sexton's.

Blake's draft began by stating that it was thought impossible "to construct a detailed joint report which should reconcile our differences of view on some questions," and that "the reasonings and conclusions of the Commissioners in such matters might be better elucidated by separate reports." It added, however, that the commissioners were able to express their agreement, subject to the qualifications noted, in the following findings on the first two questions submitted to them. The report then outlined a number of conclusions regarding the first two terms of reference to the commission.

In considering the principles of comparison upon which the relative capacity of Great Britain and Ireland to bear taxation might be most equitably determined, Blake began with two statements almost identical with those which formed the first and fourth points of agreement in the majority report:

> We are of opinion that Great Britain and Ireland must, for the purpose of this inquiry, be regarded as separate entities.
> We think that identity of rates of taxation does not necessarily involve, and in the case of these two countries has not resulted in equality of burden.

---

[13]For the full text of Blake's memorandum, see *Report of Royal Commission on Financial Relations*, 106–8.

The conclusions which followed were very similar to those stated by Sexton in his report. Chief among them was the assertion that the main principle "upon which the relative capacity of Great Britain and Ireland to bear taxation may be most equitably determined is that of a comparison of the money value of the aggregate annual income or return possessed by the people of each country." Blake added that "in fixing the proportion, regard should be had also to the comparative progress and consequent rate of increase of capacity, if any, to bear taxation in each country."

In dealing with the second part of the first term of reference, Blake concluded that "the specific standard which in the actual circumstances of each country may be most fairly applied in order to estimate the proportion of the gross annual income of each is that derived from the assessment to the income tax." He felt that, in the majority report, the commissioners should have expressed their agreement on this point. In his draft, Blake went on to relate that some of the commissioners, as their separate reports would show, thought that the net assessment, or the actual produce of the tax, afforded a more appropriate standard than the gross assessment.

Concerning the second term of reference to the commission, Blake's draft, like the majority report, asserted that "the true proportion . . . of the taxable capacity of Ireland to that of Great Britain does not exceed one-twentieth part of that of Great Britain." Blake added that some of the commissioners thought it was much less, and, in signing Sexton's report, he indicated his own agreement with this view.

The Conference

The report of the financial relations commission aroused widespread interest throughout Ireland, for Nationalists, Parnellites, and Unionists were generally agreed that their country was over-taxed. In many parts of Ireland, public meetings, attended by all classes in the community, passed resolutions requesting the government to take immediate steps to effect the suggestions made in the report, and calling on Irish members of Parliament of all shades of political opinion to act together in this matter. At some of the meetings, committees were appointed to watch the progress of the movement and to take such action as might be considered necessary to ensure its success.

On December 28, 1896, at an especially important meeting in Dublin, a committee was formed to co-operate with such committees as might be appointed by other cities, counties, and public bodies in Ireland to secure the success of the movement. This committee held weekly meetings, and on February 9, 1897, at a conference of delegates from twenty-seven of the thirty-two Irish counties, its constitution and membership were greatly enlarged. It came to be known as the All-Ireland Committee.

Meanwhile, Irish members of Parliament had begun to consider what action should be taken. At first, it was thought that the question should be brought forward at the beginning of the parliamentary session of 1897 as an amendment to the address in reply to the speech from the throne. There was a rumour that, in an effort to secure united action on the part of all Irish members, the Parnellites and Healyites might ask a Unionist to move such an amendment. Dillon, however, hoped that this would not take place, for, fearing that a Unionist amendment would not be strong enough, he felt that his party should take the initiative.[14] And since he considered Blake the only member of the party capable of opening the debate,[15] he began urging him to draft an amendment and propose its adoption in the House of Commons.[16]

Blake was not at all anxious to undertake the task. After telling Dillon that when he had entered Irish politics it had been his intention to take an active part in parliamentary debates, but that circumstances had altered his plans, he went on to say: "It is now a good while since I settled down to the rôle of the silent member, and I think I had better stick to it, not absolutely, of course, but substantially. This would not conform very well with the effort to deal with a subject so dull and dry and difficult of treatment within

[14] See Blake Papers, Dillon to Blake, Dec. 29, 1896.
[15] It will be remembered that Sexton, the other financial expert of the Irish parliamentary party, had retired from Parliament early in 1896.
[16] Blake Papers, Dillon to Blake, Nov. 20, 1896.

reasonable limits and at the same time so vitally important as is the Financial Relations Report. I daresay I ought as a member of the Commission to speak during the debate, but I think you had better open it."[17] Dillon urged Blake to reconsider his position, adding that it would be "a very great misfortune" if he did not see his way to move the amendment, and that the chances of party success would be lessened if he decided to settle down to the role of a silent member. While realizing that some of Blake's experiences in Irish politics had been "painful and disgusting," Dillon believed that if he (Blake) would make up his mind to throw himself actively into the business of the House of Commons, he would very soon occupy a position which would be some slight compensation for what he had had to face.[18]

If a Unionist was asked by the Parnellites and Healyites to move an amendment, he evidently refused, for the motions prepared for submission to the House were in the names of J. J. Clancy, a Parnellite, and Blake, who, in the end, had acceded to Dillon's request. It was generally understood, however, that, if the government agreed to give time later in the session for a discussion of the financial grievance, the motions would not be moved as amendments to the address, but would be postponed to a later date.

It was the opinion of the government that the financial relations commission had been guilty of sins of omission and that therefore a judgment could not be formed on some aspects of the controversy without further investigation. For that reason the government proposed to appoint a new investigating body to carry out the necessary inquiry. This was announced on January 19, 1897, by A. J. Balfour, government leader in the House of Commons, in the course of the debate on the address. Balfour added that he hoped to be in a position, in a very few days, to announce the terms of reference to this new investigating body.

Immediately after Balfour's announcement, Dillon inquired whether the government would promise to give time, at an early date, for the discussion of the financial relations question by way of a special motion. When Balfour replied that the government would

[17] Dillon Papers, Blake to Dillon, Dec. 21, 1896.
[18] Blake Papers, Dillon to Blake, Dec. 29, 1896.

be glad to do so, on the understanding, of course, that there would be no discussion of the matter during the debate on the address, Blake announced that he would not persist in the motion he had intended to submit, since he thought it better to take advantage of Balfour's proposal.[19] Clancy also agreed not to move his amendment.[20]

The terms of reference to the proposed new commission were announced by Balfour in the House of Commons on February 11, 1897. They were:

(1) To inquire and report how much of the total expenditure which the State provides may properly be considered to be expenditure common to England, Scotland, and Ireland, and what share of such common expenditure each country is contributing after the amount expended on local services has been deducted from its true revenue.

(2) How the expenditure on Irish local services which the State wholly or in part provides compares with the corresponding expenditure in England and in Scotland, and whether such Irish expenditure may with advantage be readjusted or reduced.

(3) Whether, when regard is had to the nature of the taxes now in force, to the existing exemptions, and to the amounts of the expenditure by the State on local services, the provision in the Act of Union between Great Britain and Ireland with regard to particular exemptions or abatements calls for any modification in the financial system of the United Kingdom.[21]

The day after the terms of reference had been announced in the House of Commons, the All-Ireland Committee, at a meeting in Dublin, protested strongly against the appointment of a new commission. Then, at a meeting on the sixteenth, it passed a resolution suggesting that Irish parliamentary representatives regardless of party should hold a conference for the purpose of taking immediate united action on the financial relations question.[22]

This resolution was greeted with considerable enthusiasm by Irish members of Parliament, and much correspondence took place between representatives of the Parnellite, anti-Parnellite, and Unionist parties. It was finally decided to issue a circular, signed by lead-

[19]For the remarks of Balfour, Dillon, and Blake, see *Hansard*, 4th Series, XLV, 77–80.
[20]*Ibid.*, 103.
[21]*Ibid.*, XLVI, 184–5.
[22]For the full text of the resolution, see Kennedy, *Irish Protest Against Over-Taxation*, 130.

ing members of each party, calling a conference of all Irish members of Parliament. Colonel Saunderson, Horace Plunkett, J. E. Redmond, and T. M. Healy signed the circular.[23] Two Unionists, one Parnellite, and one anti-Parnellite might have seemed to make up a representative group, had it not been well known that Healy had the confidence of only one wing of the anti-Parnellite party, and that Dillon, who represented the other wing, had refused to sign. Although he said he would be prepared to advise his friends to attend the conference, many regarded the absence of his signature as an indication that he would not support its work.[24]

As the date for the conference approached, there was considerable speculation regarding its chairmanship. It was understood that both Healyites and Parnellites were prepared to support the Unionists in their effort to have Colonel Saunderson elected to the position. There were, however, rumours that Dillon and some of his supporters intended to oppose Saunderson's candidature. On March 9, the day on which the conference was to be held, the *Irish Times* reported that some of the Dillonites "had declared for supporting Blake as chairman instead of Saunderson," and added: "If those who have suggested the Blake nomination proceed to propose him, there will be trouble, of course, but it is hoped that on finding that the bulk of those who attend are against him, they will refrain from disturbing the harmony of the gathering." The *Irish Independent*, on the same day, stated: "Mr. Dillon has been manœuvring to get Mr. Blake nominated for the chair, but it is now practically certain that Colonel Saunderson will preside." Nothing was said by the *Freeman's Journal* of the proposal to nominate Blake, and, when the conference assembled in London, Saunderson was "unanimously called to the chair."[25]

Dillon, in accordance with his expressed intention of advising his friends to attend the conference, had called a meeting of the Irish

[23]For an excerpt from Dillon's letter in reply to the request, see *ibid.* The date of the letter is not given, nor is the name of the person to whom it was written.
[24]For the full text of the circular, see *ibid.*, 131.
[25]*Irish Independent*, Dublin, March 10, 1897.

parliamentary party at which a resolution was unanimously adopted calling on every Nationalist member of Parliament to be present. There was, therefore, at the conference a large number of both Dillonites and Healyites. The Parnellites were also well represented. For a time, it had been expected that at least eight Irish Unionists would be present, but, in the end, only Saunderson and three others attended.

After the chair had been taken by Colonel Saunderson, a proposal was made that the press should be admitted to the conference. Dillon and two of his friends spoke in support of this motion, which was, however, withdrawn without a division when not only the Unionists, but also Redmond and Healy had expressed their opposition to it. William Abraham, T. B. Curran, Patrick O'Brien, and Horace Plunkett were then unanimously elected secretaries to the meeting,[26] and were instructed to supply a secretarial report of the proceedings to the press.[27] Following the election of the secretaries, it was suggested that leading Irish members should express their views upon the main issues involved in the financial relations controversy. The chairman therefore called on a number of them to address the meeting.

Healy expressed his opposition to the appointment of a new commission, declaring that the conference should aim at finding some common ground on which to act and then appoint a committee to consider the matter and report to a subsequent meeting. T. C. Harrington,[28] a Parnellite member, made a similar suggestion in his address to the gathering. W. E. H. Lecky, a Unionist, believed that the appointment of a new commission was inevitable, but he

[26]Abraham was a Dillonite; Curran, a Healyite; Patrick O'Brien, a Parnellite; and Plunkett, a Unionist.
[27]On March 10, an official account of the conference appeared in Irish newspapers. On the same day, the *Freeman's Journal* published a more detailed report by its London correspondent, who claimed he had secured it from an authentic source. This account, unlike the official one, included summaries of many of the speeches made at the meeting, and it is from it that much of the material in this section is taken.
[28]Timothy Charles Harrington (1851-1910), born Co. Cork; lawyer; active in Land League and National League; first elected to Parliament, 1883; Parnellite, 1890-1900, but became one of leading advocates of national unity; elected Lord Mayor of Dublin, 1901.

felt that some attempt should be made to have the terms of reference amended. Another Unionist, Edward Carson, declared that he had never been enthusiastic about the report of the financial relations commission and that he was in favour of the appointment of a new commission. Redmond, on the other hand, felt that an attempt should be made to frame a resolution simply stating Ireland's case and making no reference to the proposed new commission. This resolution should be adopted by the conference and submitted to the House of Commons.

Dillon, unlike Redmond, believed that the main efforts of the conference should be directed towards preventing the appointment of a new commission. Public meetings all over Ireland had protested strongly against its appointment; and the conference, if it properly represented the views of the people of Ireland, would do likewise. A new commission might take two or three years to complete its inquiry; and, in the meantime, the answer of the government to any claim for redress would be that the matter was still under consideration.

Blake emphatically expressed his agreement with Dillon's views regarding the proposed new commission, saying that Ireland's cause would be lost if any compromise were entered into on this point.

The chairman, Colonel Saunderson, while personally opposed to the appointment of a new commission, felt that it would be unwise to insist on a resolution which was sure to be rejected by the government.

Some time before the conference met, both Clancy and Blake had given notice in the House of Commons of the motions which they had originally intended to move as amendments to the address. So, following the foregoing expressions of opinion at the conference, these motions were read and discussed. They were:

That, in the opinion of this House, the Report of the Royal Commission appointed to inquire into the Financial Relations between Great Britain and Ireland discloses a serious grievance which affects all classes of the people of that country, and demands the immediate attention of Her Majesty's Government with a view to meeting the just claims of Ireland in respect thereof. (Clancy)[29]

[29]*Hansard*, 4th Series, XLVI, 4.

That in the opinion of this House, the report and proceedings of the Royal Commission on the Financial Relations of Great Britain and Ireland establish the existence of an undue burden of taxation on Ireland, which constitutes a great grievance to all classes of the Irish community, and makes it the duty of the Government to propose at an early day remedial legislation. (Blake)[30]

Redmond suggested the adoption of Clancy's motion as the less contentious of the two, but Dillon declared that Blake's motion had been drafted as a non-aggressive and non-contentious one and that it represented the low watermark of the Irish demand.

After a long discussion as to whether a committee should be appointed to consider further the possibility of issuing a united declaration, a vote taken on the question showed twenty-six in favour and fifteen against. Thereupon, since neither Dillon nor any of his supporters would consent to serve, Colonel Saunderson, T. M. Healy, J. J. Clancy, and W. E. H. Lecky were appointed to the committee. The meeting was then adjourned to March 12, at which time the committee was to report to the conference.

When the conference reassembled, Clancy read the following resolution, which had been framed by the committee: "That the findings of the Royal Commission on the Financial Relations between Great Britain and Ireland disclosed a disproportion between the taxation of Ireland and its taxable capacity as compared with other parts of the kingdom which deserves the immediate attention of Parliament."[31] In moving the adoption of this motion, Clancy explained that it was not one he would propose if he had the power of substituting a stronger one. Since, however, the object of the conference was to secure united action on the part of all Irish members of the House of Commons when the report of the financial relations commission came to be discussed, it would be unwise to propose a more forcible resolution. Clancy realized that even this comparatively mild motion would not have the unanimous support of the Irish Unionists, for Carson and the Belfast members would undoubtedly oppose it, but he believed that many of the other Unionists could be induced to vote for it if it were put forward in

[30]Edward Blake, *Over-Taxation of Ireland*, 1.
[31]*Freeman's Journal*, Dublin, March 13, 1897. A detailed account of the meeting of March 12 is given in this issue of the paper.

the House on behalf of Ireland. Those who felt that the resolution did not go far enough might, Clancy added, indicate this in their speeches to the House. Clancy's motion[32] was seconded by the chairman, Colonel Saunderson, who said he thought it moderate enough to meet the views of most of the Irish Unionists.

Blake spoke at considerable length against the motion. He was in favour of going as far as possible to secure unity of action, but he felt that the Irish representatives were as men holding a fort, and that if they put Clancy's resolution forward as an adequate statement of Ireland's case, they would be abandoning the fort in order to secure a few recruits to the garrisons. Clancy's resolution, if adopted, would settle nothing, for it contained no expression inconsistent with the appointment of a new commission and no demand for legislation on the basis of the report. Moreover, the reference to a comparison between Ireland and "other parts of the Kingdom" was inaccurate, since the comparison had been only between Ireland and Great Britain. And the meaning of the expression "deserves the immediate attention of parliament" was so vague that the government might properly say that the findings of the Royal Commission were receiving immediate attention because Parliament was debating the subject and was about to appoint a new investigating body to collect supplementary information.

At this stage of the proceedings, Healy, who had not been present when Clancy addressed the meeting, observed that it was not intended to submit to the House of Commons the resolution drafted by the committee. Blake, however, pointed out that Clancy had presented the resolution as one to be moved in the House. The chairman was understood to agree with Blake.

A number of other prominent members addressed the conference. Dillon, speaking against the committee's resolution, expressed views similar to those of Blake. Harrington, on the other hand, strongly urged the adoption of the resolution, saying that it was quite as strong as Blake's. After further discussion, Dillon suggested that the chairman, Colonel Saunderson, should be asked to move the resolu-

---

[32]From this point in the chapter, "Clancy's motion" is the one framed by the committee, not the one standing in Clancy's name on the notice paper of the House of Commons.

tion standing in Blake's name on the notice paper of the House of Commons. T. P. O'Connor supported this suggestion, but, after several other members had expressed their views, the chairman proposed that the proceedings be brought to a close, since there was no likelihood of arriving at a unanimous conclusion. When, however, Healy insisted on a division on Clancy's motion, Dillon moved as an amendment that the motion standing in Blake's name should be adopted. Thereupon, Clancy, feeling that a division could do no good, withdrew his motion, and the proceedings were brought to a close without any united declaration being made.

For their attitude towards the conference and especially for refusing to support the resolution framed by the committee, the Dillonites were severely criticized. The Healyites, in particular, argued that although, from the Nationalist viewpoint, the resolution was not as strong as would have been desired, its passage could not have done any harm, and would have shown that there was at least some degree of unity among the Irish members of Parliament. However, as Blake pointed out to the conference, there were many good reasons for opposing the adoption of too weak a resolution, and the Dillonites, unlike the Healyites, believed that positive harm might result from the Irish party's approving a motion which did not express definite opposition to the government's declared policy of appointing a new commission.

The Debate in Parliament

Less than three weeks after the close of the financial relations conference, the promised debate on the report of the Royal Commission took place in the House of Commons. On March 29, 1897, Blake addressed the House for more than two hours in support of the motion standing in his name.[33] He described in detail the economic condition of Ireland under the union, quoting statistics

[33]Blake's speech is recorded in *Hansard*, 4th Series, XLVII, 1577–98. It is also published in book form under the title, *The Over-Taxation of Ireland*. Quotations are from the latter.

to prove that her population had decreased sharply, the scale of existence of large masses of her people and the incomes of her wage earning classes were extremely low, her manufactures had declined, and she had scarcely any foreign commerce or investments. During the same period Britain's population had increased greatly and her people were enjoying "a steady and rapid advance in the standard of comfort." The incomes of her wage-earning classes were, man for man, almost double those of Ireland. Moreover, Britain was still the great manufacturer, merchant, carrier, and leader of the world. Thus, conditions in the two islands were "wholly different and increasingly diverging in the extent of their resources, in the kinds of their resources, and in their economic circumstances and interests."

The one area in which Britain showed a decline and Ireland an advance was that of taxation. Study of this anomaly had led the commissioners, both British and Irish, who signed the majority report to conclude that the relative taxable capacity of Ireland as compared with Britain was very much smaller than its actual tax burden. The fact that Ireland's annual contribution reached a minimum excess of £2,750,000 created an urgent case for relief on the grounds of fair play.

Blake explained that the inability of Ireland to bear the British rate of taxation had been recognized in the Act of Union, which had fixed the proportion of Irish to British taxation at one to seven and a half (two to fifteen) although the population was at that time one to two. The proportion of taxation was excessive, but the principle that the relative taxable capacity of Ireland was lower than that of Great Britain was at least recognized. And from it followed the conclusion stated in the majority report that Ireland must be treated in this matter as a separate fiscal entity. "Indeed," Blake added, "it is absurd to argue that a country full of contrasts with Britain in all respects, for which you are every day legislating separately, whose whole body of law is different from yours, should be in this matter, in which also its distinctions are fundamental, recognized and increasing, treated as one with you."

In describing the financial relations between Great Britain and Ireland after the union, Blake spoke of the enormous cost of the

Napoleonic Wars and the subsequent increase in taxation in Britain and Ireland. He mentioned Ireland's inability to meet her quota and added that there had been practical unanimity on the Royal Commission in the finding that: "The Act of Union imposed on Ireland a burden which, as events showed, she was unable to bear." Ireland's experience in the years immediately following the union showed that there should have been some definite limitation to the amount she was asked to contribute, for "a joint expenditure, the proportion of which, though heavy, may be tolerable on a lower scale of joint expense, becomes intolerable to the poorer nation when the scale is raised, while it may be no more than heavy, and quite tolerable still to the richer nation. . . ."

The general effect of changes in British fiscal policy since the close of the Napoleonic Wars had been to abolish nearly all duties on raw materials and food, substituting direct taxation on income and property and heavy duties on three or four articles of wide and general consumption. This policy had been detrimental to Ireland's interests, for these heavily taxed commodities were most largely consumed there. Moreover, the freeing of raw materials and food was of greater benefit to Britain than to Ireland. Though not objecting to the adoption of free trade, Blake insisted that the relative advantages and disadvantages to each country ought to be considered.

The biggest increase in taxation had come between 1853 and 1860. In the former year the income tax had been extended to Ireland and at intervals thereafter the spirit duties were raised until they became equal to those of Britain. The result was to increase Ireland's annual taxation by more than two million pounds. Since this had to be borne by a diminishing population at a time when the country was suffering from the effects of famine the majority report naturally concluded that "the increase of taxation laid upon Ireland between 1853 and 1860 was not justified by the then existing circumstances."

Protesting against the proposed new commission of inquiry, Blake explained that the Act of Union gave no support to the principle now put forward by the government regarding application of United

Kingdom taxation. There was no justification for dividing the expenditure into four sets of estimates, one each for England, Scotland, Ireland, and the United Kingdom, and applying proportionate contribution only to the last of these. The government claimed that the Royal Commission had failed to discharge its duty by not reporting on this question of division. But most of the commissioners held the view that that portion of the reference had had regard to the political condition existing under the Liberal government when, in view of the proposal for Irish home rule, it was necessary to consider the division of what had been United Kingdom expenditure into imperial and local expenditures. Following the change of government in 1895, it seemed unnecessary to report on this question since it had no foundation under the union. Nevertheless, all the materials necessary for a decision had been collected and were to be found in the proceedings of the commission. There was, therefore, no need for the further inquiry which the government intended to make.

It had been suggested in ministerial quarters that the commission should have indicated the precise form of remedy for the financial grievance. Blake replied that this question had not been referred to the commission, since it was obviously one to be dealt with by Parliament on the initiative of the government. The majority of the Irish people felt that home rule would constitute the most effective remedy, but the Unionists refused to adopt this solution. Their refusal to do so entailed on them added responsibilities towards Ireland, for, both as the depositories of power and as the special defenders of the existing form of union, it was their duty to find a remedy for this injustice, prevailing under the system which they maintained and controlled. Several plans, some of which were to be found in the separate reports, had been suggested. The government should now decide which it considered best, and the Irish Nationalist members would then be glad to give their opinions of the plan.

Finally, Blake predicted that, if the government refused to remedy the financial grievance, serious consequences might result for those who supported the union as a compact under which Ireland was assured of just and generous treatment. If it were now demonstrated that under it she must continue to suffer this injustice, a keen and powerful weapon would be placed in the hands of the advocates of home rule.

In seconding Blake's motion, John Redmond, leader of the Parnellites, said that there was practical unanimity amongst all Irishmen on the main issues involved in the financial question. Some Irish representatives might, however, vote against this motion, and he expressed his regret, as the Dillonites had feared he might, that it had not been modified so as to enable all Irish members to support it. Nevertheless, Ireland's case for redress was being put forward on behalf of all her people, without regard to class or party.[34]

Following Redmond's speech, an amendment to the motion was moved by an English member, T. P. Whittaker, who, although an advocate of home rule, believed that the United Kingdom must be regarded as a single fiscal entity so long as the exchequers of the two countries remained consolidated. His proposed amendment therefore stated that, if there were any tangible grievance, it could be satisfactorily removed only by so adjusting the existing fiscal system as to render it just and equitable to all persons in whatever part of the United Kingdom they might reside.[35]

After this amendment had been seconded by Colonel Waring, an Ulster Unionist, whose political views differed considerably from those of Whittaker, Sir Michael Hicks-Beach, the Chancellor of the Exchequer, proceeded to explain the attitude of the government.[36] He admitted that, as events had shaped themselves, the burden imposed upon Ireland by the proportionate contribution required of her by the act of union had been more than she could bear. He pointed out, however, that when the exchequers of the two countries were consolidated, the whole of the United Kingdom became responsible for the debt which Ireland had been unable to pay. Moreover, the committee which had been appointed in 1864

[34] But it should be noted that Blake's resolution had been adopted as the motion of the Irish parliamentary party. See Dillon Papers, Minutes of the Irish parliamentary party, March 22, 1897. For Redmond's speech, see *Hansard*, 4th Series, XLVII, 1598–1607.

[35] For the text of the amendment and Whittaker's speech, see *Hansard*, 4th Series, XLVII, 1607–24.

[36] For Waring's speech, see *ibid.*, 1624–6; for Hicks-Beach's, *ibid.*, 1631–2.

to study the question had concluded that Parliament had been justified in consolidating the debt and amalgamating the exchequers of the two countries. In the opinion of the government, this arrangement of a consolidated debt, a common exchequer, and equal taxes levied on articles in both countries was, in principle, a far more equitable arrangement than any system based on taxable capacity. Since, however, the consolidation act had included a provision that exemptions and abatements should be granted when the circumstances of Ireland and Scotland were considered to require them, the government proposed that the subject should be impartially and judicially investigated. When the facts were fully known, the government would endeavour to do justice to the poorest part of the United Kingdom. But nothing would be done to impair the permanence of either the financial or the political union between Great Britain and Ireland.

The most noteworthy speech delivered on the second night of the debate was that of Sir Edward Clarke, a Conservative who had refused office in the government. Although he agreed with Sir Michael Hicks-Beach that nothing should be done to impair the permanence of the financial or political union between Great Britain and Ireland, he felt that there was much to be said regarding the existing financial relations between the two countries. It was his opinion that the inquiry which had already taken place established beyond dispute the fact that Ireland was over-taxed at the present time. Whittaker's argument, that until home rule was granted Ireland was not entitled to separate financial consideration, should not be taken up by those who desired to maintain the union and whose duty it was to show that, under it, justice could be done to Ireland. If the union were to be maintained, a remedy would have to be found for Ireland's financial grievance.[37]

Colonel Saunderson took part in the second night's debate because he did not want it to be thought that all Ulster Protestants agreed with the views of Colonel Waring. It had been suggested that, since the late commission had been appointed by a home rule government with home rule objectives, its report could not be accepted as impartial. With this opinion Colonel Saunderson did not agree. He

[37]For Clarke's speech, see *ibid.*, XLVIII, 129–44.

believed that it had been conclusively proved by the commission that Ireland was over-taxed. There was, therefore, no need for a further inquiry, and Great Britain should make some generous proposal to the Irish people.[38]

The principal speeches delivered on the third and concluding night of the debate were those of W. E. H. Lecky, John Morley, and G. J. Goschen.[39] Lecky believed that there was a large amount of agreement on the financial question among the different Irish parties. They were all impressed with the conclusion of the Royal Commission regarding the taxable capacity of Ireland relative to that of Great Britain, and he felt that the government should not treat this conclusion as a matter of insignificance. Another point on which all Irish parties were generally agreed (he evidently did not consider Colonel Waring's opposition serious) was that, in financial matters, as in other branches of legislation, Ireland ought to be treated as Ireland, and not as a mere group of English counties. There could be no reasonable doubt that, constitutionally and historically, she had a right to this separate treatment. Regarding the form of financial redress which should be adopted, Lecky did not believe it would be possible to make extensive remissions and abatements of taxation. He proposed instead a larger expenditure on Ireland from the imperial exchequer. The United Kingdom should take the initiative in developing Ireland's resources, and there should be an inquiry into the doctrine of what constituted imperial taxation and into the question of imperial expenditure in Ireland as a set-off against over-taxation.

Speaking on behalf of the Liberal opposition, Morley asserted that Ireland was a community with certain covenanted rights and claims to special consideration. He also denied that the late commission had been appointed by him to settle home rule questions and that he had directed it to approach the inquiry from the home rule point of view. In his opinion, the proposed inquiry by a new commission was an unnecessary and futile process, since all the required information was already available.

[38]For Saunderson's speech, see *ibid.*, 171–7.
[39]For Lecky's speech, see *ibid.*, 197–211; for Morley's, *ibid.*, 211–26; for Goschen's, *ibid.*, 227–33.

Goschen declared that, since the majority of the members of the late commission believed that a sum varying from £2,250,000 to £2,750,000 was paid by Ireland in excess of what she ought to pay, those who considered that all the facts had been collected were bound to accept that conclusion. The true question before the House was, therefore, whether this sum should be transferred from Irish to British taxpayers.

When the House finally divided on the question, Blake's resolution was negatived by 317 to 157 votes.[40] Parnellites and anti-Parnellites voted for the motion, but only two Irish Unionists, Horace Plunkett and Richard M. Dane, joined them, while three others, Saunderson, Lecky, and Sir Thomas Lea, abstained. One English Unionist and the majority of the Liberals present, including Morley, Bryce, Sir Henry Campbell-Bannerman, Herbert Gladstone, Serjeant Hemphill, Thomas Ellis, and A. H. D. Acland, voted for the motion. But many Liberals were absent, and a few joined the large majority of Unionists, both Irish and British, who supported the government.

Blake's address on the over-taxation of Ireland created much interest and was widely praised. He described the reaction in a letter to J. S. Willison, editor of the Toronto *Globe*:

> The reception of the speech was very extraordinary; a necessarily dull and over condensed statement of figures, history, law, political economy and statutes with numerous *deadly* quotations was listened to with attention, hardly anyone went out, and I think the last forty minutes was received better than the middle. Many old stagers said they had never seen anything like it; and I had very warm congratulations from all quarters, including old Tories, Healyites, Parnellites and Irish Unionists. If you knew how bitter is the feeling in these quarters you could understand what that means. I undertook the business with the greatest reluctance and am rejoiced to be so well out of it. . . .[41]

The Irish parliamentary party, recognizing the importance of Blake's speech, determined that it should be given as wide circulation as possible. Alfred Webb, who, at the request of the party, undertook the task of arranging for the publication and distribution of the speech, declared:

[40]*Ibid.*, 242.
[41]Willison Papers, Blake to J. S. Willison, April 22, 1897.

The speech delivered by Mr. Blake on that occasion was generally felt to be a masterly and comprehensive statement of the Irish case; and as a mark of their sense of its great and permanent value, and of the service to the National cause rendered by Mr. Blake in making it, it was unanimously resolved at a meeting of the Irish Party—

"That the speech delivered by the Hon. Edward Blake in moving the resolution on the Financial Relations between Great Britain and Ireland be printed and published at the expense of the Party."[42]

But the government ignored the findings of the Royal Commission and the financial grievance remained to trouble Irish politics for many years to come. In 1898, 1900, and 1902, motions similar to Blake's were proposed in the House of Commons, but all were defeated. At least so long as a Unionist government remained in power, there appeared to be no hope of redress.

[42]Blake, *Over-Taxation of Ireland*, Introduction, ix.

VII. THE IRISH SITUATION AND BLAKE'S RELATIONSHIP TO IT, 1896-7

The Irish Race Convention

AT THE BEGINNING of the election campaign of 1895, Healy and his followers, apparently believing that they were stronger in the country than in the party, had demanded that a national convention be summoned to choose an impartial electoral committee to conduct the campaign. Later, when the depth of the divisions which existed within the Irish party had been revealed to the public, there were demands from various quarters that a national convention should be called to determine the feeling of the country. Although McCarthy, Dillon, and many of their colleagues would have liked the sanction of a national convention for whatever steps they decided to take in an effort to restore unity and discipline to the party, they realized that the summoning of one would be a most dangerous experiment. Much of the work of organizing it would fall to the Irish National Federation, and since its executive was controlled by the Healyites at that time, there was a danger that the convention would be sufficiently packed with Healy's supporters for him to carry it. It was therefore not until several months after the election that a decision was reached on the subject of holding a convention.

Reports of events in Ireland during the election campaign had, of course, reached the United States, and as a result the secretary of the Irish National Federation of America, Joseph P. Ryan, wrote to McCarthy making a suggestion which was eventually put into effect. Believing that there would be an open split in the Irish party at its sessional meeting in August, 1895, and that, in an attempt to restore unity, McCarthy would summon a national convention, Ryan advised McCarthy "that as they would undoubtedly have a Convention to make it a Race Convention and call for representatives from the millions of our race who have been supporting the movement abroad."¹ McCarthy replied that Ryan's suggestion was "original and bold, but all the more worthy of the fullest consideration." He would bring the suggestion to the attention of his colleagues, he wrote and expressed his own opinion that "it would be a great stroke towards success if we could have the affirmation of a Convention thus composed to any line of policy that might be adopted. . . ."²

On September 1, 1895, Ryan again wrote to McCarthy. The split which he had expected to take place at the sessional meeting had not occurred, but although it was because he had considered a break inevitable that he had previously suggested a race convention as the only remaining hope of unified action, there were other reasons almost as good for holding one. Not only was it possible that such a convention would renew interest abroad in the Irish cause, but, if delegates of the Irish race in all parts of the world attended it, thus showing their sympathy with the Nationalist movement, the Irish at home would be reassured of the popularity of their cause among members of their race in other countries. Furthermore, Britain might be brought to a fuller realization of the strength of the Irish demand for home rule.

Ryan added that his suggestion of a race convention was not a demand for representation by Irishmen abroad. What he proposed was that the people of Ireland, through the executive of the Nationalist party, should invite Irishmen abroad to share their counsels at this critical period in the history of the movement; the duties of the delegates from abroad would, however, be mainly advisory. If results at the convention seemed to ensure future harmony, each delegation on returning home could call a public meeting and make a favourable report, thus stimulating renewed interest in the cause.³

During Blake's visit to Canada in the late summer and autumn of 1895, Ryan wrote to him also on the subject of holding a race convention. By that time, Ryan realized that, although an open

¹This quotation is from a letter written by Ryan to Blake telling what was in the letter to McCarthy. See Blake Papers, J. P. Ryan to Blake, Sept. 20, 1895. Ryan's letter to McCarthy, written on Aug. 5, has not come to light.
²Blake Papers, McCarthy to Ryan, Aug. 16, 1895.
³*Ibid.*, Ryan to McCarthy, Sept. 1, 1895.

split had been avoided at the sessional meeting of the party, the situation was still very serious. He was, therefore, becoming more and more convinced of the need for a race convention. "I am still of the same opinion," he wrote to Blake, "that there is no hope for the National Cause if the present conditions continue and the people are grouped into factions supporting majority and minority parties within the party."[4]

In replying to Ryan's letter, Blake expressed the opinion that, if delegations of weight and influence could be induced to attend such a convention, Ryan's plan, though involving certain elements of risk, might be of very great advantage. There was, of course, the danger of its being regarded as an attempt by non-residents of the United Kingdom to interfere in British and Irish politics, but this might be met, as Ryan had suggested, by giving the delegates from abroad an advisory position. In closing, Blake summarized his views of the whole situation:

> If it is possible to obtain a decisive expression of opinion from the Irish at home and abroad, and to consolidate the people in favour of discipline, and if it is possible to maintain the forces during next Session and there to show a united front and press forward the Irish cause in Parliament, I should hope for a revival of spirit and for an early and rapid improvement in the whole condition. Whether this is possible I cannot tell. I own it seems to me better to stake everything upon a Convention, since the Convention seems to me the only chance. I have so advised. Should our views fail at that convention, at any rate the people will have had the opportunity of speaking and the responsibility will be theirs; should they succeed, we may, without any great delay, be able to bring the cause into better shape.[5]

Although it appears from the foregoing correspondence that the idea of holding a race convention originated with Ryan, the same suggestion was evidently made by Archbishop Walsh of Toronto. According to Davitt, the Archbishop "made earnest and touching appeals to the disputants at home to end their quarrels" in a letter to Blake in October, 1895.[6] It was apparently in this letter that the Archbishop made the suggestion of a race convention, to which, as will be seen presently, reference was later made in a resolution of

---

[4]*Ibid.*, Ryan to Blake, Sept. 20, 1895.
[5]*Ibid.*, Blake to Ryan, Sept. 24, 1895.
[6]Michael Davitt, *The Fall of Feudalism in Ireland* (London and New York, 1904), 676.

the Irish party. Though it is quite possible that Ryan and Archbishop Walsh made their suggestions independently of each other, since Ryan's proposal would be known only to McCarthy, Blake, and their closest colleagues, it appears rather odd that no credit was given to Ryan for his part in the proposal. Perhaps it was felt that, if emphasis were placed on Archbishop Walsh's desire to see the Nationalists truly united, those of the Irish clergy who supported Healy might be persuaded to modify their views.

The elements of risk, foreseen by Blake, were reduced by the events which occurred at the beginning of November, 1895. On November 7, Healy was expelled from the Irish National League of Great Britain, and six days later he and four of his strongest supporters were expelled from the Irish National Federation.[7] Both organizations gave as the reason for their action the conduct of the Healyites in a by-election in South Kerry.[8] Then, on November 14, at a meeting of the Irish parliamentary party, Healy and Arthur O'Connor were, on the same grounds, removed from membership on the party committee.[9]

No further time was lost therefore in considering the advisability of holding a convention. At the same meeting at which Healy and O'Connor were dismissed from the party committee, Dillon moved a resolution expressing approval of "the suggestion made by the Archbishop of Toronto in favour of a National Convention representative of the Irish race throughout the world," and authorizing the chairman and committee of the Irish party to arrange, in conjunction with the executive of the Irish National Federation, for the holding of such a convention.

After this resolution had been seconded by one of Dillon's supporters, Healy moved an amendment proposing that a committee be appointed by the council of the Federation to arrange the basis

[7]F. S. L. Lyons, *Irish Parliamentary Party 1890–1910* (London, 1951), 57. But it must have been the executive committee of the Federation from which they were expelled. All members of the Irish parliamentary party were automatically members of the council of the Federation, so it is difficult to see how they could be expelled from it, while remaining members of the party.
[8]For details of this by-election, see *ibid.*, 53–6.
[9]Dillon Papers, Minutes of the Irish parliamentary party, Nov. 14, 1895.

of representation at "a convention of the people of Ireland . . . according to the established precedents in times past." Though adding that invitations to prominent and representative Irishmen and organizations might be issued by the chairman of the Irish party, the amendment, which was seconded by a Healyite, Dr. Fox, made no mention of attendance by Irishmen from abroad. Probably Healy realized that their influence would be on the side of unity and discipline. From the amendment it can also be inferred that although the Healyites, through the expulsion of their leader and four of his colleagues, had lost control of the executive of the Irish National Federation, they still retained considerable power on its council.[10] Before the close of the meeting, however, Healy's amendment was negatived and Dillon's resolution carried, each without a division.[11]

It was not until May 20, 1896, that a plan for electing delegates to the proposed race convention was submitted to the Irish parliamentary party, considered by it, and finally adopted. Among the Blake papers is a copy of this "Constitution for the Irish National Convention," which was drawn up by the executive of the Federation and the chairman of the party, since the committee had by this time been abolished. After stating that the convention would meet in Dublin on September 1, 1896, this document went on to give lengthy instructions regarding the election of delegates. Ireland was to send to the race convention three delegates from each branch of the Irish National Federation, and, if there were more than 300 members in the branch, one additional delegate for each 100 members in excess of 300; one delegate from each parish in which there was no branch of the Federation; clergymen of all denominations; Nationalist members of local public bodies; three delegates from each Gaelic Athletic Club, Young Ireland Society, National Literary Society, and labour organization having not less than 50 members, and, if there were more than 300 members in the branch, one additional delegate for each 100 members in excess of 300. From Great

---

[10]The council consisted of 32 county delegates, 13 civic delegates, and all the anti-Parnellite members of Parliament; the executive committee, of 25 members of the council, elected by it. See Lyons, *Irish Parliamentary Party*, 185–6.

[11]The meeting is reported in Dillon Papers, Minutes of the Irish parliamentary party, Nov. 14, 1895.

Britain would come one delegate from each branch of the Irish National League of Great Britain having not less than 100 members, and one additional delegate for each 100 members in excess of 100.

Since distance and expense precluded the possibility of a very large number of delegates coming from abroad, and local knowledge was required to adjust the distribution of representation intelligently, no express limitation of their numbers would be made. In the United States, delegates were to be chosen by the Irish National Federation of America, the Ancient Order of Hibernians, and the Ancient Order of Hibernians (Board of Erin). Canadian delegates were to be chosen for their own cities and the country at large by the Irish National organizations in Ottawa, Montreal, Toronto, Quebec, Saint John, and Halifax. In Australasia, delegates for the city and district and for the country at large were to be chosen by the local branch of the Irish National Federation, or, where there was no such branch, by the concerted action of local Nationalists. The cities mentioned in Australia were Sydney, Melbourne, Adelaide, Brisbane, and Perth; in New Zealand, they were Auckland, Wellington, Dunedin, and Westland District; in Tasmania, Hobart and Launcestown.

At the party meeting of May 20, a resolution was adopted inviting Redmond and his supporters to join the anti-Parnellites in arranging for the convention. The hope was expressed that a meeting with the Parnellites "on fair and equal terms" would lead to the reconstitution of a united home rule party.[12]

In the months which followed, Blake, who had returned from Australia in March, 1896, took an active part in the preparations which had to be made for the convention. Anxious that Canada should send a strong delegation, he wrote to many influential men there, urging them to allow their names to be put forward as delegates. From his correspondence with Dillon in August, 1896, it is also clear that Blake gave much assistance in drafting the resolutions which were submitted to the convention.[13]

The Irish party's invitation to the Parnellites to join in the race convention met with no friendly response. In fact, neither Parnel-

[12] The meeting is reported in *ibid.*, May 20, 1896.
[13] See Blake Papers, Dillon to Blake, Aug. 19 & 20, 1896, and Dillon Papers, Blake to Dillon, Aug. 16, 19, 20, & 21, 1896.

lites nor Healyites attended the convention, which they regarded as a farce. The Roman Catholic bishops of Ireland, with one exception, also absented themselves, and, although there were many clerical delegates from abroad, the number of Irish clergy attending the gathering was comparatively small.

For a time, it had been hoped that Thomas Sexton would consent to preside at the gathering, but, remaining determined to take no further part in public life, he declined. Finally, the Most Rev. Dr. O'Donnell, Roman Catholic Bishop of Raphoe, the one member of the Irish episcopate who attended the convention, agreed to act as chairman.

The main work of the convention, which lasted three days, September 1, 2, and 3, 1896, was to adopt a number of resolutions which had been prepared in advance by the leading members of the Dillonite wing of the Irish parliamentary party. Since the convention was really an advisory body, having no power to carry its resolutions into effect, it could not be argued that the delegates from abroad were exercising powers which did not belong to them. In unanimously adopting the ten resolutions submitted to it, the convention was simply voicing its acceptance of certain principles and lines of policy. It was hoped that the action of the convention would encourage Irish Nationalist members of Parliament to carry the resolutions into effect, but it was they alone who had the power to do so.

Of the resolutions adopted, the most important were those which dealt with "reunion" and "unity,"[14] for it was primarily to consider these questions that the convention had been summoned. The first was directed mainly towards the need for reunion with the Parnellites. In words similar to those used in the recent resolution of the Irish party, it expressed the desire of those present "to meet on fair and equal terms all Nationalists who will join in the attempt to constitute a united Home Rule Party," and invited the Irish parliamentary party to take such steps as might seem calculated to promote the cause of reunion. The second resolution, directed mainly

---

[14] The others dealt with home rule, amnesty for political prisoners, the land question, over-taxation, labour, local government, education, and the Gaelic language.

towards the Healyites, dealt with the need for unity within the existing majority party. Condemning the public disputes which had so gravely impaired the power of the party, it called on all its members to forget old differences and act together for the good of Ireland and requested the party to take whatever steps proved necessary to establish unity and discipline in its own ranks.

Speaking on the second of these resolutions Blake emphasized the need for a real union. Although numbers were important and the convention was therefore in favour of reunion with the Parnellites, it would be better to have a small number of truly united men than a larger number divided against themselves. He then outlined what he felt to be the best plan for establishing the unity which was desired. Whenever possible, questions of policy should be discussed at party meetings, where every man was free to speak his own mind, but after a decision had been reached by the majority it must be accepted by all. Any who felt they could not support it should "withdraw quietly from the council," instead of publicly opposing their colleagues. If sometimes it happened that the chairman of the party, having no opportunity for consultation with his colleagues, had to act on his own initiative, it was the duty of the members of the party to stand by their leader, unless the majority felt that he had proved himself unworthy of their confidence. Though this rule regarding consultation was important to any political party, it was especially so to the Irish party which was "waging a war for a nation's cause." The enemies of Ireland rejoiced at the discord in the ranks of her representatives, feeling that it would render the Irish race powerless and ensure that the domination which the Nationalists sought to overthrow would remain unshaken.

Blake recalled that even Healy had once recognized the importance of supporting majority decisions. Speaking of the Parnellites shortly after the general election of 1892, Healy had said that although they had pledged themselves before conventions and the country to abide by the rule of the majority, they had broken that pledge. He had added that the Parnellites stood aloof from their fellow-countrymen not on a question of principle, but on the merest personal matter. Commenting on Healy's address, Blake agreed with the sentiments expressed, but reminded the convention that they were applicable not only to Parnellites, but also to "other men and more modern situations."

The resolution did not attempt to argue the merits of the disputes within the party; it was the publicity given them that it deplored. Nor did Blake wish to discuss the "squalid details" of the past; instead he made a dramatic appeal for unity:

> Our hearts are for peace; your hearts are for peace; the keynote of this Convention is peace—a real peace, a genuine peace, founded not on the vain protraction of disputes and differences about the past, but forgetfulness of all that. Let us turn the bitter and shameful page; let us tear it and destroy it, and let us write a new page of unity and forgetfulness of the evil past, and go forward again as comrades to a glorious future. The lessons are obvious; the utility is plain. I implore and entreat. In the course of this struggle some wounds, undeserved, may have been inflicted upon me. I freely forgive them all. I am fully sure that with every desire to say no unnecessary word, or do any unnecessary act in the heat and strain of this struggle I may have been tempted into words which others may consider undeserved. I do not wait to be asked, I humbly ask pardon for any offence of that kind. This should be the occasion for the exhibition of peace, charity and goodwill.[15]

Since the management of the Irish parliamentary party's funds had caused much controversy between Healyites and Dillonites, it was thought advisable at the race convention to make a statement on this subject. On the closing day of the proceedings, Blake endeavoured to justify the existing form of management, which had been severely condemned by Healy and his followers. He said that the Irish parliamentary party, in comparison with British political parties, was poor in worldly wealth. While some of its members were able to offer gratuitous services to the country which they loved, many others needed financial assistance. But the Irish party, though poor, was independent and self-respecting, and it was mainly because of this fact that he and the colleagues with whom he generally acted held very strong views regarding the management of its funds. The party provided for the distribution amongst its own members of the funds entrusted to it for that purpose and was its own paymaster. Critics argued that this system threatened the independence of Irish members who accepted allowances, and that the task of distributing the party funds should be entrusted to

[15]For the full text of this speech, see *Freeman's Journal*, Dublin, Sept. 3, 1896.

some body or group of men outside the party. Blake declared that he did not believe it to be consistent with the independence and respect of the party that any other group of men should act as paymasters; instead such a system would endanger that independence, for allowances might then be cut off from members who did not obey the dictates of the men who distributed them. This could lead to the domination of the party by men outside it. Surely this constituted a much greater threat to independence than did the existing system under which only the treasurers of the party knew the amount of money paid to members.

In order to refute the false charges made by the Healyites, some change in the details of administration might be needed, but Blake refused to believe that the Irish party could be divested of the control and responsibility of managing its own funds, and still retain its self-respect and independence. "If you trust the Irish party in Parliament with the most sacred interests of your country . . . is it not," he demanded, "absurd and foolish to say you cannot trust [it] . . . to observe the commonest dictates of honest fair play and decency in the distribution of the funds which you give for the support of these men?" He emphatically denied that there had ever been any foundation in fact for the suggestion that members of Healyite sympathies had been deprived of allowances; both he and his colleagues were entirely above such a sordid and unworthy action.[16]

In the course of the convention several references were made to the work Blake was doing for Ireland. The Rev. Dr. Frank Ryan of Toronto, in an address delivered on the opening day, spoke of the response of Canada to Ireland's appeals for aid. In doing so, he gave a very dramatic, if somewhat inaccurate, account of Blake's entry into Irish politics. Saying that Ireland had first appealed to Canada for sympathy and moral support, he declared that in response to this appeal resolutions in favour of home rule for Ireland had been adopted in the Canadian Parliament. Secondly, Ireland had asked for and received financial aid from Canada. Father Ryan then described Ireland's third appeal thus: "And the third time Ireland appealed to Canada—this time not for moral support, not for financial aid—she asked for more. Ireland asked Canada for a man, and we

[16] For the full text of this speech, see *ibid.*, Sept. 4, 1896.

looked round about and we selected one of our ablest, bravest, and best—a knight without reproach, and we know him—the Hon. Edward Blake; and we answered your appeal and sent you a man to help you in your Parliamentary work and warfare."[17] On the closing day of the convention, the Rev. Dr. Flannery of St. Thomas, Ontario, reiterated Father Ryan's remarks, saying that Canada had sent to Ireland "that great, grand man, the Hon. Edward Blake," who, if he had wished, "would to-day be Prime Minister of Canada instead of his friend Mr. Laurier."[18]

Present at the convention was the Hon. John Costigan, a prominent member of Canada's Conservative party, and special emphasis was laid on the fact that although he and Blake had long been opponents in Canadian politics, they were united in their advocacy of home rule for Ireland. The Reverend W. R. Harris, a delegate from St. Catharines, Ontario, remarked that these two men proved by their presence at the convention that "Canadian Irishmen could bury their differences for the sake of Ireland." Blake and Costigan, "who had fought face to face for thirty years, showed how they could stand shoulder to shoulder when Ireland's cause was at stake." Surely this was a good example for Irishmen at home to follow.[19] On September 2 the *Freeman's Journal* also drew attention to the presence of Blake and Costigan in an effort to prove that the gathering was truly representative of all types of Irishmen: "Two great Canadian statesmen, the Hon. John Costigan, and the Hon. Edward Blake, now of the Irish party, the one a Catholic, the other a Protestant, and leaders of opposing sides in Canadian politics, were on the platform united on the Irish question."

The Parnellites and Healyites did all in their power to make the Irish race convention a failure. Not only did they refuse to attend it, but they filled their newspapers with articles and editorials condemning it as a sectional or Dillonite gathering and levelling insults at the delegates from abroad. On September 1 the *Irish Independent* declared that the convention was a "brazen attempt . . . to delude the Irish people and to obtain money under false pretences," and

[17]*Ibid.*, Sept. 2, 1896.
[18]*Ibid.*, Sept. 4, 1896.
[19]*Ibid.*, Sept. 2, 1896.

added that the overseas delegates had no authority to speak for the millions of the Irish race abroad. "They represent nobody but themselves," it wrote, "and that is tantamount to saying that, from the Irish National point of view, they represent nobody at all." And the following day the same newspaper asserted that the "foreign delegates . . . in coming to Ireland, confessedly ignorant of the facts of the situation, and in throwing themselves into the arms of the Dillonites before making themselves acquainted with the state of feeling in the country, made a mistake which is only excusable on the grounds of ignorance. . . ." The Healyite *Nation*, a weekly journal, in its issue of September 12, alleged that the convention had "settled nothing and secured nothing," and that "the whole thing fizzled out like a damp squib."

It must be concluded from the results of the race convention that it did more harm than good. While it had been summoned in an effort to restore unity in Irish ranks, it had the opposite effect, for the actions of Healy and his sympathizers in response to it widened the division between the two wings of the Irish parliamentary party. About the end of 1896, Healy began to receive subscriptions from various parts of Ireland, and from these a fund for the maintenance of the Healyite members of the Irish party was started. It became known as the People's Rights Fund, and on January 12, 1897, the subscribers to it held a meeting at which they resolved that the Irish National Federation, as then constituted and controlled, was not representative of the country and announced their intention of forming a new organization known as the People's Rights Association. This new body, which came into existence shortly afterwards, sought, among other things, to establish the freedom of the constituencies, to have members' allowances provided by each constituency or from a central fund uncontrolled by any member of Parliament, and to limit the time during which any one man would be allowed to hold the chairmanship of the party.

In yet another way the race convention proved detrimental to the Irish cause. Reports of dissension within Nationalist ranks had already deterred many Irishmen abroad from contributing to the Irish party funds, but those who attended the convention were brought into much closer contact with that dissension. Reading the accounts of the convention in Parnellite and Healyite newspapers and noting the attitude of the Irish bishops and clergy towards it, they became even less hopeful that unity would be achieved, and naturally reported the situation on their return home. The result was that the task of collecting funds among Irishmen abroad for the cause of home rule became even more difficult after the convention than it had been before.

Party Resolutions

It was, of course, clear to the Dillonites in the months following the race convention that neither Parnellites nor Healyites intended to respond to the appeal of that gathering for "reunion" and "unity." Nevertheless, Dillon and his supporters could still act in accordance with the section of the convention's resolution on unity which asked the party to take whatever steps it considered necessary to restore unity and discipline in its own ranks. In fact, the action of Healy's sympathizers in organizing a rival fund made it imperative that the Dillonites take such steps without further delay. So, in December, 1896, it was decided that resolutions dealing with the question should be proposed at a party meeting in January.

Actually, the advisability of proposing resolutions at a party meeting had been considered much earlier. Immediately after the race convention, Blake had left to spend a short time in Canada, and before the end of September, 1896, he had drafted a number of resolutions and sent copies of them to Dillon.[20] But the actions of the Healyites in December, 1896, and January, 1897, necessitated much stronger resolutions than he had suggested. The work of framing them was begun in December when it was known that a rival fund had been started and that a meeting of subscribers to it was to be held on January 12. Since, however, the meetings at which the resolutions were proposed did not take place until after that date, references to the proceedings at that meeting were included in one of them.

[20]See Blake Papers, Blake to Dillon, Sept. 30, 1896. The draft resolutions were enclosed with this letter.

Although Dillon, Blake, and Davitt all seem to have had a part in framing the resulting two resolutions, the first was primarily the work of Davitt, the second that of Blake.[21] The object of the resolutions was to set forth the duties of party members and to make the Healyites choose between performing these duties and ceasing to be members of the party. A special effort was also made to prevent members from receiving allowances from the regular party funds if they were accepting money from the rival fund of the Healyites.

At a meeting of the party on January 19, 1897, Dillon was reelected to the chairmanship. Three further meetings were held on January 23, 25, and 26 to consider the resolutions.[22]

The first resolution, known as the resolution on unity and discipline, was proposed by Davitt at the meeting of January 23. After emphasizing the need for all members to join loyally in carrying out the party policy as settled after full discussion by the judgment of the majority, it provided that, to facilitate such discussion and settlement, party meetings should be held regularly on the first day of each session and on the second Tuesday—or the nearest convenient day—of each month during the session. Other meetings might be summoned from time to time on the judgment of the chairman or on the requisition of not less than five members. Not only was it the duty of all members, if at all possible, to attend party meetings, but it was contrary to their duty to oppose publicly in the House of Commons any decision reached by the party or any action taken by the chairman when he had had no opportunity of consulting the party. In the latter case, however, all members retained their right to criticize such action at party meetings. Finally, Davitt's resolution stated that it was "irreconcilable with the position of any member of the Irish party to associate himself" with the rival fund instituted by the Healyites or with the organization which they proposed to form in opposition to the Irish National Federation. Should any member disregard this warning or, in some other way, violate the spirit of the resolution, a special meeting of the party could be

---

[21] For details regarding the preparation of the resolutions, see Dillon Papers, Davitt to Blake, Dec. 12, 1896; Blake to Dillon, Dec. 14, 17, & 21, 1896.

[22] For an account of the four meetings, including the full text of the two resolutions, see Dillon Papers, Minutes of the Irish parliamentary party.

called at not less than one week's notice to decide whether he should be expelled from the party.

After Davitt's resolution had been seconded, the meeting was adjourned to January 25, and when it reassembled on that day a Healyite proposal that the press should be admitted was defeated. Healy then moved and one of his supporters seconded an amendment stating that the party pledge taken by every Nationalist member was an adequate guarantee of unity and that the only conditions binding on members were those imposed, before election, by their constituents. No section of the party, the amendment asserted, had the right to enforce additional obligations or to confer on the chairman "new and unusual powers." This amendment was defeated by 33 votes to 16, and, when a division was taken on Davitt's resolution, it was carried by 33 votes to 21.

Blake then proposed the second resolution which concerned the payment of members' allowances—or indemnities, as they were usually called. It provided that during the week following the passing of the resolution, the secretaries of the party should keep in the whip's room for signature by members applying for allowances a paper setting forth the party resolution on unity and discipline, as well as the following declaration:

I, a member of the Irish Parliamentary Party, whose signature is hereto appended, do hereby for myself declare as follows:
(1) That I did not before my election undertake to maintain myself in Parliament without indemnity from the Party funds.
(2) That I have not received, and that I do not expect or intend to receive, in respect of this or any future Session, any indemnity from any public fund, general or local, other than the Irish National Fund.
(3) That I am not in a position to keep up my attendance in Parliament without an indemnity.

The foregoing declaration paper, together with a statement of funds on hand and an estimate of funds expected, was to be laid before a special meeting of the party, which would, by resolution, assign to a Members' Indemnity Fund such sums as it deemed expedient. Then, from time to time as funds allowed, the sums so assigned would be placed by the party treasurers to the credit of this account. All who signed the declaration, so long as they remained members of the party under its rules, would be entitled "share and share alike, without preference or priority, to the same proportion of the instalments," which would be distributed by the treasurers in six monthly payments as nearly equal as the funds on hand would allow. Finally, all money in the hands of the treasurers not assigned to the Members' Indemnity Fund would be disposed of by party resolution, and the treasurers' accounts would be audited yearly by public accountants named by the party. The accounts would then be laid before the party and published.

In his resolution Blake sought to carry into effect the views he had expressed at the race convention and to add certain provisions made necessary by the recent action of Healy's sympathizers in starting a rival fund. A study of the resolution reveals that it brought about several important changes in the administration of the party funds. First of all, members who were unwilling to ascribe to the party's resolution on unity and discipline or were accepting money from any fund other than the one provided for the payment of members' indemnities could not receive allowances. Secondly, the resolution lessened the powers of the treasurers so that they could not be charged with showing favouritism in the granting of allowances. Thirdly, with the same aim in view, it provided that all allowances should be equal. Fourthly, it made definite rules for auditing and publishing the treasurers' accounts.[23]

After Blake's resolution had been seconded, the meeting was adjourned to the next day, January 26. On reassembling, it was found that Healy and all but five of his followers had absented themselves; so when the resolution was put to the meeting, it was carried by 32 votes to 5. The resolution was, however, severely criticized by Healy and his sympathizers. In its issue of February 6, the *Nation* asserted that Blake's resolution put "the members of Mr. Dillon's majority on the outdoor relief list." Here it was copying an expression used by the Parnellite *Independent*, which on January 27 had declared that to belong to the anti-Parnellite party "after Mr. Blake's 'outdoor relief resolution' has been passed is to confess an entire absence of ordinary feelings of self-respect."

[23]The names of those who received allowances still remained secret. A Healyite proposal to publish them was defeated by 20 votes to 5. See *ibid.*, Feb. 4, 1897.

Blake evidently heard many unfavourable comments regarding his resolution, for on January 28 he wrote a letter on the subject to the editor of the *Freeman's Journal*. In this letter, which was published the next day, he began by saying that a system which had been worked by the treasurers with absolute fairness, but which rested on mutual trust, had been assailed for years. At the same time, some had demanded that the funds be administered by outside trustees, on the ground of distrust in the fair play of the party and of its officers. Though the Irish party felt it impossible to allow any outside body to become paymasters for its members, it was thought best, in view of this criticism, to frame a new plan. Blake then proceeded to describe and justify the plan put into effect by his resolution:

> The present plan gives to every member of the Party, no matter what his individual views or preferences, no matter what his votes in Party meeting, the absolute right, so long as he remains a member of the Party under its rules, to share on equal terms with every other member on one single condition, namely, that he signs the declaration.
> Those who have voted this session against the Party resolutions on the election of the chairman, on unity and discipline, or on the funds, and those who may hereafter vote against any other resolution carried by the Party, are palpably as secure as if they had happened to be in the majority.
> Thus is removed at one stroke all possible pretence for the propagation of degrading and unfounded suspicions of favouritism, influence, dependence, or insecurity.
> Provision is made for audit and publication so that the country may know what has been done. The ancient and higher sentiments of loyalty and trust, confidence and good fellowship, having been shaken, publicity is the only substitute, and it is also the best defence against continued imputation of evil.

Next, Blake dealt specifically with the declaration. Some provision had to be made for the allocation of the fund, he said, and no plan more tender of the honour and independence of a colleague could be suggested than this one, which made his own statement the proof of his claim and the title to it. He then examined and accounted for each of the terms of the declaration:

> There are members who have before election agreed not to become a charge on the scanty National funds.
> Would it be right that they should, notwithstanding, quarter themselves thereon? To prevent this is the first precaution taken.

Then, there are members whose constituencies have, instead of contributing to the National Fund, provided for them individually by a local subscription, and there is also another fund opened, not for the Party as a whole, but, to quote its originator's words, "in support of those members of the Irish Parliamentary Party who work with Mr. Healy, and act with him outside as well as inside the House of Commons."

Would it be right that those paid locally by their constituents, or those accepting the grants offered by the paymasters of the Healy Fund, should also deplete the National Fund? To prevent this is the second precaution taken.

Lastly, the only purpose of the National Fund is to provide indemnity for those whose circumstances do not enable them to attend Parliament at their own expense.

Would it be right that those who are able so to attend should come upon such a fund? To prevent this is the third and last precaution taken.

It had been suggested in some quarters that it was humiliating to have to sign the declaration. But Blake pointed out that ex-cabinet ministers of the imperial government signed an analogous declaration as a prerequisite for pension. It was no humiliation for a member to accept the indemnity if unable to attend Parliament without it, and there could be no humiliation in avowing the existence of the true condition of acceptance.

The clearest expression of Healy's opposition to the resolution, and especially to Blake's proposing it, is to be found in the book on Irish politics which he published in 1898. After quoting a lengthy passage from the speech delivered by Blake at the Irish race convention, in which Blake denies that members of Healyite sympathies had ever been deprived of allowances, Healy declares that the resolution moved in the Irish party by Blake in January, 1897, directly conflicts with this speech.[24] Of course, what he means is that, by moving a resolution which provided that allowances be denied to those who would not ascribe to the party's resolution on unity and discipline, Blake was proposing that discrimination be exercised against members who differed in opinion from the majority of the party. Had Blake replied to this charge, he would undoubtedly have repeated what he had said in his letter to the *Freeman's Journal*, namely, that those who voted against the majority in party meetings were just as certain of their allowances as any other members, so long as they signed the declaration. This meant, of course, that they would have to agree not to criticize the decision of the majority

[24]T. M. Healy, *Why Ireland Is Not Free* (Dublin, 1898), 166.

outside party meetings, and it was to this that Healy objected. But before charging Blake with inconsistency Healy should have remembered that the situation had changed considerably between September, 1896, and January, 1897, for he and his sympathizers, by forming both a rival fund and a new national organization, had virtually forced the majority of the party to take some sort of action against them.

Although the passage of the resolutions on unity and discipline and on the party funds helped to re-establish the centralization of control which had existed in the Irish party before the Parnell split and which Dillon wished to restore, it did not bring into existence what the Irish people really desired—a reunited Nationalist party. Shortly after the passage of the resolutions, Vesey Knox, one of Healy's leading colleagues, was expelled from the party, in accordance with the resolution on unity and discipline, for denouncing its "new constitution" in a letter to his constituents.[25] And although Healy and most of his colleagues managed to remain within the party, it was perfectly clear to the country that they still did not support the policy of the Dillonites. The Healyites continued to recognize the People's Rights Association as opposed to the Irish National Federation, and those among them who required allowances obtained them from the rival fund, thus avoiding signing the declaration required for the regular indemnity. Moreover, about the middle of 1897, the Healyites, who had not had the support of a Dublin daily newspaper since the amalgamation of the *National Press* with the *Freeman's Journal*, founded the *Daily Nation*.[26] Thus in 1897 the division between the two wings of the Irish parliamentary party became even more pronounced than previously.

Blake and Canada

In a study of Blake's Irish career, two aspects of his relationship with Canada in the years 1896–7 are important: the one, his efforts to stimulate the collection of money in that country for the Irish

[25]Lyons, *Irish Parliamentary Party*, 66.
[26]It was under the direction of William Murphy, a leading Healyite, who had bought the weekly *Nation*.

cause; the other, the question of whether he would return to Canadian public life. Since the two subjects recur frequently in this period and would be difficult to separate, they will for the most part be treated conjointly.

In June, 1896, a general election in Canada resulted in the defeat of the Conservative government. After eighteen years in opposition, the Liberals returned to power, and Wilfrid Laurier, Blake's successor to the leadership of that party, became Prime Minister of Canada. It was not surprising that this event soon gave rise to rumours that Blake would return to Canada either to become a member of the cabinet or to accept some other prominent position to which the new government had the power to appoint him. For there now existed no serious difference of opinion between Blake and his former colleagues in Canada, the Liberals having virtually discarded, at a national convention in 1893, the plank in their platform to which he had been opposed.

Not long after the Liberal victory a rumour arose concerning a post for Blake, acceptance of which would not actually have involved his return to Canada. In August, 1896, it was stated in the press that the new Canadian Prime Minister, having the right to nominate one judge to be added to the Judicial Committee of the Privy Council, had offered the post to Blake in recognition of his long service to the Canadian Liberal party. This rumour was not at all unreasonable in view of the fact that Blake, since his entry into Irish politics, had developed a large practice in colonial appeals to the Judicial Committee. The Toronto *Globe*, commenting upon the reported offer in its issue of August 23, remarked that Blake's ability, knowledge, and standing would have made the appointment a good one, but added that he had turned it down and was continuing to devote himself to the Irish cause.[27] It does not appear, however, that there was any foundation for the rumour that he had been offered the post at this time, for, in a letter to Dillon, Blake remarked jokingly that the cable reports had made him a judge on the Privy Council.[28]

[27]The *Globe*'s article was copied by the *Freeman's Journal*, Dublin, Sept. 3, 1896.
[28]Dillon Papers, Blake to Dillon, Aug. 21, 1896.

When Blake arrived in Canada in September, 1896, his attention was drawn to unfavourable reports of the Irish race convention which had reached that country. He was much distressed, for he felt that the reports made the situation appear considerably worse than it actually was. In a letter from Toronto he told Dillon that he believed the good effect which the convention had been calculated to produce abroad was already almost lost, and would, unless reparative steps were taken, be absolutely destroyed.[29]

Early in October, 1896, Blake, together with Hugh Ryan and J. J. Foy, two of the Canadian delegates to the race convention, had an interview with the Archbishop of Toronto. In reporting this interview to Dillon, Blake explained that the Irish hierarchy's lack of interest in the convention had greatly affected the Archbishop, who had assumed that there would be an earnest display of interest in the proceedings from that quarter. The Archbishop believed that a great opportunity had been lost, while Hugh Ryan remarked that he could come to no other conclusion than that many of the Irish clergy did not wish for home rule, and that this view was shared by many of his colleagues in the Canadian delegation. Blake did his best to explain the situation, including the attitude of members of the hierarchy and many of the clergy to the dissension within the Irish parliamentary party. He told the Archbishop that to himself and his colleagues, who, "knowing how things were, had expected less, the Convention appeared to be a great success, and to give fair promise, if only the Nationalists—lay and clerical—would build vigorously upon its foundation, of a restoration of the cause."[30] Blake must have realized later that the views he expressed on this occasion were unduly optimistic, but allowance must be made for the fact that he was anxious to counteract the reports which had reached Canada and to assure the Archbishop that there was still hope for the cause of home rule.

Shortly after the race convention, it was decided to make an appeal to Ireland for money to sustain members at Westminster during the next session of Parliament. Blake had understood that this appeal was not to be made until the late autumn of 1896, but,

[29]Blake Papers, Blake to Dillon, Sept. 16, 1896.
[30]For a report of the interview, see *ibid.*, Blake to Dillon, Oct. 8, 1896.

while in Canada in September, he received a letter from Dillon stating that most of their colleagues felt that it ought to be issued at once.[31] Not wishing to oppose them, Blake cabled Dillon his acquiescence in this plan, and promised that for every thousand up to five thousand pounds he would add as his personal subscription a tenth of the amount collected.[32] On December 10, 1896, just after Blake, who had returned from Canada in October, had sent in his second subscription of £100, the *Freeman's Journal* published an editorial warmly praising him for all the aid he had given and adding that he had "done not one but a dozen men's part in saving the cause of Ireland."

It has been seen that, in December, 1896, and January, 1897, the split in the Irish party became even more serious. As a result of this, Blake grew especially downhearted about the prospects of the Irish cause and his own relationship to it. Hence, when certain opportunities for service to Canada presented themselves, he felt that he must consider seriously the advisability of accepting them.

The rumour that Blake had been offered a judgeship on the Judicial Committee of the Privy Council appears to have been premature rather than false, for, in a letter to Dillon on December 8, 1896, Blake referred to certain offers, apparently including the judgeship in question, which had been made to him by Laurier. It appears that Laurier made a number of offers, in the hope that Blake would choose at least one of them, but unfortunately Laurier's letter submitting the proposals has not come to light. What it contained can only be conjectured from Blake's correspondence with Dillon.

With his letter of December 8 to Dillon, Blake enclosed Laurier's letter, remarking that the matters discussed in it had previously been presented to him informally.[33] But now that the offers were given definite formulation, he felt it necessary to consider them carefully. He told Dillon that the only position which really attracted him was the judgeship on the Judicial Committee, but that he had thought when he joined the Irish party that he was giving up that aspira-

[31]*Ibid.*, Dillon to Blake, Sept. 19, 1896.
[32]*Ibid.*, Blake to Dillon, Sept. 28, 1896.
[33]Possibly during his visit to Canada in Sept.–Oct., 1896.

tion. As to the other offers, he felt that he must think of his future a little, since the Irish situation now appeared to him hopeless. Even in his own constituency, South Longford, the Healyites were increasing in strength, and, if this situation continued, he did not believe that he would seek nomination there in another general election. "Indeed," he remarked, "it is painful to me to be representing the division in view of the hostility of such a large body of my former supporters." Blake then told of the work he would probably do if he returned to Canada: "It is not at all likely that I would take a judgeship for keeps;[34] I would either (so far as I can fathom my mind just now) take up the threads of certain openings in Toronto which remain available, or go back to the Canadian Parliament as an independent Liberal,[35] but I might probably try the Bench." Finally, he reiterated that, in view of existing circumstances, it would not be reasonable for him to refuse to consider prospects in Canada unless he could see with certainty the opportunity of continuing in public life in Ireland. But he was "puzzled and worried" about the best course to take and therefore wished to have Dillon's advice.[36]

In his reply, Dillon expressed sympathy with Blake's position, but added that the latter's retirement from Irish politics during the coming session would destroy whatever chance remained of adequately reconstructing the Nationalist party. He therefore urged him to postpone his decision until the close of the parliamentary session.[37] In view of Dillon's attitude, Blake agreed to remain in Irish politics for the time being, although it meant declining an office which was to become vacant in Toronto in April, 1897. But he added: "It is not an exhilarating prospect to feel that one does no good staying, but will do harm going, and therefore must stay!"[38] To this Dillon replied that Blake should not take such a view of the situation,

[34]Here he is referring to a judgeship not on the Judicial Committee of the Privy Council, but in the Supreme Court of Canada, probably, indeed, to the chief justiceship, which he was certainly offered about this time.

[35]It will be seen presently that by an independent Liberal he meant a private member of the Liberal party.

[36]Dillon Papers, Blake to Dillon, Dec. 8, 1896. There is a rough draft of this letter in the Blake Papers.

[37]Blake Papers, Dillon to Blake, Dec. 20, 1896.

[38]Dillon Papers, Blake to Dillon, Dec. 21, 1896.

since the party would have long ago been destroyed or captured by unscrupulous adventurers if Blake had not joined it.[39]

Although the appeal to Ireland in the autumn of 1896 met with considerable response, the financial position of the Irish party in the following year once more became desperate. In 1897, it was difficult to raise additional funds in Ireland for parliamentary purposes, because a collection was under way for the evicted tenants and the country was again threatened with agrarian distress approaching famine. In view of this situation, Blake determined to do his best to raise money in Canada. He arrived there in August, 1897, but spent the remainder of the summer at Murray Bay, Quebec, and it was not until he reached Toronto at the end of September that he really started the work of stimulating the collection of funds for the Irish cause. It was then that he became fully aware of the effect produced on the Canadian delegates by the attitude of the Parnellites, Healyites, and Irish ecclesiastics towards the race convention.

On September 29, 1897, Hugh Ryan gave a dinner at his home in Toronto to reunite the Canadian delegates to the Irish race convention. The Archbishop of Toronto and Blake were also invited to attend the dinner, and the latter took advantage of the opportunity thus afforded to begin his campaign for funds. Though he made no direct public appeal, he told the delegates, in private, of the urgency of the financial situation. Then, after the dinner was over, some of them discussed the question and, on the following day, went to see Blake about it. In giving Dillon an account of the dinner and subsequent activities, Blake remarked that there was now going to be a gathering at the Archbishop's and that he hoped a good deal could be done to raise funds.[40]

It was not until a few days later that Blake told Dillon of an unpleasant incident which had occurred at Ryan's dinner. Sir Frank Smith, who had several times contributed generously to the Irish cause, had "delivered a most bitter invective against the Irish hierarchy and clergy in respect of their attitude towards the Canadian delegates and towards the convention."[41] Blake told Dillon that the

[39] Blake Papers, Dillon to Blake, Dec. 29, 1896.
[40] *Ibid.*, Blake to Dillon, Oct. 1, 1897.
[41] *Ibid.*, Blake to Dillon, Oct. 6, 1897.

speech was inaccurate and that Smith had finally admitted having made it in an attempt to excuse the inaction of Canadians in subscribing to the Irish cause in 1896. But Blake feared it would also be used as an excuse for inaction now. He was therefore opposed to the publication of the speech, at least in its original form, and was consequently much relieved that, when it did appear, most of the damaging statements had been omitted.[42]

Shortly after the Ryan banquet, Blake decided that it would be unwise to delay any longer in making a public appeal for funds. Consequently he wrote to the editor of the Toronto *Globe* a letter, which appeared in that journal on October 5, describing the financial situation in Ireland and appealing to Canadian friends of Irish home rule for aid. He added that, in the case of communities where no local committees or organizations were available, he would be pleased to enter into correspondence with friends who were willing to take charge of subscriptions.

Blake's next letter to Dillon showed that the situation in Canada was not at all encouraging. On October 14, Blake had had a long interview with Archbishop Walsh and the Rev. Frank Ryan. The Archbishop had been very kind and was ready to do all he could, but he had added that the worst possible effect had been produced by the attitude of the Dublin people and particularly the Dublin ecclesiastics towards the convention and the Canadian delegates. He had told Blake that Sir Frank Smith and Hugh Ryan had returned to Canada saying that they would never give another shilling to the Irish cause. Blake believed that Hugh Ryan had now softened, but that Sir Frank Smith had not, and, although he could afford to contribute generously, he would probably decline to do so. To add to this discouraging situation, Blake had not, at the time of his interview with the Archbishop, received a single letter in response to his public appeal. He told Dillon that other cities were probably waiting for Toronto to act, but that, nevertheless, this lack of response was discouraging.[43]

At a dinner given by Archbishop Walsh on October 27, Hugh Ryan brought up the subject of subscriptions, admitting that it was mainly his personal admiration for Blake which was making

[42]*Ibid.*, Blake to Dillon, Oct. 7, 1897.
[43]*Ibid.*, Blake to Dillon, Oct. 15, 1897.

him contribute. Sir Frank Smith, after repeating his charges and saying that he would give nothing, finally decided that, for Blake's sake, he would subscribe $1,000, but he emphasized that this was the last time he would do so. Several others agreed to contribute, and before the close of the evening a total of $4,300 had been promised.[44] Partly through the efforts of Hugh Ryan, several more subscriptions were secured the next day.[45]

A meeting to arrange further action was held the day after the Archbishop's dinner. There it was decided that an appeal should be made by circular to Irish-Canadians in all parts of the country. But it was the unanimous opinion of the meeting that the circular should be issued by Blake personally, rather than by the central committee which was being formed in Toronto to take charge of the subscriptions.[46] This was a recognition of the fact that Irish-Canadians had become discouraged about the prospects of the home rule cause and that Blake was the only person who might be able to persuade them to give money at this time. Many Irish-Canadians might, like Hugh Ryan and Sir Frank Smith, subscribe because of their admiration for Blake.

In the weeks which followed, Blake did all in his power to persuade Irish-Canadians to subscribe to the fund which was being organized in Toronto. Having agreed not only to send out the circulars in his own name, but also to act as general treasurer of the central committee, he began his work by writing to friends in many Canadian cities and towns, asking them to list the names of people in their part of the country to whom he might send his appeal. As he received each list, he sent out to every person whose name appeared on it a copy of the circular making the appeal, together, in many cases, with a short private letter, asking attention to it. By December 20, he had sent over 900 circulars and about 250 special letters.[47] In addition to this, he corresponded with a number of influential men who were organizing the appeal in various centres, and made a trip to Ottawa to encourage the work there. Moreover,

[44]For Blake's account of the dinner, see *ibid.*, Blake to Dillon, Oct. 28, 1897.
[45]See *ibid.*, Blake to Dillon, Oct. 29, 1897.
[46]For Blake's account of the meeting, see *ibid.*
[47]These figures are given in *ibid.*, Blake to W. O'Brien, Dec. 20, 1897.

THE IRISH SITUATION, 1896-7 191

to all those who responded in any way to his appeal, either by sending lists or subscriptions or by aiding in organization work, he wrote letters of thanks. And finally, he had the task of transmitting returns to the treasurers in Dublin.[48]

Blake's efforts met with considerable success. Before he left Canada at the end of December, 1897, subscriptions to the fund amounted to $7,093.75.[49] Although the bulk of this amount consisted of the large Toronto subscriptions, the total was nevertheless impressive in view of the fact that Irishmen in other parts of the world contributed almost nothing to the cause of home rule in 1897. In Ireland, as a result of the situation already described, no appeal was made; only about £50 was obtained from Australia;[50] while in the United States it was evidently considered useless to make an appeal. In referring to the Canadian subscriptions in a letter to Dillon, Blake remarked that "in no other quarter of the globe was it possible to raise anything for the movement."[51]

As had been expected, the Canadian subscriptions were given mainly as a personal tribute to Blake. "Most of what was given, was in compliment to your own magnetic and magnificent personality," he was told by a resident of Hamilton, who had been active in collecting funds there.[52] Blake believed that, had he been able to stay in Canada another month and to hold public meetings in several cities, he might have been able to collect even more. But his services were required elsewhere, and he could not remain longer. He therefore left his son, Edward F. Blake, in charge of his correspondence in connection with the Canadian fund, and before it was closed at the beginning of May, 1898, several hundred dollars more had been collected. The fund's total by that time was $7,670.[53]

[48]For correspondence in connection with the appeal, see *ibid.*, General Irish Political Correspondence, 1897.
[49]This figure is given by Blake in a letter dated Dec. 27, published in the *Globe*, Toronto, Dec. 28, 1897.
[50]This is reported in Blake Papers, Davitt to Blake, Nov. 20, 1897.
[51]*Ibid.*, Blake to Dillon, Dec. 16, 1897.
[52]*Ibid.*, Frank O'Reilly to Blake, Nov. 9, 1897.
[53]The receipt book of the fund is among the Blake Papers. See also *ibid.*, E. F. Blake to the treasurers of the Irish parliamentary party, May 5, 1898.

But Blake realized that it would not be possible to appeal to Canada in the following year, for it had been pointed out by several besides Sir Frank Smith that their subscriptions would not be repeated. Feeling it his duty to make this clear to the leaders of the party in Ireland, Blake mentioned it in at least two of his letters to Dillon.[54] And, telling William O'Brien of the large Toronto subscriptions, he remarked that they had "taken all the nuggets and nearly exhausted the mine."[55]

For his work in Canada in the autumn of 1897 Blake received wide acclaim. The Archbishop of Toronto declared: "What splendid confidence, dauntless courage, undying devotion to the cause. In this selfish, sordid, material age, it is a sunburst from the days of chivalry."[56] On November 13, the day it published the first subscription list from Canada, the *Freeman's Journal* wrote of Blake: "He has done not a man's service merely, but a giant's service, to the Irish cause. He has been lavish alike of his private fortune, of his time, his influence, and his eloquence in its support. This latest service of once more reviving the generosity and enthusiasm of the sterling friends of Ireland in Canada is, if we may so say, but an ordinary incident in his extraordinary career." And Michael Davitt, in a letter to Blake, remarked: "The opinion of your friends over here is that you have achieved a miracle! To have even issued an appeal under all the discouraging circumstances was an act of supreme courage, but to have realized the sum you say will come in as a result of the appeal is a really marvellous performance."[57]

But, while doing his best to collect money in Canada for the home rule cause, Blake did not forget that the situation in Ireland was very discouraging and that it might be well for him to consider what opportunities there were for service to Canada. Nevertheless, when he was offered the chief justiceship of the Canadian Supreme Court in September, 1897, he rejected it. It appears that he had

[54]*Ibid.*, Blake to Dillon, Oct. 28 & Dec. 16, 1897.
[55]*Ibid.*, Blake to W. O'Brien, Oct. 29, 1897.
[56]The Archbishop's tribute is contained in an undated letter to Blake from the Rev. Frank Ryan, which is among the 1897 correspondence in the Blake Papers. A copy of the tribute, in an envelope marked "Tribute to Blake—October 1897" is also contained in the Dillon Papers.
[57]Blake Papers, Davitt to Blake, Nov. 20, 1897.

refused this position several times before, for he announced in a letter to Dillon: "I have just written—I hope for the last time—declining once again the proposal of the Chief Justiceship of Canada."[58]

However, from some of Blake's activities during his visit to Canada in the autumn of 1897 it is clear that he was anxious to show his interest in returning to Canadian politics. On previous trips he had taken practically no part in public gatherings except those directly connected with the furtherance of the cause of Irish home rule. But in 1897 he participated in a number of purely Canadian functions and expressed his views on current Canadian questions, including the policy of the Liberal government then in power at Ottawa.

On October 5, Blake attended a reception at Massey Hall, Toronto, in honour of Sir Wilfrid Laurier. Two days later, as Chancellor of the University of Toronto, he conferred on Sir Wilfrid the honorary degree of doctor of laws. On December 8, he attended a dinner at the National Club in Toronto in honour of the Governor-General, Lord Aberdeen, and replied to the toast, "Canada and the Empire." His interest in Canadian politics was evidenced in the addresses he delivered on these three occasions, but it was at Strathroy, Ontario, on November 24, that he made his most significant speech, explaining his own relationship to the Liberal party and expressing his desire to return to Canadian politics.[59]

Blake began by speaking of the years he had spent in the federal Parliament and the Ontario legislature. Of those twenty-four years, the last two or three had, he asserted, been "the pleasantest of all," for, with health restored and free from the cares of leadership, he had been able "to take a part as an independent Liberal in the discussion of public affairs and in the advancement of true Liberal principles." This was the only part for which he had ever cared, he said. "I confidently expected . . . to continue in that special service to the end; but far different has been the issue." It was now more than seven years since he had addressed his fellow-countrymen

[58]*Ibid.*, Blake to Dillon, Sept. 27, 1897.
[59]Press reports of all these gatherings are to be found in the Blake Scrap Books.

upon Canadian politics, and, since he had sometimes been accused of neglecting his duty to his own country during that period, he now wished to remind his audience of the facts which he believed to be his vindication. He described the circumstances which had led to his break with the Liberal party in 1891—his opposition to its advocacy of unrestricted reciprocity with the United States and his refusal to contest a seat in the general election of that year. Then, while he was thus estranged from the Liberal party, he was invited to accept an Irish seat in the Imperial House of Commons. Because he was convinced of the justice of the Irish cause and of his own inability, for the time being, to serve Canada, he felt it his duty to accept this invitation "which seemed to open another door for public service elsewhere."

In 1893, the Canadian Liberal party laid down a fresh policy on the trade question, to which, Blake explained, "it was my satisfaction to give my adhesion, for it was that which I had always maintained myself." He then told his audience why this event had not led him to return to the service of Canada:

> But, though the difference which had caused my severance from Canadian public life had thus ended, yet, as I have said, new conditions had been meantime created for myself, and anxious as I have been to return to my own people, there has never since that day been a time at which, in the opinion of my confidential friends in the Imperial Parliament, it was possible for me to resign my seat without detriment to the cause in which I had enlisted; and so it happens that I remain. For the occasion of return I have looked and longed without ceasing, and still I look and long, earnestly desiring that the path of duty may some day approximate closer to the path of comfort and of pleasure, and may lead me back to the land of my birth, where my children, my grandchildren, and my lifelong friends abide, and may so afford me, during the short interval which remains to me, the greatest solace and purest gratification which an old man can hope to have.[60]

In making this speech, Blake was obviously paving the way for a return to Canadian public life if the situation in Ireland rendered such a step possible or advisable. At the same time, he explained the role which he hoped to play if he returned to Canadian politics.

[60]The foregoing account of Blake's Strathroy speech is based on the text printed by the *Advertiser*, London, Ontario, Nov. 26, 1897. For the *Advertiser*'s account, which Blake regarded as the most accurate one published, see the Blake Scrap Books.

It is clear that by an independent Liberal he meant not what would be understood by the term to-day, but a private member of the Liberal party. Although he apparently had no desire to hold a cabinet post, he did wish to be a regular member of the Liberal party, for it was only when it had ceased to advocate a policy which he could not support that he thought of returning to the Canadian House of Commons.

In an address delivered at the annual dinner of the University of Toronto medical faculty on December 9, Blake spoke again of his plans for the future. He mentioned that he would never again lead a party or accept office in a government, but the Toronto *Globe*, in reporting his speech the next day, misinterpreted what he had said. In an article headed "Mr. Blake's Intentions. Will Not Return to Canadian Public Life. A Definite Statement," it said, "Hon. Edward Blake, speaking last night at the University of Toronto medical dinner, announced that he would never return to Canadian public life." Blake was much disturbed by this inaccurate report, and the speed with which he sought to correct it showed that he was anxious to prevent its gaining wide circulation. On the very day the report appeared, he wrote to J. S. Willison, editor of the *Globe*, saying that he had made no such announcement as that contained in the newspaper. He told Willison that it was the leadership of a party or office in a government which he wished to avoid, but that in a recent address he had spoken in the most distinct terms of his desire to serve as an independent Liberal in the Parliament of Canada.[61] Willison replied that he had heard Blake's speech at the University dinner and that, as soon as he saw the paper, he realized that Blake's statement as to his connection with Canadian public life had been "bungled."[62] Consequently, the next day, December 11, a correction appeared in the *Globe*.[63]

[61]Blake Papers, Blake to Willison, Dec. 10, 1897. The original is in the Willison Papers.
[62]For this letter dated Dec. 10, 1897, see the Blake Scrap Books. A clipping of the *Globe*'s account of Blake's speech is also included here.
[63]For further details of Blake's relations with Canada during his Irish career, see Margaret A. Banks, "Edward Blake's Relations with Canada during his Irish Career, 1892–1907," (*Canadian Historical Review*, XXXV, no. 1, 1954), 22–42.

But Blake was not destined to return to Canadian politics. His colleagues in the Irish party continued to fear that his withdrawal from the British Parliament would prove disastrous to the Irish cause, and feeling that he could not abandon them, Blake remained for nearly ten years more an Irish member of the British House of Commons.

VIII. NATIONALIST REUNION

IN THE YEARS preceding 1898, disputes among the various factions of Irish Nationalists had become so acute that many Irishmen began to despair of achieving home rule through the efforts of their representatives in Parliament. They felt that it would be many years before the self-government which they desired would be established and that, in the meantime, instead of concentrating on the attainment of this distant goal, efforts should be made to improve the social and economic conditions of the country.

Some reforms were, in fact, obtained from the Unionist government which had come into power in 1895. This government had decided not to resort to coercion in its attempt to defeat the Irish Nationalist movement, but to adopt a new policy based on what was afterwards called the principle of "killing home rule with kindness." As a result, two important measures became law—the Land Act of 1896 and the Local Government Act of 1898. The first, relating to land purchase, lessened the burdens on the tenants, although, since it made no provision for compulsory sale, it could not be regarded by the Nationalists as a final settlement of the land question. The second provided for the establishment in Ireland of a complete system of local government by elective bodies—county councils, urban district councils, and rural district councils—to replace the old grand juries which had always been controlled by the landowners. Although some Irish Nationalists criticized the bill when it was before the Commons, it proved, from their point of view, to be an excellent measure of reform, for Nationalists soon gained control of the new elective bodies and obtained wide experience from serving on them.

During the years of dissension, several attempts were made to bring together representatives of all political parties in Ireland to consider social and economic questions on which there might be a possibility of reaching agreement. During the parliamentary recess of 1895, Horace Plunkett, hoping to secure united action in the promotion of social reform, summoned both Nationalists and Unionists to a conference. The anti-Parnellites refused their co-operation, but Parnellites and Unionists took part in it. At the conference a "recess committee" was appointed, and in the summer of 1896 it submitted a report to Gerald Balfour, the Irish chief secretary, recommending a number of measures of social reform. Among the most important of the committee's suggestions were those concerning government encouragement of agriculture, and it was as a result of the report that a Department of Agricultural and Technical Instruction was founded in 1899. Plunkett, who became head of this new department, was well qualified for the position, for he was deeply interested in the promotion of agriculture and had already, in 1894, founded the Irish Agricultural Organization Society for the organization and instruction of farmers in the best agricultural methods.[1]

We have already seen what efforts were made in 1897 to settle the financial relations question by co-operative action and in 1898 meetings again took place in many parts of Ireland to discuss this important problem. One held in Blake's constituency on January 12 shows vividly how, on questions such as this, those who differed politically were willing to work together. Although there were still a good many Parnellites in Longford, and the growing strength of the Healyites had already alarmed Blake, he received a very cordial reception on this occasion. According to Dillon, who was present at the meeting, the Parnellites all turned out to welcome Blake; and the bishop and priests, though supporters of Healy, were also most friendly.[2]

The United Irish League

In the years which followed his retirement from Parliament in 1895, William O'Brien had been living in Westport, County Mayo, where he became deeply interested in the agricultural problems of that part of the country. Like many of his fellow-countrymen, he began to feel that the settlement of these problems was more urgent

[1]For a fuller account of these attempts at social reform, see Horace Plunkett, *Ireland in the New Century* (London, 1904), chaps. VII–IX.
[2]Dillon Papers, Dillon to William O'Brien, Jan. 13, 1898.

than was the attainment of home rule. The problem in Mayo and in the west of Ireland generally centred around the fact that much of the country was taken up by large cattle ranches, while the remaining land was unproductive and quite insufficient for the needs of the large peasant population. Faced by this situation O'Brien proposed a new movement with the motto "the land for the people," which would support a local programme of transplantation of the people from their small barren plots to the more fertile land around them. It did not at first occur to him that any political object should be connected with it. But to carry out such a programme "a great accumulation of national strength" was needed, and for this reason O'Brien decided to form a new organization to be known as the United Irish League.[3]

Even before the League was actually founded, O'Brien began to visualize larger plans for it than he had originally intended. The Irish National Federation, especially since the formation of the People's Rights Association, could no longer be regarded as a truly national organization, for many of its branches had fallen into decay. O'Brien hoped that its place might be taken by the United Irish League, whose membership would be open to all sections of Nationalists, and in this way, the Irish people would, perhaps, become truly unified and a reunion of the political parties might follow. So, although O'Brien's primary aim was to improve the lot of the peasants in the west of Ireland, his long-range scheme was to bring about reunion, which in turn might lead to the achievement of home rule.

In promoting the United Irish League, O'Brien sought the cooperation of Dillon, who, he believed, was sufficiently discouraged with the dissension in his party to welcome this new movement. Dillon, however, was not at all enthusiastic about O'Brien's scheme, for he continued to believe that home rule was the primary need of the country and feared that the League would detract attention from it. So, although he agreed to attend the meeting at Westport on January 16, 1898, at which the League was founded, he and

[3]For a fuller description of conditions in the west of Ireland and the founding of the United Irish League, see William O'Brien, *An Olive Branch in Ireland and Its History* (London, 1910), 85ff. and F. S. L. Lyons, *The Irish Parliamentary Party 1890–1910* (London, 1951), 69–70.

O'Brien discovered, in the months which followed, that they differed considerably in their attitude towards the new organization. Dillon felt that, as leader of the Irish party, he ought not to take an active part in the League, for, knowing that the authorities regarded it with disfavour, he feared that they might take action against it and imprison its leaders. With the existing state of dissension in the party an extremely serious situation might result from the imprisonment of its chairman, and Dillon thought it unwise to take such a risk.

It is true that at times during 1898 Dillon became so discouraged with the situation in the Irish party that he seriously thought of resigning its chairmanship. In fact, he was advised to do so by Blake who felt that this action on Dillon's part might provide the only possible hope for a reunion of the various factions of Nationalists. Shortly before the sessional meeting of the party in January, 1898, Blake proposed that Dillon should decline re-election to the chair, so that "personal questions" could no longer be "made or pretended as obstacles" to reunion. He felt that this action would place Dillon on a very high plane and would almost force the members of other factions to make some move towards unity.[4] Dillon did not refuse re-election at this time, but he later told William O'Brien that he thought he would resign shortly after the session was over and recommend that a convention be called with the object of restoring unity in Nationalist ranks. "Blake," he went on, "sticks to his opinion that I ought to have resigned at the opening of this Session, but I am convinced that I did right to hold the field through the Session."[5]

Shortage of funds, the ineffectiveness of the Irish National Federation, and "the persistent advice of Blake" regarding the need for resignation had led Dillon to believe that his position was hopeless. But he had really little faith in a convention's settling a plan for union,[6] and in April he admitted to O'Brien that if he could count on sufficient money he would carry on.[7] Before the session ended in August he had almost decided to retain the chairmanship

[4] Dillon Papers, Blake to Dillon, Jan. 27, 1898.
[5] W. O'Brien Papers, Dillon to O'Brien, March 30, 1898.
[6] See *ibid.*, Dillon to O'Brien, April 4, 1898.
[7] *Ibid.*, Dillon to O'Brien, April 8, 1898.

and attempt to raise sufficient money to maintain the party at Westminster and carry it through another general election.⁸

It was O'Brien's attitude rather than Blake's which kept him from reaching a definite decision. Blake's advice was straightforward enough, but O'Brien's point of view was difficult to understand. He was troubled at Dillon's threats of resignation;⁹ yet he had become so deeply engrossed in the work of the League that he had little interest in the fate of the party. According to Davitt, who was in close communication with O'Brien and was very enthusiastic about the new organization, he was opposed to the raising of any funds for the party since the country ignored its existence and he felt it was the League which really required a fund.¹⁰ Although O'Brien wished Dillon to retain the leadership of the party, he took the unreasonable stand that he should carry on the parliamentary movement without funds, and Dillon realized that O'Brien's lack of support would make the raising of money increasingly difficult.

In view of O'Brien's attitude, Dillon thought that, before coming to a definite decision regarding the chairmanship and the raising of funds, he and his principal colleagues should confer with O'Brien. He therefore asked Blake, who was in London, to come to Ireland for ten days or two weeks early in September.¹¹ Blake agreed to do so and at the same time expressed dissatisfaction with O'Brien's attitude:

> I return O'Brien's two letters with thanks. It is no use criticising them. I can't help thinking they do disclose his mind, and that his mind is that you and all of us should be sacrificed, if need be, on the Mayo movement. If there is not an aroused and excited country this fall, then let the party go, which of course means let the cause and all go, damned by us. If there is such a country, then there is to be a new or reconstructed party after Redmondism and Healyism have rotted away. So that even such a country is to involve a recast.¹²

---

⁸See Dillon Papers, Blake to Dillon, Aug. 4, 1898. In this letter Blake comments on Dillon's proposal to try to raise money for "2 or 3 sessions and an election."
⁹See *ibid.*, W. O'Brien to Dillon, April 1 and 7, 1898.
¹⁰See Lyons, *Irish Parliamentary Party*, 74n.
¹¹Blake Papers, Dillon to Blake, Aug. 19, 1898.
¹²Dillon Papers, Blake to Dillon, Aug. 21, 1898. O'Brien's letters have not come to light, but their contents can be conjectured from Blake's remarks.

Before Blake's arrival in Ireland, Dillon had a preliminary interview with O'Brien. Afterwards he reported to Blake that O'Brien was completely wrapped up in the League and that, to his mind, everything else was of secondary importance, and, in fact, of little or no importance. "He protests violently," Dillon wrote, "that if I resign I assign Irish politics to ruin and degradation for a quarter of a century, but proposes that I should face next session without a shilling, get elected at a meeting in Dublin and go over with a few members, leaving the bulk of those who voted for me behind, and he apparently thinks me most unreasonable because I cannot accept this programme." Dillon admitted, however, that O'Brien had worked almost a miracle in the districts to which his League had spread and that if he had taken a rational view of the necessities of the parliamentary situation and had given a fair amount of help in keeping the Irish National Federation alive, his League might have been an exceedingly useful movement. But O'Brien's preoccupation with the League and consequent lack of interest in the party was very discouraging.[13]

On September 6, Dillon, Blake, Davitt, and O'Brien met in Dublin to discuss the situation. According to O'Brien, Dillon again threatened resignation and expressed displeasure that the Sligo branches of the Irish National Federation has resolved to become branches of the United Irish League. O'Brien pointed out that the Federation had received practically no money from County Sligo during the past year and that he could therefore see no reason why Dillon should object to the move. In his account of this discussion, O'Brien added that Davitt strongly supported his view.[14] No mention is made of Blake's attitude, but from his correspondence in August it can be assumed that he would support Dillon, for he feared that the break-up of the Federation would be blamed on Dillon and his colleagues and that this would prove detrimental to the Irish cause.[15]

Many other aspects of the situation were discussed by the four men, and it appears from their later correspondence that O'Brien agreed to some sort of compromise in order to prevent Dillon from

[13] Blake Papers, Dillon to Blake, Aug. 29, 1898.
[14] O'Brien, *An Olive Branch in Ireland*, 103n.
[15] See Dillon Papers, Blake to Dillon, Aug. 10, 1898.

resigning. At any rate, O'Brien, contrary to his previously expressed intention, decided to support an appeal by Dillon for funds for the party. But exactly what other views were expressed proved to be a matter of controversy in the months which followed.

From the correspondence between Dillon and Blake in the days immediately after the latter's return to England, it appears that they had begun at once to write to influential Irishmen who might be able to aid them in the raising of funds for the party. Very soon, however, certain actions of O'Brien led Blake to believe that the former was unwilling to give sufficient support in this campaign. From O'Brien's remarks at their conference in Dublin, Blake had received the impression that no attempt was to be made to spread the League beyond a few counties in the west of Ireland, but in a letter which O'Brien wrote later in September he spoke of the extension of his new organization all over Ireland. This Clondalkin letter, as it was called, greatly disturbed Blake, for, as he told Dillon, it attempted "to fix men's minds everywhere, not in 5, or 8, or 10 counties, on the League; and its purpose not as a lever for relief to congested districts but as a unifying machinery in Irish National politics." It was Blake's opinion that O'Brien's policy would impair the party's chances of obtaining even a humble share of public support and that it was inconsistent with the spirit of the conference of September 6 and of the *modus vivendi* reached on that occasion.[16]

Dillon, however, was not at all surprised at the views expressed by O'Brien in his Clondalkin letter. As he told Blake, he had not expected any real change in O'Brien's attitude or any co-operation in raising funds for the party beyond what he thought necessary to prevent Dillon's immediate resignation.[17]

Dillon evidently wrote to Davitt about Blake's views regarding O'Brien, for shortly afterwards, in a letter to Blake, Davitt gave his version of O'Brien's attitude and of the agreement reached on September 6. Before the conference of that day, Davitt related, O'Brien had spoken to him "of the Parliamentary Party as virtually a cypher in the National movement and of the Federation as a

[16]*Ibid.*, Blake to Dillon, Sept. 22, 1898.
[17]Blake Papers, Dillon to Blake, Sept. 27, 1898.

shadow or a sham." Being convinced that neither was worth saving, he wanted whatever funds were raised to be devoted not to them, but to the spread of the League. After learning these views, Davitt feared that, if O'Brien adhered to them, Dillon would have no alternative to resignation.

At the conference, however, Davitt went on, O'Brien modified his position so as to accept both an appeal by Dillon for party funds and efforts on the part of his colleagues to help in this task by writing to friends who might subscribe. On Davitt's suggestion, it was decided that money for the party should be sought mainly in Ireland and Great Britain, while America and Australia would be left as fields for the League. It was also agreed that the Federation should remain as a necessary skeleton organization behind Dillon, but that he should also support the League. Although there was some talk of the League's being confined to about ten counties, Davitt did not recall that any definite decision had been reached on this point. His only other recollection was of a general understanding that Dillon should retain the chair and do the best he could.[18]

Blake had never ceased to believe that Dillon ought to resign. At the conference he had reiterated this conviction, though he had agreed to support Dillon in his efforts to raise funds if he decided to carry on.[19] By the middle of November, 1898, Dillon, realizing that it was quite hopeless to look to O'Brien for support either of the Federation or of the party, finally seemed ready to accept Blake's advice. He was, he told Blake, directing all his efforts towards forcing a conference and general union,[20] and if he succeeded in bringing about a conference, he would resign at once and throw on it the responsibility of reuniting the parties. If he did not succeed before the next sessional meeting, he would have to consider the situation carefully, but, judging from present appearances, he did not think he would stand for re-election. Dillon had also come to accept Blake's views on O'Brien's Clondalkin letter: it was absurd

[18]*Ibid.*, Davitt to Blake, Sept. 30, 1898.
[19]See Dillon Papers, Blake to Dillon, Sept. 28, 1898.
[20]It will be seen presently that, in Oct., 1898, Dillon had proposed a conference between representatives of the Parnellites and anti-Parnellites.

and entirely inconsistent with their understanding, and there was no doubt that O'Brien's idea was to spread the League over the country as far as possible. And he added a word of praise for Blake: "I may say that of those who were at the conference, you, whose advice was not taken, are the only one who has fully acted up to the assurances of support on which I decided to hold on."[21]

It seemed unlikely to Blake that Dillon would succeed in bringing about a conference between Parnellites and anti-Parnellites, and even if he did it would be difficult to determine the role of the Healyites, should they wish to take part. And regarding the question of retiring from the chair, Blake expressed the opinion that Dillon should do so without waiting to see if a conference could be arranged, since he would then "have done something, not merely offered or promised something, towards reunion."[22]

By December, 1898, the United Irish League had spread through much of the west of Ireland; and towards the end of that month O'Brien proposed that, in order to place the organization in the province of Connaught on a permanent footing, a convention or congress should be held. He expressed the hope that Dillon would attend this gathering and offer suggestions regarding its programme.[23] Dillon, however, in replying to O'Brien's invitation, declared that he felt he should not attend a provincial congress unless he and O'Brien were "in accord as to the future conduct— not only of the United League—but generally of the national movement," and he feared they were not.[24]

O'Brien was convinced that the party could be saved and united only from the outside. He hoped that the League, as an organization welcoming all Nationalists, would be able to promote so strong a public opinion in favour of reunion that the parliamentary factions would be unable to stand out against it. As to Dillon's proposal for a conference between the parties, he considered that "in the temper

[21] Blake Papers, Dillon to Blake, Nov. 16, 1898.
[22] Dillon Papers, Blake to Dillon, Nov. 17, 1898.
[23] Blake Papers, W. O'Brien to Dillon, Dec. 22, 1898. This is a copy sent to Blake by Dillon.
[24] W. O'Brien Papers, Dillon to O'Brien, Dec. 25, 1898. There is a copy of this letter in the Blake Papers.

of Healy, Redmond and those fellows," such negotiations would be useless.[25] In hoping that the League, and not the party, would be chiefly responsible for bringing about reunion, O'Brien was really proposing that his new organization should be supreme over the party. This was something to which Dillon would not agree, for, although by this time he had come to recognize that the Federation was dead (killed, he believed, by O'Brien) and was willing that the League should replace it as the national organization, he wanted the party to predominate over the League as it had over the Federation. And although in the end he attended the provincial congress held at Clare Morris on January 30, 1899, he made it clear to O'Brien that he would not let the League or anything else interfere with his work for the party.[26]

In this controversy Blake's views were closer to Dillon's than to O'Brien's. Like Dillon, he was opposed to the new organization's becoming more powerful than the party, and although he was not very hopeful that a conference between Parnellites and anti-Parnellites could be arranged, he was not in principle opposed to direct negotiations between the parties. The main point on which he differed from both Dillon and O'Brien throughout 1898 was his insistence that Dillon should delay no longer in resigning the chairmanship of the party.

Negotiations for Reunion

By the end of 1898, there seemed at least some likelihood that reunion might be effected by direct negotiations between Parnellites and anti-Parnellites. During the few years preceding, a number of proposals for reunion had been made by prominent members of both parties. Davitt had written to William O'Brien in March, 1897:

[25]*Ibid.*, O'Brien to Dillon, Dec. 26, 1898. There is another copy in the Blake Papers.

[26]See *ibid.*, Dillon to O'Brien, Dec. 27, 1898. There is a copy of this letter in the Blake Papers. Lengthy excerpts from the foregoing correspondence between Dillon and O'Brien in Dec., 1898, are quoted in Lyons, *Irish Parliamentary Party*, 75-8.

"I am convinced that without union with the Parnellites the constitutional movement is doomed before the next general election."[27] Moreover, according to Healy, Davitt had, in January, 1896, expressed himself in favour of such a union under the leadership of a member of the minority party, other than Redmond.[28] Some of the Parnellites were also looking towards reunion at this time, for it was in 1897 that Redmond put forward a proposal for the formation of an association of "Independent Nationalists," which he hoped would unite members of different factions in Irish politics in the advancement of a common policy. But Redmond's plan came to nothing, and for some time afterwards T. C. Harrington appeared more eager than Redmond or any of the other Parnellites to bring about reunion. Harrington, in fact, frequently criticized Redmond and his colleagues for not doing enough to advance the cause of unity, and there were sometimes rumours that he might join the anti-Parnellites. It was fortunate, however, that he did not do so, for when negotiations eventually took place his more or less independent position enabled him to act as a link between the parties.

The need for reunion was more apparent in 1898-9 than it had ever been before, for with the widening of the division between Dillonites and Healyites neither of these factions nor the Parnellites could raise sufficient funds for their parliamentary work or their organizations. Perhaps this was the main reason why many members of all factions became more willing to consider seriously the advisability of negotiations.

It was in October, 1898, in a speech at Glasgow that Dillon publicly proposed such a policy—what he suggested was a conference of five men nominated by him and five by Redmond. Redmond at first took no notice of this proposal, but the Limerick board of guardians, composed mainly of Parnellites, took up the work of encouraging negotiations. It made a number of practical proposals, and, by submitting them to other public bodies, obtained strong expressions of opinion from all parts of Ireland condemning the continued disunity of Nationalist forces. One of the proposals of the Limerick board of guardians was that there should be a con-

[27] *Ibid.,* Davitt to O'Brien, March 1, 1897.
[28] T. M. Healy, *Why Ireland is not Free* (Dublin, 1898), 140.

ference of all Nationalist members of Parliament. Dillon agreed to this proposal, but Redmond regarded it as impracticable, and suggested instead a modification of Dillon's original plan for a conference by the addition to it of five men nominated by Healy.

This was the stage which had been reached when Blake, in an important speech at Glasgow on December 11, 1898, described his views regarding the existing situation.[29] His remarks on this occasion proved that he, like Dillon and unlike O'Brien, continued to regard home rule as the dominating and vital question in Irish politics. But he spoke especially of the need for a reunion of Nationalist forces, without which home rule would never be attained. Though he agreed with O'Brien that the leaders of the parliamentary factions "could not make a union without the people" of Ireland, he believed that it was their responsibility to "set the seal to that union for which the people crave."

Speaking of the conference proposals which had recently been made, Blake expressed the opinion that the suggestion of the Limerick board of guardians for a conference of all Nationalist members should first be put into effect. If agreement were reached there on the desirability and principles of reunion, a meeting of a small number of Parnellite and anti-Parnellite representatives (similar to that proposed by Dillon) might then take place to arrange the details. Regarding Redmond's proposed modification of Dillon's plan by the addition of five men nominated by Healy, Blake thought that, in view of the unfortunate relations existing between Healy and Dillon, it would be better for the conferees to be nominated by the anti-Parnellite party rather than by Dillon. But although there was no doubt that some Healyites would be among them, Redmond's proposal was inadmissible, for it would involve the recognition of Healy as the leader of a separate party.

Blake expressed disappointment at the attitude of Redmond towards reunion. Commenting on a statement of Redmond's that, when certain conditions were met, he and his colleagues would not be found anxious to stand in the way of reasonable union, Blake said that it was not by agreeing "not to be anxious to stand in the

[29] Blake's speech is published in a pamphlet entitled "The Irish Situation," Speech at Glasgow, Dec., 1898 (Dublin, 1899).

way" that people came together. They wanted Redmond "to be anxious to find the way, to make smooth the rough places in the way, to walk in the way, and to press forward in the way of reunion." Nor was Blake encouraged by the attitude of Healy who had lately suggested that, since the question of leadership caused so much difficulty, the election of a party chairman should be abandoned. He had also recommended that Irish Nationalists should no longer ally themselves with a single political party in Britain, but should take a lesson from Irishmen in the United States, some of whom belonged to the Democratic and some to the Republican party. These remarks of Healy's led Blake to conclude that the former did not wish Irish Nationalists to be independent of British political parties, but to divide and attach themselves to one or the other. But so divided and attached the Nationalists would be powerless, and Blake could not see that a policy of non-election of a chairman and the division of Nationalist forces would make for unity.

So although Blake thought that negotiations should be attempted, the attitude of Redmond and Healy led him to fear they might at this time fail. In conclusion, he summarized his views on the existing situation:

Candidly speaking, I do not see that either of these gentlemen [Redmond and Healy] has as yet given signs of that cordial adhesion to reunion which is essential to success, and therefore I fear that a conference just now may fail.
On what, then, do I base my hope? On the growing strength of the popular demand, on the flowing tide of National sentiment, on the rise of a spirit of self-abnegation among leaders, which may prove by practical action, stronger than mere words, their whole-souled devotion to their country.
May the proof come soon! For I warn you that, though Ireland's cause be immortal, yet this like other phases of her struggle cannot last forever, nay, will not under existing conditions much longer live. And should it unhappily so end, I do not choose to conjecture by what weltering chaos it may be followed, or how many weary years of degradation may elapse ere we regain our present ground.

Not long after Blake's speech at Glasgow, another effort to encourage reunion was made by a representative group of Irishmen. At the invitation of the Limerick board of guardians, a convention of delegates from elective councils in Munster met in Limerick and resolved to summon a conference of all Irish Nationalist members of Parliament in an effort to bring about reunion. The convention appointed a committee to make the necessary preparations for this conference.

On January 31, 1899, at a meeting in Dublin, the Irish parliamentary party, in a resolution which was adopted unanimously, expressed its satisfaction with the work of the Limerick board of guardians and the Munster convention and its willingness to cooperate with the committee appointed by the latter.[30] Then, on February 7, at the sessional meeting of the party in London, Dillon took the step which he had been contemplating and Blake had been advising for more than a year. He declined re-election to the chairmanship, stating that, in the interests of reunion, he would "not be a candidate . . . for any office, in this or any other Irish Party during the continuance of the present Parliament." At the same time, he proposed and secured the unanimous adoption of a resolution adjourning the election of a chairman until the second Tuesday after the Easter recess "with a view to the holding of a Conference of Irish Nationalist members on the subject of reunion."[31]

The next step towards reunion was taken by the Parnellites, who considered the invitation of the Munster convention at a meeting on February 13. They decided that before replying to the invitation their secretary, Patrick O'Brien, should communicate with Sir Thomas Esmonde, senior whip of the anti-Parnellites, who was fulfilling the functions of chairman of that party while the post remained vacant. O'Brien was to suggest to Esmonde that an interchange of opinions should take place between representatives of

[30] For the text of the resolution, see Dillon Papers, Minutes of the Irish parliamentary party, Jan. 31, 1899.
[31] For the text of Dillon's resolution and speech, see *ibid.*, Feb. 7, 1899. At a party meeting on April 13, 1899, the election of a chairman was again postponed, this time until the sessional meeting of 1900. See Minutes of the Irish parliamentary party. It should be noted that, while Blake had advised Dillon's resignation, he was not in favour of postponing the election of a new chairman. He felt that some not too prominent member should hold the chair until reunion had been achieved. See Blake Papers, Blake to Dillon, Oct. 23, 1899.

the different parties to ascertain whether any basis of agreement could be reached and submitted to the proposed general conference.[32]

O'Brien wrote at once to Esmonde, but the anti-Parnellites did not hold a meeting to consider the Parnellite proposal until March 28, and during that interval no reply was sent to O'Brien. In an editorial published on March 18, the Healyite *Daily Nation* blamed this long delay on "the syndicate of politicians composed of Mr. Blake, Mr. T. P. O'Connor, Mr. Davitt, and others, who now control the affairs of the majority of the Irish Party, whose salaries they distribute." Since the unity conference summoned by the Munster convention was to be held on April 4, the choice of so late a date as March 28 for an anti-Parnellite meeting to consider the Parnellite proposal was indeed absurd. For even if the anti-Parnellites agreed to preliminary discussions between representatives of the parties, there would be hardly any time left before the unity conference to hold them. The *Nation*, however, placed the blame for the delay in the wrong quarter, and Blake was able to show that, although he was opposed to preliminary discussions, he had done all in his power to have an earlier date set for the anti-Parnellite meeting. When asked by the London correspondent of the *Freeman's Journal* about the allegations made by the *Nation*, Blake supplied him with a statement, which read in part:

> I beg to say that I belong to no syndicate, control no affairs, and distribute no salaries. I am but one of the rank and file of the Party, and am responsible only for my own action. But for that action I am ready to account.
> From the moment, about mid-February, when I heard of the Parnellite resolution, I have been constant in pressing on everyone who spoke to me on the subject the necessity of an early meeting. I had hoped that the meeting might be fixed by those concerned early in March. This failing I had hoped for the second week of March, but on the 8th March I was thunderstruck to hear that the 28th had been fixed.

In order to prove the truth of his assertions, Blake then quoted the text of a letter which he had written to Captain Donelan, the

---

[32] The details of the Parnellite proposal are contained in Dillon Papers, Minutes of the Irish parliamentary party, March 28, 1899.

whip in charge, on March 8, immediately after hearing this announcement. Blake had told Donelan that he had emphasized from the first the need for an early meeting to deal with the Parnellite proposal. Having now heard of the choice of a date just before the adjournment for the Easter recess, he wished to say that he thought it "far too late either to obtain any proper representation of our Party or to dispose in a timely and effective manner of a suggested preliminary to the Recess Conference." Adding that the delay was placing their party in a false position before the Parnellites and the country, he declared that, though reserving his final decision, his "present mind" was against attending a meeting convened under such extraordinary conditions.

After stating that Donelan had told him of the transmission of his letter to the proper quarter, but that three days later the summons to the meeting had been issued, Blake closed his statement to the *Freeman's Journal* with the remark: "I hope I have shown that on whomsoever it must lie, no part of the responsibility for the transaction condemned by the *Nation* rests on me."[33]

T. P. O'Connor also told the London correspondent of the *Freeman's Journal* that he had had nothing to do with the fixing of the date of the anti-Parnellite meeting and that he understood the illness of Sir Thomas Esmonde had been the reason for the delay in holding it.[34]

When the anti-Parnellite party assembled on March 28, Patrick O'Brien's letter to Esmonde was read to the gathering. Thereupon, Arthur O'Connor proposed a resolution agreeing to the appointment of a committee to confer with representatives of the Parnellites. But Blake, who attended the meeting after all, moved and secured the passage of an amendment which, after expressing regret at the delay caused by Esmonde's illness, proposed that, if discussions between the parties at the unity conference showed it to be expedient, "any questions connected with any plan of reunion" might be referred for consideration and report to a smaller body composed of represen-

[33]*Freeman's Journal*, Dublin, March 21, 1899. In the Blake Papers is a copy of Blake's letter to Donelan, together with Donelan's reply, which is undated. Donelan told Blake that he had sent his letter to Esmonde.
[34]*Freeman's Journal*, Dublin, March 21, 1899.

tatives chosen by each party.³⁵ This was just the reverse of what the Parnellites had proposed.

The rejection by the majority party of the Parnellite proposal was communicated to Patrick O'Brien on April 1. The Parnellites were annoyed at this rejection, for they continued to think that the basis for union should be laid by a small number of representatives from each party, rather than at a meeting of all the Irish Nationalist members of Parliament. Doubtless, one of their reasons was that at a general conference they would be greatly outnumbered.

It was not surprising, in view of the Parnellite attitude, that Redmond and most of his followers absented themselves from the unity conference which met on April 4. Two Parnellites, J. J. O'Kelly and T. C. Harrington, did attend, however, and, in fact, the latter presided. Both sections of the anti-Parnellite party were well represented, a total of 53 being present.

Since the conference was composed mainly of anti-Parnellites, Sir Thomas Esmonde proposed and T. M. Healy seconded that it should appoint a committee to meet representatives of the Parnellite party and discuss with them conditions of reunion. But as this was really a repetition of the Parnellite proposal that the basis of unity should be laid by a small group of representatives of each party rather than by a general conference, it met with opposition from a large majority of those present. Even Harrington, although a Parnellite, declared that the conference, and not a committee, should propose terms. Esmonde's proposal was therefore rejected, and Dillon then suggested an alternative plan.

As it was generally felt that the conference should suggest the terms of unity, Dillon outlined a five-point plan, which had been framed by Blake.³⁶ The first of these points was that all Irish Nationalists should be reunited in one party on the principle and constitution of the old Parnellite party as it had existed from 1885 to 1890. Secondly, the reunited party was to be absolutely independent of all British political parties. Thirdly, the main object of

³⁵For the text of the resolution and amendment, see Dillon Papers, Minutes of the Irish parliamentary party, March 28, 1899.
³⁶Michael Davitt, *Fall of Feudalism in Ireland* (London and New York, 1904), 692–3. The *Freeman's Journal*, on Jan. 18, 1900, also mentions that the plan was drafted by Blake.

the united party would be to secure for Ireland a measure of home rule as ample as that embodied in the bills of 1886 and 1893. Fourthly, the party was also to fight on the old lines for the redress of all Irish grievances, notably those connected with the land, labour, taxation, and education. The fifth and final proposal read:

> That since a genuine reunion involves a real reconciliation we declare our view that all the adherents of a reunited party should accord to and receive from each other recognition and standing based on past public service to Ireland, absolutely irrespective of the course any adherent may have felt it his duty to take since the division of 1890; and that the reunited party and its adherents should exert all legitimate influence in favour of the adoption of this principle in the selection of candidates for parliamentary and party offices, and as the earliest practicable exemplification of the spirit of this resolution, this meeting, mainly composed of those belonging to the larger party, declares its readiness to support the choice of a member of the Parnellite Party as first Chairman of the United Party.

Each of these five proposals was put separately to the conference, and the first four were carried, apparently without discussion. There was, however, considerable controversy regarding the fifth. T. D. Sullivan, Healy's father-in-law, complained that it bound the united party to force its choice of a candidate on a constituency, regardless of the wishes of the constituency. Harrington, however, interpreted the words of the resolution otherwise. He explained to Sullivan that "the reunited party and its adherents" meant the party and its followers in the constituency, and that it was stated that they should exert all legitimate (not improper) influence. In order to settle the controversy, Blake suggested the insertion of the words, "fully recognising the right of every constituency to select its own candidate," making the portion of the resolution in question read ". . . that the reunited party and its adherents should, while fully recognising the right of every constituency to select its own candidate, exert all legitimate influence in favour of the adoption of this principle in the selection of candidates for Parliamentary and party offices. . . ." The change in wording settled the controversy and the first portion of the fifth proposal was carried unanimously. There was then some discussion about the portion dealing with the election of a Parnellite to the chair of the reunited party, but eventually it was adopted with only one dissentient.

The question of how this scheme for reunion should be presented to the Parnellites remained to be solved. Dillon, when outlining it, had proposed that those present at the meeting should express their readiness to attend a future conference for the purpose of discussing it or any other proposals which the Parnellites wished to submit. He had added that if the minority party refused to attend such a conference, the anti-Parnellites might consider any other means suggested for the purpose of bringing about such discussion.

When, however, the five proposals had been adopted by the conference, Healy again brought up the suggestion that a committee should be appointed to confer with representatives of the Parnellites, but he added that he did not wish to serve on it. Since the conference had now at least put forward a possible plan for reunion, Healy's proposal did not meet with so much opposition as had Esmonde's motion earlier in the proceedings. The chairman asked Dillon if he would accept it as a substitute for his motion, but, before he replied, Blake expressed the opinion that the general feeling of the conference was that it should terminate in the appointment of a committee. Dillon then agreed to accept Healy's suggestion, but expressed the wish that the latter should serve on the committee. The chairman appealed strongly to Healy to accede to this request, and Blake added that the whole practical chance of the proposal's success depended upon Healy's undertaking with the other members responsibility in connection with the committee. His position in the ranks of the Irish party and the country demanded it, and, moreover, it was known that the Parnellites would insist on his presence. Healy, however, still declined to act on the committee, although he promised to abide by its decisions. In view of his attitude, both Blake and Dillon also refused to serve, and in the end, the idea of a committee was given up, and Dillon's original resolution, proposing a future conference, was put to the meeting and carried unanimously.[37]

By their action at the unity conference, and especially by their proposal that a Parnellite should be chosen as the first chairman of the re-united party, the anti-Parnellites showed that they genuinely desired reunion. It appeared, however, at least at the beginning of the conference, that the Healyites were more anxious than the

[37] The foregoing account of the meeting is based on the report given in the *Freeman's Journal*, Dublin, April 5, 1899.

Dillonites to meet the Parnellites' demand that the main negotiations should be carried out by representatives of the parties rather than at a meeting of all Irish Nationalist members of parliament. But later in the proceedings, when Dillon and Blake expressed their willingness for a committee, it was really the attitude of Healy which made its appointment impossible.

In spite of the generous terms offered by the majority party, the Parnellites refused to consider them, mainly because they objected to discussing them at a general conference. Patrick O'Brien explained in a letter which appeared in the *Freeman's Journal* on April 8 that his party continued to believe that reunion could be brought about only by negotiations between a small group of representatives from each party.

In the months which followed, further attempts were made to bring about reunion. In May, the Rev. John Fitzpatrick, an Irish priest living in France, wrote to Dillon, Redmond, and Healy, suggesting that they join in inviting Sir Charles Gavan Duffy, the veteran Irish patriot who had been associated with "Young Ireland" and had later worked for land reform, to act as arbitrator in their dispute. Though Healy was in favour of the idea, Dillon refused to accept it, and Redmond felt that it would be well for representatives of all sections to consult on the basis of reunion before replying definitely to Father Fitzpatrick's proposal. So, some time later, Redmond wrote to both Dillon and Healy suggesting that a meeting of the anti-Parnellite party be called to appoint representatives of both its sections to confer with Redmond and a few of his friends. He added that if it were inconvenient to call a meeting he would be ready to confer with Dillon, Healy, and any friends they wished to name. Healy agreed to Redmond's plan, but Dillon rejected it, on the grounds that he was no longer a leader and that, in any case, he believed reunion could best be achieved, not by negotiations between the parties, but by the people of Ireland. Thus no meeting between representatives of the parties was held, and nothing came of Father Fitzpatrick's proposal.[38]

[38]For correspondence relating to Father Fitzpatrick's suggestion, see the *Irish Independent*, Dublin, July 29, 1899; also Denis Gwynn, *The Life of John Redmond* (London, 1932), 93.

Dillon's assertion that unity could best be achieved by the people of Ireland indicated an important change in his attitude. It is clear, in fact, that by the summer of 1899 both Blake and Dillon had come to accept O'Brien's view that there was more likelihood of reunion's being achieved through the efforts of the United Irish League than by direct negotiations between the parties. At the end of July, immediately before leaving for a short visit to Canada, Blake wrote to William O'Brien enclosing a subscription for the United Irish League fund, and stressing the importance of reunion and the work which he hoped the League would do in effecting it:

. . . I have ceased to hope for reunion through the exertions of Parliamentary leaders. The long continued efforts from within have now failed beyond remedy, and the people must work out their own salvation.
I believe that they realise this, and that, in the country at any rate, to the paralysis of dissension is succeeding a determination to achieve reunion.
But to this end organization is essential. Now, to revive as a truly National instrument any of the old institutions is hopeless. To multiply new ones is as impossible as it would be fatal.
But the United Irish League is founded on a principle so comprehensive, and has already done so much for reunion, that it seems to me the duty of every lover of the country to give it a helping hand.
Its extension over all Ireland, its development as the great National instrument, and the achievement by its means of a genuine, effective, and organised reunion, should be the immediate aim.
The task is difficult, the labour is arduous, the cost is great, the time is short, the event may be uncertain. But the object is supreme; it is our best hope, and the prospects justify the effort.[39]

O'Brien was naturally delighted with this change of attitude, for there could be no doubt that Blake's support of the League would have a beneficial effect on its progress. He therefore sent Blake's letter to the *Freeman's Journal*, which published it on August 3. With it appeared a letter from O'Brien, stating that when Blake, who had no responsibility for the origin of the divisions in the Irish party and no personal interest in continuing them, saw in the League's appeal to the people the only means of restoring unity, no one could suspect that sectional prejudice had anything to do with his conclusion.

Dillon expressed much the same view as Blake in a letter which he wrote to William O'Brien at the end of August: "To me, it is

[39]Blake Papers, Blake to W. O'Brien, July 28, 1899.

quite clear that the time for negotiations has gone by, and that the only safe way in which we can look for unity is for all to unite without reference to the past on the platform of the United League."[40]

Meanwhile, Healy, who was strongly opposed to the League, was attempting to negotiate with Redmond. According to Healy's own account of this period, Arthur O'Connor acted as a go-between, but he himself had two interviews with Redmond before the beginning of August. Apparently Healy wished these negotiations to remain secret, for he continues: "I had to conceal from the Dillon Party my friendly relations with Redmond and pretend to be hostile to the projects of reunion. I, therefore, treated them in a grudging spirit, while at the same time I was caucusing with Redmond and his friends."[41]

At least one member of the Irish party, Dr. M. A. MacDonnell, was impressed by Healy's efforts to bring about reunion. Writing to Blake several months later, MacDonnell declared: "In August last Mr. Healy appeared to me to be anxious for a settlement. He then told me he would work under J. J. Clancy as Chairman, if Clancy was acceptable to all sections of Nationalists, and if the Redmondites did not come in, he (Healy) would support you as Chairman and he felt sure you would have the support of all his friends."[42]

This was not the first time that Healy had suggested Blake as a possible chairman of the anti-Parnellite party. He had evidently made such a proposal before Dillon's first election to the chair in 1896, and from correspondence between Dillon and Blake in December, 1899, it appears that in February of that year, just before Dillon announced his resignation, Healy and his friends had been considering the expediency of proposing Blake against Dillon for the chair.[43]

Needless to say, it was not because he admired Blake that Healy desired to see him elected chairman. But he probably regarded him as less objectionable than Dillon, and felt that, if Blake were pro-

[40] W. O'Brien Papers, Dillon to O'Brien, Aug. 29, 1899.
[41] T. M. Healy, *Letters and Leaders of My Day* (London, 1928), II, 434–5.
[42] Blake Papers, MacDonnell to Blake, Dec. 15, 1899.
[43] See *ibid.*, Dillon to Blake, Dec. 21, 1899; Blake to Dillon, Dec. 24, 1899.

posed, some Dillonites might join the Healyites in voting for him. On the other hand, it would have been useless to nominate a Healyite, for all the Dillonites would have voted against him. That Blake understood Healy's motives can be seen from a comment which he made to Dillon. Referring to the three occasions on which Healy had evidently suggested his name, Blake wrote: "I attribute each of these proposals not to love for me, but to hate for you. Unfortunately, in politics, hate seems more persistent than love."[44]

It was as a result of his negotiations with Healy that on August 12 Redmond wrote to Jeremiah Jordan, P. J. Power, and Thomas J. Healy, secretaries of the April unity conference, asking them to appoint a small committee to meet him and a few of his friends.[45] Healy urged the secretaries to call a new conference for the purpose of selecting this committee. Naturally, Dillon and his friends were somewhat troubled at this turn of events, for it began to look as though a reunion might be effected between Parnellites and Healyites, leaving the Dillonites in the apparent position of being opposed to reunion. This would indeed have been a strange situation, in view of the fact that, since the time of the split, the Healyites had been fierce opponents of any compromise with the Parnellites, while Dillon and his supporters had been the champions of both unity in their own ranks and reunion with the minority party.

When Blake, who was by then in Canada, heard that Healy was trying to bring about a new conference, he wrote to Dillon that whatever stand he and his friends decided to take, "Healy's position, as having been the obstacle to the carrying out of this plan ... of a small private conference, should be emphasized over and over again." He added, however, that, although the calling of a new conference would place him, Dillon, and many others in an awkward position, there might also be difficulty for those who sought the new meeting:

One gain to be drawn out of so much trouble is that the men who now press for the conference, having begun their pressure just at the moment when you and I declared we had ceased to hope for any results from the M.P.s, will now occupy in any conference a position wholly different from that which they had arrogated to themselves with respect to a conference before. They will be, and it should be shown that they will be, mainly re-

---
[44]Ibid., Blake to Dillon, Dec. 24, 1899.
[45]For Redmond's letter, see Irish Independent, Dublin, Aug. 30, 1899.

sponsible for the conference, and they can no longer assume the attitude of waiters for, and criticisers of, somebody else's plan. . . .

In the same letter, Blake told Dillon that, while they could not refuse to attend such a conference, unless they wished to have their position misconstrued, an attitude of marked reserve and of doubt as to the soundness of summoning it was not merely permissible but necessary.[46]

Writing to Blake on October 2, Dillon told him that Davitt and two or three other members of their party whom he had consulted were hostile to the proposed conference because they feared an alliance between Healy and Redmond. Harrington, however, was strongly in favour of it, for he believed that if reunion were achieved it would be through the efforts of the parliamentary leaders, rather than through the United Irish League, which he regarded as merely a Connaught movement without anything in its programme to recommend it to the other provinces of Ireland. On October 6, after a definite decision to summon a conference had been reached, Dillon wrote again to Blake, announcing that although he was "at present disposed to have nothing to do with the Conference," his mind was open.[47]

After Blake's return to Britain later in October, he and Dillon discussed the question of attending the conference. It was known that the Parnellites, apart from Harrington, were not planning to attend, but this was understandable in view of the fact that the purpose of the conference was to select a committee to meet Parnellite representatives. Nevertheless, Dillon evidently believed that the absence of the Parnellites provided an adequate reason for him and his friends to stay away, for Blake, after their discussion, wrote to him:

> As to the conference—I think it impossible to justify non-attendance on the ground of Redmond's intention to be absent . . . Redmond has consistently insisted on a joint committee, as a preliminary; and he now invites those who met before in his absence to meet again and agree to his view. In such circumstances it seems absurd to object to his non-attendance.
> I think that our non-attendance will be open to much honest doubt, to great misconception and to virulent attack.

---

[46]Blake Papers, Blake to Dillon, Sept. 14, 1899.
[47]For both these letters, see Blake Papers.

And it is difficult to make clear to the man in the street why one should refuse to attend for the purpose of discussing the question and helping to a sound conclusion.
It is certain that many will place on the shoulders of the absentees the failure of the Unity negotiations. . . .

Thus, while admitting to Dillon that their position was a difficult one, he expressed the opinion that "there was much to be said for facing the music and dealing in public meeting with the proposal" (of appointing a committee). He added that, if they decided to absent themselves, it would be impossible within the limits of a letter of declinature to compress such an argumentative statement as would show fair grounds for non-attendance. So Blake's opinion was that their choice lay between attendance and unexplained absence. He concluded, however, that it would be absurd not to keep a free hand until events developed.[48] His general view seems to have been that, although there was now little likelihood of achieving unity through direct negotiations, it would nevertheless be unwise not to consider any proposals for unity which were put forward.

There appears to have been no further correspondence between Dillon and Blake until a week before the conference, which was held on November 23. By then (November 16) both men, Blake against his better judgment, had decided not to attend. They were still, however, considering whether they should write letters of declinature. On that day, Dillon wrote to Blake saying that if he (Dillon) sent a letter, he did not think it should be until the day before the conference, but he was still uncertain whether he should write a long letter defending his position, a short letter, or no letter. On this matter he asked the advice of Blake,[49] who replied that, since he had decided on non-attendance only in deference to Dillon's views, he found it impossible to draw up for him a letter defending that policy. As to the time of sending it, Blake's idea had been that the publication of Dillon's decision, if announced in advance, might influence some members. But the date of the conference was now so close that hardly any choice remained.[50]

[48]*Ibid.*, Blake to Dillon, Oct. 23, 1899.
[49]*Ibid.*, Dillon to Blake, Nov. 16, 1899.
[50]Dillon Papers, Blake to Dillon, Nov. 18, 1899.

Three days later, Blake again wrote to Dillon stating: "I am almost decided to send no letter myself to the Conference, but this decision obviously is reached on grounds which not merely do not apply, but rather point to another line as applicable to your case."[51] And finally, on the twenty-second, Dillon told Blake that he too had almost decided to send no letter, adding that, by some curious oversight, he had not received an invitation to the conference and therefore had nothing to which he ought to reply![52]

So, in the end, neither Dillon nor Blake wrote to the conference, and when it assembled on November 23 it was found to be mainly a Healyite gathering. The Parnellites, apart from Harrington, did not attend, while only five of Dillon's supporters—two of whom, having been secretaries of the April unity conference, had summoned this new gathering—were present. Patrick O'Brien, on behalf of the Parnellites, sent a letter explaining that "it must have been under some misapprehension that the invitation was sent to them," since the purpose of the conference was to appoint an anti-Parnellite committee to meet representatives of the Parnellite party.

A number of Dillon's supporters including T. P. O'Connor sent letters to the conference giving their reasons for non-attendance. O'Connor, after expressing his desire for reunion, stated that in his opinion the time for negotiations between parties had passed, since the people of Ireland had taken the question of reunion into their own hands. In building up a great popular organization, the United Irish League, they were providing a means whereby Nationalists of all sections could work together for the good of their country. Under these circumstances, O'Connor thought that the best course which Irish Nationalist members of Parliament could adopt towards reunion was "to throw themselves into the work of reorganizing the country."[53]

After these and other letters of declinature, together with Redmond's letter of August 12 requesting the appointment of an anti-

---

[51]*Ibid.*, Blake to Dillon, Nov. 21, 1899.
[52]Blake Papers, Dillon to Blake, Nov. 22, 1899.
[53]O'Brien's and O'Connor's letters are dated Nov. 22. For the full text of both, see *Daily Nation*, Dublin, Nov. 24, 1899.

Parnellite committee, had been read to the conference, Healy proposed that a committee should be named to confer with the Parnellites in an effort to bring about the reunion of the Irish National representation. His resolution was seconded by one of his supporters and, following a short discussion, it was adopted by the conference, P. J. Power alone dissenting.

The question of what members of the party should be named to the committee was then considered. There was some controversy as to whether members who were absent from the conference and could not therefore give their assent should be appointed. But since no prominent Dillonite was present, it was impossible to appoint a representative committee without the inclusion of some absent members. Healy therefore proposed that the committee should consist of T. C. Harrington, T. M. Healy, John Dillon, Edward Blake, Sir Thomas Esmonde, and Jeremiah Jordan.[54] This resolution, like the first, after being seconded, was adopted by the conference, P. J. Power again dissenting.[55]

For not attending the conference, Dillon and his followers were severely criticized. This was, indeed, not surprising, for while the Parnellites were justified in absenting themselves, those of the Dillonites who wrote letters of declinature to the conference gave no really adequate reason for their non-attendance. Their principal excuse was that the conference seemed unlikely to do any good and that reunion would eventually be brought about by the people of Ireland through the United Irish League. But even if they thought there was little likelihood that the conference would be successful, it would surely have done them no harm to attend it. Moreover, the main reason for the failure of the April conference to appoint a committee was the refusal of Healy to serve on it. But now, as Redmond pointed out in his letter of August 12, Healy was willing to serve on a committee. Thus an important obstacle to negotiations

[54]The fact that Harrington was on the committee appointed by the convention, rather than on the Parnellite committee which was named later, illustrates his position in relation to the two parties.
[55]The debates at the conference are fully reported in the *Daily Nation*, Dublin, Nov. 24, 1899.

between the parties had been removed. It was therefore difficult for the Dillonites to refute the charge made against them, that by refusing to attend the November conference they were acting inconsistently with their conduct in April. Of course, there was another reason—one which could not be stated in public letters—why they did not attend the November conference. This was their fear that if reunion were achieved, Redmond and Healy, who now seemed to be working together, might manage to control the party. But even if this were the case, with the country so eager to see its parliamentary representatives reunited, it would surely be better for Dillon to be a member of that party than to remain outside it where, as an apparent opponent of reunion, he would have no influence at all.

It was undoubtedly because he was deeply conscious of this situation that Blake had wished to attend the conference and had found it impossible to write a letter justifying his absence. But he did not think that his own decision not to write such a letter excused Dillon's failure to do so, and he was somewhat annoyed at Dillon's last-minute decision to remain silent. After hearing that the conference had appointed a committee to meet Parnellite representatives, he wrote to Dillon: "Your unexpected reversal, on the eve of the Conference, of the decision that you would write a refusal has created such a change in my situation that I fear I must consider whether I may not be driven, however reluctantly, to attend the committee."[56] To this Dillon replied that if he had had the slightest idea that his abstaining from writing could have such an effect, he would most certainly have written. He had not, however, been under the impression that Blake regarded his writing to the conference as a matter of vital importance. And finally, he stated: "Under all the circumstances, your attendance at the Committee would—so far as my judgment goes—be a great misfortune and very seriously aggravate the evils of the present situation."[57]

Correspondence between Blake and Dillon in the weeks which followed shows that they continued to disagree as to the proper course to take. Moreover, early in December, Dillon wrote to Jeremiah Jordan and Thomas J. Healy, secretaries of the November

[56] Dillon Papers, Blake to Dillon, Nov. 25, 1899.
[57] Blake Papers, Dillon to Blake, Nov. 26, 1899.

conference, advising them that he did not intend to act on the committee to which he had been appointed.[58] Blake, however, did not communicate with the secretaries at this time, and they, together with the conference chairman, wrote reminding him that he had been appointed to the committee.[59] In reply Blake stated that, even before the April conference, he had had little hope that reunion would be achieved through the efforts of parliamentary leaders. Nor had he believed that, in the temper of those leaders, a small committee consulting in private would make the best of the faint chances of success. Convinced that if a committee were to be appointed, it was essential that Dillon, Redmond, and Healy should all serve on it, he had withdrawn his name at the April conference when Healy declined to act on the committee. Now it was known that Dillon would not serve on the proposed committee, and Blake therefore declined to participate in its proceedings.[60] So, in spite of the disagreement between Blake and Dillon, both had now decided not to serve on the committee.

Notwithstanding the attitude of Dillon and Blake, the Parnellites, at a meeting held on January 3, 1900, unanimously agreed that three of their members—John Redmond, Patrick O'Brien, and J. P. Hayden—should meet the committee appointed by the November conference.[61] Redmond explained the reasoning of the Parnellites in a letter which he wrote to the conference chairman and secretaries. He declared that, under normal circumstances, the absence of Dillon and most of his colleagues from the November conference, together with the recent declarations of Dillon and Blake that they would not serve on the committee, would have led Redmond and his friends to proceed no further in the matter. But at this time conditions were not normal, and the outbreak of the Boer War made it especially important that all Irish Nationalists should be united. The Parnellites had therefore decided to send representatives to the proposed consultative gathering in the hope that, even if

[58]Reference to this is made in *ibid.*, Elizabeth Dillon to Blake, Dec. 13, 1899.
[59]*Ibid.*, Harrington, Jordan, and T. J. Healy to Blake, Dec. 20, 1899.
[60]*Ibid.*, Blake to Harrington, Jordan, and Healy, Dec. 23, 1899. The original is in the Harrington Papers.
[61]See *Irish Independent*, Dublin, Jan. 4, 1900.

permanent reunion could not be effected, united action might be secured at least during the next session of Parliament, when opportunities for serving Ireland, which might not soon recur, were likely to arise.[62]

The two committees finally came together on January 17, and, although both Dillon and Blake adhered to their decision not to attend the meeting, considerable progress was made towards reunion. The five-point plan which the April conference had submitted for the consideration of the Parnellites was now adopted by both committees as the programme of what they hoped would be a reunited party. Moreover, it was agreed that a joint meeting of Parnellites and anti-Parnellites should be held in London on January 30, at the beginning of the parliamentary session. Harrington, who had been chairman of both the April and November conferences and of the January 17 meeting of representatives, was authorized to summon this joint meeting.[63]

Dillon and Blake were now in a more awkward position than ever, for the plan of reunion adopted by the two committees was the very one which had been framed by Blake and proposed by Dillon at the April conference. If these two men now refused to accept their own plan, their action would appear most inconsistent to the country. Dillon, however, continued to fear that Redmond and Healy would control the reunited party, and was therefore still uncertain as to the best course to take. But Blake, who had stayed away from both the November conference and the January meeting of delegates out of deference to Dillon's views, determined to act on his own initiative and attend the joint meeting of the parties in London. So, without waiting for Dillon to reach a decision on the question and even before the invitations to the meeting had been sent out, he wrote a letter to the editor of the *Freeman's Journal* announcing his decision to attend. It began:

> Those of us who had been driven to the conclusion that Parliamentary leaders were not disposed to real conciliation and general reunion should be

---

[62]Harrington Papers, Redmond to Harrington, Jordan, and T. J. Healy, Jan. 3, 1900.
[63]See *Irish Independent*, Dublin, Jan. 18, 1900.

glad to see that the proposed performance by a small committee has been abandoned, that the attitude of ignoring or declining the proposals of the majority has been reversed, and that some acceptance has at last been vouchsafed of that most liberal basis which we long ago presented, and of our request for a general Conference with a view to reunion on its lines. No ampler vindication of the policy of the majority could be desired.

Blake went on to say, however, that he understood the acceptance of the plan was limited and that it diminished rather than eliminated the differences between the sections. But he supposed that any controversial questions would be brought up at the conference. He also mentioned that some temporary arrangement for provisional agreement during the next session had been foreshadowed and that he had little sympathy with this idea. Both reason and experience, he declared, had proved its futility.

Having expressed regret that the offers made at the April conference had not been "earlier and otherwise accepted," Blake remarked that he believed the change of attitude was due "to the course and pressure of events, not in Africa, but in Ireland, where the spread of the United Irish League is fast settling the question of reunion." Indeed, the political factions were so far discredited that they could no longer assume to lead, but must be content to follow the existing popular movement. To the League's programme, Blake went on, he had for many months stood publicly committed, and, since under it Ireland had become once more organized and united, he could not be a party to any act which might thwart its work. To do so, he believed, would be "to throw away the greater for the infinitely lesser chance of reunion." He preferred, however, to think that the present change, which he had attributed to the League, involved a recognition of that organization, rather than an attack on it. He assumed also that, as at the last two general conferences, the press would be admitted, for he was convinced that the parliamentarians should have no secrets from the people in this matter.

Having thus outlined his views on the existing situation, Blake concluded his letter with the following announcement regarding his attendance at the forthcoming conference in London: "On these assumptions I propose to attend the Conference, and to do what little I can towards the recognition, even at this eleventh hour, of the popular demand for genuine reunion."[64]

Blake's letter proved to be a decisive factor in completing the reunion of the parties, for it was the means of bringing both Dillon and T. P. O'Connor to the conclusion that they should attend the meeting. T. P. O'Connor appears to have strongly favoured Dillon's policy of staying away from the November conference and the committee meeting in January, and it was undoubtedly because of this that as soon as Dillon heard of Blake's letter to the *Freeman's Journal* he wrote to O'Connor on the subject. His letter shows very clearly the effect which Blake's action had upon him:

> ... The first I heard of his [Blake's] letter was in the Freeman office last night. His attitude, and the impossibility of coming to any working understanding with him is an important element in the situation. If we were to remain away from the meeting on the 30th, what would be our position during the session? Would we not hand over the whole parliamentary position absolutely into the hands of Redmond and Healy? And as we could not think of setting up any rival parliamentary party—or of holding meetings of our friends—the tendency would in my judgment be irresistible for our friends to drift into the ranks of the men who were holding meetings and conducting the Irish business.
> Then what would be our resources in regard to holding our own on the floor of the house, Blake having separated himself from us? It appears to me that the inevitable and logical consequence so far as I am concerned of remaining away from the meeting—specially after Blake's letter—would be to abandon attendance in Parliament and remain in Ireland. This is of course what O'Brien is working for, but it is a course I am resolved not to take. If I were to decide not to attend I should resign my seat. I have not finally made up my mind yet. But I am disposed to support Blake's attitude. His letter is a very able one, will do much good, and with the general lines of it I am in thorough accord.[65]

To this O'Connor replied: "When I saw Blake's letter last night, I saw at once that our hands were forced. It is a very able letter, as you say; and it marks out the lines on which, I think, we should go." He added that he had spoken to two other members of the party who agreed that Blake's letter forced the hands of Dillon and his friends and gave the right lines of strategy to be adopted by them

[64]For the full text of Blake's letter, dated Jan. 20, see *Freeman's Journal*, Dublin, Jan. 22, 1900.
[65]Dillon Papers, Dillon to T. P. O'Connor, Jan. 22, 1900.

at the conference.⁶⁶ Two days later Dillon again wrote to O'Connor: "I agree—Blake's letter makes it quite impossible for us to remain away from the meeting—and on the whole I am very glad he wrote it."⁶⁷

Thus, at last, all sections of Irish Nationalists were to be present at a conference, and although Redmond and Healy had played the leading part in the negotiations immediately preceding this meeting, Blake's role was also of considerable importance. Not only had he framed the plan which the committee meeting of January 17 had accepted as the basis for reunion, but he had also been responsible for bringing Dillon and O'Connor into the work of reunion.

A United Irish Party

Shortly after the conference of Irish Nationalist members of Parliament assembled on January 30, it was decided, as Blake had hoped, that the press should be admitted. When representatives of several Irish newspapers and English press agencies had entered, T. C. Harrington, as chairman, opened the main part of the proceedings. He began by thanking members of all sections for attending the conference and expressed the hope that the unhappy quarrel which had divided them in the past would now be brought to a close.

Redmond then spoke at considerable length in a most conciliatory manner, stating that he wished to avoid every possible topic of irritation and that, since he was not going to repudiate his action in the past, he did not ask any man to repudiate his. He voiced his acceptance of the plan for reunion put forward by the April conference, and said that he hoped the Irish Nationalist members would now constitute themselves into one party and lay down a good plan of campaign for the session which was just opening. But while expressing this desire, he did not assert that the five-point programme provided a complete scheme of reconstruction—he realized that other matters would have to be considered when the proper

⁶⁶*Ibid.*, T. P. O'Connor to Dillon, Jan. 23, 1900.
⁶⁷*Ibid.*, Dillon to T. P. O'Connor, Jan. 24, 1900.

time came, and urged, for instance, the holding at some suitable date of a national convention in Ireland to place the movement upon a sound foundation. Nevertheless, the reunion of all Irish Nationalists in one party ought to be the first step taken, and, with that in mind, Redmond proposed a resolution declaring the existing division at an end and proclaiming the formation of a united party under the constitution which had been in effect between 1885 and 1890.

After Redmond's resolution had been seconded by a Healyite, Dillon proceeded to address the conference. He said that he reciprocated the principle laid down by Redmond in his speech that if there were to be a useful reunion it would have to be based on a spirit of conciliation and on the determination of all Irish members to forget any harsh words spoken in the course of party struggles in the past. But having begun his speech in this conciliatory tone, he soon brought up a subject which might easily have divided the conference and delayed the reunion of the Irish parliamentary representatives. He said there was a feeling—which he shared to a considerable extent—among a number of his friends that some indication ought to be given, before the Irish members were reunited into one party, of the attitude which that party intended to adopt towards the United Irish League. When, however, he referred to violent attacks which had been made against the League, the chairman asked whether he thought any good purpose could be served by alluding to those attacks. Dillon insisted on speaking somewhat longer on the subject, saying that he feared the reunited party might take up a position in opposition to the League. Redmond denied that anything of the kind was contemplated by him.

After Dillon had completed his address, the chairman requested Healy to say a word upon the resolution. That gentleman, however, was unusually reticent on this occasion, stating simply that he was in favour of it. When the chairman told him that the conference would like him to trespass a little longer on its time, he replied that he had nothing further to say.

The chairman then proceeded to put Redmond's resolution to the meeting, but he was interrupted by J. F. X. O'Brien, who said that he did not want to be a party to any reconstruction scheme if the united party was to be antagonistic to the League. Thereupon Blake remarked that he was in the same position as O'Brien, but that he had not observed any antagonism. The chairman then declared that Blake had said precisely what he desired to say. A number of others, including T. P. O'Connor, expressed the opinion that there was no antagonism between Redmond's resolution and the League. O'Connor, in particular, spoke strongly in favour of the resolution, and, when he had completed his remarks, it was finally put to the meeting and carried unanimously.

Healy then proposed that the election of a party chairman be postponed for a few days, but that the whips be chosen at once. He moved the election of Sir Thomas Esmonde, Captain Donelan, and Patrick O'Brien to these offices. After this motion had been seconded, Redmond expressed his agreement with Healy's proposal that the whips be chosen immediately, since their services would be required from the beginning of the session. He added that he had no objection to the names suggested. There being no opposition to Healy's motion, the chairman declared it carried.

It having been pointed out that, with the passage of Redmond's resolution, the conference had become a party meeting, the chairman now intimated that further proceedings would be conducted in private, and the press accordingly withdrew.[68]

There is no record of what occurred after the withdrawal of the press, but a brief outline of two further meetings, held on February 1 and 2, is contained in the party minutes. At these meetings the parliamentary business of the session was discussed and the party's course of action decided. In addition to this, there was one resolution adopted at the meeting of February 2 which is of interest here. The following is an excerpt from the party minutes:

> A discussion having arisen concerning the future custody of the minute books, it was moved by P. A. McHugh, seconded by T. M. Healy, and resolved unanimously: "That the records of this Party and of the Committee be left in the custody of Mr. Blake and no access to them be accorded to any person until permission shall have been previously obtained at a meeting of the reunited Irish Party."

The meeting of February 2 is the last recorded in this minute book. Following the account of that meeting, however, there is a note to the effect that this volume of minutes and the other volumes were

---

[68] The foregoing account of the conference is based on the report given in the *Freeman's Journal*, Dublin, Jan. 31, 1900.

handed over to Blake on March 28, 1900. How long the minute books and any other party records entrusted to Blake remained in his possession has not been ascertained, for the minutes of later party meetings have not come to light.

One important question which remained to be settled after the meeting of February 2 was the election of the united party's first chairman. Although it had already been agreed that the office should be held by a Parnellite, there was much discussion behind the scenes as to which member of the minority party should be chosen. The Parnellites were so few that they could not hope to control the election, so the choice really lay with those who had been members of the majority party. Naturally, its leaders wished to secure a chairman who would not be too much of an autocrat and who might be influenced to a considerable extent by their advice. Moreover, as was to be expected, the Dillonites and Healyites were each anxious to prevent the other from exercising too much influence over the chairman.

From the time of Parnell's death, Redmond had been leader of the minority party, and he was now suggested as a possible candidate for the chairmanship of the united party. But the very fact that he possessed many of the qualities of leadership and had had wide experience as chairman of a party made some who desired a less able and independent leader oppose his candidature at first. Healy was strongly in favour of electing Redmond, undoubtedly because he believed the latter would accept his advice in preference to Dillon's. Dillon was not on good terms with Redmond, and would have preferred to see either Harrington or O'Kelly in the chair. Indeed, Harrington's work in reuniting the party gave him a strong claim to the chairmanship, for he had tactfully conducted the various conferences leading up to reunion and had also presided at the party meetings on February 1 and 2. However, a number of Dillon's friends felt that he was being unwise in opposing Redmond and urged him to change his course. William O'Brien did not wish Harrington to be elected, for he regarded him as a treacherous "friend" of the United Irish League and as a man who could bring no strength whatever to the movement. He felt that, if Redmond became chairman, his followers would probably fall in with the League, or at any rate cease to oppose it. Furthermore, O'Brien thought that Dillon could do more to kill Healyism by proposing Redmond for the chair or at least supporting his candidature than by dividing against him. Shortly before the election of a chairman took place, Davitt explained O'Brien's views to Dillon, adding that he (Davitt) had no confidence in Redmond, but had less in Harrington, and that the election of Redmond would undoubtedly be more acceptable to the country than would that of Harrington.[69] It was presumably the influence of O'Brien and Davitt which led Dillon to reverse his course and support Redmond.

Whether Blake, from the first, was in favour of Redmond's election is not clear. The only evidence on the subject is a statement of Healy's that Blake's breakaway from Dillon in January elected Redmond to the chair,[70] but it is doubtful whether this statement is accurate. Healy was probably thinking of Blake's letter to the press which had virtually forced Dillon to attend the conference on January 30. This action of Blake's had enabled reunion to take place, but had had nothing to do with Redmond's election.

At any rate, when, on February 6, a meeting of the united Irish party was held to elect its first chairman, it was Blake who proposed Redmond's name. His motion was seconded by Healy and carried unanimously.[71]

It is possible that Dillon, noting the advice of O'Brien and Davitt, but not wishing himself to propose Redmond, asked Blake to do so. But as there is no evidence on this subject it must remain a matter for conjecture.

The Party and the League

In the months following the reunion of the party and the election of Redmond to its chairmanship, the relationship between the party and the United Irish League caused much controversy among lead-

[69] Dillon Papers, Davitt to Dillon, n.d. (The postmark on the envelope is Feb. 4, 1900.) Healy states erroneously that O'Brien was in favour of Redmond's election because he was under the false impression that Healy was supporting Harrington. See Healy, *Letters and Leaders*, II, 444. It is clear from Davitt's letter that O'Brien knew that Healy was supporting Redmond.
[70] Healy, *Letters and Leaders*, II, 448.
[71] *Freeman's Journal*, Dublin, Feb. 7, 1900.

ing Irish Nationalists. As already seen, this question had threatened to mar the harmony of the proceedings of January 30, and it was one on which, following reunion, the distrust still existing among former political opponents was most apparent.

By the beginning of 1900 the United Irish League had become a most important organization. It was undoubtedly true, as Blake asserted in his letter to the press in January, that its extension had been largely responsible for bringing the political leaders to accept proposals for reunion. By then the League was very strong in the west of Ireland and was beginning to spread to other parts of the country. There was little doubt that it would become the national organization, for the Irish National Federation had continued to decay. Moreover, the Federation would have been unacceptable to many members of the reunited party as a national organization, since it had been founded by the anti-Parnellites and in the end been regarded as purely a Dillonite organization.

It was certain, therefore, that some decision would have to be reached regarding the part which the League would play in the national movement. Earlier national organizations had always been subordinate to the party, but just as there had been a widespread belief that the League, and not the politicians, should take the lead in bringing about reunion, so now there were some who thought that the League should predominate over the party in the national movement. O'Brien, of course, took this view of the situation, and Dillon, because he still feared the power of Redmond and Healy in the party, supported him. But had it not been for this fear, Dillon would undoubtedly have favoured the supremacy of the party as he had during his earlier career.

Redmond, in the days before reunion, had had nothing to do with the League, but immediately after his election to the chair of the united party, he wrote to O'Brien expressing his desire to work in harmony with him.[72] There was much correspondence between them in the months which followed, and O'Brien believed that Redmond was sincere in desiring to forward the work of the League. Dillon, on the other hand, suspected that he was, at heart, an

[72] The letter, dated Feb. 10, 1900, is quoted in Gwynn, *Life of Redmond*, 95.

opponent of the League and would do his utmost to establish the supremacy of the party. At the conference of January 30, Redmond had proposed the holding of a national convention to consolidate reunion and place the movement on a sound foundation. This convention was to be under the auspices of both the party and the League, and Redmond was anxious that it should meet as soon as possible. Dillon, however, was afraid that Healy, because of his antagonism towards the League, would persuade Redmond to attempt to have the convention controlled by those in opposition to it. He was therefore opposed to the holding of a convention until Redmond had given definite proof of his support of the League. O'Brien, although more trustful of Redmond, was also inclined to take this view.

On March 23, the question of holding a national convention was discussed at a meeting of the Irish party in London. The next day, the *Freeman's Journal* reported simply that the fifty-five members who attended this meeting unanimously accepted a resolution recommending that a convention be held "if possible at Whitsuntide" and that a committee of the party be appointed to confer with the League and report to the party on the subject.

It is clear, however, from a letter which Dillon wrote to O'Brien that, although the resolution was unanimously adopted, there was much controversy regarding it which was not revealed to the press. Dillon told O'Brien that he had objected to the mention of any date in the resolution and that he thought this had also been the general feeling of the meeting. When, however, Redmond stated that O'Brien had said he saw no objection to holding the convention at Whitsuntide, Dillon was "jumped upon by Blake and Harrington," who asked whether after this important statement he could reasonably object to the date's being mentioned. Finally, Blake suggested as a compromise that the words "if possible" be inserted. Dillon, though adhering to his own views, agreed to accept this, but Healy, all the time "snarling and carping" at the League, moved the omission of Blake's words. After "somewhat acrimonious debate," in which Harrington and Blake opposed him rather violently, Healy was induced to withdraw. It was then that the resolution, as amended by Blake, was adopted. Dillon also wrote that the committee proposed in the resolution was appointed at this meeting and consisted of: John Redmond, Edward Blake, T. C. Harrington, J. F. X. O'Brien, Patrick O'Brien, W. Abraham, and Captain Donelan. Dillon explained that he had declined to serve because he would have had little or no support on the committee and because he did not believe in the policy of allowing the convention to be held so soon. Finally, Dillon told O'Brien that he believed there was an understanding between Redmond and Healy and that the object of hurrying on the convention was to take the movement in Ireland out of O'Brien's hands and to put Redmond at the head of it.[73]

In his reply to Dillon's letter O'Brien stated that the resolution adopted at the party meeting was a miserable compromise and that Redmond should have explained that he (O'Brien) had agreed to the holding of a convention at Whitsuntide only on the condition that Redmond would "throw himself heart and soul into the League work in the meantime."[74]

At this time and in the months which followed, Blake, though taking a rather moderate stand between the two sides in the dispute, appears to have been on better terms with Redmond than with Dillon. There is no record of any correspondence between Dillon and Blake during the first half of 1900—this in itself suggests some disagreement—but from letters which Dillon wrote to O'Brien it can be seen that the former now regarded Blake as a friend of the party rather than of the League. Late in March, Dillon warned O'Brien that Redmond, in order to prevent the domination of the party by the League, wanted to be president of the latter organization, and added: ". . . As you apparently have not offered him that position, he will of course endeavour so to arrange the Convention that, with the assistance of Healy, Harrington and Blake, he may be then nominated head of the League or the new National organization then started."[75] In another letter, while considering the composition of the committee which had been named by the party to meet the executive of the League, Dillon remarked to O'Brien: ". . . You will have against you a very formidable trio—

[73]W. O'Brien Papers, Dillon to O'Brien, March 24, 1900.
[74]Ibid., O'Brien to Dillon, March 26, 1900.
[75]Ibid., Dillon to O'Brien, March 28, 1900.

Redmond, Blake and Harrington—Blake will support Redmond and go for conciliation with Healy."[76]

From these statements of Dillon's, it is evident that he believed he and O'Brien were opposed in their plans for the League not only by Healy, who was openly antagonistic, but also by Redmond, Blake, and Harrington, who professed to be friendly towards that organization. While Redmond and Harrington had never had the faith of O'Brien and Dillon in the League, Blake had, for many months before reunion, regarded it as the most important power in nationalist Ireland. Thus, it would have been strange if he had now taken a stand in opposition to it, and, indeed, it is not likely that he did so. Blake's position was probably similar to O'Brien's; that is, he trusted Redmond and believed him to be sincerely desirous that a satisfactory understanding should be reached between the party and the League. It seems improbable that Blake would have gone in for conciliation with Healy, at any rate on the question of the party's relations with the League—Dillon himself had admitted that Blake had opposed Healy when the latter criticized the League at the party meeting of March 23.

Further correspondence between Dillon and O'Brien indicates that for some time Dillon continued to distrust Redmond, mainly because the latter was still on good terms with Healy. O'Brien, though not sharing Dillon's distrust of Redmond, believed that, in order to work with him, it would be necessary to break up his alliance with Healy. What he would have liked was closer co-operation between Dillon and Redmond, thus leaving Healy without any support. This, however, was difficult to attain, for Dillon believed that Redmond and Healy were so closely allied that it would not be possible to separate them. Moreover, it was not easy for Redmond to break away from Healy and identify himself completely with the League, as O'Brien desired, because Healy had been very helpful in the negotiations of the previous year and also because Redmond was anxious for an amalgamation between the *Irish Independent,* which was in serious financial difficulties, and the Healyite *Daily Nation.* Nevertheless, O'Brien did his best, before the meeting of the convention, which was finally set for June 19, to bring about

[76] *Ibid.*, Dillon to O'Brien, April 15, 1900.

better relations between Redmond and Dillon. When Dillon continued to complain that Redmond wished to be president of the League,[77] O'Brien replied that, if Redmond behaved well, he (O'Brien) saw no very great difficulty about his getting the honour if he cared for it.[78] In attempting to improve relations between Redmond and Dillon, O'Brien was aided by T. P. O'Connor, who shared his views on this matter and believed that Redmond's election to the presidency of the League was desirable.[79] The advice of O'Brien and O'Connor finally produced an effect upon Dillon, for, a few days before the convention met, he agreed that if it were decided to propose Redmond as its chairman, he (Dillon) would be prepared to second the nomination. He really thought, however, that it would be better for the proposing and seconding to be done by members of the committee which had arranged for the convention.[80] In agreeing to support Redmond if he were nominated for the chairmanship of the convention, Dillon was practically admitting that he would not oppose the election of the leader of the Irish party to the presidency of the League.

When the convention assembled on June 19 and it was proposed by one of the clerical delegates that Redmond should take the chair, Dillon, in accordance with his agreement, seconded the motion, which was then carried unanimously. On the first day of the convention, two important questions were settled. First of all, the United Irish League was officially recognized as the national organization, taking the place of the National Federation, the National League, and the People's Rights Association, which had all been sectional. Secondly, Redmond was elected president of the United Irish League, a move to which Dillon offered no opposition. The remainder of the first day's proceedings and those of the second day were devoted to a discussion of the constitution and programme of the United Irish League. The constitution, which had been drawn up mainly by O'Brien, was dealt with and adopted clause by clause.

[77]*Ibid.*, Dillon to O'Brien, April 5, 1900.
[78]Dillon Papers, W. O'Brien to Dillon, April 6, 1900.
[79]See *ibid.*, T. P. O'Connor to Dillon, June 12 and 13, 1900.
[80]W. O'Brien Papers, Dillon to O'Brien, June 16, 1900.

It left no doubt that the League, and not the party, was to be the dominant partner in the national movement.

Speaking on the second day of the convention Blake complained of the nature of the representation afforded to the party in the government of the League. The sixth and seventh clauses of the constitution provided as the League's supreme governing body, a National Directory, which was to be appointed according to a scheme drawn up by the members of the four Provincial Directories, together with the chairman and officers of the Irish parliamentary party. But until the election of a Directory for all the provinces of Ireland, the general government of the League was to be administered by the members of the Provincial Directories already appointed, or which might be appointed, together with the chairman and officers of the party. Blake asserted that either the government of the League should be left entirely in the hands of its own delegates and officers, or, if the party were to be joined to them, it should be with equal numbers. But the proposal under consideration was to add nine members of the party to eighty or ninety from the League. Blake remarked that he happened at the moment to be an officer of the Irish parliamentary party (he was one of the treasurers during the year 1900) and looked at the question from that point of view. If the League were to be governed by its own executive, it should appoint its own executive, but if the party were to be given a portion of the responsibility it should have equal representation. Otherwise, it would not be able to exercise a potent influence by voting at the deliberations of the Directories.

Some of the speakers who followed Blake, notably William O'Brien, expressed their disagreement with him on this matter. O'Brien stated his belief that the party should be subordinate to the League. Remarking that the objection had been raised that the party was not, under the proposed constitution, to have the same predominant power as it had once had in the management of the national movement, he declared that this was quite true and he believed it to be a salutary and absolutely inevitable arrangement. But he added that the representation was not so disproportionate as Blake suggested, in view of the fact that members of the party might also be members of the League. Later in the proceedings Blake explained that he had not asked for a preponderance of the party; what he desired was not preponderance but equality. In spite of his protests against the two clauses they were adopted.

It would appear from Blake's statements that, as already suggested, the stand which he took was a moderate one—he wanted the party and the League to be equal partners in the national movement. The fact that a reunion of Irish parliamentary forces had been achieved evidently led him to have more faith in the party than he had had during the last six months of 1899.

Towards the end of the proceedings, Blake again addressed the convention, proposing the following resolution: "That the Nationalist candidate for Parliament be chosen by a Divisional Convention called for the purpose; that no candidate be adopted save on the condition of adhesion to the old Party pledge; and that unless asked by the Divisional Executive or the Convention no suggestion as to candidates be made by any central organisation." This resolution, like Blake's previous speeches, indicated the middle of the road position which he was now taking towards the relationship between the party and the League. While he wished to ensure that all Nationalist candidates should pledge themselves to "sit, act, and vote" with the Irish party, he also wanted to prevent unasked for interference by any central organization of either the party or the League. The resolution, together with another one concerning the payment of members, which Blake proposed in conjunction with it and which will be examined in the next chapter, was adopted by the convention.[81]

The proceedings at the convention did much to establish better relations between Redmond and Dillon and to break up the alliance between the former and Healy, for while Redmond had now definitely identified himself with the League, and, with the approval of Dillon, had become its president, Healy continued to oppose it. He took no part in the "O'Brien convention," as it was termed on June 21 by the *Daily Nation*, and refused to disband the People's Rights Association. Although Redmond and Healy remained on

[81]For a full report of the proceedings at the convention, see *Freeman's Journal*, Dublin, June 20 and 21, 1900.

fairly good terms for some time longer, it will be seen that, by the end of 1900, their alliance had been broken.

The general election which took place in the autumn of 1900 showed more plainly than any other event that the League, and not the party, was now the dominant partner in the national movement. In 1892 and 1895, it was a committee of the party which directed the election campaign; now, however, the League's National Directory, which had been established some time after the June convention, performed this task. It drew up rules for the selection of candidates in the constituencies, including the provisions made in Blake's resolution adopted at the convention. Thus, the National Directory did not take over all the powers of the old party committee, for much more freedom was now allowed to the constituencies. The work of summoning and arranging for conventions was done by local League officials, and all that the National Directory did was appoint one representative to attend each convention as an observer; he was to offer no advice regarding the selection of candidates unless requested by the convention to do so.[82]

Although Healy had always posed as the champion of the freedom of the constituencies and had been the principal objector to the system of committee control of the elections, it was he and his followers who now opposed the new system established by the League. In the election of 1900 Healy refused to recognize the conventions summoned under the auspices of the League, and, in a number of constituencies, put forward candidates of his own. But the fact that all the Healyite candidates, except Healy himself, were defeated by official League candidates indicated the strength of the new national organization throughout Ireland.[83] One specific example of its power was the defeat in Cork City of Healy's brother, Maurice, by William O'Brien, the founder of the League, who now, after an absence of more than five years, returned to the House of Commons.

With Healy now standing alone, the party leaders decided that it would be safe to take the step which many of the anti-Parnellites

[82]For a complete list of the rules drawn up by the National Directory, see Lyons, *Irish Parliamentary Party*, 151–2.

[83]Blake was in Canada when Parliament was dissolved in September and did not return to Britain until the election campaign was almost over. He did not, therefore, take part in it, but was re-elected for South Longford.

would have liked to take several years earlier. At a national convention held in Dublin in December, 1900, Healy, because of his action during the general election campaign, was expelled from the Irish parliamentary party. The motion of expulsion, which was moved by William O'Brien, had the support of Dillon. Harrington, however, strongly opposed it, while Redmond, the chairman, expressed his personal disapproval, but added that he would accept the verdict of the convention.[84] Thus, the alliance between Redmond and Healy, which had been weakening for several months, was now completely broken, and, with the Healyite influence removed from the party, the unity which existed in Nationalist ranks was more cordial than it had been during the preceding months.

[84]*The Annual Register, 1900,* p. 253.

IX. IRISH NATIONALIST ACTIVITIES, 1900-2

Imperial Issues

IN THE EARLY MONTHS of 1900, Irish Nationalist members of Parliament were confronted with a number of current imperial questions, the most important of which was probably the Boer War which had begun in October, 1899. It was not the first time since Blake entered the British House of Commons that the situation in South Africa had given rise to serious problems. At the end of 1895, the Jameson raid into the Boer republic of the Transvaal had precipitated a crisis and in the ensuing inquiry Blake had a considerable part.

There was, at the time of the raid, much disaffection among the Uitlanders, as the foreign residents of the Transvaal were known. These Uitlanders, the majority of whom were British, had entered the Boer republic following the discovery of gold in its territories. By 1895, they numbered about 60,000, and their complaint was that they were denied all the rights and privileges of self-government by the Boers, who numbered only 15,000. In that year, the Uitlanders were planning to stage some sort of uprising against what they regarded as a most unsatisfactory state of affairs. It appears, however, that what some of them wanted was an "absolutely bloodless revolution."[1]

News of a proposed uprising reached Cecil Rhodes, the internationally known English mining magnate in South Africa, who hoped to see the federation of the two Boer republics of the Transvaal and the Orange Free State with the two British possessions in South Africa, Cape Colony and Natal. In addition to being Premier of Cape Colony at this time, Rhodes was managing director of the British South Africa Company and director of the De Beers Consolidated Mines and the Gold Fields of South Africa. On hearing of the projected uprising, Rhodes secretly offered the Uitlanders the aid of the armed forces of the British South Africa Company.

[1] J. A. Spender, *The Life of the Right Hon. Sir Henry Campbell-Bannerman* (London, 1923), I, 190.

A large force of mounted police was to be drawn up along the Transvaal border on a strip of land recently acquired by the company for the extension of the Capetown-Kimberley railroad into Rhodesia. When the uprising in Johannesburg occurred, this force, commanded by L. S. Jameson, a Scottish doctor who was the company's administrator, would invade the Transvaal and go to the aid of the Uitlanders.

Late in December, 1895, while Jameson's force was on the Transvaal border waiting for the signal to cross it, a dispute arose among the Johannesburg Uitlanders regarding the use of the British flag. Those among them who were not British did not wish the new régime which they sought to establish in the Transvaal to be under British rule. Rhodes, on learning of this quarrel believed that the movement had collapsed and that a raid into the country would be useless. But Jameson, although he had heard discouraging news from various sources, received no message from Rhodes himself. He therefore decided to act on his own initiative, and, on December 29, without waiting for instructions, invaded the Transvaal.

The raid was a complete failure. Jameson and his men were stopped before they reached Johannesburg and forced to surrender to the Boers. Both the Colonial Secretary, Joseph Chamberlain, and the British High Commissioner at the Cape, Sir Hercules Robinson, condemned the raid, which they asserted had been made without their knowledge or authority,[2] and a select committee of the House of Commons was appointed in 1896 to inquire into its origin and circumstances. Among the fifteen persons on this committee were prominent members of both the government and the opposition, including Joseph Chamberlain, Sir Michael Hicks-Beach, Sir Henry Campbell-Bannerman, and Sir William Harcourt. Blake was named to the committee as the representative of the Irish party. Since the committee was appointed late in the parliamentary session, it did very little in 1896, but, at the beginning of the next session, early in 1897, it was reappointed and, beginning its work in February, sat for five months.

[2]For a detailed account of the raid and the circumstances surrounding it, see Jean van der Poel, *The Jameson Raid* (London, 1951).

Before the select committee began its sittings, the Parliament of Cape Colony had held an inquiry of its own into the raid. Those taking part in the inquiry had concluded that Jameson, in starting when he did, had acted on his own initiative, but that Rhodes was an active instigator of the Johannesburg conspiracy and had intended Jameson's force to be used in its support at the proper moment.

In the course of the British inquiry, most of the Liberal members of the committee appeared anxious to prove that the British South Africa Company had, under Rhodes's advice, contrived the uprising in Johannesburg to advance its material interests. Henry Labouchere and Blake, in particular, took this view of the situation.[3] Blake's main contribution to the work of the committee was his masterly cross-examination of Rhodes, the worth of which was widely recognized in the British and American press.

While the inquiry was going on, there were persistent rumours that Chamberlain and the Colonial Office had known in advance about the raid and that certain telegrams, sent from London to Capetown before it took place, contained evidence to this effect. The committee sought the production of these telegrams, and forty-four out of a series of fifty-one were produced. The remaining seven were, however, withheld at Rhodes's order, and naturally, in the eyes of the general public, this gave rise to the suspicion that they were the incriminating ones.[4] Most of the members of the committee, however, including both the Unionists and the leading opposition representatives, Campbell-Bannerman and Harcourt, did not regard the withholding of these telegrams as a very serious matter, and were satisfied that Chamberlain and the Colonial Office had not been implicated. Only Blake and Labouchere took a different view of the situation. On the ground that, in the absence of the seven telegrams, the inquiry was incomplete, Blake not only refused

[3]*Annual Register, 1897*, p. 83.
[4]For an attempt to vindicate Chamberlain by publishing excerpts from the missing telegrams, see J. L. Garvin, *The Life of Joseph Chamberlain* (London, 1934), III, 110–113. But see also Ethel Drus, "A Report on the Papers of Joseph Chamberlain Relating to the Jameson Raid and the Inquiry" (*Bulletin of the Institute of Historical Research*, May, 1952). In this article Garvin's arguments are refuted.

to take part in considering the report of the committee, but also withdrew altogether from that body.[5] Labouchere submitted a report of his own, in which he asserted that, owing to the absence of the telegrams and the reluctance of some witnesses to tell all they knew, the inquiry was incomplete and it was therefore possible to draw conclusions only from the evidence which had been obtained. After strongly condemning the conduct of Rhodes, Labouchere admitted that there was no evidence to prove the alleged complicity of the Colonial Office in the raid, but he expressed regret that this question had not been thoroughly investigated.[6]

The select committee's report, which was signed by the remaining thirteen members, condemned the raid and severely censured Rhodes, but acquitted Chamberlain and the officials of the Colonial Office.[7] But among the public there was much dissatisfaction with the situation, especially after the government decided not to punish Rhodes and, during the Commons debate on the committee's report, very little was said against Rhodes by the members of the committee. It was naturally regarded as somewhat peculiar that the men who had censured Rhodes in their report should refrain from doing so in the House of Commons and there were suspicions that something was being kept secret.

Although the Boer War did not begin until October, 1899, the Jameson raid was directly responsible for it. That raid had naturally angered the Boers and united them firmly against the British. And, at the same time, it had made the position of the Uitlanders worse than ever. In March, 1899, they appealed to the British government to intervene on their behalf, and, in the months which followed, complicated negotiations took place between the British and Transvaal governments. But, in October, upon receipt of an ultimatum from Paul Kruger, President of the Transvaal, the British government declared war.

[5] *Annual Register, 1897*, p. 158.
[6] For a summary of Labouchere's report, see Algar Thorold, *The Life of Henry Labouchere* (London, 1913), 429–31. In the course of describing Labouchere's work on the committee, Thorold remarks: "Mr. Labouchere found his chief support in Mr. Blake, but even he fell off towards the end. . . ." See *ibid.*, 427.
[7] For a list of the report's conclusions, see *Annual Register, 1897*, pp. 162–3.

The war, in which the Transvaal was joined by the other South African Boer republic, the Orange Free State, did not have the unanimous support of the British Parliament. Some of the Liberals, notably Morley, felt that it should have been avoided, though other members of that party, including Rosebery, thought otherwise. The principal critics of the war were, however, the Irish Nationalists, and it will be remembered that Redmond had regarded the outbreak of the war as one of the principal reasons why an attempt should be made to reunite all Irish Nationalists.

The day after he was elected leader of the reunited Irish party, Redmond proposed an amendment to the address in reply to the speech from the throne, stating that the time had come to recognize the independence of the Transvaal and the Orange Free State and bring the South African war to a close. In the speech which he made on this occasion, Redmond declared frankly that the sympathy of Ireland was with the two South African republics. Referring to the charge made in some quarters that Ireland knew nothing of the merits of the case and sympathized with the Boers simply because they too were against the British, Redmond, though admitting that his country's attitude was partly due to its antagonism to England, claimed that Ireland would be on the side of the republics no matter what power was attempting to oppress them.[8] The amendment did not receive any support outside Redmond's party and was defeated by 368 to 66 votes.[9]

Although Blake did not take part in the debate on this amendment, he joined the Irish Nationalist members in voting for it. In doing so, he made himself decidedly unpopular among English-speaking Canadians, whose sympathies were on the side of the British. Conservative and independent journals in Canada took advantage of the opportunity to criticize him, saying that he had never done anything which met with such general condemnation in Canada as in voting for the Redmond resolution, and that his loyalty to his home rule colleagues surely had not placed him under

[8]For the text of the amendment and Redmond's speech, see *Hansard*, 4th Series, LXXVIII, 830–43.
[9]*Ibid.*, 892.

any obligation to vote as he had.[10] But many Canadian Liberals also were displeased with Blake's action, and some of them wrote letters rebuking him. One correspondent, who described himself as "an Irish Canadian and a Canadian Liberal," told Blake that his course as a Canadian Irishman had alienated thousands of his friends in Canada,[11] while another remarked that it was with "heartfelt pity" that the loyalists of Canada had read of Blake's support of Redmond's "infamous resolution."[12]

From the remarks of some Canadians it might be inferred that they believed Blake had voted for the Redmond amendment merely because his Irish colleagues had done so. In view of this attitude, it is important to understand his personal opinion regarding the war and the stand of the Irish party upon it. He expressed his views very plainly in a letter to a friend in New Zealand:

> I was always conscious, as, I believe, indeed, were most Irishmen, of the injury (more or less temporary, I hope,) to the cause of Home Rule which would be done by an Irish Nationalist opposition to the war. Nevertheless, I personally believe (as I apprehend did almost all Irish Nationalists, and, as I know, a very large number of Irish Conservatives) that the war was both unjust and in the highest degree impolitic. Accordingly I felt no difficulty in agreeing in the general judgment of the Nationalist Party. At the same time, my own opinion on which I acted, and, as far as I could, insisted, was that our views should be expressed without extravagance of language, and in terms which, though unmistakable, should not needlessly add to the disfavor in which their expression would plunge the Nationalist Cause.[13]

Two weeks after Redmond's suggested amendment was defeated in the House of Commons, a Liberal member proposed that the inquiry into the Jameson raid should be reopened.[14] Several of the men who had been members of the South Africa committee, including Sir William Harcourt, Henry Labouchere, and Blake, spoke in favour of this motion. In his address, Blake pointed out that it was only within the last few months that the country had realized the gravity of the issues involved in the Jameson raid and that those

[10]*News*, Toronto, Feb. 9, 1900. See also *ibid.*, Feb. 12, 1900 and *Mail and Empire*, Toronto, Feb. 12, 1900.
[11]Blake Papers, Joseph Connors to Blake, Feb. 10, 1900.
[12]*Ibid.*, R. E. A. Land to Blake, Feb. 11, 1900.
[13]*Ibid.*, Blake to Hon. Morgan Grace, Sept. 27, 1900.
[14]*Hansard*, 4th Series, LXXIX, 599.

issues would not end even with the close of the war since it would be necessary to rehabilitate affairs in South Africa. Thus, it was important that the inquiry into the raid should be complete, and he asserted that it had not been so in 1897 because all the necessary materials for judgment had not been obtained.[15] The proposal that the inquiry should be reopened was, however, defeated by 286 to 152 votes.[16]

There were other occasions on which Irish Nationalists expressed their sympathy with the Boers, for peace was not restored until May, 1902. But since it was clear long before then that the Boers had been defeated, interest in the war was not so intense during its closing stages.

It has been seen that, in the months following the reunion of the party, Blake was on better terms with Redmond than with Dillon. That Redmond regarded Blake's advice to be of considerable importance is evidenced by an incident which occurred early in 1900, when it was announced that Queen Victoria was planning to visit Ireland. Although it was made plain that her visit, to take place in April of that year, was not prompted by political motives, extremists in Ireland wished to boycott it, and Redmond, as leader of the Irish Nationalists, was undecided as to the attitude he and his party should adopt. He therefore sought the advice of Healy, who suggested that he should take the stand that, politics aside, the Queen was a venerable lady to whom not even an extremist could be discourteous. According to Healy, Redmond hesitated but promised to consult Blake. Shortly afterwards, Blake met Redmond and Healy to take counsel as to the reception of the Queen, and, on Blake's advice, Redmond accepted Healy's view that he should welcome the royal visit.[17] So, in a brief statement to the House of Commons, Redmond announced that the Irish people would "treat with respect" the Queen's visit, knowing that no attempt would be made to give it a party significance, and that their hospitality would not be taken to mean any abatement of their demand for national rights.[18]

[15]For Blake's speech, see *ibid.*, 660–73.
[16]*Ibid.*, 696.
[17]T. M. Healy, *Letters and Leaders of My Day* (London, 1928), II, 448.
[18]*Hansard*, 4th Series, LXXX, 402–3.

Dillon's opinion on this subject differed from that of Redmond, Healy, and Blake. In a letter to William O'Brien, he expressed his annoyance at what he termed Redmond's "crawling statement" in the House of Commons on the subject of the Queen's visit.[19]

In May, 1900, a Commonwealth of Australia Constitution Bill was introduced into the House of Commons by the Colonial Secretary, Joseph Chamberlain. This bill sought to establish a federal union of the Australian states. In its original form it had been drawn up by a convention of the Australian state governments and approved by the legislatures of the states and by the majority of the Australian voters to whom it had been submitted in referenda.

There was only one clause of the bill, as drafted by the Australian convention, to which the British government took serious exception. This was clause 74, which dealt with the right of appeal to the Judicial Committee of the Privy Council. According to the draft bill, such appeals were to be greatly restricted in the case of private litigants and completely forbidden on questions of the interpretation of the new Australian constitution. The argument put forward in support of the latter provision by the Australian delegates, who were sent to London to press for the bill's adoption by the British Parliament, was that the Australians had framed their own constitution and should therefore be the sole authority as to its interpretation. But the British government took the view that the appeal to the Privy Council was a right which the mother country should preserve as much in the interests of all British subjects as of her own dignity. So, in introducing the bill, Chamberlain declared that the government felt bound to propose some modification in the interests of Australia and the Empire as a whole.[20]

Before the beginning of the debate on the second reading of the bill, negotiations on the subject took place between Chamberlain and the Australian delegates. Fortunately, a settlement was quickly reached and announced by Chamberlain when he moved the second reading of the bill on May 21. It had been agreed that in all cases in which other than Australian questions were concerned, the right

[19] W. O'Brien Papers, Dillon to O'Brien, March 14, 1900.
[20] For a summary of Chamberlain's speech, see *Annual Register, 1900*, p. 100.

of appeal should be fully maintained, while purely Australian questions—i.e., differences arising between two states as to the interpretation of the constitution, or as between a state and the federal parliament—would be finally decided by the High Court of Australia, unless both sides consented to refer the matter to the Privy Council.[21]

The Commonwealth of Australia Constitution Bill was of considerable interest to the Irish party, for the fact that the government was willing to sponsor such a bill indicated that it did not object to a distant part of the Empire choosing its own form of government. Thus, while praising the bill, Irish Nationalists took advantage of the opportunity to criticize the government for ignoring the national rights of Ireland, while recognizing those of Australia. Blake's interest in the bill was especially great because of his experience in the working of the federal system in Canada.

Speaking during the debate on second reading,[22] Blake expressed satisfaction with Chamberlain's statement regarding appeals to the Judicial Committee of the Privy Council. Although he had been prepared to affirm the absolute right of the Australian people, if they so pleased, to ask that there should be no appeal outside their country in matters wholly internal, he was glad that their delegates had agreed to some slight modifications in the expression of that view. In Canada it had been found that, in matters over which bitter controversies had arisen, it was a great advantage to have the opportunity of appealing to an external tribunal such as the Judicial Committee for the interpretation of the constitution.

The remaining and by far the greater part of Blake's speech was devoted to a consideration of the principles and application of self-government and of the place of self-governing communities in the British Empire. He expressed the hope that Parliament, which was now dealing so fairly with Australia, would some day realize that "it is not merely in Australia or Canada, or the remote corners of the earth, that the principles of liberty lead to Imperial unity, reconciliation, and common action." They would do so with even greater

[21]*Ibid.*, 119–20. The revised clause was, however, somewhat altered in committee. See *ibid.*, 137.
[22]For the full text of Blake's speech, see *Hansard*, 4th Series, LXXXIII, 773–84. The speech is also published in a pamphlet entitled "Commonwealth of Australia Constitution Bill—Speech by Edward Blake in the British House of Commons on Monday, 21st May, 1900." (London, 1900).

force at "the heart and centre of the Empire." Australia's position in the Empire, he declared, would be strengthened by the establishment of a federal system, for his experience in Canada led him to believe that it would be easier for Britain to conduct negotiations with the Commonwealth of Australia than with the separate states, whose outlook was naturally more restricted. Blake then proceeded to express his views on imperial parliamentary federation, a scheme which he had once favoured, but had long ago abandoned as impracticable:

> I have said Imperial negotiations, because for many years I, for my part, have looked to conference, to delegation, to correspondence, to negotiation, to quasi-diplomatic methods, subject always to the action of free Parliaments here and elsewhere as the only feasible way of working the quasi-federal union between the Empire and sister nations like Canada and Australia. A quarter of a century past I dreamed the dream of Imperial Parliamentary federation; but many years ago I came to the conclusion that we had passed the turning that could lead to that terminus, if ever, indeed, there was a practicable road. We have too long and too extensively gone on the lines of separate action here and elsewhere to go back now. Never forget—you have the lesson here to-day—that the good will on which you must depend is due to local freedom, and would not survive its limitation. Never forget what has passed in the course of this brief controversy. It is another evidence that the real link is good will, and that the root and foundation of that link is the local freedom, which you give so freely everywhere except in one small part of the Empire. I do not think Pan-Imperial Parliamentary federation is within the bounds of possibility. And this conviction it was which made it impossible for me, with every sympathy, to join in the efforts of the late Imperial Federation League. I do not in the least degree think this Bill is a step towards Imperial Parliamentary Federation. On the contrary, I believe it is distinctly a step the other way.

The Commonwealth of Australia Constitution Bill, after passing both Houses of Parliament, received the royal assent on July 9, 1900.

Payment of Members

At a meeting of the reunited Irish party on February 28, 1900, a resolution, embodying a temporary plan for the payment of members who required financial assistance, was adopted. It provided that the sum of £400 be set aside for distribution, in equal amounts, to those members who intimated to the treasurers before March 10 that they intended to give a substantial attendance but were unable to do so without indemnity.[23] Under the terms of this resolution, 35 members of the party requested financial assistance, but it is not altogether clear whether allowances were granted to all of them. Nor is it possible to determine the total allowance received by each member who was granted assistance during 1900.[24]

When the Irish national convention met in Dublin in June, 1900, no permanent plan for the payment of members of the party had yet been devised. It was, however, thought advisable to make some reference to the question and it was for this reason that Blake had moved a resolution dealing with the subject. His resolution, which was adopted by the convention, proposed that all funds devoted to members' indemnity should, from time to time, be distributed in equal shares among those members who intimated to the treasurers of the party their inability to attend Parliament without this assistance. But it added that such payments should be subject to deduction for non-attendance, as certified by the member concerned, according to a general plan, applicable to all alike, to be framed by the party.

The chief innovation proposed by this resolution was deduction for non-attendance. Under the scheme framed by Blake and adopted by the party in 1897, no such provision was made, and although allowances were granted for the specific purpose of enabling members to attend Parliament, it had been found that many were drawing allowances without giving regular attendance. Some provision to prevent this was therefore considered necessary.

In moving the resolution at the June convention, Blake declared that he attached great importance to the principles laid down in it. But because he understood from the chairman of the Irish party that it was "deemed more convenient that that question should be left to be disposed of by the Party itself," he did not wish to speak at length on the resolution. Nevertheless, though believing that the

---

[23] A copy of this resolution, together with letters requesting indemnity under its provisions, is contained in the J. F. X. O'Brien Papers.
[24] See F. S. L. Lyons, *The Irish Parliamentary Party, 1890–1910* (London, 1951), 209.

general principles stated as to the disposition of members' indemnity were shared by the party and that there would be no difficulty in enforcing them, he felt that the proposition should receive the consideration of the convention. He therefore explained why he believed the Irish party should grant allowances to those of its members who could not keep up their attendance at Parliament without them:

> I urge the necessity for the proposition, coming, as I do, from a democratic country, where the State pays for the public services of their members. That is the democratic view which enables men, no matter what their rank, who are chosen, to fill these representative positions. Anything else simply puts a premium on the rich man over the poor, and we, of all people in the world, are bound to carry out that sound principle. I believe it is of the last importance and consequence that we determine that the bulk of the representatives of the Irish Parliamentary Party should be drawn from the soil from the localities they represent. They should be men who, toiling and labouring and suffering in those districts, are familiar with the griefs and wrongs of their fellow-men, men responsive to the temperaments of those who surround them. I believe that these are the men who ought to form the great bulk and force of the Irish Parliamentary Party, and such men you cannot have unless you recognize it is your duty to pay them for their services. You want men of that class, racy of the soil, knowing the Irish tradition, knowing the Irish sentiment and feeling, and you want men deeply imbued with the National spirit and deeply imbued with the love of their country; in fact you want men possessing all those qualifications except, I hope I may say, love for Ireland and belief in the National spirit—possessing all those qualifications which I lack.[25]

In speaking on the resolution, Blake did not elaborate on the suggested deduction for non-attendance. He simply proposed that the general practice of paying the poorer members of the party, which had been established long before the Parnell split and continued during the years of dissension, should be retained permanently by the united party.

Some months elapsed and the general election of 1900 intervened before a definite plan for the payment of members' indemnity was drawn up and submitted to the party. This scheme, like the one adopted in 1897, was primarily the work of Blake, a fact which indicates that Redmond, like Dillon, greatly valued Blake's advice on such matters.

[25]For the full text of Blake's resolution and speech, see *Freeman's Journal*, Dublin, June 21, 1900.

Early in February, 1901, Redmond wrote to Blake proposing that they discuss a plan for the distribution of the parliamentary fund. The number of men in the new party (i.e., the party elected in 1900) who desired assistance was, he explained, so large that it was absolutely necessary to base payments strictly on attendance.[26] Consultations between Redmond, Blake, and other leading Nationalists followed, and shortly after this Blake drew up and submitted to Redmond a "Draft Plan for the Administration of the Members' Indemnity Fund."[27]

In the draft plan, it was stated that, in view of the urgent necessity of securing a full attendance from the opening of the parliamentary session, the chairman of the Irish party had written to each member, asking whether, while intending to give a substantial attendance, he was unable to do so without indemnity. To this inquiry, 46 members had answered in the affirmative. Thereupon, the chairman had given a list of these members to the treasurers, who, at his request, had remitted to each of them the sum of £20. It was proposed in Blake's draft plan that the action of the chairman and the treasurers should be approved by the party. The plan then went on to suggest that, subject to any withdrawals from the list and to new applications which might be considered, the list already in the hands of the treasurers should be the one used in future. Any application for indemnity from a member who had pledged himself not to be a burden on the party fund could not be considered.

Definite provisions for the payment of allowances and for deduction for non-attendance were next outlined by Blake. Allowances were to be distributed to the members on the list by monthly payments in advance at a rate (for the time being) of £20 a month for a maximum period of six months, or "at such higher or lower rate and for such longer or shorter time as in view of the funds available, the length of the session and the general condition, may from time to time be fixed by the party." The provision regarding deduction for non-attendance read:

[26] It will be seen that 46 members of the new party desired allowances, while only 35 members of the old party had applied for them under the provisions of the resolution of February, 1900. For Redmond's letter, see Blake Papers, Redmond to Blake, Feb. 5, 1901.

[27] For a copy of the plan, see the Redmond Papers.

A deduction at the rate of 15/— a day from the allowance hereby settled, and a proportionate deduction to be fixed on the settlement of any higher or lower scale of allowance shall be made for every day on which the Member does not attend a sitting of the House provided the House sits on such day. But each day after the first on which the Member attends on which there has been no sitting of the House, or on which the Member was within 10 miles of the Palace of Westminster but was prevented by sickness from attending the sitting, shall be reckoned as a day of attendance at the session for the purposes of this plan.

The £20 allowance already paid would be treated as the first payment in advance. Thereafter, monthly payments in advance were to be made during the session to any member on the list who, on or about the fourteenth day of each month, signed a declaration regarding his attendance while public business was in progress during the preceding month. On receipt of this declaration, the treasurers were to calculate the amount of any deduction for non-attendance and to pay only the balance of the next instalment after charging the said amount against it.

Blake's plan was evidently submitted to William O'Brien, for the latter wrote to Redmond expressing his general agreement with it, but adding that he thought, if funds allowed, special provision should be made for the months when Parliament was not sitting. Moreover, it was his opinion that any time spent on League business in Ireland at the request of the party should count as if it were time spent at Westminster.[28]

It appears that Redmond was unwilling to accept O'Brien's suggested additions and that the latter finally agreed not to propose them when the plan was laid before the party. O'Brien's attitude was described by Redmond in a letter to Blake. He wrote: "I have further discussed the proposed administration of the fund with O'Brien and he has come round to the view which I pressed upon him as to his proposed additions. He will support the scheme as drafted by you just as it stands and will propose no changes. . . ."

In the same letter, Redmond expressed the hope that Blake would agree to propose the scheme at the party meeting which was to be held on February 25. Though he knew that Blake was not well, he attached "enormous importance" to his moving the scheme him-

[28]*Ibid.*, W. O'Brien to Redmond, Feb. 18, 1901.

self.²⁹ Despite his ill health, Blake acceded to this request and at the party meeting of February 25 proposed the plan which he had drafted for the distribution of members' indemnity. According to the *Freeman's Journal*, the plan, as amended, was unanimously adopted. Unfortunately, however, there is no mention of the way in which Blake's scheme was amended, the press reports stating only that the plan, as adopted, provided for an equal division among those members of the Irish party who declared themselves unable to attend Parliament regularly without indemnity, but that a deduction was to be made for any period during which a member was absent from the House of Commons while public business was in progress.³⁰ Since all this was provided by Blake's plan, it is impossible, in the absence of any party minutes, to ascertain the manner in which it was amended. It does not seem likely, however, that O'Brien decided, after all, to propose the additions which he had wanted. From later correspondence it will be seen that one of them, at any rate, was not included in the plan which was adopted by the party. Assuming, therefore, that the amendments adopted were not of very great significance, it can be concluded that the main provisions of Blake's plan were accepted by the party. Thus, presumably, the conditions imposed in 1897, under which the payment of indemnity depended on adherence to the party's resolution on unity and discipline, were abandoned. It was indeed natural that this course should be taken, for the circumstances which had led to the adoption of Blake's 1897 resolution on the party funds no longer existed.

From correspondence of the period shortly before Blake's retirement from Irish politics in 1907, it is clear that certain of the provisions of his 1901 resolution proved somewhat unsatisfactory. Towards the end of February, 1907, Redmond told Blake that his resolution had not been re-enacted since the general election of January, 1906, and that it would soon be necessary to put forward some proposal on the subject. From the start, it had been difficult to carry out all the provisions of the resolution, for many members

²⁹Blake Papers, Redmond to Blake, Feb. 23, 1901.
³⁰The party meeting is reported briefly in the *Freeman's Journal* and the *Irish Independent and Nation*, Dublin, Feb. 26, 1901.

receiving allowances had objected to the monthly declaration which they were required to sign. "Indeed," Redmond added, "it (the resolution) may be said never to have been carried out at all in its full strictness." He went on to explain that when men were absent through illness, whether in Ireland or elsewhere, it had been found impossible to deprive them of their allowance. The same was true when they were absent on political business at his request or with his sanction. In view of this situation, Redmond had drawn up a draft resolution on the subject and discussed it with Dillon and the party treasurers. But not wishing to lay it before the party without Blake's approval, he now sent him a copy so that he might give his opinion.[31] Redmond's draft resolution proposed that if a member were absent from Parliament for a full week he would lose his allowance for that period unless he were ill or on political business elsewhere with the sanction of the chairman.[32]

In his reply to Redmond's letter, Blake explained that, in drawing up the resolution of 1901, he had had to guide him only the experience and forms of the Canadian House of Commons and the legislature of Ontario. As to the special conditions relating to the Irish party he had had less experience than many other members. Some of the provisions had, indeed, been submitted to rather than cordially accepted by him, and the resolution had been "the fruit of consultation with leading members," though he had, of course, taken full responsibility. After adding that he had heard very little of the practical working of the scheme before he received Redmond's lettter, he went on:

> It seems to me plain that such a matter as this must be judged by its working and by the lessons of experience; and that the plan should be modified according to the best judgment of those who have been working it.
> I am not in that position; and accordingly make no suggestions on the draft you are kind enough to send me; nor shall I take any part in the discussion of the matter. But I have not the least objection in the world to the revision and modification by those in charge; and hope you will go on at once with any changes you find expedient. I felt at the time that the

---

[31]Blake Papers, Redmond to Blake, Feb. 27, 1907.
[32]The copy of the draft resolution sent by Redmond to Blake is among the Blake Papers.

proposal was an invidious one, which I would gladly have been relieved from making, but which I undertook at the earnest instance of leading friends; and personally I am glad that it should be reviewed.[33]

At a meeting of March 6, 1907, a resolution on the lines of the draft sent by Redmond to Blake was adopted.[34] This did not mean, however, that the resolution of February, 1901, was completely abandoned. In a list of party rules and regulations drawn up in May, 1907, it was explained that the resolution of February, 1901, as modified by the resolution of March, 1907, remained in full force and effect.[35]

Protest against Coercion

As the United Irish League, following its recognition as the national organization, continued to expand rapidly, the Unionist government, which was returned to power in the general election of October, 1900, became more and more alarmed. It therefore revived the policy of coercion which had been used against many Irish agrarian movements of the past. Actually, from the first, the government had regarded the League with disfavour, and there had been some coercion of it even before 1900. It was, however, in 1901 and 1902 that the strongest government action was taken against it.

The principal weapon used by the government against the League was the Crimes Act of 1887. Under the terms of this act, many of the League's meetings were declared to be unlawful assemblies, and the principal participants in them were prosecuted and imprisoned. Since many Irish Nationalist members of Parliament were among the most active organizers of the League, it was not surprising that some of them were punished in this way for their activities.

Naturally, the government's policy of coercion was frequently debated in the House of Commons. From time to time, during the

[33]*Ibid.*, Blake to Redmond, Feb. 28, 1907.
[34]For a report of the meeting, see *Freeman's Journal*, Dublin, March 7, 1907.
[35]There is a copy of this list among the Redmond Papers.

sessions of 1901 and 1902, motions condemning coercion were proposed, the government being attacked in the strongest terms by Irish Nationalist members. These motions were always defeated by large majorities.

In 1901, Blake took some part in the work of the House; he was, in fact, at the end of February, nominated by the Speaker as one of the temporary chairmen of committees.[36] But his intervention in debate was usually very brief and he did not speak on any subject of major consequence. It was not until March 13, 1902, that, in an important address, he publicly condemned the policy of coercion adopted by the government.

The speech was delivered in the course of a debate on the civil service estimates. Redmond, having proposed a reduction in the salary of the Chief Secretary for Ireland,[37] had taken advantage of the opportunity to condemn that gentleman's policy of coercion. He had asserted that there was in Ireland practically no ordinary crime and less agrarian crime than ever before, but that there was intense political and agrarian discontent accompanied, no doubt, by cases of boycotting. Insisting that remedial measures were needed, he had complained that, instead of introducing them, the government dispersed lawful meetings, suppressed the rights of free speech, and imprisoned the leaders of the people in the west of Ireland. In his reply to Redmond's address, George Wyndham, Irish Chief Secretary, had asserted that the executive carefully inquired into any case in which the police were accused of brutality, and that the number of acquittals of defendants by the resident magistrates who tried the cases proved that these officials were not subservient to the government. He had insisted that the government was in duty bound, under the ordinary law if possible, but under the Crimes Act if necessary, to protect individual liberty and prevent illegal combinations.[38]

---

[36]*Hansard*, 4th Series, LXXXIX, 2400.
[37]His motion to this effect was defeated by 215 to 125 votes. See *Annual Register*, 1902, p. 94.
[38]For Redmond's speech, see *Hansard*, 4th Series, CIV, 1298–1312; for Wyndham's, *ibid.*, 1313–29.

Blake was among the speakers who followed Wyndham.[39] In an effort to show the unjustness of the government's policy towards Ireland, he described the administration of the law in that country, dealing especially with the operation of the Crimes Act. After complaining that the laws of Ireland, unlike those of England, were not framed with the assent of the people, Blake spoke of the general clause of the Crimes Act,[40] which had been made the common law of Ireland regarding unlawful assemblies. It was very difficult to determine whether an assembly was unlawful, because there were so many delicate and difficult points involved—the shadowy line between political and seditious action, the subtle point of intent, the application of former speeches at other places, the doubtful result of such a general change of intent during the meeting as would convert a lawful into an unlawful assembly—all of which had to be considered. In connection with the last point, there had recently been made in the House of Commons statements of law regarding unlawful assembly which Blake altogether repudiated. It had been suggested that an assembly which was lawful up to a particular moment became unlawful when one speaker had said, or even was supposed to be about to say, something unlawful. While agreeing that an absolutely lawful assembly might become unlawful in its progress, Blake "utterly denied" the proposition that it could be made so by the thoughts or words of one or another of its participants. His address continued:

> It might turn out that ten or fifteen men might come to a perfectly lawful meeting with intent to promote something unlawful. If so, those ten or fifteen were of themselves an unlawful assembly gathered within the mass of the lawful assembly. But surely that did not turn into criminals the lawful men assembled for lawful purposes. It did not turn those men who came to a meeting upon their lawful business, in pursuance of their rights as supposed free citizens of a free country, into criminals, because enough men to constitute of themselves an unlawful assembly had come into their meeting for

---

[39] Blake's speech is reported in *ibid.*, 1339–53. The *Hansard* account is reproduced in pamphlet form. See Edward Blake, "Speech, 13th March, 1902, on Supply—Civil Service Estimates (Irish situation)."
[40] The general clause of the Crimes Act as to unlawful assemblies could be applied all over Ireland without a proclamation. The other clauses were applied in various districts by proclamation of the Lord-Lieutenant.

an unlawful purpose. He denied altogether that one man rising in a lawful assembly and uttering unlawful sentiments turned that meeting into an unlawful assembly. That was a monstrous assertion. To produce any such result it must be made to appear that an unlawful intent, not before existent, had been created in the mass by the speech.

Since such difficult questions were involved in determining the lawfulness of an assembly, the securities which obtained in England —precise formulation of a charge, trial by jury, and an independent judiciary—were especially necessary, but in Ireland, under the Crimes Act, they did not exist. The excuse given for this improper administration of justice was that the maximum penalty was very short; the resident magistrates (who took the place of an independent judiciary) could not give a sentence longer than six months. But they had the power, substantially without appeal, to turn even a one month sentence into six, nine, or twelve months, or perhaps even more, by holding to bail for good behaviour, a practice which, though legal under ancient law, was most unjust. Moreover, the resident magistrates, sitting under the special jurisdiction conferred by the Crimes Act, had no real authority to convict under the bail law. "The questions of holding to bail for good behaviour should," Blake declared, "be decided by another Bench, and under the ordinary law of the land, and should not be touched under the special jurisdiction."

After dealing with a specific case in which a meeting had been declared unlawful, Blake condemned the government and Parliament for not realizing their responsibilities and redressing the terrible evils which existed in Ireland. The House of Commons was allowing itself to be made an instrument and accomplice of tyranny by not insisting on the abrogation of the laws from which these evils sprang and by adopting force instead of redress as its Irish policy. Admitting that things which he regretted were sometimes said in Ireland, he insisted that this was no reason for cutting away the main foundation of British liberties. He referred to free speech as a jewel and held that circumstances in Ireland were such as ought to make England very tolerant and lenient towards the language employed by a long suffering people. If English members realized the dreadful conditions in which the poorer classes in Ireland lived, they would, he asserted, be amazed, not at the occasional agitation and breaches of the law, but at the extraordinary patience and endurance of the people.

The attacks of Blake and other Irish Nationalists did not lead the government to abandon its policy of coercion. In fact, it was not even satisfied with applying all over Ireland the general clause of the Crimes Act for which no proclamation was necessary. A month after Blake's address, the Lord-Lieutenant of Ireland issued proclamations putting into force in many parts of the country several additional provisions of that act. These provisions, which related to special juries, change of venue, and summary jurisdiction in cases of intimidation and illegal conspiracy, were applied, with some variation, in the counties of Cavan, Clare, Cork, Leitrim, Mayo, Roscommon, Sligo, Tipperary, and Waterford, and in the cities of Cork and Waterford.

The League Delegation to America

Just as in Ireland the United Irish League had taken the place of the National Federation and other sectional organizations, so in the United States the Irish National Federation of America had been replaced by the United Irish League of America. Branches of the new organization were formed in many parts of the United States, and in 1902 it was decided that the time had come to hold a national convention. It was therefore arranged that one would meet in Boston on October 20-21 of that year. Delegates from many branches of the organization attended, and the United Irish League sent its president, John Redmond, and two of its most distinguished members, John Dillon and Michael Davitt, to take part in the proceedings.

At the time that preparations for the convention were being made, Blake was in Canada, and although he had not been named as an Irish delegate, John O'Callaghan, national secretary of the United Irish League of America, wrote inviting him to attend and address the gathering.[41] Blake replied that he did not occupy any representa-

[41] Blake Papers, J. O'Callaghan to Blake, Sept. 8, 1902.

tive position in connection with the convention and therefore hesitated to accept. He supposed, however, that the committee arranging the convention had considered this and he would defer to its judgment.[42]

Blake arrived in Boston on October 17, the same day as the delegates from Ireland.[43] On the nineteenth, the night before the convention opened, two mass meetings were held in their honour. Redmond, Dillon, and Davitt spoke at both meetings, while Blake spoke at one of them. At both the meetings there was adopted a series of resolutions with a preamble expressing "horror and indignation" at the British government's treatment of Ireland and promising the Irish delegates that "so far as in us lies," no alliance would ever take place between the United States and "a nation which so tramples on the rights of humanity." The resolutions expressed the need for a settlement of the land question, the establishment of home rule, the promotion of Irish industries, and the study and revival of the ancient language and literature of the Irish race.[44]

On October 20, the first day of the convention, resolutions similar to those passed at the mass meetings were adopted. But in pledging their undying allegiance to the Irish cause and appealing to all Irish-Americans to subscribe to it, the delegates of the United Irish League of America expressed their recognition of the fact that the American organizations were but auxiliaries and advisers and that the Irish people at home, through their chosen representatives, were best fitted to decide on the means by which their battle was to be fought.[45]

Several important speeches were delivered on the first day of the convention, but it was not until almost the close of the second day's proceedings that Blake addressed the gathering. Once more, as in the House of Commons on March 13, 1902, he described the

[42]*Ibid.*, Blake to O'Callaghan, Sept. 12, 1902.
[43]The arrival of the delegates is reported in the *Globe*, Boston, Oct. 18, 1902. See Blake Scrap Books.
[44]A full account of both meetings is given in *ibid.*, Oct. 20, 1902. See Blake Scrap Books.
[45]A detailed account of the first day's proceedings is given in *ibid.*, Oct. 21, 1902. See Blake Scrap Books.

operation of the Crimes Act in Ireland.⁴⁶ The *Boston Globe* commenting on the proceedings of the second day remarked:

> But perhaps the most significant speech of the day was that of Hon. Edward Blake. It was an arraignment of the judicial system in vogue in Ireland under the crimes act.
> It was more than an arraignment, for it was an exposé by an able jurist of the entire judicial farce which is being enacted in Ireland.
> He understands not only the history and practice of English law, but its application. He analyzed the whole thing in a merciless manner.⁴⁷

Afer the close of the national convention in Boston, the delegates from Ireland spent several days addressing meetings in different parts of the United States under the auspices of the United Irish League of America. Blake accompanied the official delegates, speaking at New York, Philadelphia, and Elizabeth, New Jersey. On each occasion he described the situation in Ireland, condemning the policy of coercion enforced by the British government. He also stressed the fact that he was not an official delegate of the League, but the American press, though reporting his statements to this effect, otherwise ignored them, referring to him continually as one of the delegates.⁴⁸

Shortly after these meetings, Redmond sailed for Ireland and Blake returned to Canada, but Dillon and Davitt remained in the United States to address meetings in other important centres.

In Canada, as well as the United States, branches of the United Irish League were being formed, and some of them were being affiliated with the American organization. Several of the Canadian branches were anxious to have Blake and one or more of the delegates from Ireland address meetings under their auspices. It was therefore arranged that Blake and Dillon should speak in Toronto, Montreal, and Ottawa on December 1, 2, and 3 respectively. But towards the end of November, Dillon, who was in Chicago, became seriously ill with intermittent fever and was unable to keep his

⁴⁶Blake's speech at the convention is published in a pamphlet entitled "Speech of Hon. Edward Blake, M.P., delivered before the First National Convention, United Irish League of America, Faneuil Hall, Boston, Mass., October 20–21, 1902" (Boston, n.d.).
⁴⁷*Globe*, Boston, Oct. 22, 1902. An account of the second day's proceedings is contained in this issue. See Blake Scrap Books.
⁴⁸For American press reports of all these meetings, see Blake Scrap Books.

Canadian engagements. In informing Blake of his illness, Dillon suggested that Joseph Devlin, a young Irish Nationalist member of Parliament who was then in the United States, might take his place.[49] Blake at once informed the branches; they agreed, and it was therefore decided to go ahead with the meetings.

In addressing the Canadian meetings, Blake did not approach the Irish situation in quite the same way as he had in the United States, for he realized that, on some questions, the sentiments of Irish-Americans were not shared by Irish-Canadians. While Irish-Americans had supported the stand taken by Irish Nationalist members of the British House of Commons on the Boer War, English-speaking Canadians, including those of Irish descent, had, for the most part, opposed it. As Blake pointed out in a letter to Dillon before the latter was forced to cancel his Canadian engagements, the overwhelming sentiment of the majority of the Canadian population towards the war was not the same as theirs; they would find a different atmosphere in Canada and would have to act accordingly.[50] Moreover, although Irish-Canadians were strongly opposed to the British government's coercion policy in Ireland, they were beginning to feel that the Irish Nationalists, in condemning this policy, were adopting too much of an anti-British and perhaps separatist tone; they feared therefore that the form of home rule proposed by Gladstone would no longer satisfy them. Content that Canada should remain within the British Empire, they did not wish Ireland to depart from it. Naturally, their sentiments of loyalty to the Empire were not shared by Irish-Americans.

So, with the attitude of the Irish-Canadians in mind, Blake began his address at Toronto on December 1 by referring to the expressions of sympathy with the Irish cause which had been passed by the Canadian House of Commons in the 1880's. Having added that he was sure Canada had not changed its views regarding the benefits of self-government, he went on to deal with the assertion which was sometimes made that the situation in Ireland had changed and that

[49]Blake Papers, Dillon to Blake, Nov. 24, 1902. Devlin, at Redmond's request, had come to the United States to ease the work of the League delegates.
[50]*Ibid.*, Blake to Dillon, Nov. 1, 1902.

the Irish demand was not what it had been. In one sense, he admitted, this was true; Irish-Nationalists regarded the principle and general provisions of the Gladstonian home rule measure as a compromise of the extreme national demand, but it was equally true that they accepted that compromise and had never withdrawn their expression of consent. Then, in answer to the charge sometimes voiced that Ireland was disloyal, Blake declared that he saw no objection to that country's being discontented when injustice was done, disaffected when it had nothing to be well affected to, and disloyal to a constitution of which it had no practical enjoyment. Ireland had not been loyal, well affected, nor contented when Gladstone took up the question of home rule, but he "had learned that the way to make people loyal, contented, and friendly is to give them something to be loyal to, contented with and friendly towards...."

After dwelling upon the transcendent importance of settling the troublesome Irish question, which caused discontent, disaffection, and disloyalty at the very centre of the Empire, Blake evidently felt that it was safe to deal with the current Irish situation. He therefore proceeded to describe it as he had to his American audiences.[51]

At Montreal on December 2 and at Ottawa the next day, Blake's remarks followed the same pattern as at Toronto. Devlin too, undoubtedly on Blake's advice, addressed the Canadian meetings in a similar strain. In Montreal, both Devlin and Blake spoke of the blessings of self-government in Canada and explained that they wanted the same sort of government in Ireland.[52] At Ottawa, both men emphasized repeatedly that Ireland would loyally accept partnership in the Empire if given self-government at home. And, by the use of an amusing analogy, Blake accounted for Ireland's current disloyalty:

> Do they say that Irishmen are not loyal and do they say that Ireland should be loyal first and then ask for home rule? Why, what has Ireland to be loyal to? It is like a man being sick, and you tell him he is sick and needs a dose

[51]The foregoing account of Blake's speech is based on that given by the *Globe*, Toronto, Dec. 2, 1902. For it and accounts from other Toronto papers, see Blake Scrap Books.
[52]For Montreal press reports of the meeting, see Blake Scrap Books.

of medicine. And then you tell him to get well first and you will give him the medicine afterwards.[53]

Blake was well satisfied with the Canadian meetings. In a letter to O'Callaghan, he declared that, considering conditions in the Dominion, they had been very successful and had produced subscriptions to the amount of about $3,500.[54]

It had been arranged that Dillon, Davitt, and Blake should address a meeting in Washington on December 7. Dillon was to be the first and principal speaker, but when he became ill it was evidently decided that it would be better for Blake to precede him in speaking. In view of the circumstances, Blake agreed to this arrangement, writing to Davitt as follows: "I suppose I am to go first at Washington in order to ease off Dillon? In that view, I very gladly consent; though I own to you nothing else would induce it. . . ."[55] In the end, Dillon was unable to attend the Washington meeting, and Blake, in accordance with his agreement, was the first and principal speaker. Nevertheless, he told his audience that he would leave some great topics, such as the object, work, and claims of the League and the vital subject of the land, to be elaborated by Davitt, the delegate of the League.[56]

The proceedings at the American and Canadian meetings addressed by Blake and other Irish Nationalists in the closing months of 1902 indicated that there was growing indignation among Irishmen abroad, as well as at home, at the policy adopted in Ireland by the British government. It is true that Irish-Canadians, fearing that Ireland would soon demand complete separation from Britain, did not share the views of Irishmen at home and in the United States on all aspects of the current situation. Although Blake had, therefore, to change his line of approach to suit the different attitudes of his American and Canadian audiences, nevertheless, there was

[53]*Evening Journal*, Ottawa, Dec. 4, 1902. See Blake Scrap Books.
[54]Blake Papers, Blake to O'Callaghan, Dec. 15, 1902.
[55]*Ibid.*, Blake to Davitt, Nov. 29, 1902.
[56]Blake's address is published in a pamphlet entitled "The Case for Ireland Stated, Speech delivered by Hon. Edward Blake, M.P., in Washington, U.S.A., on December 7th, 1902" United Irish League of Great Britain Leaflets, no. 5 (London, n.d.). Press reports of the Washington meeting are contained in the Blake Scrap Books.

no inconsistency in what he said in the two countries. In both, he described the Irish situation, but in Canada he added a preliminary justification of the attitude of the Irish Nationalists; in the United States, where feeling against England was so strong, as indicated in the preamble to the resolutions adopted at the mass meetings in Boston, he refrained from suggesting that the granting of home rule to Ireland would be beneficial to the British Empire. In stating at the Canadian meetings that Ireland would accept the Gladstonian scheme of home rule, Blake was undoubtedly sincere, for, although he and his colleagues in the Irish parliamentary party did not regard that scheme as perfect, most of them were not seeking complete separation from Britain.

X. BLAKE'S ACTIVITIES CURTAILED, 1903-6

IN PROTESTING against the Unionist government's policy towards Ireland in 1901-2, the Irish Nationalists had insisted that agrarian unrest in that country would be cured not by coercion but by settling the land question on the United Irish League's principle of "the land for the people." Even while continuing its policy of coercion, the government evidently realized that some land reform was necessary, for, in March, 1902, George Wyndham, the Irish Chief Secretary, introduced in the House of Commons a Land Purchase Bill. This bill, as the name implied, was designed to facilitate land purchase, but it was a weak measure, whose provisions would have operated so slowly that the purchase would not have been completed for at least a century. In the end, the bill, which was denounced by the United Irish League, was withdrawn by the government. The following year, however, a much more important and far-reaching Land Bill became law.

The passage of the Land Act of 1903, as will be seen later, was largely the result of a land conference held a few months previously between representatives of the Irish Nationalists and moderate Irish Unionists. The success of that conference led several influential men, including its chairman Lord Dunraven, to see in such a policy of conference and conciliation a possible solution to the university question. However, Lord Dunraven's proposal for a Roman Catholic college to be added to the University of Dublin, although supported by moderate men of all religious faiths, came to nothing.

In spite of the government's attitude towards his university proposals, Lord Dunraven continued to hope that some reforms might be achieved through conference and conciliation with the Nationalists. So, in August, 1904, he and other moderate Unionists who shared his views formed an organization known as the Irish Reform Association, the general aim of which was to secure "the devolution to Ireland of a larger measure of self-government than she now possesses." More specifically, it proposed, first of all, that the administrative control of Irish finances should be vested in an Irish financial council, partly nominated and partly elected; and secondly, that a statutory body should be established and given the power to legislate on certain Irish affairs which were considered unsuitable for the attention of Parliament. It was not surprising that these proposals were denounced by both British and Irish Unionist members of Parliament who regarded them as suggestions for giving Ireland what was really a form of home rule. When it became known that, in drafting them, Lord Dunraven had been aided by the permanent Under-Secretary for Ireland, Sir Antony MacDonnell,[1] the Irish Unionist press accused the government, and especially Wyndham, of secretly promoting the devolution scheme. Actually Wyndham was opposed to the plan, but when MacDonnell had written informing him of his support for it, he had somehow misunderstood or ignored the letter. Although Wyndham publicly expressed his opposition to the programme of the Irish Reform Association, the Unionists continued to distrust him and finally secured his resignation in March, 1905. The devolution proposals came to nothing.[2]

During the years that Lord Dunraven and his associates were advocating a policy of conciliation, Irish Nationalists were sharply divided as to the attitude they should adopt towards it. While Nationalist opinion was generally favourable to the land conference and the Land Bill, Dillon had, from the first, regarded the new policy with suspicion, and it was only his loyalty to his party which prevented him from opposing the bill in committee and voting against it on third reading. Although, at a public meeting in Ireland shortly after the bill became law, he admitted that it had some good points, he added that Ireland owed the bill "not to the goodwill of English ministers or Irish landlords but to the agitation of the United Irish League." He made it clear that he was not con-

[1]In Oct., 1902, Sir Antony MacDonnell had, at Wyndham's request, accepted the post of Under-Secretary on the understanding that he would be given the opportunity of influencing the policy of the Irish government. His appointment was looked upon with suspicion by most Unionists, for Sir Antony, who had had a distinguished career in the Indian civil service, was an Irish Roman Catholic, and his brother, Dr. M. A. MacDonnell, was a member of the Irish parliamentary party.

[2]For a fuller account of the devolution scheme, see F. S. L. Lyons, "The Irish Unionist Party and the Devolution Crisis of 1904–5" (*Irish Historical Studies*, March, 1948).

vinced of the good intentions of Irish landlords who talked of conciliation and going into conference with the leaders of the Irish parliamentary party; finally, in fact, he stated bluntly that he had no faith in the doctrine of conciliation.[3] There were other prominent Nationalists who shared Dillon's views, chief among them being Davitt, Sexton, and T. P. O'Connor. William O'Brien and Redmond, on the other hand, had been delegates to the land conference and were supporters of the policy of conciliation; O'Brien's faith in it was, however, stronger than Redmond's.

With men of such prominence as Dillon, Davitt, Sexton, and T. P. O'Connor against conciliation, Nationalist opinion, which had generally welcomed the Land Bill, gradually altered. Although neither Davitt nor Sexton was at this time a member of Parliament, both had considerable influence in the country. Davitt was one of the leading members of the National Directory of the United Irish League, and Sexton controlled the *Freeman's Journal* which he was able to turn against the new policy. Being outside the party, these two men had, in fact, been freer than Dillon and T. P. O'Connor to criticize the Land Bill when it was before the Commons, and the *Freeman's Journal* had, since the issue of the report of the land conference, taken a hostile attitude to its proposals, which it regarded as too favourable to the landlords. In the months following the passage of the Land Act, the difference of opinion between prominent Nationalists became more acute; it was clear that there was growing hostility to further co-operation with moderate Unionists. William O'Brien, conscious of the situation and of the difficulties of his own position, urged Redmond to take a firm stand against the policy of the *Freeman's Journal*, but Redmond, though in general agreement with O'Brien, realized that it would be unwise to risk a breach with such influential men as Dillon, Davitt, Sexton, and T. P. O'Connor. He therefore refused to act as O'Brien wished, and, in consequence of this, the latter, in November, 1903, announced his intention of resigning both his seat in Parliament and his position on the National Directory of the United Irish League.

As in the early days of the United Irish League, Dillon and

[3]For a fuller account of Dillon's speech, see F. S. L. Lyons, *The Irish Parliamentary Party, 1890–1910* (London, 1951), 103–4.

O'Brien were divided on the land question. In 1898, O'Brien had regarded land reform of primary importance, while Dillon had felt that the demand for home rule should be kept in the foreground. Although Dillon had come to accept O'Brien's views regarding the United Irish League, he was, by 1903, reverting to his earlier opinion that the settlement of the land question might lessen Ireland's chances of attaining home rule.

There was much to be said for the attitude of Dillon and those who supported him, for, in the years when Lord Dunraven and his associates were advocating the policy of conciliation, the Unionist government was becoming steadily weaker. For its decline in popularity and power there were several reasons, most important of which was the growing dissension within Unionist ranks in Parliament. In September, 1903, Joseph Chamberlain, the Colonial Secretary, who earlier that year had begun a campaign for tariff reform, a subject on which Unionists were sharply divided, withdrew from the cabinet. The devolution crisis of 1905 and the resignation of Wyndham as Irish Chief Secretary at the demand of a section of his own party further increased the dissension in Unionist ranks. There was also a serious decline in the prestige and popularity of the government as a result of the publication in August, 1903, of the report of the Royal Commission appointed to inquire into the conduct of the South African war. This report, though moderate and restrained in its tone, showed clearly that the government had been quite unprepared for the war. Dillon and his supporters regarded co-operation with the Unionists at such a time as ridiculous. It appeared to them much wiser to seek co-operation with the Liberals and to induce them, if returned to power at the next general election, to introduce a satisfactory home rule measure.

O'Brien's retirement from public life had a profound effect on the course of the national movement. In view of the fact that he was the author and principal advocate of the idea that the United Irish League should predominate over the Irish parliamentary party and that he was also the leading Nationalist supporter of the new policy of co-operation with moderate Unionists, his resignation did much to ensure that the Nationalists would revert to their earlier policies. This became apparent in the reception given by the

Nationalists in 1904 to the devolution proposals of the Irish Reform Association. Most Nationalists were openly hostile to the scheme which, they feared, would lessen the chances of securing the type of self-government for which they had long been striving. Dillon spoke of the plan as the discreditable climax of a long campaign to "kill home rule with kindness," while Davitt denounced it as "a wooden-horse stratagem." Only Redmond who was, at that time, in America retained his faith in the policy of co-operation with moderate Unionists. On hearing of the proposals of Dunraven and his associates, he cabled: "The announcement is of the utmost importance. It is simply a declaration for Home Rule and is quite a wonderful thing. With these men with us Home Rule may come at any moment."[4]

It must not be supposed, however, that O'Brien's influence on the national movement ended abruptly with his retirement. In County Cork, and more especially in Cork City, one of the two divisions of which he had represented in the House of Commons, there was much support for his views. The Cork branch of the United Irish League greeted with pleasure the establishment of the Irish Reform Association and praised "the statesmanlike spirit" in which Redmond, on hearing of the devolution proposals, had cabled from America.[5] O'Brien's popularity in his former constituency was, in fact, so great that when, after several months' delay, a by-election was held, he was, despite his protests, re-elected unopposed. He then became a serious danger to Nationalist unity, for he did not sign the party pledge and was therefore free to advocate his own policies. But, in one sense, O'Brien's re-election strengthened national unity, for Redmond, who had been inclined to support O'Brien, now worked in greater harmony with Dillon and those who shared his views in order to maintain the unity of the party.

There is comparatively little information about Blake's activities during this period. His health, never good, was growing worse, and he was therefore unable to take as active a part as formerly in Irish politics. But it must not be inferred that his work for the cause

[4]The remarks of Dillon, Davitt, and Redmond are quoted in Denis Gwynn, *Life of John Redmond* (London, 1932), 106.
[5]Lyons, *Irish Parliamentary Party*, 110.

ceased altogether; on the contrary, the Irish leaders continued to seek and receive his advice on many questions of the day. Nor did Blake completely abandon the work of the House of Commons, although he found it increasingly difficult to attend night sittings, and there were sometimes long intervals during which ill health forced him to be absent. But he continued when possible to act on committees of the House and to serve, on the Speaker's nomination, as one of the temporary chairmen of committees. The part he played in Irish politics from 1903 to 1906 and the many difficulties, including ill health and other afflictions, with which he was faced are described in the following sections.

The Land Question

On September 3, 1902, there appeared in the Irish newspapers a letter from Captain John Shawe-Taylor, a hitherto unknown gentleman living in County Galway. The letter invited representatives of the landlords and tenants (four of each) to attend a conference in Dublin with the object of finding a satisfactory settlement of the land question.[6] Captain Shawe-Taylor had not consulted any of the eight men to whom he publicly issued this invitation, and his letter would undoubtedly have been forgotten had not Wyndham, two days after its appearance, expressed his approval of the idea of holding a land conference. Efforts were therefore soon made to put the idea into effect.

Many landlords were, of course, hostile to the scheme. The landlord representatives named in Captain Shawe-Taylor's letter—the Duke of Abercorn, Lord Barrymore, Colonel Saunderson, and the O'Conor Don—refused to attend the proposed conference, and a landlords' convention, representative of conservative Unionist opinion, also expressed itself opposed to the plan. But a number of more enlightened landlords, chief among them being Lords Dunraven, Castletown, Mayo, Powerscourt, and Meath, Colonel

[6] For the text of the letter, see Gwynn, *Life of John Redmond*, 99; or William O'Brien, *An Olive Branch in Ireland and Its History* (London, 1910), 140.

Hutcheson-Poe, and Mr. Talbot Crosbie, were anxious that a land conference should take place, and, in an effort to bring it about, formed a conciliation committee. This committee submitted to the landlords of Ireland a plebiscite asking them to state whether they were for or against a conference with representatives of the tenants. The plebiscite showed that the landlords were almost two to one in favour of the proposed scheme. In spite of this result, the landlords' convention still refused to take any part in the selection of landlord representatives, so the conciliation committee appointed Lord Dunraven, Lord Mayo, Colonel Hutcheson-Poe, and Colonel Nugent Everard to attend the conference.

The conciliation committee's next move was to request John Redmond, as leader of the Irish parliamentary party, to furnish it with the names of four gentlemen who would act as representatives of the tenants at the land conference. In Captain Shawe-Taylor's letter, the tenant representatives named were John Redmond, T. C. Harrington, William O'Brien, and T. W. Russell. Redmond, Harrington, and O'Brien were, of course, all Nationalists, Harrington being at this time Lord Mayor of Dublin. T. W. Russell, though still a Liberal Unionist in politics (he later became a Liberal Home Ruler), was, in matters relating to the land question, the principal spokesman for the tenant farmers of the north of Ireland. During the general election campaign of 1900, he had, by speaking in favour of compulsory expropriation of all Irish landlords, shown himself opposed on this question to most of his Unionist colleagues. On receipt of the conciliation committee's request, Redmond felt that it would be inconvenient to hold a party meeting for the selection of representatives; moreover, he regarded it as unnecessary, since the names suggested by Shawe-Taylor appeared to him quite satisfactory. He thought, however, that it would be wise to give the members of the party some say in the matter, so on December 2, 1902, he sent to them a circular letter asking whether or not they approved of the original selection.[7]

While most of the replies expressed approval of the four names in question, a few objected to one or other of them. One member of the party disapproved of the choice of Harrington, complaining

[7] There is a copy of the circular letter in the Blake Papers.

that his position as Lord Mayor of Dublin did not qualify him to appear as a representative of rural Ireland; he thought that either Davitt or Dillon would be a better choice. Another member objected to the party's naming Russell and proposed that Sexton or Davitt should replace him. Two others, while approving of the proposed representatives, suggested that, if the number were not restricted to four, Dillon's name should be added.[8]

At the time the circular letter was sent out, Blake was in Canada. When he received it, he realized that the matter in question would be arranged before his reply could reach Redmond; nevertheless, he decided to express his views upon it. He therefore wrote to Redmond, stating that since, so far as he could gather from the newspapers, there had been no objection to the proposed representatives in any quarter save that of the executive of the landlord organization (i.e., the landlords' convention), he thought it best to name them. But it occurred to him that Russell ought to be suggested with approval as the special representative of the northern farmers, instead of being named by the Nationalist party. "He would," Blake added, "thus occupy his true position, and be disembarrassed of the suggestion—awkward to both of us—that he is 'our man.' "[9]

Since the majority of Irish members expressed satisfaction with the four tenant representatives originally suggested, they were named to attend the conference which assembled in the Mansion House, Dublin, on December 20, 1902. Lord Dunraven was unanimously elected chairman of the conference. The representatives of the landlords and tenants evidently had comparatively little difficulty in reaching an agreement, for, two weeks later, after holding six sittings, the conference adjourned, and on January 4, 1903, issued a unanimous report.

The report asserted that the tenants should become the owners of the holdings which they rented, but it did not recommend compulsory sale, the method previously advocated both by the Nationalists and by T. W. Russell. Instead, it proposed that the landlords should be encouraged to sell by the promise of aid from the govern-

[8]For the four letters, see Redmond Papers, John McKean, J. O'Shee, K. E. O'Brien, and John O'Donnell to Redmond, Dec. 5, 1902.
[9]*Ibid.*, Blake to Redmond, Dec. 16, 1902. There is a copy of this letter in the Blake Papers.

ment, and that the sale price should be determined by agreement between the owner and the occupier. Purchase and resale of estates by the government was discouraged except in the congested districts or where the owner and half the tenants desired that procedure.

It was further proposed that the landlords should be paid a price for their lands which would yield incomes of not less than those derived from second-term rents.[10] If the landlords received a sum which upon investment at 3 or 3¼ per cent would equal the income they had received in rent from the land, they would probably be willing to sell. A fair price would also encourage them to remain in Ireland. With that in view the conference recommended that the purchase arrangements be such as would insure the landlords against any diminution of the capital sum on account of delays, costly title search, guarantee deposits, or losses pending reinvestment. A still more important inducement, suggested by the report, was a provision enabling the owners to purchase their demesne lands on the same terms as the tenants purchased their holdings. Thus freed from burdensome mortgages, the landlords would probably remain.

The report went on to recommend that the tenants should be permitted to purchase on terms that would secure a reduction of from 15 to 25 per cent on second-term rents. The money required by the tenants to pay the landlords should be advanced by the treasury which would recover it by a series of annuities payable by the tenants over a period of years. In addition to this, the treasury should give a bonus to the landlords in order to make good the differences between the price which the tenants were ready to pay for their holdings and the price which the owners could afford to accept.

There was much enthusiasm in Ireland over the report of the land conference. Even the executive committee of the landlords'

[10] The first- and second-term rents to which reference is made in the land conference report and the Land Act of 1903 are the judicial rents established under the provisions of the Land Act of 1881. Under that act, either landlord or tenant could apply to a legal tribunal to have a fair rent fixed on the holding. The rent was to endure for fifteen years—the first term—at the end of which either party could apply for a revision. If a revision were granted, the new rent was called a second-term rent.

convention, at a meeting held in Dublin on January 7, 1903, unanimously recognized the valuable nature of the report and urged the government to give it serious consideration. On February 16, both the Irish parliamentary party and the National Directory of the United Irish League held meetings, at which resolutions expressing satisfaction with the land conference report were unanimously adopted. But Dillon, who was a member of both these bodies, and Davitt, who was on the National Directory, did not attend these meetings.

That the landlord and tenant representatives at the conference had reached an agreement had been a matter of much surprise. It was even more amazing that the government accepted the principal recommendations of the report and embodied them in a Land Bill which was introduced in the House of Commons by George Wyndham on March 25, 1903. There were, it is true, some differences between the scheme proposed by the government and that recommended in the land conference report. Moreover, since the report was in general terms, it had been necessary, when preparing the bill, to work out many details, some of which proved to be rather controversial. Except in the case of the congested districts, the government did not accept the report's recommendation to proceed by sale of individual holdings. Principally, the operation of purchase was to take the form of the purchase of estates. Landlords were to be permitted to make arrangements with their tenants, subject only to the supervision of estates commissioners who were to be appointed to oversee and conclude the transactions. With the consent of the tenants of three-fourths of the holdings, the estates commissioners might arrange for the purchase of the estate. If the remaining tenants refused to purchase, they were to be deprived of the right of having their rents fixed judicially. Thus, an indirect sort of pressure to compel the minority to purchase would be applied.

As had been recommended in the report, the money required by the tenants to pay the landlords was to be advanced by the Treasury. The tenants were to repay it by a series of annuities extended over a period of $68\frac{1}{2}$ years. It was important to the government, as well as to the tenants, that these annuities should amount to less than the current annual rent, for the government had obligations to meet which depended entirely on the ability of the tenants to pay their instalments. The bill therefore provided for a system of price "zones" with the object of reducing to a minimum the likelihood of nonpayment. Under this system the annuities were to be 20 to 40 per cent less in the case of first-term rents and 10 to 30 per cent less in the case of second-term rents.

In a further effort to induce the landlords to sell, the Treasury was to provide for the payment of cash bonuses the sum of £12,000,000. It was proposed that the bonus should be graduated inversely with the purchase price; i.e., 15 per cent on an estate worth £5,000, 10 per cent on one worth £20,000, and 5 per cent on one worth £40,000.[11]

The bill was generally well received in the House of Commons except by a few extreme Unionists. There was, however, opposition among Irish Nationalists to some of its provisions. It was argued that the proposed bonus was insufficient to induce the larger landlords to sell, for, under the graduation scheme, they would receive a proportionately smaller amount than would the landlords with less valuable estates. Another aspect of the bill to which the Nationalists took exception was the "zonal" system, for they felt that if free bargaining were allowed the tenants might, in some cases, be able to secure greater reductions than the maximums allowed in the price zones. There was also Nationalist opposition to the provision designed to compel the minority to purchase its holdings.

In public, at least, Blake's role in relation to the Land Bill was not a major one. He did not participate in the debates on first and second readings in the Commons, and it was only during the committee stage that he intervened briefly from time to time. It appears that there were at least two, and probably three reasons for his comparative inactivity in the Irish debates of this period.

Because a dispute had arisen between the United States and Canada over the boundary of Alaska, it was agreed in 1903 that

[11] For further details of both the land conference report and the Land Bill, see John E. Pomfret, *The Struggle for Land in Ireland, 1800–1923* (Princeton, 1930), 284–96.

the interpretation of the treaties establishing that boundary should be referred to a tribunal of "six impartial jurists of repute."[12] At the request of Sir Wilfrid Laurier, Prime Minister of Canada, Blake agreed, in March of that year, to act in the case as counsel for Canada.[13] Between that time and the end of July, 1903, he devoted much of his time and energy to the difficult task of preparing the Canadian case, and, since these were the months during which the Irish Land Bill was before the Commons, it was not surprising that his participation in the debates upon it was limited.

A second reason for Blake's comparatively minor role in relation to the Land Bill was the state of his health. Long overwork had led him to the verge of a nervous breakdown, and, from his correspondence during this period, it is evident that he was constantly struggling to keep up his labours in the face of increasing ill health. His condition was aggravated by his work on the Alaska boundary dispute and, as will be seen presently, illness eventually forced him, much against his will, to give up his association with that case before the work on it was completed.

It is possible that a third reason for Blake's reticence during the debates on the Land Bill was his disagreement with Redmond on some aspects of the question and his desire that these differences of opinion should not become known to the public. This, at any rate, can be inferred from a letter of Blake's, reference to which will be made later.[14]

But it must not be supposed that Blake did not assist or advise

[12]The task of the jurists was to interpret the Anglo-Russian treaty of 1825, by which the boundary of Alaska had been fixed at ten marine leagues from the sea, and the American-Russian treaty of 1867, by which the United States had acquired Alaska from Russia. At the time these treaties were signed, the exact boundary was of little concern to anyone, but the discovery of gold in territory, part of which belonged to the United States and part to Canada, made the accurate delimitation of the boundary important. For a detailed account of the Alaska boundary dispute, see C. C. Tansill, *Canadian-American Relations, 1875–1911* (New Haven, 1943), 121–265.

[13]See Laurier Papers, Blake to Laurier, March 6, 1903. The text of Laurier's letter to Blake, dated Feb. 5, 1903, requesting him to act as counsel, is included in this letter. There is much correspondence between Blake and Laurier and between E. F. Blake and Laurier regarding the Alaska case among the Laurier Papers.

[14]Blake Papers, Blake to Redmond, March 20, 1903.

his Irish colleagues in their work on the Land Bill. On the contrary, although his public role in relation to the measure was a minor one, he was active behind the scenes. Together with other Irish Nationalist leaders, he took part in negotiations with Wyndham and Sir Antony MacDonnell. Indeed, it may be inferred from the following statement made by William O'Brien regarding the Irish national convention held in April, 1903, to consider the Land Bill, that Blake was one of the chief spokesmen for the Nationalist side: "Mr. Wyndham told Mr. Redmond and Mr. Blake that unless it was made clear that the Convention heartily accepted the Bill in its main principles it would not be possible for the Government to proceed with it further."[15]

It appears that, some time before the introduction of the Land Bill in the House of Commons, Blake, together with Redmond and William O'Brien, attended a private conference with Sir Antony MacDonnell at the Westminster Palace Hotel in London. Sir Antony's brother, Dr. M. A. MacDonnell, was also present at this meeting. Some additional meetings seem to have been held and then, only a few days before the introduction of the bill, Blake, at the request of Dr. MacDonnell, had a further interview with Sir Antony. This interview was reported by Blake in a lengthy letter to Redmond. It is from it that the following account is taken.

On March 19, Dr. MacDonnell requested Blake to accompany him to see Sir Antony and showed him (Blake) a note of some suggestions. Blake said that he did not see how he could engage in any discussion of these points without Redmond and O'Brien; he felt, at any rate, that he should not go without Redmond's knowledge and assent. When, however, Dr. MacDonnell told him that he had just seen Redmond, who had expressed a strong desire that Blake should go, he agreed to do so.

By this time, Sir Antony was aware that an Irish national convention was to be held after the introduction of the Land Bill to consider what stand the Irish parliamentary party should take upon it in the House of Commons. What seemed most obvious to Blake during his interview with Sir Antony was that the latter was very anxious about the convention and was desirous of expressing his

[15] O'Brien, *Olive Branch*, 226.

views as to resolutions. Sir Antony thought that the convention's general resolution should be one of acceptance of the principles of the bill as a settlement, or, as he once put it, as the basis of a settlement, of the land question. It was his belief that this course would be consistent with claiming amendments on certain aspects. On its being pointed out, however, that acceptance, authorized conditionally on the concession of amendments, involved rejection if the amendments were not conceded, he took the ground of pressing for amendments, but not in such a way as would involve rejection in case of failure. But it was repeated that whatever the convention should make absolute conditions of acceptance could not afterwards be abandoned.

Sir Antony was next reminded of the conviction of Redmond and O'Brien that the amount of the bonus was inadequate to settle the question. Later in the interview Blake expressed his concurrence with his two colleagues in this matter. In response to a question asked by Dr. MacDonnell, Sir Antony said it would be "perfectly legitimate to press" for an increase of £3,000,000 to the bonus. He could not, however, give any assurance that such an increase would be granted, and Blake doubted that he felt at all certain that it would.

At this point in his letter to Redmond, Blake expressed some of his general views on the land question. It is this part of the letter which gives the impression that he was not altogether in agreement with Redmond and that, for this reason, he could say little in public upon the subject. He wrote:

> I must here diverge to state my personal position as affecting this point. You will remember, when I saw you immediately on my return [from Canada], I told you that my own impression formed without having seen the speeches, criticisms and articles on the [land] Conference, was that the conference terms to the landlords were extravagant, that the Treasury would not make them good, that the tenants would be squeezed, and that the possible but strange result of the affair might be to find the tenant party engaged in an agitation to secure to the landlords an unjustifiable price. I have since read all the material available and I grieve to say this impression has not been changed.
>
> I also then told you that I recognized that a critical situation had been created, that much was irrevocable, that it was a clear duty to seek to make the very best of that situation, that I was determined to act with a single eye to that object, and had not the least idea of making public any impressions

which I could properly keep private. On these lines I have since acted; but of course, the most I can do on some points is to keep silent where I am unable to argue in line with you. . . .

The next important subject discussed in the interview with Sir Antony was the maximum of reductions specified under the zonal system. Blake reminded the Under-Secretary that, in earlier interviews, a suggestion had been made as to the absolute elimination of the maximum; this proposal had, however, been set aside by the Nationalists who were present on the ground that a dangerous impression might be created in the tenants' minds that this change was in the landlords' interests. Since then, however, the *Freeman's Journal* had adopted the view that there should be no maximum, and Blake's personal opinion was that this tended to remove the danger. He thought, therefore, that Redmond might now be willing to accept the elimination of the maximum. But Sir Antony spoke strongly as to the difficulty of eliminating the maximum; he believed that it would involve individual inquiry in every case. He suggested that the Nationalists request an increase of the maximum, in the case of second-term rents, from 30 to 35. Blake said that 40 had been mentioned earlier. The Under-Secretary did not strongly dispute this but did not quite yield it. Blake spoke of 40 throughout the discussion. When Sir Antony added that an increase in the second-term maximum would involve a proportionate increase in the first-term maximum (he suggested 50), Blake replied that this was one of the difficulties which made him tend to favour elimination, rather than raising, of the maximum. He reminded Sir Antony that Wyndham had expressly said that he could not contemplate any increase as to the first-term maximum. The Under-Secretary did not seem to remember this, but Blake felt quite clear upon it. Sir Antony reiterated that the one seemed to involve the other and Blake could not differ. When Dr. MacDonnell spoke to his brother about assurances as to the government's yielding on the question under discussion, the latter did not, of course, commit himself. Blake felt, however, that his tone was much more encouraging than it had been on the bonus and that he believed it could be accomplished.

After giving Redmond the foregoing detailed account of the interview, Blake summarized Sir Antony's views in the following words:

> Speaking generally, it seemed pretty plain that Sir Antony had considerably modified some views expressed at the Westminster Palace Hotel. I judged that he thinks now that the Convention may pass or wreck the bill; that the resolutions and the speeches there are of the last consequence; that the power behind the Government largely depends on the idea of the new departure of goodwill, concerted action and settlement by practically mutual agreement of the Land Question; and that language and resolutions which would dissipate these notions would be dangerous or fatal. The idea he wished to convey was that "judicious management" would procure amendments and success, while other courses would result in the failure of the Bill, which he said represented more than we could ever hope to get again.[16]

Further correspondence between Redmond and Blake shows that the latter gave much assistance in drawing up the resolutions which were adopted at the national convention held in Dublin on April 16. Writing from London on April 10, Blake told Redmond, who was then in Dublin, that he was enclosing a few suggestions which might serve as rough drafts in connection with the resolutions on the Land Bill. Unfortunately, Blake's draft resolutions have not come to light, but his general view regarding the attitude to be taken at the convention can be ascertained from this letter. By way of comment on his draft resolutions he wrote:

> The attitude I desire to see adopted is such as will show acceptance of the Bill in principle as a large effort to settle the question; coupled with declarations of its inadequacy in our opinion to accomplish that work unless amended in indicated respects; making a call on the Parliamentary Party to put amendments as serious and urgent as is consistent with some freedom of action later; but declaring no present *ultimatum*; and the reserving of final decision till after the Committee stage.
> I wish the party to be armed with all the strength which can be given to it by the Convention to occupy every position and use every weapon useful for attack; and for important amendments.
> But I repeat I wish no *ultimatum* now.[17]

It was generally felt among leading Nationalists that some reference to national political objectives should be made at the convention; this would make it plain that, no matter how beneficial

[16] Blake Papers, Blake to Redmond, March 20, 1903.
[17] *Ibid.*, Blake to Redmond, April 10, 1903.

the Land Bill proved to be, Ireland and her representatives would continue to press their demand for home rule. With this in mind, Blake, a few days after drafting the resolutions on the Land Bill, wrote again to Redmond, enclosing his suggestion for a general resolution on the political question. "I have," he explained, "sketched and enclosed a very rough draft which will show you at any rate what I aim; and may serve like the others as material out of which you may construct worthier work."[18] This draft, like the earlier one, has not been located.

Various proposals for amending the provision designed to compel the recalcitrant minority on an estate to purchase were evidently under discussion at this time, for in a further letter Blake told Redmond that the more he thought of it, the more dissatisfied he was with the proposal for compulsion. There did not seem to him to be any sound basis for the allegation that there existed among the tenants a common interest similar to that which in companies justified the decision of the majority of shareholders or bondholders being made binding on the minority. On the whole, he concluded, "I wish to say that I do not see my way to compulsion as at present advised—tho' of course I keep a very open mind. . . ."[19]

From the two last mentioned letters, it is clear that Blake was struggling to keep up his work under very serious difficulties. On the thirteenth, he told Redmond that he was "very far from well," but was "striving to get on" with his Alaska work. Then, on the fourteenth, he reported that he had planned to start for Dublin the next day, but that now, having suffered "a sharp attack," he feared he would be unable to stand the journey and the convention. Adding, however, that he would not yet give up hope, he told Redmond that, if compelled to cancel his trip, he would wire him the next day. As he had feared, ill health prevented his attendance at the convention in Dublin on April 16. It was announced to the gathering that he had "wired an excuse for not being present owing to illness."[20]

A letter which Redmond wrote to Blake the day before the con-

[18]*Ibid.*, Blake to Redmond, April 13, 1903.
[19]*Ibid.*, Blake to Redmond, April 14, 1903.
[20]*Irish Independent and Nation*, Dublin, April 17, 1903.

vention shows that the latter's suggestions proved very helpful to those who were working on the resolutions in Dublin. Redmond reported that he and his colleagues had carefully considered Blake's drafts and had added to the first resolution the words proposed by him. Furthermore, most of his suggestions on other points had been embodied in the resolutions outlining desired amendments.[21]

The convention proved to be almost unanimously in favour of accepting the general principles of the bill, while seeking amendments on certain points. William O'Brien proposed the adoption of a resolution expressing satisfaction at the introduction of the bill, declaring that it required serious amendment on a number of vital points, and entrusting to the Irish parliamentary party the power and responsibility of deciding the attitude to be adopted towards it in its subsequent stages. A clerical delegate who moved as an amendment the unconditional rejection of the bill found only one supporter. Nor was Michael Davitt, who brought forward what he described as a "friendly" amendment, any more successful. His proposal was that the convention should, at the present time, come to no final decision regarding the bill but should wait until it was in its amended third reading form, when it might be brought before an adjourned meeting of the convention. On seeing that there was little support for his amendment, Davitt withdrew it, and O'Brien's original resolution was carried unanimously. On the second day of the convention, a resolution was adopted asserting that Ireland's first and greatest need was national self-government, and that no other remedy for her needs and grievances either could or would be accepted. Following this, a resolution calling for amendments on seventeen specific points in the Land Bill was carried. Among the matters on which amendments were sought were those mentioned by Blake in some of his letters to Redmond—the cash bonus to the landlords, the zonal system, and compulsory purchase by the recalcitrant minority on an estate.[22]

O'Brien's resolution, adopted on the first day of the convention, was undoubtedly the one referred to by Redmond as the first one,

[21] Blake Papers, Redmond to Blake, April 15, 1903.
[22] For a fuller account of the work of the convention, see O'Brien, *Olive Branch*, 222-9.

to which the words suggested by Blake had been added. When Blake's attitude, as outlined in his letter of April 10 to Redmond, is examined, it is not difficult to see that there is a strong resemblance between it and the views expressed in O'Brien's resolution. It is probable too that Blake's draft resolution on national political objects aided those who prepared the resolution on self-government, which was adopted on the second day of the convention.

During the Commons debate on the second reading of the Land Bill, which began on May 4, Irish Nationalist members took the stand which had been advocated at the convention in Dublin. While expressing satisfaction with the spirit and general purpose of the measure, they spoke strongly of the need for numerous amendments. The proposal and consideration of specific amendments had, of course, to be delayed until the committee stage, and the second reading of the bill was carried by a very large majority—443 votes against 26.

When the bill was in committee, the Nationalists succeeded in securing the adoption of many of the amendments which they considered necessary. Their proposed changes in the zonal system were not accepted in full, but Redmond and Wyndham reached a compromise upon this question. It was agreed to allow free bargaining outside the zones if this were desired by both tenants and landlords. In such cases, however, the bonus would have to be treated as part of the purchase money until it had been ascertained whether the terms agreed upon were fair to all parties concerned. Wyndham's scheme of graduating the bonus inversely with the purchase price was replaced by a provision for a uniform bonus of 12 per cent of the sale price. The powerful landlords, as well as the Nationalists, had pressed for this amendment. The clause regarding the treatment of the recalcitrant minority on an estate which had been sold was also amended. Originally, an indirect sort of pressure to compel them to purchase had been proposed; as will be remembered, they were to be deprived of the right to have their rents fixed judicially. To replace this, an amendment proposed not by a Nationalist, but by T. W. Russell, was adopted. It provided that the estates commissioners might, if they thought fit, "order that the remaining tenants, or any of them" should be "deemed to have accepted the offers" which they had not accepted. Although this was a more direct form of compulsion, it was regarded by Nationalist members as preferable to the indirect form, for under it there was a possibility of securing consideration of individual cases. It met, at least in part, the objection put forward by Blake in his letter of April 14 to Redmond.

On July 21, the third reading of the bill, like the second, was carried by a large majority—317 votes against 20. Then, in August, having passed the House of Lords and received the royal assent, it became law.[23]

By this time Blake's health had broken down completely, and, at the end of July, he was forced to give up further association with the Alaska boundary case. Writing of his enforced decision to Sir Wilfrid Laurier, he declared that he had devoted much time and energy to the case, but "with ever increasing difficulties, owing to nervous debility arising out of long continued overwork." He then described in some detail the current state of his health:

> At last and within a few days the malady became so acute that my energies, and powers of concentration, recollection and continuous application—in short my capacities for discharging the duties of the position—so far failed that I was driven to consult the best physician available; and after a second consultation, he has to-day reiterated his first and decided opinion that I am suffering from a severe attack of *neurasthenia*, and absolutely require complete rest and change for about six months.[24]

This breakdown in health, in addition to forcing Blake to relinquish his brief in the Alaska case, naturally removed him for a time from active participation in Irish politics. On the advice of his physician, he left England in August and remained on the continent, mainly in Switzerland and Italy, until almost the end of 1903.

From Blake's correspondence during March and April, 1903, it has been seen that he co-operated closely with Redmond and O'Brien in their private discussions on the Land Bill. Obviously, he was in sympathy with the general purpose and spirit of the bill, though he desired amendment on various aspects of it. From his

[23]For a more detailed account of the debates on the Land Bill and especially of the changes made in committee, see *Annual Register, 1903*, pp. 127, 154–7, and 181–2.
[24]Laurier Papers, Blake to Laurier, July 31, 1903.

expressed dissatisfaction with the land conference report, it might however be implied that he was not overly enthusiastic about the policy of conciliation with the Unionists, and the fact that, as will be seen in the next chapter, he had from the first been opposed to Sir Antony MacDonnell's appointment as Under-Secretary strengthens this view. Unfortunately, there is no record of what Blake thought of Dillon's attitude towards the Land Act. Since, however, Dillon was abroad during March and April when negotiations on the bill were taking place, his absence from the meetings at which Blake was present need not be taken as an indication that the latter was in complete agreement with the views of O'Brien and Redmond as opposed to those of Dillon. The only piece of evidence on this subject is a statement of Dillon's—in a letter written in November, 1903,—that there was, so far as he could see, no difference of opinion between him and Blake as to conciliation.[25] But since the letter to which Dillon's was a reply has not been located, no definite conclusion can be drawn regarding Blake's views on this subject.

The Cork Writ

With his health at least partially restored by the rest and change on the continent, Blake was able to return to London in time for the opening of the parliamentary session of 1904. He took part in the debate on the address, speaking mainly of the need for a settlement of the Irish university question,[26] and, from the Irish leaders' correspondence of that year, it is clear that he gave much valuable advice and assistance during the session. But it is also evident that Blake's health had not been completely restored and that he was thus prevented from taking as active a part in political life as he would have wished. The Irish party was, in fact, greatly handicapped by illness during the session of 1904. Dillon's health at the beginning of the year had forced him to go abroad for several months; and Redmond, writing to him in May, reported that Blake

[25] Blake Papers, Dillon to Blake, Nov. 27, 1903.
[26] For Blake's speech on this occasion, see *Hansard*, 4th Series, CXXIX, 243–52.

and T. P. O'Connor had been "laid up off and on during the whole session."[27]

In the closing days of the session, an incident occurred which called for a difficult and immediate decision on the part of the Irish leaders. Redmond, however, had by that time gone to Ireland, leaving the affairs of the party at Westminster in charge of Blake. Thus, the chief responsibility for making the decision rested on him.

To understand what occurred in August, 1904, it is necessary to go back to November of the previous year, when William O'Brien announced his intention of resigning both his seat in the House of Commons and his position on the National Directory of the United Irish League. The reason for his decision was his annoyance at the attitude adopted by Dillon, Davitt, and Sexton towards the Land Act, and, at the time he announced his proposed resignations, he attacked these men in letters to the press. Irish Nationalists were both surprised and dismayed at O'Brien's action, for they feared that not only would the retirement of so prominent a public figure weaken the cause, but also that his attacks on leading Irish Nationalists would result in a return of the dissension of the previous decade. They decided therefore to call a special meeting of the party in the hope that it would urge O'Brien to reconsider his decision. On November 18, 1903, Redmond issued a circular letter to the members of the party inviting them to attend a meeting in Dublin on the twenty-fourth of that month to consider the adoption of a resolution expressing regret at O'Brien's proposed resignations and urging him "for the sake of Ireland" to abandon his intention and continue to aid the cause which he had so long and ably championed. Redmond proposed to move this resolution from the chair.[28]

It is clear from Blake's reply to Redmond's circular letter that he did not approve of O'Brien's attack on Dillon and those who shared his views. Writing from Rome, he told Redmond that he was sorry he could not get to Dublin for the meeting—there was not sufficient time and, in any case, his health would not allow it. He then went on to say that he had read O'Brien's letters with the greatest surprise and regret and that he trusted he would not reiterate his personal

[27] Dillon Papers, Redmond to Dillon, May 17, 1904.
[28] There is a copy of the circular letter among the Blake Papers.

attacks. It was also Blake's hope that those directly concerned might, in the interests of peace, make the great sacrifice of silence and that O'Brien might—though he judged this to be improbable—be induced to recall his proposed resignations.[29]

The Irish party, at its meeting of November 24, adopted Redmond's resolution urging O'Brien to reconsider his decision.[30] In spite of this, O'Brien persisted in carrying out his expressed intentions.

Not only the Irish party, but also O'Brien's constituents in Cork City, wished him to retain his seat in the House of Commons. In view of this situation, the Irish leaders decided to delay the motion for the issue of a writ for a by-election in that city in the hope that O'Brien would, after a few months' retirement, agree to return to Parliament. As a result, the seat remained vacant for several months, and it was generally understood that no attempt would be made to fill it during the session of 1904. But on August 10, as the session was drawing to a close, Blake was warned that Jasper Tully, an Irish Nationalist member of Parliament, was going to move the writ for Cork the next day.[31] Tully, although a Nationalist, was not a member of the Irish parliamentary party and frequently criticized its policies. He evidently believed that the leaders of the party were attempting to keep the seat vacant because they were opposed to some of O'Brien's views and did not wish him to be re-elected.

In view of the attitude of the Irish party and the electors of Cork City, Blake realized that the issue of the writ would not be a popular move. Yet he feared that there was no constitutional ground for resisting the motion. Though the writ for a vacant seat in the House of Commons was generally moved by a whip of the party to which the retiring member belonged, there was nothing to prevent any member of the House from moving it. If, however, a member proposed to take such action, it was customary for him to give notice of his intention to the whips of the party concerned. For

[29]Redmond Papers, Blake to Redmond, Nov. 23, 1903. There is a copy of this letter among the Blake Papers.
[30]For an account of the meeting, see *Irish Independent and Nation*, Dublin, Nov. 25, 1903.
[31]See Blake Papers, John Murphy to Blake, Aug. 10, 1904; W. Abraham to Blake, Aug. 10, 1904.

BLAKE'S ACTIVITIES CURTAILED 293

the moment, therefore, all Blake could do was to ascertain whether such notice had been given. What he discovered was revealed in his remarks the next day in the House of Commons.

On August 11, Jasper Tully announced to the House of Commons that "he wished to move that a writ should be issued to fill the vacancy in the representation of the City of Cork, caused by the resignation of Mr. William O'Brien." After complaining that the representation of the constituency had been vacant for nearly a year, he revealed that he had "given notice to the three Whips of the Nationalist party that unless they moved for the issue of the writ on Wednesday [August 10] he would move for it the following day." When he began to discuss related matters, the Speaker interrupted him to say that they could not "be gone into in moving for a new writ" and that he understood Tully to base his action on the fact that the seat was vacant and the constituency unrepresented. Thereupon Tully stated simply that he moved that the Speaker issue the writ.

At this point Blake rose to ask the ruling of the Speaker on a question of order. Noting that the vacancy had existed for a considerable time and that a period of the session had been reached when it would be impossible for an election to take place and a member to be returned early enough to take his seat before Parliament prorogued, he asked whether there did not arise a question of privilege connected with the recency and urgency of the matter and with the inability of a new member, if returned, to take his seat until Parliament next assembled. And there was another question requiring consideration. When it was desired that a writ be moved, the practice usually observed, so far as his experience went, was that notice was given to the whips of the party which had held the seat. Tully had given notice, but it had been addressed to the three whips who were absent in Dublin on political duties, while the remaining whip, who was in London, had not received it. Thus the question was whether reasonable and sufficient notice had been given to the representatives of the party to which the former holder of the seat belonged.

After Tully had reported that he had not been aware of the absence of the three whips, the Speaker declared that he did not think there was any reason why he should not put the question regarding the issue of the writ. The fact that the election could not be held in time to enable the new member to take his seat during the present session was not, he asserted, a ban to the motion. After further interruptions by Tully, who wished to speak of certain charges made against himself and O'Brien, the Speaker said that the writ might, of course, be moved for by any member, but that it was customary to give notice to the whips of the party concerned. He added that although Tully had given such notice there appeared to be some doubt as to whether it had been a sufficient notice. Accordingly, he recommended that Tully postpone his motion, for he thought that the House would hardly approve of proceeding with it immediately. With Tully's consent, the motion was therefore postponed until the next day.[32]

In view of this situation, Blake felt that it would be advisable to attempt to ascertain Redmond's views on the issue of the writ before the motion was again proposed the next day. Consequently, he wired Redmond asking his advice.[33] When Redmond received the telegram, he was just leaving Dublin for his country home, "Aughavanagh," in County Wicklow. He therefore sent the telegram to Dillon, who was at Ballybrack, near Dublin, expressing the opinion that Blake should make it plain that they had abstained from moving the writ in accordance with the wishes of the Cork people. Redmond asked Dillon, if he agreed, to wire Blake in both their names to that effect. Finally, Redmond told Dillon that he was wiring Augustin Roche, the Lord Mayor of Cork, telling him of Tully's action.[34] Dillon wired Blake accordingly, but also advised him to communicate fully with Redmond the next day.[35] Dillon's telegram did not, however, reach Blake before he had to speak again in the Commons on the issue of the writ. The only communication which he did receive from Ireland was a telegram from

[32]For the full text of the foregoing proceedings, see *Hansard*, 4th Series, CXL, 228–30.
[33]This telegram has not come to light.
[34]Blake Papers, Redmond to Dillon, Aug. 11, 1904.
[35]*Ibid.*, Dillon to Blake, Aug. 11, 1904.

the Lord Mayor of Cork reading: "Better defer application for writ for the present."[36]

Blake also considered it wise to seek the opinions of leading members of the major parties in the House of Commons upon the matter in question. He therefore spoke to Herbert Gladstone, son of the late Prime Minister, who promised to consult influential persons and let Blake know their views. Later the same day (August 11), he wrote to Blake:

> As regards the Cork writ I have spoken to Bryce and Acland Hood and others. It seems to be generally agreed that delay in moving a new writ beyond a certain point cannot be defended in "constitutional" argument. Practically it is never done as regards England, Wales and Scotland, so that you must not count on Liberal support if you oppose Tully's motion. I quite understand how the delay in respect to the Cork writ has occurred, but at the same time delay does mean disfranchisement and on constitutional grounds as well as on grounds of general convenience we should have to support the general practice if we took any part.[37]

Since Acland Hood was chief whip of the Conservative party (Gladstone was chief whip of the Liberals), this letter really indicated that neither Liberals nor Conservatives were likely to support Blake if he opposed the issue of the writ. In fact, by the time he received this communication, Blake had already spoken to Acland Hood, who had expressed views similar to those stated in Herbert Gladstone's letter.[38]

On August 12, Jasper Tully, in moving the issue of a new writ for Cork City,[39] said that, according to Sir Erskine May (a distinguished lawyer and historian, who had been clerk of the House of Commons), the acceptance of office legally vacated a seat[40] and

[36]*Ibid.*, Augustin Roche to Blake, Aug. 11, 1904.
[37]*Ibid.*, Herbert Gladstone to Blake, Aug. 11, 1904.
[38]For an account of Blake's interviews with Herbert Gladstone and Acland Hood, see *ibid.*, Blake to Dillon, Aug. 14, 1904.
[39]For Tully's speech, see *Hansard*, 4th Series, CXL, 413–14.
[40]By English law a member of Parliament cannot resign his seat, but if he accepts an office of profit under the Crown he *ipso facto* vacates it, though in some cases he can be re-elected. A member who wishes to resign therefore petitions for a nominal office, that is, to be made Steward of the Chiltern Hundreds (namely, Stoke, Burnham, and Desborough in Buckinghamshire), or of the Manor of Northstead.

obliged the House to order a new writ. The same authority laid it down that in the case of an acceptance of the Chiltern Hundreds, the statutory power of the Speaker to issue a writ on his own authority during the recess did not apply. What Tully meant to emphasize by this latter statement, though he did not explain it very clearly, was that if the writ were not issued before the close of the current session it would not be possible to hold a by-election in Cork City until some time after Parliament reassembled; thus, the constituency would not be represented in the early days of the next session.

As on the preceding day, Tully attempted to outline O'Brien's views; but after a few statements he was interrupted by the Speaker, who asserted that the question was not the opinion of O'Brien, but whether the vacancy caused by his acceptance of the Chiltern Hundreds was to be filled by someone, not necessarily O'Brien. In spite of the Speaker's attitude, Tully was determined to speak of O'Brien's position at least in relation to the vacant seat. He feared that further delay in issuing the writ might weaken O'Brien's position, for O'Brien had been described in the *London Gazette* as having accepted the stewardship of the Chiltern Hundreds and it was a serious thing in Ireland for anyone to be described as the paid bailiff of His Majesty's government. In America and elsewhere, O'Brien would be branded as holding paid office under the British government.

Finally, Tully asserted that a serious precedent would be established by allowing the seat to remain vacant for so long a period and that it might result in grave consequences. It might be necessary to hold an autumn session to consider a question of peace or war, the decision of which might rest upon a single vote—the vote of the member for Cork City. Moreover, the period during which the seat remained vacant would be used to undermine O'Brien's position, and, just as any fortress might be reduced in six months, so, before next session, O'Brien might be deprived of the right of representing Cork City. Tully therefore begged to move the issue of the writ.

When the motion had been made and the question proposed, Blake rose to address the House.[41] He explained that he had been unsuccessful in his attempt to communicate by wire with Redmond,

[41] For Blake's speech, see *Hansard*, 4th Series, CXL, 414-17.

but that he had had a personal conversation with him on the subject of the Cork vacancy some two or three months previously. Thus, he was able to explain why the writ had not been moved and was not now moved from the benches occupied by the Irish party. After the vacancy occurred, those who were responsible for the conduct of political affairs in Cork told Redmond that they did not desire the issue of the writ. Redmond had expressed his readiness to move for the issue of the writ as soon as he received an intimation of their desire for it, but at the time of Blake's conversation with him, he had received no such intimation either from these men or from any other quarter. Moreover, Blake was quite confident that no such desire had been expressed by the people of Cork since that date. The wishes of the political authorities in that city had been to the contrary for reasons which were well known, but which were not of the character indicated by Tully. Blake told the House of the telegram which he had received from the Lord Mayor of Cork, who was known to be a supporter of O'Brien's views, expressing the desire that the application for the writ should be deferred for the present.

But the House would have to dispose of the question regarding the writ "upon general constitutional considerations and nothing else." There was, in Blake's opinion, only one circumstance which could justify the non-issue of the writ and the leaving of the city of Cork or any other place unrepresented for a time beyond that which was reasonable and which both sides might require to make their arrangements. This was the existence of an almost unanimous feeling on the part of the constituency in favour of that view. The right of any member to move for the issue of a writ was a valuable security, although it might occasionally be abused, against a seat being left vacant for any other reason. Any member who assumed to himself to represent that general feeling of the body in favour of representation was free to exercise this right. It was true that if the writ had been moved for earlier, more could have been said for the motion than was now possible. A new representative of Cork City would not be able to take his seat this session, so no urgency existed from that point of view. Nevertheless, it was quite true that, in this case, the ordinary right of two members to address the speaker during the recess and thus secure the issue of a writ did not obtain; consequently, if the writ were not now issued, Cork City would be unrepresented during the early days of the next session. His speech continued:

> The Nationalist Party had all along recognised that their abstention from moving for the writ could only operate so long as no member availed himself of his privilege to move independently. That was the extent of their responsibility and the limit of their power. According to the practice of the House any hon. member had a right to move after giving 24 hours notice. As far as he and his colleagues were concerned, they were satisfied that the rights of Parliament and of the City of Cork, and of any minority in that city to be represented in Parliament, were amply secured by the powers possessed by any hon. member to move for the issue of a writ if he thought fit to do so. Having received no intimation with reference to this matter from any person in the City of Cork, the Nationalist Party had left to others the task of moving for this writ.

Blake concluded his speech with the announcement that the Irish party had no desire to resist Tully's motion. But he added that the responsibility for this course was his alone, since he had had no opportunity of consulting Redmond. The question regarding the writ was then put to the House and it was agreed, without a division, that it should be issued.[42]

The day after, Redmond wrote to Blake assuring him that he had done "absolutely the right thing about the Cork writ."[43] Before receiving this letter, however, Blake had become much disturbed by the comments on the subject which had appeared on August 13 in the London correspondence of the *Freeman's Journal*. In this column, after Tully's action had been described as "a proceeding which is outside the recognised rules of Parliamentary warfare," it was remarked that Blake had "stated the case, politically and constitutionally, with perfect lucidity, and while registering a protest against the breach of Parliamentary usage which Mr. Tully had perpetrated, at the same time did not feel able on constitutional grounds to oppose the issue of the writ." The London correspondent added that, if the Irish members had wished to divide against the motion, it would have been defeated, since Tully would have had

[42]*Ibid.*, 417.
[43]Blake Papers, Redmond to Blake, Aug. 13, 1904.

the support of only "a few of the more rabid tories," while the bulk of the ministerial party and the opposition would have voted to prevent "the breach of the established usage."

Blake believed that these remarks constituted a veiled attack upon him for not opposing the issue of the writ. In a letter to Dillon he complained that if matters were to remain before the Irish people as that issue of the *Freeman's Journal* left them, it would be assumed that the party had been injured by his action. Consequently, "an intolerable injustice" would be inflicted upon him, and his "poor power of serving the cause" would be so impaired that he might well hold himself free to take any opportunity of retirement. After quoting the remarks of the London correspondent, Blake declared that if these statements were true he would have been guilty of a grave fault. "I was bound," he asserted, "to avail myself of any 'established usage' or any 'rules of Parliamentary warfare' which might furnish a ground for defeating Mr. Tully's motion." But the Speaker had indicated plainly that there was no established usage or rule which, the condition of preliminary notice to the whips being performed, interfered with Tully's right to move for the writ.

> Again, as to the fate of the motion resisted, had the views of "all the opposition" and of "the bulk of the ministerial party" been such that they would have voted against the motion it would have been my plain duty to take the best steps I could to develop that feeling.
> And I am in effect charged with having thwarted the wishes of the House and secured the issue of the writ, which would have been prevented had the House been challenged by me to exercise its judgment.
> This is an absolutely false position in which no man or party has the right to place or leave me.

Then, by telling Dillon of his interviews with Herbert Gladstone and Acland Hood and enclosing the letter which he had received from the former, Blake showed that the general view of the House of Commons was just the reverse of that stated by the London correspondent of the *Freeman's Journal*. He concluded, therefore, that had there been a division Tully would have carried the motion "by the whole house less a handful of men," thus inflicting on the members of the Irish party a defeat in which they "would have been discredited not only by the numbers and character of the majority (to which in a good cause one attaches less weight) but also by the indefensible and anti-popular nature of the position" which they had vainly defended.

Finally, after complaining of the abbreviated report given by the *Freeman's Journal* of his speech in the House of Commons, and the editorial silence on that subject, Blake remarked: "I may add that the Speaker to others as well as to myself expressed the highest approval of my statement of the constitutional and parliamentary position and of the course I had taken; and I have had from several other quarters intimations of the favourable way in which it impressed the House."[44]

Having asked Dillon to send his letter on to Redmond, Blake wrote a short note to him, explaining that he was disturbed at the attitude of the *Freeman's Journal*, but that he had thought it better to write to Dillon, who would forward the letter to him.[45]

On receipt of Blake's letter, Dillon immediately wired and wrote him expressing deep distress at its contents, stating that he was communicating with Redmond, and begging Blake to take no step until he heard from them. Dillon declared that he was indignant at the conduct of the *Freeman's Journal*, but hoped that the wrong done to Blake in the issue of August 13 would be righted as far as possible. He added that the situation in Ireland was extremely critical and that any such disaster as Blake's retirement would make it quite hopeless.[46]

To Dillon's telegram, Blake, who had by then received Redmond's letter of August 13, wired the following reply: "Gratified for wire. Did not dream of embarrassing by precipitate action. Redmond kindly wrote saying management absolutely right."[47] He also sent a letter expressing the same views and saying that he was sorry he had used words which might be interpreted into an intention of taking some public action, embarrassing or precipitate in its nature. He had meant only that he must hold himself "in all conditions free, and in some conditions obliged, to take decisive action later."

[44]*Ibid.*, Blake to Dillon, Aug. 14, 1904.
[45]*Ibid.*, Blake to Redmond, Aug. 14, 1904.
[46]Dillon's telegram and letter, both dated Aug. 15, 1904, are among the Blake Papers.
[47]There is an undated copy of the telegram among the Blake Papers.

But he would do so only when he judged it least embarrassing to the cause.[48]

On seeing Blake's letter of August 14 to Dillon, Redmond appears to have felt that Blake was unduly upset. But since he (Redmond) was about to sail for America and would be making a speech at Queenstown, near Cork, just before his departure, he decided to deal briefly with the Cork writ in the course of that address. His view of Blake's attitude can be seen from two letters which he wrote on August 18. To Dillon he remarked: "I am writing Blake and intend to say a word on the matter this morning. It is a pity he is so sensitive. . . ."[49] He then wrote to Blake as follows:

> Dillon has sent me your letter and I am extremely sorry you have been so worried. Your action, as I intend to say to-day, was of course the right one and the only possible one.
> I have not heard even a whisper of disapproval or even misunderstanding. The Freeman Correspondent was very stupid, but really people don't mind these statements.[50]

In accordance with his promise, Redmond spoke of the Cork writ in the course of the address which he delivered immediately before his departure for America. He stated that members of the Irish party had abstained from moving the writ for Cork because they knew this to be the wish of the people of that city. The writ had now been moved and an election forced upon the citizens of Cork by the action of a gentleman who did not belong to the Irish party. Redmond then explained, in case there might be some misunderstanding, that, according to constitutional practice, a writ could be moved by anyone and, once moved, it was, except for some overpowering reason, always issued. Thus it had been impossible for the Irish party to prevent the issue of the writ once it had been moved. Understanding this situation, Blake, though protesting against Tully's action, had not divided the House against it. This course had been very wise, for, had there been a division, both Liberals and Conservatives would have voted for the issue of the writ, thus putting the Irish members who were against it in a minority. Finally,

[48]*Ibid.*, Blake to Dillon, Aug. 16, 1904.
[49]Dillon Papers, Redmond to Dillon, Aug. 18, 1904.
[50]Blake Papers, Redmond to Blake, Aug. 18, 1904.

Redmond told his audience that he had "said these few words" so that Blake's action would be thoroughly understood and the citizens of Cork would realize that the Irish party had not been responsible for forcing an election at a time when it was not desired.[51]

Redmond's remarks closed the question regarding the Cork writ. It will be recalled, however, that, as Tully had hoped, O'Brien was returned unopposed to represent his former constituency.

Visits to Canada

In earlier chapters it has been seen that Blake, on his frequent visits to Canada and the United States, devoted much of his time and energy to arousing interest in the Irish cause and raising funds for it. But during his sojourns in Canada in 1904, 1905, and 1906 his health was so poor that he was unable to continue this work. His visits to his native land in those years are interesting chiefly because they show very clearly the difficulties with which he was faced during his later years in Irish politics.

Shortly after Redmond's departure for the United States in August, 1904, Blake sailed for Canada. On September 26 Redmond addressed a meeting in Toronto, but Blake was too ill to attend. The chairman of the meeting, Edward J. Hearn, read a letter from Blake, expressing his regret at his inability to be present and enclosing a cheque for $500 for the Irish cause.[52]

Blake benefited somewhat from his rest in Canada and was able to return to Britain for the parliamentary session of 1905. But once more he had difficulty in keeping up his attendance in the House of Commons and, indeed, some months previously, he had come to the conclusion that, if he were to remain in Irish politics, he would have to give up the greater part of his Privy Council work. Accordingly, he was arranging to bring his general practice to a close by the summer of 1905, though he intended to continue the special

[51]For the full text of Redmond's speech, see *Irish Independent and Nation*, Dublin, Aug. 19, 1904.
[52]The meeting is reported in the *Mail and Empire*, Toronto, Sept. 27, 1904.

work of two or three clients, such as the Canadian government, involving constitutional and other important questions. But even this plan proved too ambitious for him to carry out, and in March, 1905, he was forced to return all his Privy Council briefs. Announcing his decision to Dillon, he remarked: "All pointed to the conclusion that I could not do my duty here [in the House of Commons] and in P.C., and that I should have a breakdown worse than Alaska!" But he expressed sorrow at having to take the step.[53]

Relieved of his Privy Council work, Blake was able, even in his weak state of health, to continue to advise and assist his Irish colleagues. In June, he aided Redmond, T. P. O'Connor, and Joseph Devlin in drawing up a resolution designed to strengthen the party against William O'Brien (who was now back in the House of Commons, but had not taken the party pledge) and the few Irish Nationalist members of Parliament who supported his policy. The resolution, which stressed the importance of the party pledge as an instrument for preserving the unity and discipline of the party and expressed the belief that the policy pursued during the past two years had had the support of the country, was adopted at a party meeting in June by 58 votes to 4.[54]

By the summer Blake was again much in need of rest. He therefore went to Canada with the intention of staying at his summer home in Murray Bay until about the middle of October. With the rest and quiet there, his health was steadily, though slowly, improving when, in September, he was summoned urgently to Toronto, where his second son, Edward Francis, had taken seriously ill. The death of his son on September 15, in addition to being a terrible personal loss to Blake, greatly increased his financial responsibilities, for his son left a widow and four small children, for whom some provision had to be made. Moreover, Blake was faced with considerable work concerning his property and other business affairs which, during his years in Irish politics, had been left in charge of his second son.

Grief stricken as he was at the death of his son, Blake nevertheless retained his interest in Irish politics. Writing to Redmond of his

[53]Dillon Papers, Blake to Dillon, March 28, 1905.
[54]See Lyons, *Irish Parliamentary Party*, 112.

own feelings and those of his wife, he declared: "We do not even yet find ourselves able to realize what has happened, in its full sense, and we know that for us there is a void which can never be filled." He went on, however, to say that they were, of course, "trying to take up their burdens again," and that he was watching with interest the course of public affairs in Ireland.[55]

The death of his second son was not the only affliction which Blake had to bear at this time. He was also worried about the health of his youngest son, Samuel, who was "making a fight against an obstinate illness,"[56] and to whose support Blake had also to contribute. Then, in November, 1905, the death of Mrs. Blake's brother added to the family's sorrow. Naturally, all these troubles did not help to restore Blake's health.

Having heard that a national convention was to be held in Dublin in December, Blake had, towards the end of October, written to Joseph Devlin, asking its exact date, so that he could try to be over for it. A month later, however, he wrote again to Devlin, explaining that the many troubles with which he was faced in Canada made his attendance impossible. He also sent a cable to be read at the convention expressing his regret that "health and urgent private affairs" prevented his presence.[57]

By this time it was clear that a general election was approaching, and Blake had declared in his cable that, if he were again chosen to contest South Longford, he would "cross for the coming Home Rule campaign." The Unionist government had actually been defeated in July, 1905, but it was not until December 4 that A. J. Balfour, who had succeeded Lord Salisbury as Prime Minister in 1902, resigned that position. Thereupon, a Liberal government, led by Sir Henry Campbell-Bannerman, took office, and a general election followed in January, 1906.

On hearing of Balfour's resignation, Blake realized that a general election might be held so soon that he would be unable to return in time for the contest. So the day after he had sent his cable to the convention, he wrote again to Devlin saying that he did not think he could leave before the middle of January, but that, if it were

[55]Blake Papers, Blake to Redmond, Oct. 27, 1905.
[56]See *ibid.*, Blake to Redmond, Sept. 19, 1905.
[57]*Ibid.*, Blake to Joseph Devlin, Oct. 24, Nov. 22, and Dec. 4, 1905.

urgent that he go to Ireland earlier, he would make the attempt.[58] Later in December, Devlin assured Blake that his interests were being properly looked after.[59]

Blake's health, instead of improving, grew worse. He was stricken with grippe, bronchitis, and finally pneumonia. Writing to Devlin shortly before Christmas, he reported that he would try to sail the second or third week in January, but that he feared he would be very weak and quite unfit for public speaking when he arrived in Ireland. He was very sorry about this as he would have liked, for many reasons, to hold some meetings in Longford. In spite of his weakness, he declared that if he were not too late in arriving he would very much like to help a little in connection with the Irish vote in Britain at the office of the United Irish League of Great Britain. In this letter Blake also expressed his regret that, for the first time since he entered Irish politics, he was unable to contribute to the parliamentary fund of the Irish party.[60] His added family responsibilities were, of course, the reason for this change in his financial position.

As it turned out, Blake was unable to give any help in the election campaign, even with the work of the United Irish League of Great Britain to which he had been so anxious to render assistance. He had made arrangements to sail on January 17, 1906, but his illness forced him to postpone his departure first to January 24, then to February 3. Meanwhile, on January 17, he received a cable from Redmond telling him that he had been elected unopposed for South Longford.[61]

From Blake's correspondence at this time, as well as from the fact that he once more accepted nomination and election in South Longford, it is clear that, despite his ill health, he was determined to make an attempt to remain at least a little longer in Irish politics. But realizing that his political career probably could not last much longer, he had, during his visit to Canada, approached Sir Wilfrid Laurier as to the possibility of useful though less strenuous service in another field when retirement from Parliament could no longer

[58]*Ibid.*, Blake to Devlin, Dec. 5, 1905.
[59]*Ibid.*, Devlin to Blake, Dec. 21, 1905. (Cablegram)
[60]*Ibid.*, Blake to Devlin, Dec. 21, 1905.
[61]*Ibid.*, Redmond to Blake, Jan. 17, 1906.

be postponed. What he would have liked was not "a post of great emolument and high dignity" (i.e., a judgeship on the Judicial Committee of the Privy Council), such as had been contemplated some years previously, but rather an "appointment to the [Privy] Council, with a view to being summoned to assist in the Judicial Committee."[62] Laurier, though stating that the Canadian government would be glad to secure his services on the Judicial Committee if this were what he desired, urged him to accept instead the chief justiceship of the Supreme Court of Canada.[63] Blake replied, however, that the work of the Supreme Court would be too arduous and that, in any case, he intended for the present to continue his parliamentary service. It was only if he found his impaired health prevented the discharge of his duty as an Irish member that he wished for an appointment to the Privy Council.[64]

Blake's feelings on the subject of retirement from Irish politics were also revealed in a letter which he wrote to Dillon. After remarking that the failure of his general health made it difficult for him to keep up his parliamentary work and that he feared his continued insomnia would prevent his attendance at night sittings, he concluded: "I intend to try the experiment of next Session, but cannot help feeling considerable apprehension that it may be my duty before long to give up the attempt to serve further in Parliament, an attempt which I fear, as I have said, can, at best, be very imperfectly performed."[65]

The general election of January, 1906, resulted in a decisive victory for the Liberals, who obtained 377 seats, a majority of 84 over all other parties combined. Unionists of all shades of opinion received only 157; Irish Nationalists, 83; and Labour, 53. This Liberal victory was naturally a matter of great consequence to the Irish parliamentary party which, after indicating its opposition to the policy of conciliation with the Unionists, had, in the months before the election, tried successfully to secure a declaration from

[62]*Ibid.*, Blake to Laurier, Aug. 30, 1905. The letter was not mailed until Nov. 9, 1905.
[63]*Ibid.*, Laurier to Blake, Nov. 11, 1905.
[64]*Ibid.*, Blake to Laurier, Nov. 20, 1905. The original is in the Laurier Papers.
[65]Dillon Papers, Blake to Dillon, Jan. 12, 1906.

the Liberals in favour of home rule. On November 14, 1905, in a private conversation with Redmond and T. P. O'Connor, Sir Henry Campbell-Bannerman had committed himself to the policy of home rule, though he had added that it might not be possible to achieve it completely in the next Parliament. In proposing this "step by step" policy, which he publicly expounded in a speech at Stirling on November 23, Sir Henry made it plain that each step "should lead up to and be consistent with the final goal of a Parliament in Dublin."[66]

There was, however, little time during the first session of the new Parliament to devote to the question of home rule for Ireland, for the Liberals had won the election mainly because of the social reforms which they had promised the British people, and it was necessary to begin at once to put this part of their programme into effect. Moreover, the fact that the Liberal government was not dependent on Irish votes for its majority undoubtedly made it feel that there was no need to hurry with the preparation of a home rule measure. The leading members of the Irish parliamentary party understood the difficulties with which Campbell-Bannerman and his colleagues were faced and therefore did not trouble them about the Irish question until the summer recess of 1906. The negotiations which followed will be examined in the next chapter.

Blake's health continued to be very poor during the parliamentary session of 1906 and, at the beginning of the summer recess, he again left for Canada to spend several months at Murray Bay. He hoped that he would be well enough to attend a convention of the United Irish League of America which was to be held at Philadelphia from October 1 to 3, but by the end of August he realized that this would be impossible.[67] The leaders of the American organization were most upset on learning this, and, fearing that his absence would discourage a good many delegates from attending, they did not announce it in the press until shortly before the convention opened.[68]

[66]For further details of the negotiations between Liberals and Irish Nationalists, see Gwynn, *Life of John Redmond*, 111–17.
[67]See Blake Papers, Blake to O'Callaghan, Aug. 27, 1906.
[68]See *ibid.*, O'Callaghan to Blake, Sept. 1 and 28, 1906, and Blake to O'Callaghan, Oct. 1, 1906.

For a time it appeared that Blake's place at the convention would be taken by Charles Devlin, a former Liberal member of the Canadian House of Commons, who, in 1903, had followed Blake's example by entering Irish politics. This plan was upset when, towards the end of September, 1906, financial difficulties forced Devlin to apply for the Chiltern Hundreds.[69] His short career as member for Galway City thus ended, Devlin later entered the legislature and cabinet of Quebec.

T. P. O'Connor was the delegate from the League in Ireland to the convention in Philadelphia and also attended a meeting in Boston on October 7. After this, he spent about ten days in Canada and addressed meetings in Ottawa and Toronto. In the course of his Toronto speech, he paid a warm tribute to Blake. Remarking that only those on the inside of the Irish movement could fully appreciate the greatness of Blake's services to the cause, he declared that "in all their councils he had been their greatest and most trusted guide and their most generous friend in their hours of difficulty." And despite his ill health, which prevented him from attending this meeting, he had promised, in an interview with O'Connor that afternoon, to return to Ireland immediately "if in the negotiations for the preparation of the proposed Home Rule Bill his presence was required."[70]

[69]See *ibid.*, Charles Devlin to Blake, Sept. 14 and 21, 1906.
[70]*Mail and Empire*, Toronto, Oct. 15, 1906.

XI. BLAKE'S CLOSING MONTHS IN IRISH POLITICS

The Irish Council Bill

WITH A LIBERAL GOVERNMENT once more in office, it was Blake's hope that before his retirement from Irish politics he would be privileged to take part in negotiations for the preparation of a new Home Rule Bill, which might institute, at least to some degree, the object for which he had been striving during the preceding fourteen years. For although the House of Lords would undoubtedly reject such a bill, the Liberals, with their large majority in the Commons, would be in a much better position to appeal to the country against the action of the Upper House than they had been in 1893; moreover, it seemed reasonable to suppose that they would do so, because the Lords were opposed not only to Irish home rule, but also to the programme of social reform advocated by the Liberals.

At this time, however, the Irish leaders were not at all pleased at the attitude which the British government was adopting towards Ireland. James Bryce, the Irish Chief Secretary, appeared to be too much under the influence of the Under-Secretary, Sir Antony MacDonnell, who, it will be recalled, had helped to draft the devolution proposals. In view of Campbell-Bannerman's declaration in 1905 that Irish home rule might not be achieved completely in the next Parliament, it was feared by the Nationalists that some sort of devolution scheme, which they would regard as wholly inadequate, might be proposed as the first step towards home rule. By the autumn of 1906, it was known that the government intended to introduce some form of "administrative home rule," a proposal which Redmond, in a speech at Limerick in September, indignantly repudiated. He was annoyed not only at the government's intention of proposing such a makeshift scheme, but also at the fact that neither he nor his colleagues had been consulted as to the measure which was then in preparation.[1]

[1]For an account of Redmond's speech, including excerpts from it, see Denis Gywnn, *Life of John Redmond* (London, 1932), 132–4.

Early in October, Bryce, who had just arrived in Dublin, informed Redmond that the cabinet had prepared a rough draft of the scheme and had consented to its being shown in strict confidence to him and Dillon. On being shown the draft, Redmond "said practically nothing to Bryce except that at first sight it seemed beneath contempt," but he asked if he might show it to Sexton as well as Dillon.[2] Permission was evidently secured from Campbell-Bannerman, for, in the following week, Redmond, Dillon, and Sexton discussed the plan together.[3]

It appears that the cabinet's original scheme, shown to Redmond and his two friends at this time, was to establish in Ireland a Lord-Lieutenant's council, which was to be appointed rather than elected. The Nationalists who were consulted, being of the opinion that a body generally representative of the people could be constituted only by direct popular election, naturally told Bryce that the cabinet's proposal was absolutely unacceptable.

Shortly after this, the cabinet reconsidered and revised its original plan to allow a certain percentage of the members of the council to be elected. But even under this scheme, it was doubtful whether the Nationalists would have been able to secure a working majority on the council, for Ulster was to elect 14 members, as against 12 for Leinster and 8 for Munster (no record has been found of the number to be elected for Connaught), and the appointed or nominated members would probably not be of Nationalist sympathies. Moreover, the Irish executive was not to be responsible to the council and there was no provision for the immediate devolution of legislative powers to the new body, though it might petition the Imperial Parliament for permission to legislate on any subject. Thus, it was not surprising that when Redmond and his colleagues were shown the revised scheme by Bryce, they declared that, while it was an improvement on the previous proposal, it was nevertheless open to the gravest objections.

Bryce was disappointed at the attitude of the Nationalist leaders and asked them to submit an alternative plan for the constitution

[2]Redmond's interview with Bryce is reported in Dillon Papers, Redmond to Dillon, Oct. 8, 1906. See also *ibid.*, Bryce to Dillon, Oct. 11, 1906.
[3]Gwynn, *Life of John Redmond*, 135.

of the new body, since he thought it best that this matter should be settled before other aspects of the scheme were discussed. Redmond and his colleagues therefore prepared a memorandum proposing that the new council should be composed of "the Irish members of the House of Commons, together with such a number of additional members nominated by the Lord-Lieutenant, as will give the minority in Ireland a strong representation while leaving a working majority to the representatives of the great majority of the Irish people." They also took strong exception to the proposal of the cabinet that the Lord-Lieutenant should have power to appoint a vice-chairman to preside over the council in his absence. While expressing their willingness that the Lord-Lieutenant, when present, should preside, they felt that the council should have the right to elect his surrogate. Finally, they suggested that the name of the new body should be "the Irish council" instead of "the Lord-Lieutenant's council."[4]

But, having made these proposals, Redmond realized that they might not be accepted, for with the large Liberal majority in Parliament independent of the Irish vote the Nationalists could not expect to exercise much influence on the government's policy. Feeling, therefore, that the Irish party could not afford to dismiss without serious consideration any plan which the cabinet offered, Redmond decided that it would be wise to consult a number of prominent Irish Nationalists in various parts of the world. Accordingly he prepared a memorandum outlining the proposals already made by the government and relating the attitude of himself, Dillon, and Sexton towards them. Among those to whom he sent this memorandum were John O'Callaghan, secretary of the United Irish League of America; Joseph Devlin, who was in Australia on a fund raising mission; and Blake, who was in Canada. In a letter to O'Callaghan, with which the memorandum was enclosed, Redmond explained the need for absolute secrecy in the matter, adding that O'Callaghan and Blake were "the only persons on the continent of America" to whom

[4] Redmond Papers, "Memorandum on the Constitution of the proposed New Administrative Body to be set up in Ireland." It is from this memorandum that the foregoing details of the cabinet's original scheme and the first of the three revisions of it were obtained.

this information regarding the cabinet proposals was being sent.[5]

Writing to Blake at the same time, Redmond thanked him for his self-sacrificing offer, conveyed through T. P. O'Connor, to come over at once if he were needed. Should it appear necessary, he would not hesitate to ask Blake to do so, but meanwhile he was anxious to have his advice on this memorandum. He added that the Irish administration was "lamentable in the extreme," since Bryce was under the domination of Sir Antony MacDonnell, who utterly disregarded the views of Ireland's representatives. Indeed, it was Redmond's opinion that Bryce was deeply discouraged and might before long abandon his task.[6]

Blake's reply is valuable not only because it gives in detail his views upon the proposed scheme, but also because it supplies considerable information about the first revised draft of the Irish Council Bill which is not available elsewhere. It was his opinion that the Irish leaders should impress upon the cabinet their view that "a halfway house, or a step by step advance," would not be satisfactory, and that they could therefore "only aim at finding a result the least objectionable" under the limitations imposed by the government. He was not surprised at the general character of Bryce's administration and, in view of his failure to communicate freely with the Irish leaders, he had little hope of his ever becoming a great success as Irish Secretary. As to MacDonnell, he reminded Redmond that, from the moment he had heard of his proposed appointment in 1902, he had "felt despondent as to his really forwarding the cause of Irish self-government."

Early in his letter Blake stated his general views regarding the type of bill which could be accepted:

I have from the beginning felt and spoken strongly as to the vital importance of the *constitution* of the governing authorities, legislative and executive; deeming this of infinitely greater consequence than the *extent* of the powers, whether executive or legislative, to be in the first instance conferred. We can always, and with increased force as we prove our capacity to use wisely what we have got, press for addition to the powers, and, therefore, in a confessedly partial and tentative scheme, temporary exclusions are of less conse-

---

[5] *Ibid.*, Redmond to O'Callaghan, Nov. 13, 1906. The memorandum has not come to light.
[6] *Ibid.*, Redmond to Blake, Nov. 13, 1906.

quence. But to permit the building of an unsound and anti-popular constitutional foundation would be a grave error, to which we should, even if we found ourselves obliged to submit, yield only under earnest protest and of necessity.

This would be, not merely the non-concession of self-government, but the denial in the directest form of our right to any effective self-government, and our first work would have to be, not to build on the foundation or enlarge the superstructure, but to tear down the edifice erected by professedly friendly architects. This would, in truth, be an added obstacle to Home Rule set up by professed adherents.

Blake referred to the fact that, under the proposed scheme, no legislative powers were to be conferred upon the Irish council, but that it might petition the Imperial Parliament for permission to legislate on any subject. Redmond, in the memorandum sent to Blake, had evidently expressed opposition to this latter proposal, complaining that it would really renew Poyning's Act, a statute of 1495, which provided that no parliament should meet in Ireland until the King and his council had approved of the meetings and of the acts which were to be passed. Redmond felt that the proposed provision would create a precedent for an Irish legislature when it was established. Blake, on the other hand, took the attitude that the proposal for petitions of itself conceded that the council should possess the fundamental characteristics of a popular legislative assembly. He regarded it not as a dangerous precedent, but rather as a valuable recognition of the incomplete nature of the scheme and the probable extension of it. It might, indeed, provide a method whereby powers of legislation on different topics might be granted to the Irish council gradually and, as each extension of power was granted, it would become, from the constitutional standpoint, substantially irrevocable. But, though favouring the principle behind the proposed provision, Blake did not approve of the plan for dealing with petitions. The suggested procedure was that petitions would lie on the table of both Houses of Parliament for a certain time and, if not disallowed, it would be assumed that permission had been granted. Blake's objection was that the House of Lords would almost certainly disallow them.

After remarking that administration formed an important part of free government, Blake asserted that the more limited was to be for a time the legislative power exercised in Ireland, the more necessary it was to attain "the essential elements of effective *administrative* Home Rule, comprising executive or administrative officers responsible for their acts to a popular elective body." With this in mind, Blake concluded that since, in his opinion, the principle of introducing "a greatly preponderating element directly elective" was vital, and since the political heads of the administrative departments should be drawn from the elected members and be responsible to the council, the present scheme of constituting the new Irish body was fundamentally unsound.

Blake agreed with Redmond that it would be best to elect the same members for both the Imperial Parliament and the council. Regarding the question of admitting additional members to the new body, although he did not favour "nominated members, or delegates, or indirectly elected members," he would not inflexibly oppose any of these plans so long as they did not imperil the principle of popular control by the directly elected members. His own choice would, however, be for a small additional number of members directly elected for wide areas comprising five or seven seats within specified districts, each of which would extend over a large part of Ireland. "And," he added, "I would offer to apply to these elections the principle of the single, or transferable, vote within the large district, so as to secure proportional representation and to enable scattered Unionist and scattered Nationalist minorities within the large district each to combine effectively in the choice of a Member." But in view of the transitory nature of the scheme and the fact that so much of concern to Ireland would still be controlled by the Imperial Parliament, he thought there was a good deal to be said for yielding one or two *ex officio* seats on the council to representatives of certain United Kingdom departments.

The next proposal made by Blake was that a certain number of ministers or political officers should be chosen by the Lord-Lieutenant from among the members of the council to take charge of and be responsible for the Irish departments of state which were to be administered by the council.

Blake expressed his agreement with the principle contained in Redmond's memorandum to the government that the council should choose its own presiding officer or chairman from amongst its members. He added, however, that its choice should be subject to approval by the representative of the Crown (the Lord-Lieutenant), but he did not mention whether he thought the Lord-Lieutenant, when present, should preside.

The administration of education would be under the control of the council. As had been the case in preparing the Home Rule Bill of 1893, the chief problem was to provide adequate safeguards for minorities. Blake declared that he would take grave exception to an imperially appointed director of education, but would not be inflexibly opposed to some sort of *modus vivendi* whereby the fears which would be aroused by Orange and Tory partisans in Britain might be minimized. After suggesting that "declaratory, or negative, or limiting words protecting minorities and enjoining justice and equality might serve the turn," he added: "You know I have no fears. But neither have I any distaste to the consecration of fundamental principles of justice in written constitutions as was done to some extent in the Home Rule Bill, and in the U.S. constitution." But, regarding the whole question of education, he felt that it was necessary to walk warily and have due regard for the views of the hierarchy. In educational matters which seemed to him difficult and doubtful, he had, as a rule, deferred to the opinions of certain political friends and colleagues who were more familiar with the views of the clergy and educational staff and with the whole involved educational situation, being himself, for obvious reasons, but little competent to form a judgment. It was his intention to continue to pursue this course.

Turning to the proposed financial scheme, Blake remarked that it seemed to him very unsatisfactory. It was evidently suggested that a block sum be voted by the Imperial Parliament for use in those branches of the Irish administration which were to be controlled by the council in Dublin. He regarded the principles on which this block sum was to be ascertained as a question of cardinal importance, involving, in theory, the whole business of the financial relations and, in fact, perhaps the failure of the Irish local administration through starvation. Another aspect of the financial scheme to which Blake took exception was the proposed formation of a finance committee with which the powers of initiation were to rest. It was his opinion that there should be no departure from the recognized system of cabinet initiative, a committee of the council being in this case more or less equivalent to the cabinet. Like the cabinet, this committee would deal with all matters of administration coming within its jurisdiction, and, so far as Blake could see, there would be no need for a special or separate committee on finance. He also told Redmond that an imperially appointed Treasurer of Ireland was, in his opinion, a very undesirable anachronism, but that the degree to which he would oppose this proposal might depend, to some extent, upon other details. Blake concluded that the Irish leaders should do all in their power, "consistently with principle, to bring the scheme to fruition," while pressing "to the uttermost, consistently with prudence, for its improvement."[7]

On hearing that the parliamentary session of 1907 would probably begin on February 18, Blake arranged to sail for England on January 26, so that he would arrive in good time for the opening day. In a letter to Redmond, he reported that, as a result of his long rest in Canada, his health was to a considerable extent restored, but that his insomnia continued as obstinate as ever. It was mainly on this account that he looked forward to the session with considerable apprehension, but he intended to make the best of the situation. Increased financial obligations and diminished means had led him, very reluctantly, to accept a few briefs in the Privy Council, but under conditions which he hoped would not appreciably interfere with his parliamentary work.[8]

Before the opening of the session, a change of considerable importance from the point of view of the Irish Nationalists took place in the personnel of the British cabinet. James Bryce, having been appointed British Ambassador at Washington, resigned the Irish chief secretaryship and was replaced in the latter post by Augustine Birrell, who until then had been President of the Board of Education. Birrell was known to be more sympathetic than Bryce towards Ireland, and it was hoped that, through him, satisfactory

[7]*Ibid.*, Blake to Redmond, Dec. 6, 1906. There is a copy of this letter in the Blake Papers.
[8]Blake Papers, Blake to Redmond, Dec. 24, 1906.

amendments to the cabinet's scheme for establishing an Irish council might be obtained.

Shortly after Birrell was established in his new post, Redmond sent him a memorandum outlining some of his objections to the policy and plan adopted by the cabinet. He told Birrell that he considered the constitution of the council, as proposed, so hopelessly impossible that he thought it useless, unless important changes were made, to discuss seriously the powers to be given to the body or the machinery for carrying them out. Moreover, he condemned the cabinet for drawing up its original plan without consultation with the Nationalist leaders, asserting that he had warned Bryce again and again against putting a cut-and-dried scheme before them.

From Redmond's criticism of details of the cabinet's scheme in this memorandum, it can be seen that, despite Blake's arguments to the contrary, he continued to object to the council petitioning the Imperial Parliament for permission to legislate on any subject. He repeated that such a provision would renew Poyning's Act and create a precedent for an Irish Parliament when it was established. It would be better, he told Birrell, for the council to have no legislative power at all than to create such a precedent.[9]

Very soon after Redmond had sent this memorandum to the new Chief Secretary, Birrell was able to submit a revised draft of the scheme for the consideration of the Irish leaders. Among the Redmond Papers is a copy of this draft entitled "Skeleton of Plan." It provided that the new body should be called the Irish council and should consist of from 80 to 90 members, of whom about three-fourths would be elected and one-fourth nominated. For the election of members of the council new constituencies were to be established; thus Redmond's proposal for retaining existing parliamentary divisions for this purpose was refused. The non-elective members of the council were to be nominated for or during their first term of office by the king, but, after the expiration of that term, by the Lord-Lieutenant. The Irish Under-Secretary was to be, *ex officio*, a member of the council, and the Chief Secretary, though not a

[9]For excerpts from Redmond's memorandum, see Gwynn, *Life of John Redmond*, 141-2.

member and not entitled to vote, was to have the right to be present and to speak at meetings of the council. One of the members of the council was to be its president and his salary would be such as the council might determine. The Lord-Lieutenant, through the council, was to have control of all matters concerning the Local Government Board, the Department of Agriculture and Technical Instruction, Public Works, the Primary and Intermediate Education Boards, and the Congested Districts Board. The Lord-Lieutenant was to have the power to defer action upon any resolution of the Irish council, pending reference to the King-in-Council (i.e., the British government). Any matter alleged to be *ultra vires* might be brought before the Judicial Committee of the Privy Council within a year, its decision to be final. Standing committees of the council to deal with finance, education, local government, public works, and possibly other matters were to be established. The financial provisions remained much the same as those criticized by Blake in his long letter to Redmond. It was proposed that an Irish fund, to be paid over by the imperial exchequer, should be created. Out of this fund Irish expenses, under specified heads, were to be met. It was stated, however, that the financial clauses in the "Skeleton of Plan" were "especially of a tentative character."

Blake's comments on this "Skeleton of Plan" are contained in a lengthy memorandum which he sent to Redmond and which is among the latter's private papers. Much of Blake's criticism concerned the organization and wording of the clauses, which he considered highly unsatisfactory. He told Redmond that the "Skeleton of Plan" was, in form, not a skeleton but a jumble of bones; in this respect, it was far inferior to the previous scheme. Moreover, the inferiority was much more than a matter of form. It rendered the task of grasping the true meaning and effect of the plan most difficult.

Among other things, Blake complained that the new draft, before completing its description of the constitution of the council, dealt with its functions. This section he regarded as very disappointing, for from certain information received he had inferred that a responsible member of the council was to be in charge of one or more of the departments of administration and act as the political head.

No provision was, however, made for this, and Blake was convinced that nothing else would give the scheme a fair chance. Furthermore, he considered that the wording of this part of the plan was very awkward and demanded the scrutiny of the Irish leaders in consultation.

Dealing with the composition of the council, Blake remarked that he did not see why the first nominations to the non-elective seats should not be made by the Lord-Lieutenant. He did not, however, attach great importance to this matter. It was not stated in the draft whether the president of the council was to be nominated by the Lord-Lieutenant or elected by the council. Blake supposed that the former method was intended, but, if nothing were stated on this point, he did not see why the council should not elect its own president.

By the end of February, 1907, Blake's health was again so poor that he realized it would be impossible to continue his parliamentary work beyond the close of the current session. Explaining the situation to Redmond, he wrote:

> I am sorry now that I did not resign when I found myself unable to attend in the autumn. But I did then hope to be thus enabled to serve in my last session as I had served in my first fifteen years ago, when the Home Rule Bill of 1893 was being prepared.
>
> Fortune forbids, and I have quite abandoned the idea. I have said "my last session"; for I am about closing up my small concerns on this side of the Atlantic, and I expect to retire at the close of this session, if my health does not constrain me to leave even earlier.[10]

Redmond replied that it would be a serious blow to him and his colleagues if they were deprived of Blake's advice and guidance during the negotiations on the government scheme. He hoped that if Blake did not overtax himself by remaining too late at the House of Commons his health would improve.[11]

In April Birrell submitted to Redmond a further revision of the scheme for establishing an Irish council. Redmond and his colleagues regarded it as an improvement on the previous plans, insofar as it enlarged the number of members on the council and modified in

[10]Redmond Papers, Blake to Redmond, Feb. 28, 1907. There is a copy of this letter in the Blake Papers.
[11]Blake Papers, Redmond to Blake, March 1, 1907.

some slight degree the anomalies which had existed in the previous schemes. But they told Birrell that the objections which they had previously expressed remained substantially unaffected by these changes.[12] The British cabinet refused to make further concessions to the Nationalist leaders and, on May 7, the Irish Council Bill was introduced in the House of Commons. In an address during the debate on first reading, Redmond criticized many details of the bill and dissociated himself from responsibility for it. He decided, however, to vote with the government until the opinion of the Irish people had been ascertained at a national convention. Plans were being made to hold such a gathering before the beginning of the debate on the second reading of the bill.

As the Nationalist leaders had expected, the Irish people were both angry and disappointed at the type of bill which the Liberal government had introduced. Conscious of their attitude and in accordance with his own views, Redmond proceeded, a few days after the introduction of the bill, to draft a resolution for submission to the national convention. It began by reaffirming Ireland's demand for self-government and declaring that she would never be prosperous or contented so long as she was governed by "the alien laws of an alien parliament." Then, after expressing disappointment that the government, made up of men who for twenty years had been pledged to home rule, now declined to grant it, Redmond's draft resolution asserted that Birrell's bill was not calculated to promote a settlement of the Irish question and, even when considered merely as a measure of small administrative reform, was marred by several provisions of an unjust and unworkable character. Among these were the constitution of the proposed council, its finance, the appointment of chairmen of committees by the Lord-Lieutenant, the system of exercising control over departments through committees, and the power of the Lord-Lieutenant to override the decision of the council on all matters. In the closing words of the draft resolution it was recommended that, unless these and other defects were

[12]See Redmond Papers, "Memorandum on Constitution of Irish Council—Sent to Birrell, 25 April, 1907."

remedied, the Irish party should not support the second reading of the bill.[13]

By this time, Dillon had gone to Dublin and was, therefore, in a better position than Redmond, who was still in London, to gauge Irish feeling towards the bill. In view of this situation, Redmond was especially anxious to have his opinion of the draft resolution, so he sent him a copy at once. Dillon considered it a very strong one, but was certain that, if proposed at the convention, it would be carried by a sweeping majority, a step which would lead to the immediate abandonment of the bill by the government. He told Redmond that he would like to see some form of words devised which, though expressing the hostile feeling of the country towards the bill, would get around the actual killing of it by the convention, a task which he thought should be left to the Irish Unionists and the House of Lords. With this in mind, he would try to draft an alternative resolution. At the same time, he advised Redmond to ascertain the views of T. P. O'Connor and Blake as soon as possible.[14]

Dillon lost no time in drafting an alternative resolution which was much more moderate than Redmond's. The principal changes he proposed were in the opening and closing words. Omitting the reference to "the alien laws of an alien parliament," he stated simply that Ireland would not be prosperous or contented so long as national self-government was forcibly withheld from her. And, in concluding, he did not give the Irish party such definite instructions as did Redmond. He merely advised its members, if the defects listed were not removed, to "abstain from giving any support to the measure and to keep themselves clear of all responsibility for its passage into Law."[15]

In a letter accompanying the draft resolution which he sent to Redmond, Dillon explained that he was not "pressing it as an alternative," for it was probable that the convention would be un-

[13]There are copies of Redmond's draft resolution in both the Redmond and the Blake Papers.
[14]Redmond Papers, Dillon to Redmond, May 12, 1907.
[15]There is a copy of Dillon's draft resolution among the Redmond Papers.

willing to adopt so moderate a resolution. "Still," he added, "I am not clear that even at the risk of some unpopularity and of having our hands forced by the Convention we are not bound to put the common-sense policy before the Convention." But he would not be in favour of trying to drive the convention or to shut off speakers who advocated more extreme courses.[16] By this time, Redmond was preparing to leave for Ireland but on the evening of his departure he gave Blake a copy of his draft resolution. From correspondence in the days which followed, it is clear that the latter, despite his failing health, gave valuable suggestions as to the course to be adopted at the national convention.

On May 16, Blake wrote to Redmond enclosing his proposed amendments to the latter's draft resolution. Unlike Dillon, he made no changes in the opening words, but he admitted to Redmond that they were not such as he would have drafted. "They are," he wrote, "more flamboyant than attune with my sluggish temperament; but you know with whom you have to deal, and the rhetorical exigencies; and with you I gladly leave them." Blake did, however, propose some changes in other parts of the resolution. Since he thought that the major points of objection to the bill should be explained in somewhat more detail, he added explanatory notes to each of the items on Redmond's list of defects. He also changed the order in which they were stated, trying to place them in their proper sequence. Thus, the resolution, as amended by Blake, condemned the following provisions:

The constitution of the proposed Council, which does not give fair security for the vital principle of popular control.
The reservation to the Lord-Lieutenant of the power to override and contravene decisions of the Council by his arbitrary decree.
The plan of exercising control over departments and officials through written resolutions of the Council and its Committees without providing effective executive power.
The appointment of chairmen of Committees by the Lord-Lieutenant without any influence of the Council or the Committee in the choice or retention in office of the chairman.
The Finance which is inadequate to the obvious, acknowledged and long neglected needs of Ireland in the matters transferred.

Blake also advised Redmond to correct and supplement the list

[16]Redmond Papers, Dillon to Redmond, May 13, 1907.

before submitting it to the convention and expressed the opinion that it might be necessary to deal with the educational provisions of the bill, since the clerical delegates would undoubtedly be most interested in this question.

With regard to the closing words of the resolution, Blake did not propose any such modification as that suggested by Dillon. Not only did he advise members of the Irish party to abstain from the division on second reading, but he added that, unless the stated defects were substantially removed, the party should, on third reading, mark its dissent from the bill.

That Blake was deeply discouraged at the current political situation can be seen from his closing remarks to Redmond in the letter accompanying his draft amendments. It was his opinion that the government, which had "disgusted Ireland and large masses of British Liberals" by introducing such a makeshift bill, would offer only inadequate concessions, while standing firm on some capital points. "I can," he concluded, "only express wishes, hearty however vain, for your good guidance in the convention and heartfelt regrets that I am unable to be with you. But I know I could do no good. Were it otherwise I would willingly take the strain and risk."[17]

The day after sending his draft amendments, Blake wrote again to Redmond reporting that, after further reflection, he had become even more convinced of the necessity of dealing with the educational provisions of the bill at the convention. He was certain that the subject would be brought up by the clerical delegates and that Redmond would have to express his views upon it. But it would be better, Blake thought, for Redmond to introduce the subject.[18]

In his reply to Blake's letters, Redmond related that he and the colleagues he had consulted in Dublin had "practically come to the conclusion that the best thing for the Party and the movement is to reject the Bill." He explained that he and Devlin had had a long talk with Dillon and that that was now his view also.[19] It was un-

[17]*Ibid.*, Blake to Redmond, May 16, 1907. There is a copy of this letter in the Blake Papers. Copies of Blake's draft amendments are to be found in both the Redmond and the Blake Papers.

[18]Redmond Papers, Blake to Redmond, May 17, 1907. There is a copy of this letter in the Blake Papers.

[19]Blake Papers, Redmond to Blake, May 18, 1907.

doubtedly because of this decision that the wording of the resolution submitted by Redmond to the convention differed considerably both from that which he had originally drafted and from the amended forms prepared by Dillon and Blake. For although the adoption of any of these draft resolutions—or, at any rate, of Redmond's or Blake's—would have led to the rejection of the bill by the Irish party if satisfactory amendments were not secured, it was evidently now thought best for the convention to recommend rejection without stating the objectionable details. From Blake's remarks in his letters to Redmond it seems unlikely that he would have regarded this as a very good policy.

When the convention assembled in Dublin on May 21, Redmond was deprived of the support of two of his principal advisers. Blake sent a letter to the gathering expressing regret that ill health prevented his attendance.[20] Dillon's absence was the result of an unexpected personal tragedy which occurred a few days before the convention. The sudden death of his wife on May 15 had left him so stricken with grief that he was unable to be present.

There had been a belief in some quarters that Redmond was in favour of accepting the Council Bill. Though his letters prove that this rumour was entirely without foundation, there was considerable surprise and relief at the convention when he proposed a resolution declaring that the bill was "utterly inadequate in its scope, and unsatisfactory in its details, and should be rejected by the Irish nation." The resolution was adopted unanimously.[21]

In view of the stand taken by the national convention, it was useless for the government to proceed further with the Irish Council Bill. Accordingly, on June 3, the Prime Minister, Sir Henry Campbell-Bannerman, announced that it had been dropped.

The Irish Council Bill was the last issue on which Blake was able to advise his Irish colleagues. His letters and draft amendments to Redmond's proposed resolution are especially interesting because, as will be seen presently, it was only a few days after writing them

[20]Blake's letter, addressed to Joseph Devlin, secretary of the United Irish League, was published in the *Freeman's Journal*, Dublin, May 22, 1907.
[21]For an account of the convention, including the full text of the resolution, see *Freeman's Journal*, Dublin, May 22, 1907.

that he was stricken with the illness which ended his Irish career. Until almost the eve of his serious illness, he had continued to give as much assistance to the Irish cause as his failing health would permit.

Retirement

It was on Friday, May 24, 1907, that Blake "was seized with an attack of effusion of blood on the brain which . . . produced paralysis of the left arm and leg with some other minor consequences." Thus he described his condition to Redmond in a letter dictated two days later against his doctor's orders. The letter continued:

> My doctor hopes for a good though rather tedious recovery and I have complete confidence in his opinion. But he advises most peremptorily that this attack, supervening on my age and long continuing general and nervous debility, makes it imperatively necessary that I should retire from Parliamentary life. Of this I am satisfied. You have known for some time my views on the question of retirement irrespective of this new development. I need not say that the matter is now placed beyond a question of choice. Deeply though I deplore my enforced relinquishment at this juncture of my seat for Longford, I *must* go.

Since Blake was at this time a member of the House of Commons' committee of selection he asked Redmond to make the necessary arrangements for filling his place there. He added that as soon as he was physically able, he would send him his application for the Chiltern Hundreds and, at the same time, communicate with his faithful constituents.[22] Redmond was deeply distressed at Blake's letter and wrote at once advising him not to worry about parliamentary business. "I will, of course," he added, "do exactly as you wish but you may take it as certain that Longford won't consent to your resignation. Need you take any step at all at present?"[23] To this Mrs. Blake replied that her husband felt he must adhere to the course set out in his letter of May 26.[24]

In the weeks which followed, resolutions of sympathy with Blake

[22]Blake Papers, Blake to Redmond, May 26, 1907.
[23]*Ibid.*, Redmond to Blake, May 27, 1907.
[24]*Ibid.*, Margaret Blake to Redmond, May 27, 1907.

and his family were passed by many groups and organizations, including the Irish parliamentary party, both the executive council and the standing committee of the United Irish League of Great Britain, and the House of Commons' committee of selection. The executive council of the United Irish League of Great Britain, of which Blake had once been a member, recorded "its profound sense of gratitude . . . for his imperishable services to the United Irish League of Great Britain and the cause of Ireland."[25]

It was not until the middle of July that Blake was well enough to carry out the necessary preliminaries to his retirement. He then wrote asking Redmond to secure for him a draft of the usual letter of application for the Chilterns or Northstead. When written, his letter would be sent to Redmond with a covering note requesting him to communicate with the United Irish League executive in South Longford as to its convenience with regard to the date of the application's presentation. Emphasizing that his decision was final and that it would be useless to consider any median course, Blake remarked to Redmond: "I . . . can only console myself by the reflection that I did not desert the cause, and that I erred, not by quitting too soon, but by struggling too long."[26]

In accordance with Blake's request, Redmond secured a draft of the letter of application for the Chiltern Hundreds, but he repeated to Blake his conviction that the Nationalist electors of South Longford would not, under present circumstances, listen to the suggestion of vacating his seat.[27] On July 19 Blake wrote to Redmond enclosing his application for the Chiltern Hundreds. Once more he declared that his retirement was inevitable and should therefore be faced as soon as possible.[28] The same day he sent the following letter to the Nationalist electors of South Longford:

After a service of fifteen years, marked by your constant kindness, I have felt constrained to place in Mr. Redmond's hands my application for the

---

[25] The letters conveying the resolutions are among the 1907 miscellaneous correspondence in the Blake Papers.
[26] Blake Papers, Blake to Redmond, July 15, 1907.
[27] *Ibid.*, Redmond to Blake, July 16, 1907. The draft letter of application for the Chiltern Hundreds is also in the Blake Papers.
[28] *Ibid.*, Blake to Redmond, July 19, 1907.

Chiltern Hundreds with the request that he would present it as soon as, after consultation with the local Executive, may be found consistent with the convenience of the constituency.

You know that I had contemplated a much earlier retirement; but the vicissitudes of the national struggle, and your own strong desire that I should remain your member moved me to continue an effort made increasingly difficult by advancing years and failing health.

My present serious illness (though I have every prospect of recovering a substantial measure of health and strength and the ability to do some quiet work) yet leaves, as I believe, no reasonable prospect that I could resume the strenuous duties of membership without danger of a recurrence of the attack; and I am advised that it is my clear duty to withdraw.

Thus it only remains for me, with grateful thanks for your goodness, and warmest wishes for the triumph of the cause, to say the sad word, "farewell."[29]

As Redmond had predicted, Blake's constituents were most desirous that he should retain his seat. On July 27, at a meeting of the South Longford executive of the United Irish League, a resolution urging him to reconsider his decision to retire was unanimously adopted. The resolution, after expressing deep regret at Blake's illness and intended retirement, went on to state that the executive would be willing to leave the representation of the county in his hands pending his restoration to better health. It also requested Redmond not to use Blake's letter of application for the Chiltern Hundreds until a reply had been received.[30]

On being informed of the terms of this resolution, Blake wrote to thank his constituency for "this last and crowning mark of its goodness," explaining that, had there been any hope of his being able to resume his duties, he would have felt "free to accept a proposal so flattering and generous." But, since there was no such hope, he was obliged to treat his resignation as "necessary and irrevocable."[31] There was nothing, therefore, for the South Longford executive to do but accept his decision, and accordingly, on August 14, Redmond

---

[29] This letter, of which there is a copy in the Blake Papers, was published in the *Freeman's Journal*, Dublin, July 22, 1907.

[30] There is a copy of the resolution in the Blake Papers. The meeting is reported in the *Freeman's Journal*, Dublin, July 29, 1907. See Blake Scrap Books.

[31] A copy of this letter, dated Aug. 6, and addressed to F. McGuiness, secretary of the South Longford executive, is in one of the Blake Scrap Books.

forwarded Blake's application for the Chiltern Hundreds to H. H. Asquith, Chancellor of the Exchequer. The next day Blake was appointed in the customary manner to be "Steward and Bailiff of the Three Hundreds of Chiltern."[32]

By this time Blake had sailed for Canada and, before the end of August, he was at his home in Toronto. Letters written later in the year indicate that there was some slight improvement in his health and that he was able to "hobble up and down stairs and move about after a fashion through the house."[33] And although, during the remaining four and a half years of his life, he never recovered sufficiently to take any further part in public affairs, he retained his interest in the Irish cause to which he had rendered such great service.[34]

There were, of course, many expressions of regret at Blake's retirement, both by his friends and colleagues and by the press. Several of the men who had been Blake's colleagues in the Irish parliamentary party during some or all of the preceding fifteen years wrote to him not only of their regret that he was leaving, but also of their appreciation of his services to the cause of home rule. Justin McCarthy, who had resigned the chairmanship of the party in 1896 and retired altogether from the House of Commons in 1900, told Blake that his retirement would be a great loss to Ireland and would be deeply regretted by Irish Nationalists in all parts of the world.[35] Letters from T. P. O'Connor and Alfred Webb were on somewhat similar lines,[36] while Stephen Gwynn, the journalist and historian who, in 1906, had been elected to the House of Commons as member for Galway City, wrote to Blake: "I hope I may be permitted to say in a line or two how deep is my regret for the loss that your illness inflicts on us, and how sincere will always be my pride

[32]The letter of appointment, dated Aug. 15, 1907, is among the Blake Papers.

[33]Blake Papers, Blake to J. C. Walsh (Montreal), Nov. 25, 1907. See also *ibid.*, Blake to Redmond, Dec. 13, 1907.

[34]In a letter dated Dec. 17, 1909, which is among the Blake Papers, Dillon acknowledges the receipt of a letter and subscription from Blake.

[35]Blake Papers, McCarthy to Blake, July 23, 1907.

[36]*Ibid.*, T. P. O'Connor to Blake, Aug. 2, 1907; Alfred Webb to Blake, July 27, 1907.

to remember that I have been part of the same party with you. . . ."³⁷

Blake also received letters expressing regret at his retirement from many friends and admirers outside the Irish party. Among those who wrote to him were Lord Aberdeen, former Governor-General of Canada and now for the second time Lord-Lieutenant of Ireland; C. P. Scott, editor and chief proprietor of the *Manchester Guardian* and a former Liberal member of Parliament; (Sir) Henry Lucy, the parliamentary correspondent who had been unfavourably impressed by Blake's maiden speech in the British House of Commons in 1893; and Sir W. Brampton-Gordon, who, for several years, had worked with Blake on committees of the House of Commons and who told him that his advice was especially missed on the committee of selection.³⁸ But perhaps the letter which Blake prized most of all was the one he received from the Prime Minister, Sir Henry Campbell-Bannerman, which read in part:

> I deeply and sincerely regret your retirement—on personal as well as public grounds. You have been invariably so friendly and kind to me that I shall miss you keenly. I owe you more than you are aware of. In the evil days of the past, with an overbearing majority against us, and with trepidation and even positive backsliding, among those who should have been our friends, I always could count on your fidelity, and many a time while endeavouring to stem the torrent against us I have been encouraged by your smile and a sympathetic twinkle in your eye.
>
> But on public grounds you will be even more missed, for you have always maintained a high level of Parliamentary idea and action, and have done as much as any man in my time to exalt and keep pure the public life of the Empire.
>
> I earnestly hope that your leisure will bring you happiness and health, and I trust that you will have kindly memories of your House of Commons days.³⁹

Blake's feelings on receiving Sir Henry's letter can be seen from his reply, the principal part of which read:

> I cannot tell you how touched I am by your kind and sympathetic words. It lightens my natural regret at leaving the House of Commons to get such

---

³⁷*Ibid.*, Stephen Gwynn to Blake, Aug. 2, 1907.
³⁸All these letters are among the Blake Papers.
³⁹*Ibid.*, Sir Henry Campbell-Bannerman to Blake, Aug. 13, 1907.

a letter. You have correctly interpreted my sentiments towards you and your general course in Opposition, but I had no idea that they were even guessed by yourself.

I value beyond expression your testimony to my general line of Parliamentary idea and action, and will preserve while I live, and leave as an heirloom to my family, the letter in which you express it.

You are right in saying that I have kindly memories of my House of Commons days. Though always decided to be outspoken on political questions, I am proud to think that I have not left, so far as I know, one enemy in the House; and I have received some touching expressions of good feeling from quarters in which I least expected them.[40]

Many British and Irish newspapers, in expressing regret at Blake's retirement, attempted to evaluate his services to the Irish cause and his achievements in the House of Commons. The *Westminster Gazette,* after remarking that his retirement would be "a source of genuine regret to all sorts and conditions of men," declared that, on the rare occasions when he had intervened in parliamentary debate, he had been "heard with the respect due to his character, his career, and his eloquence." Though he had never quite adapted himself to the manner of the British House of Commons, unusual grasp and breadth of outlook had been recognized in his speeches. The *Pall Mall Gazette* asserted that Blake had "played the part of a 'smoother' in the internecine conflicts of the Nationalist party," while the *Leeds Mercury* declared that he had many friends on both sides of the House, but that his political career in Britain had not been as interesting or brilliant as the record he had left behind in Canada. It went on: "His commanding figure and classic head seemed to mark him as a leader of men, but the course of Irish politics has not given him adequate opportunity to display his fine abilities."[41] (Sir) Henry Lucy's evaluation of Blake's Irish career was somewhat similar. Writing in *Punch,* he commented on his infrequent speechmaking, adding that "when he did interpose he bestowed upon the House the fruits of statesmanlike instinct, wide culture, and long experience in public affairs." He continued: "Nothing less like the typical Irish Nationalist member could be imagined than the grave and reverend signior, who in slow well-ordered speech reasoned with

[40]*Ibid.,* Blake to Campbell-Bannerman, Aug. 28, 1907.
[41]Excerpts from the foregoing newspapers, all dated July 22, 1907, are in the Blake Scrap Books.

the adversary. Loyal in every thought, honest in every fibre, he sat among the Irish Nationalists, but he was not of them." He carried with him, Lucy concluded, the esteem of all who had known him in public and private life.[42]

The *Freeman's Journal*, being under the control of Thomas Sexton, a former colleague of Blake's on the committee of the Irish party, was in a better position than any of the British journals to know of the many services which Blake had rendered to the Irish cause. On July 22 it wrote:

> . . . [Ireland] will always remember with gratitude the loyalty and the devotion that brought to her side in years of difficulty, doubt, and dissension the Irish-Canadian leader who turned from paths of honour, profit, and ambition in the land of his birth to serve the land of his forefathers in her hour of trial. Mr. Blake's rally to Ireland was an inspiration; his services to her have been a great example. A statesman of repute, a great constitutional lawyer, a politician skilled in party warfare, his counsel and his purse have been for the past fifteen years at the service of the Irish party. His experience and his ability entitled him to claim a leading part in the counsels of the Party. But his voice was never heard outside the Council Chamber save in preaching the duties of steadfastness, union, and common action along the decided course. . . . Mr. Blake rarely intervened in debate in the House of Commons, and his colleagues, indeed, found it hard, owing to his retiring disposition, to insist on his taking the place to which his unusual eloquence and commanding abilities entitled him. His kindly counsel and generous sympathy were, however, always at the service of those by whom they were sought, and it is no exaggeration to say that the policy of the Irish Party and its line of action in many a critical time were shaped and directed by his cool judgment and sagacious and far-sighted statesmanship.

The *Irish People*, a newspaper which was under the management of William O'Brien, who was still outside the Nationalist party and continued to criticize it, took the stand that Blake was almost its only reliable member and that his retirement was therefore a great blow to it. "He was," it asserted in an editorial on July 27, "one of the few men in the Party whose ability and attainments commanded the ear and won the respect of the House of Commons." It paid high tribute to "his great ability, his high personal character, the staunchness of his convictions, the example which he set of a deliberate avoidance of personalities in public controversy," and added

[42]Lucy's remarks are quoted in the *Globe*, Toronto, Aug. 13, 1907. See Blake Scrap Books.

that it was "an open secret" that contributions from him had materially helped to tide the party over periods of financial difficulty.[43]

From the letters which Blake received at the time of his retirement, as well as from the comments of British and Irish newspapers, it has been seen that his character and ability commanded wide respect and admiration. But, while British newspapers generally took the attitude that he had not achieved as much at Westminster as had been expected of him, Irish journals stressed the many great services which he had rendered to the home rule cause. Since both these attitudes should be considered in the light of all the available material, an attempt will be made, in the remaining pages of this book, to evaluate the work Blake did for Ireland.

[43]The comments of these Irish papers are contained in the Blake Scrap Books.

XII. CONCLUSION

AN ASSESSMENT of Blake's achievements in the Imperial Parliament and of his contributions to the Irish cause based on the opinions expressed by his contemporaries would reveal certain widely held beliefs about his activities in Irish politics. A study of his Irish career, based on the documents of the period, proves that, though some of these beliefs were true, others were wholly or partly without foundation.

The *Freeman's Journal* and members of the Irish parliamentary party frequently stated that Blake abandoned a great position in the Canadian Parliament in order to aid the Irish cause. This was not strictly true, for, when he accepted the invitation of the Irish leaders to join their party, he was not a member of the Canadian House of Commons, having broken with the Liberal party in 1891. In fact, one reason he accepted the Irish invitation was that he saw no immediate opportunity of serving Canada and therefore felt it his duty to do what he could for Ireland. However, Blake's entry into Irish politics did involve many sacrifices, for it meant the abandonment of his very lucrative law practice in Toronto and the separation from members of his family and the friends of a lifetime. Furthermore, the year after he entered the Imperial Parliament, Canada's Liberal party virtually discarded that portion of its policy to which he had been opposed, so, had he then been in Canada, he would have been in a position to return to the Liberal ranks. Thus, although it is incorrect to say that Blake abandoned a great position in the Canadian House of Commons to enter Irish politics, it is true that, in remaining in the Imperial Parliament after 1893, and especially after the victory of Canada's Liberal party in 1896, he was depriving himself of high positions in his native land.

At the time of Blake's retirement in 1907, a Canadian newspaper remarked that he was "that odd combination, an Imperialist and an Irish Nationalist."[1] There is no doubt that Blake would have agreed with this statement, except that he would not have regarded the combination as an odd one. Over and over again, in the course of

[1] *Star*, Toronto, July 22, 1907. See Blake Scrap Books.

his Irish career, he expressed the belief that the granting of home rule to Ireland, as well as to British possessions abroad, would strengthen rather than weaken the Empire. He believed, in fact, that the Empire's only chance of survival lay in the extension of the liberties enjoyed in Britain to all her possessions. His ideal for the British Isles was a federal system with provincial legislatures for England, Scotland, Ireland, and Wales, and a central parliament to deal with matters common to all. But pending the establishment of such a system, he desired that some provision should be made for home rule in Ireland. In view of his advocacy of the federal system and of the retention, even under a temporary scheme, of Irish members at Westminster, it is difficult to say whether he would have approved of the step which was taken ten years after his death—that of granting dominion status to Ireland, or, at least, to twenty-six of its thirty-two counties. Perhaps, having regard to changing conditions, he would have acquiesced in the arrangement, although the provision for partitioning Ireland would undoubtedly have disappointed him. It seems unlikely, however, that he would ever have favoured the establishment of an Irish republic.

In Britain and Canada it was frequently asserted that Blake was not an Irish Nationalist in the same sense as were his colleagues in the Irish parliamentary party. It was argued that, while Blake was an imperialist and wanted Ireland to have a form of home rule similar to, though not identical with, that enjoyed in Canada, other Irish Nationalists really desired complete separation from Britain and therefore secretly regarded such a measure as the Home Rule Bill of 1893 as a possible step towards the attainment of that goal. Though it was probably true that Blake's attitude towards the Empire was different from that of some of his colleagues, it is not correct to say that the Irish parliamentary party was seeking to establish an Irish republic. There is little doubt that most of the leading Irish Nationalists of Blake's time would have been content had their country attained home rule within the Empire. Justin McCarthy, in his biography, expressed the hope that Ireland would become a partner in the British imperial system,[2] and John Redmond was also known to be friendly towards the Empire. Nevertheless, it is note-

[2] Justin McCarthy, *An Irishman's Story* (New York, 1904), 187.

worthy that few of the leading Nationalists alluded any more than necessary to the question of what Ireland's relationship with Britain would be after the establishment of home rule. This may have been because there were many Irishmen who did desire complete independence for their country. Such organizations as the Gaelic Athletic Association, which sought to promote Irish, as opposed to English, sports, and the Gaelic League, which wanted to revive the Irish language and cultivate an Irish literature, were already in existence during the years of Blake's Irish career. Although these organizations were at first non-political, they formed the basis of a later movement for complete national independence. Moreover, at least one of Blake's colleagues desired Ireland's complete separation from Britain. Michael Davitt, in a book published in 1904, declared that he wished Ireland to be an independent nation like Holland or Denmark.[3] In view of this situation, most of the Nationalists who sought only home rule within the Empire may have thought it more tactful to avoid, whenever possible, any discussion of their attitude towards the question of complete independence. In this they differed from Blake who, on many occasions, expressed the views which indicated that he was both an Irish Nationalist and an imperialist.[4] Furthermore, there was probably another difference on this question between Blake and most of his Irish colleagues. For, while he appears to have regarded it as definitely desirable that Ireland should remain within the Empire, it may be inferred that most of his colleagues would have been content with something resembling colonial self-government mainly because they believed that Ireland's proximity to Britain made complete independence unattainable.

A study of Blake's Irish career in the light of more recent events may give rise to the belief that he was mistaken in thinking that the granting of home rule to Ireland would strengthen the Empire. Similarly, it might be argued, in view of the establishment of an Irish republic, that the Unionists were right in asserting that Ireland would not be satisfied until she had attained complete independence.

[3] Michael Davitt, *The Fall of Feudalism in Ireland* (London and New York, 1904).
[4] But in the United States in 1902, anti-British feeling was at such a height that even Blake thought it best to make no mention of the place he thought Ireland should have in the Empire.

An examination of such arguments will, however, show that the reasoning behind them is fallacious. For though Blake believed that if Britain sanctioned the establishment of self-government in Ireland, the latter would be content to remain within the Empire, he realized that if home rule were not granted Ireland's discontent would increase perhaps to the point where nothing short of complete separation would satisfy her. Thus, while the Unionists feared that the concession of any form of self-government would lead eventually to demands from Ireland for complete independence, Blake believed that such demands were much more likely to arise if home rule were not granted. When the question is regarded in this light and it is observed that home rule was not actually established until the demand for absolute independence had become very vociferous, it will be seen that the desire for complete separation from Britain increased as a result not of the granting, but of the withholding, of home rule. So, although it cannot be definitely stated that Ireland would have been satisfied either with home rule under a federal system or with something approximating dominion status, had one or the other been granted in time, it is unjust to assert that recent events have proved Blake wrong in his belief that the granting of home rule to Ireland would strengthen the Empire.

It was frequently alleged by Blake's contemporaries in Britain and Canada, and the belief persists among Canadian historians today, that he did not attain in the British Parliament the position which had been expected of him. If by this is meant that he did not become either a cabinet minister or leader of the Irish party, the assertion is, of course, true. But to anyone who understood the position of an Irish Nationalist member in the British House of Commons, it must have been clear, from the beginning, that Blake could not enter a British cabinet. Moreover, as an Irish member, his principal interest had to be in matters of direct concern to Ireland and not in the debates on British and imperial questions, in which some of his admirers in Britain and Canada had expected him to take an active part. It is true that, even in debates on Irish questions, he did not intervene very frequently, but it has been seen that, when he did speak, his remarks were generally of considerable importance. The charge was also made that, on the occasions when he did address the House, his speeches were needlessly long and redundant and that he never really adapted himself to the manner of the British House of Commons. This is largely a matter of opinion, but, though it is true that his speeches usually included a large amount of detail, it must be remembered that the principal subjects on which he spoke in the Commons, such as the Home Rule Bill of 1893 and the overtaxation of Ireland, required lengthy explanation to make them intelligible. Blake's greatest contributions to the Irish cause were, however, made outside the House of Commons and, in fact, so much of his work was done behind the scenes that only his closest colleagues realized the full extent of it. Thus, it is not surprising that, while those who judged a politician's success by his attainments in the House of Commons greatly underestimated Blake's accomplishments, those who were in a position to know how much he had really done for the Irish cause gave him high and well-deserved praise.

One of Blake's greatest contributions to the Nationalist cause was the help he gave in financing the Irish parliamentary party which in the 1890's had great difficulty in securing sufficient money to carry on its work. Not only did he subscribe generously from his own purse, but he also spent considerable time and energy in raising funds in Canada and the United States. The amount of correspondence between Blake and leading Canadians and Americans of Irish descent, together with the number of meetings he addressed in Canada and the United States in the interests of the Irish cause, gives some idea of the extent of his assistance in this most important aspect of Irish Nationalist activity. It is no exaggeration to say that in 1894, when he raised a loan on his personal security and again in 1897, the Irish party was saved from collapse by his efforts.

A quotation from a book by Michael Davitt shows the extent of Blake's success in raising funds in Canada. Writing of the financial troubles of the 1890's and of the help which was received from abroad, Davitt remarked:

> Canadian supporters, however, were, in proportion to numbers, the most helpful of the friends in need that came to the financial assistance of the federation during the financial troubles of the 90's. Each year, when aid was most required, their remittances came over the ocean to cheer on the

good work against the cruel odds with which it was contending. This doubly generous, because most opportune, help was due mainly to the great popularity of Mr. Edward Blake with all classes in Canada, and to his own untiring labors to provide the means by which the fight in Ireland and in Parliament could be continued until returning political reason among parliamentary leaders should again unlock the resources of general Irish assistance for the cause so upheld.[5]

Another way in which Blake did his best to further the Irish Nationalist cause was by speaking in favour of home rule at public meetings in Britain. This aspect of his work took place mainly during the early part of his Irish career when Gladstone was Prime Minister and home rule was a major issue in British politics. At this time, when England, unlike the other divisions of the United Kingdom, had a majority in the House of Commons opposed to home rule, it seemed most important to popularize the cause in that country. Both Liberals and Irish Nationalists felt that Blake was well qualified for this task, for he was the type of man likely to appeal to English electors. But, after Gladstone's retirement and the succession to the premiership of Rosebery, who lacked enthusiasm for home rule, and especially after the defeat of the Liberal government in 1895, home rule was relegated to the background of British politics, and Irish Nationalists were so busy with dissension in their own ranks that less time and money could be spent on British propaganda. Still, Blake had done what he could to further the cause in Britain. That he was not more successful was due to circumstances beyond his control.

Yet another very great service which Blake rendered to the Irish party was the advice he gave his principal colleagues throughout the fifteen years that he served Ireland as a member of the British House of Commons. This was the aspect of his work which was known only to his closest colleagues. From his correspondence it has been seen that his counsel was frequently sought not only by McCarthy and Dillon, but also, after the reunion with the Parnellites in 1900, by Redmond. His advice was highly valued by all these men, as well as by Davitt, T. P. O'Connor, and even William O'Brien who, from time to time, had serious differences with Blake's most intimate colleagues. The following excerpt from a letter which Mrs. Dillon wrote to Blake in 1904 shows what great importance

[5]Davitt, *Fall of Feudalism*, 673.

her husband placed on Blake's services to Ireland: "I hope you will remember . . . what *infinite* help your *infinite sacrifices* gave to Ireland when there were so few to help. John often talks now of those disheartening years when you, almost alone, one might say, helped him to carry on the Parliamentary fight; and, hard and trying as those years were, they had to be got through somehow to lead up to the renewed hope of more recent times."[6]

It was not only the Irish leaders who recognized Blake's great ability and sought his advice on the problems of the day. Several prominent British Liberals, notably Morley and Bryce, conscious of the fact that he was a constitutional expert, consulted him about the details of the Home Rule Bill of 1893. Moreover, it was Morley who, knowing of his ability in the field of finance, requested him to become a member of the financial relations commission in 1894. Even when the Unionists were in power, Blake's views were sought by those preparing a government measure on one occasion. Sir Antony MacDonnell requested an interview with him regarding the Land Bill of 1903, and he took part in other private conferences on this matter with Wyndham, MacDonnell, Redmond, and William O'Brien.

When Blake entered Irish politics it was thought that he might reunite the Parnellites and anti-Parnellites under his leadership. He was indeed anxious for such a reunion and, although he did not wish to become leader of the party, he was willing to do all in his power to bring about a reconciliation between the two factions. But feeling was too bitter for a reunion at that time, and it was not until 1900 that it was finally achieved. Although Blake did not take part in some of the principal negotiations which led to reunion, it is nevertheless true that he drafted the resolutions which were, in the end, accepted as the basis of reconciliation and that it was he who was responsible for bringing Dillon and T. P. O'Connor into that reunion.

But although Blake's contributions to the Irish cause were many and important, there is no doubt that he possessed certain qualities which, to some extent, unfitted him for the trials and difficulties of political life. While with his intimate friends and colleagues he was kind and even witty, to the public and to those who knew him only

[6]Blake Papers, Elizabeth Dillon to Blake, Dec. 4, 1904.

slightly, he often appeared cold and aloof. Moreover, he had a very sensitive nature which proved a great handicap in Irish politics, especially during the dissension of the 1890's. His reactions to Arthur O'Connor's charges made in February, 1894, to the Omagh incident in 1895, and to the attitude of the *Freeman's Journal* regarding his stand on the issue of the writ for Cork City in 1904 are the best examples of the display of his sensitive nature. From the correspondence of Blake's most intimate friends and colleagues in the Irish party it can be seen that even they found it difficult to understand this aspect of his nature.

Closely linked with this quality of sensitiveness was Blake's tendency to resign in the face of difficulties. Writing letters of resignation appears to have been almost a hobby with him. Barely a month after his entry into Irish politics he was deeply discouraged and was complaining to McCarthy that if he had realized the constant internecine warfare amongst prominent Nationalists, he would not have left his home in Canada to come over to serve Ireland. Before the end of 1892, he had expressed a desire to be allowed to resign from the committee of the Irish party, and he repeated this wish from time to time until the abolition of the committee early in 1896. On many occasions he also intimated his desire to retire altogether from Irish politics. It was generally when some form of unfounded criticism had been levelled against him that he wished to resign, feeling that, in the circumstances, he could not bear to remain in public life.

Earlier in this book it has, however, been pointed out that it would be wrong to judge Blake too severely for his frequent resort to resignation in the face of difficulties. For it must be remembered that he never enjoyed very good health and that it was not discouragement alone, but also illness, which led to his threatened resignations. Furthermore, the fact should be kept in mind that Blake served Ireland in difficult and discouraging times when more than one prominent and experienced Irish politician withdrew in disgust from the continuous struggles with which he was faced. Thomas Sexton and William O'Brien, both of whom had had more experience than Blake of the intricacies of Irish politics, retired from public life in the mid-1890's because of the dissension in the Nationalist party. Alfred Webb retired at about the same time mainly for the same reason. O'Brien's retirement was, indeed, temporary, but it will be recalled that he did not return to the House of Commons until after the reunion of the Irish party in 1900. In view of the actions of these men, it may almost be said that the surprising thing is not that Blake so often threatened to resign, but that, on being urged by his colleagues, he agreed to stay so long. The fact that he remained for fifteen years in Irish politics surely proves that he did not always submit completely to the dictates of his sensitive nature and to his feelings of despondency.

Something should be said of the position Blake held in the Irish party, for his own remarks on this subject are misleading. When he was invited to join the party, it was predicted by many of his admirers that he would become its leader. Several times in the course of his Irish career, the rumour arose that he was to be elected to that position and, on more than one occasion, he was actually suggested within the party as a suitable candidate for it. From the beginning, however, Blake attempted to make it clear both to his colleagues and to the public that he did not aspire to a position of leadership. Over and over again he alleged that he was but a rank-and-file member of the party and that it was in this capacity that he wished to serve Ireland. Perhaps it was partly because of these repeated assertions that the idea arose in some quarters that he had not attained the position in the Irish party which had been expected of him. But whether or not this be true, there is no doubt that, although Blake did not become chairman of the party, he was, despite his denials, one of its leading members. Practically all his Irish correspondence was with the most prominent Nationalists of the day; it was they who were his friends and with whom he carried on his political activities. He was probably scarcely acquainted with the ordinary members of the party. There is no doubt that the successive chairmen of the party—McCarthy, Dillon, and Redmond—together with their principal advisers, regarded Blake, not as a rank-and-file member, but as one of the leaders of the party.

Sir Wilfrid Laurier, Blake's successor to the Liberal leadership of Canada, on one occasion made an interesting evaluation of Blake's character and ability. Having been a close colleague of Blake's, Laurier was, of course, in a position to form accurate judgments upon him and, though some of his statements might be disputed, the estimate is, on the whole, a well-reasoned one, based on a long and intimate acquaintance with Blake. Although Laurier was relating Blake's character and ability to his achievements and failures in Canadian politics, the estimate is, for obvious reasons, of equal interest in a study of his Irish career. The following is the main portion of it:

> Blake was the most powerful intellectual force in Canadian political history. He had an extraordinary mental organization, a grasp that covered the whole and searched out each smallest detail. He was first and foremost the great advocate, a tremendous dialectician, analyzing and cross analyzing to the last point, major points and minor points, utterly exhaustive. But he was no mere man of words. He would have proved Canada's most constructive statesman had he held office. Why did he never reach the place his genius warranted and all men expected? I do not know whether the reason lay more in the country, in his party, or with Blake himself. . . . Patience was needed, but Blake was never patient. He was not the man to fight uphill battles. He was proud, and expected men to come to him; sensitive, for he lacked humour; honourable and earnest, and saw charlatans and men steeped in corruption holding high place in public life. . . . The kindliest of men to his intimates, he wore the sensitive man's mask of indifference to the public. Ill-health and a nervous temperament unfitted him for the drudgery and disappointments of politics. He was moody and nervous when things were not going well. Yet without any of the lesser arts, he cast a spell over every man in parliament. We felt in the presence of genius, and would have been proud to serve to the end, had he not drawn himself aloof.[7]

From the foregoing passage it can be seen that Blake's shortcomings as a public man had hindered his career in Canada as well as in Ireland. The truth is that there was a certain important similarity between the problems with which he was faced in the two countries. Indeed the essential tragedy of Blake's political career was that he served both Canadian Liberalism and Irish Nationalism in difficult and discouraging times. He was a prominent Canadian Liberal in the years in which his party had little success at the polls; his part in Irish politics was played during a period when the home rule movement made little progress. In each case, there was a change in the fortunes of the cause he served not very long after his retirement. Five years after he left the Canadian House of Commons, a Liberal government took office at Ottawa and remained in power for fifteen years; the same length of time after his retirement from Irish politics, the introduction of the third Home Rule Bill,—follow-

[7]Quoted in O. D. Skelton, *Life and Letters of Sir Wilfrid Laurier* (Toronto, 1921), I, 223–4n.

ing the passage of the Parliament Act of 1911 which reduced the House of Lords' absolute veto to a suspensory one—gave fresh hope of success to the Irish Nationalists. It was indeed sad that Blake, who had worked long and hard for both causes in discouraging times, was denied the opportunity of serving them in the brighter periods of political success. But certainly he must be given some credit for striving as he did in the years of difficulty, thus helping to make possible the more hopeful times in which he was not privileged to share.

Finally, it may be asked whether Blake, in the long run, regretted his decision to enter Irish politics. There is no doubt that, from the material viewpoint, his Irish career was a losing battle, for his health was seriously impaired by overwork and his fortune diminished by his large contributions to the home rule cause. Actually, despite his added responsibilities in later years, he was probably never in serious danger of financial need, for his Privy Council cases brought him considerable revenue and his income from private investments was probably more than he realized.[8] Yet, the expenditure which his work for Ireland entailed must have left him much poorer than he would otherwise have been. Indeed, it is natural to ask if he regretted spending so much money and energy on a cause which failed during his lifetime and in the service of which he had endured many trials and difficulties.

During his early years in Irish politics Blake sometimes, in moods of depression, expressed the wish that he had never left Canada. But his feelings at such times ought not to be taken too seriously, for it is plain that, despite his frequent threats of resignation, he could not bring himself to retire from Irish politics until his health forced him to do so. He felt it was his duty to accept the Irish invitation and to continue, if at all possible, to aid the cause as long as his services were required. He doubtless would have brooded over his neglect of this duty had he refused to accept an Irish seat or withdrawn at an early date from the struggle. As it was, he had at least the satisfaction of knowing that he had done all in his power to aid the cause until his health failed completely.

[8]This was stated by his grandson, Mr. V. Blake, in conversation with the author.

BIBLIOGRAPHY

I. Sources

1. *Collections of Private Papers*

(a) *The Edward Blake Papers.* This collection, during most of the time that I was working on it, was in the University of Toronto Library. It has since been transferred to the Ontario Department of Public Records and Archives, Toronto. That portion of the collection which deals with Blake's Irish political activities consists of approximately 5,000 letters, memoranda, and drafts of speeches, together with ten scrap books. The letters are mainly from prominent Irish Nationalists, British Liberals, and Canadian and American sympathizers with the cause of Irish home rule. There are also copies of some of Blake's replies. Some of the correspondence is arranged according to the writer—Bryce, Davitt, Dillon, Gladstone, McCarthy, Morley, J. F. X. O'Brien, William O'Brien, T. P. O'Connor, and Redmond—and chronologically within these divisions. The rest is run together under the heading, "General Irish Political Correspondence." Most of the letters received from Blake's former political colleagues in Canada during the years he spent in Irish politics are included with their earlier correspondence near the beginning of the collection. Memoranda and drafts of speeches are arranged chronologically. The scrap books, compiled by Blake himself, contain clippings from many Irish, British, Canadian, and American newspapers. They deal mainly with the offer of an Irish seat to Blake and his election for South Longford, 1892; the rumour that he was to become leader of the Irish party, 1892; T. W. Russell's visit to Canada, 1892; Blake's speeches in Britain, Ireland, Canada, and the United States, 1892–3, 1897, and 1902, including his maiden speech in the British House of Commons, 1893; and his retirement from Irish politics, 1907. The material in the scrap books is not very well organized, clippings on the same subject sometimes being scattered through two or three books.

(b) *The Sir Wilfrid Laurier Papers.* These papers are in the Public Archives of Canada, Ottawa. Arranged chronologically, they include about 45 letters from Blake (or from his son, Edward

Francis, on his behalf) written during the years he spent in Irish politics. Most useful to me were the following: (1) A letter from Blake, dated Aug. 31, 1892, commenting on his speech at the Eighty Club and on the general Irish situation and mentioning the length of time he expected to remain in Irish politics. (2) A large group of letters and cables between Laurier, Blake, and Blake's son, relating to the Alaska boundary dispute, in which Blake agreed, in 1903, to act as Canadian counsel. Ill health forced him to relinquish his brief in the case before the work was completed.

(c) *The Sir John S. Willison Papers.* These papers are also in the Public Archives of Canada, Ottawa. Arranged alphabetically, they include 11 letters from Blake written between 1896 and 1903. Most of these letters request Willison, who was editor of the Toronto *Globe* until November, 1902, to include reports of certain of Blake's speeches in his newspaper. In one or two of them are interesting remarks on Blake's activities in Irish politics.

(d) *The John Dillon Papers.* This very large collection is in private custody in Dublin. That part of it which deals with the years during which Blake was an Irish member of the British House of Commons is contained in 6 large tin boxes. The correspondence is arranged in envelopes according, in some cases, to subject, and in others to correspondent and date. There are among the papers approximately 300 letters from Blake. Of almost 200 of these there are no copies in the Blake Papers. Also of interest in a study of Blake's Irish career is the correspondence between Dillon and other leading Nationalists, for it contains some interesting references to Blake. Additional items among the Dillon Papers which have proved of considerable value are the minute books of the Irish parliamentary party from 1886 to 1900 and the minute book of the council of the Irish National Federation from January, 1893, to January, 1898.

(e) *The J. F. X. O'Brien Papers.* These papers are in the National Library of Ireland, Dublin. Since O'Brien was for many years one of the treasurers of the Irish party, this collection is made up to a considerable extent of such items as account books, bank pass books, bundles of cheque counterfoils, and letters dealing with matters relating to the party finances. There are approximately 35 letters from Blake among the J. F. X. O'Brien Papers but, except for a few, they are of minor importance. Some material relating to the

Tweedmouth incident of 1894 is of interest in a study of Blake's career. Also of considerable value are the two minute books of the electoral committee of 1892 and two other notebooks containing rough drafts of the minutes of some of the meetings of the committee of the Irish party between September, 1892, and August, 1895.

(*f*) *The William O'Brien Papers.* This collection, which is a comparatively small one, is also deposited in the National Library in Dublin. It comprises approximately 1,000 items, of which many belong to the period after Blake's retirement in 1907. There are no letters from Blake in the collection, but some interesting references to him occur in letters from Dillon to O'Brien, especially during the years 1898–1900.

(*g*) *The T. C. Harrington Papers.* These papers are also in the National Library in Dublin. The correspondence in the collection is arranged in a number of folders, of which only one, marked "Party Reunion—1897–1900," was of any value in preparing this book. It contains some interesting material regarding the negotiations for reunion, including a letter from Blake, of which there is a copy in the Blake Papers, and one from Redmond, giving his views of the situation and of the attitude of Dillon and Blake.

(*h*) *The John Redmond Papers.* This collection has now been transferred from the Library of University College, Cork, to the National Library in Dublin. During my stay in Ireland, plans for this transfer were being made and, through the kindness of Professor Denis Gwynn of Cork, that portion of the collection relating to the period of Blake's political association with Redmond (i.e., 1900–7) was sent to the National Library so that I could examine it. The most valuable items for my purposes were a "Draft Plan for the Administration of the Members' Indemnity Fund," prepared by Blake in 1901, and a large collection of documents, including letters and memoranda written by Blake, relating to the Irish Council Bill of 1907.

2. *Speeches of Blake's Separately Published*

Several of Blake's speeches, delivered during his Irish career or relating to the Irish question, have been published in pamphlet form. The following is a list of them:

(a) "The Irish Question—Speech in the Canadian House of Commons, 1882" (n.p., 1882).

(b) "The Irish Question with Special Reference to Home Rule in Canada—Speech at the Eighty Club" (London, 1892).

(c) "The Blake Demonstration—Pavilion—September 19, 1892" (n.p., n.d.).

(d) "Speech in Connection with the Frome Division Liberal Association, and in Supporting a Resolution of Confidence in Mr. Gladstone's Government, at the Guildhall, Bath, January 27, 1893" (reprinted from the *Bath and County Weekly News*).

(e) "Address in Aid of Home Rule in Ireland" (Boston, 1894).

(f) "Speech on Irish Situation—New York, 1894" (*Home Rule Bulletin*, Irish National Federation of America, November, 1894).

(g) "The Over-Taxation of Ireland" (Dublin, 1897).

(h) "The Irish Situation—Speech at Glasgow, December 1898" (Dublin, 1899).

(i) "Commonwealth of Australia Constitution Bill—Speech in the British House of Commons on Monday, 21st May, 1900" (London, 1900).

(j) "Speech in the House of Commons on 13th March, 1902, on Supply—Civil Service Estimates (Irish Situation)" (reprinted from *Hansard*).

(k) "Speeches in the House of Commons on 9th and 10th June, 1902, on the Finance Bill (Corn Tax)" (reprinted from *Hansard*).

(l) "Speech Delivered before the First National Convention, United Irish League of America, Faneuil Hall, Boston, Mass., October 20–21, 1902" (Boston, n.d.).

(m) "The Case for Ireland Stated—Speech Delivered in Washington, U.S.A., on December 7th, 1902," United Irish League of Great Britain Leaflets, no. 5 (London, n.d.).

3. *Newspapers*

In addition to the press clippings in the Blake Scrap Books, several Dublin and Toronto newspapers have been most useful in preparing this book. The Dublin newspapers used were:

(a) The *Freeman's Journal*, which was the official organ of the anti-Parnellites before 1900 and of the reunited Irish party after that date.

(b) The *Irish Catholic and Nation*, a weekly journal which strongly supported the views of the Healyite wing of the anti-Parnellite party. In June, 1896, the *Irish Catholic and Nation* was discontinued, its place being taken by two weekly newspapers, the *Irish Catholic*, which dealt exclusively with religious matters, and the *Nation*, which concerned itself with political and other questions, giving its support to Healy as had the earlier journal. About the middle of 1897, the *Nation* was purchased by William Murphy, a member of the Healyite wing of the anti-Parnellite party, who changed it from a weekly to a daily newspaper, calling it the *Daily Nation*.

(c) The *Irish Daily Independent*, which was Parnellite until 1900 and which tended, after that date, to be somewhat critical of the reunited party. In August, 1900, the *Irish Daily Independent* and the *Daily Nation* amalgamated. The newspaper thus formed was called the *Irish Daily Independent and Nation*, but after about five years it reverted to the name, *Irish Daily Independent*.

(d) The *Irish Times*, a Unionist journal.

The Toronto newspapers used were:

(a) The *Globe*, which, being a Liberal journal, naturally took some interest in Blake's Irish career, since he had previously been leader of Canada's Liberal party.

(b) The *Toronto World*, which, although a Conservative journal, showed a great deal of interest in Blake's entry into Irish politics. It gave much space to reports and comments regarding the offer to him of an Irish seat, and even sent a correspondent with him to report on his reception in Ireland and his election campaign. Thus, for accounts of the opening stages of Blake's Irish career, the *World* is more valuable than either the *Globe* or any of the Dublin newspapers.

(c) The *Mail* and the *Empire*, both of which were Conservative newspapers, strongly opposed to Irish home rule and consequently to Blake's advocacy of it. In 1895 these two journals amalgamated to form the *Mail and Empire*.

(d) The *News*, which professed to be an independent journal, but which, until a change of ownership and management took place at the end of 1902, generally expressed strongly Conservative views.

The London *Times* has also been a useful source of reference.

4. Parliamentary Records

Official Report of the Debates of the House of Commons of the Dominion of Canada (Ottawa, 1882 and 1886).

Hansard, Parliamentary Debates, 4th Series, VII–CLXXXII.

Final Report by Her Majesty's Commissioners Appointed to Inquire into the Financial Relations between Great Britain and Ireland (London, 1896).

5. Contemporary Works of Reference

The Annual Register—A Review of Public Events at Home and Abroad for the Years 1892–1907 (London, 1893–1908).

MORGAN, HENRY J., The Canadian Men and Women of the Time (Toronto, 1898 and 1912).

Who's Who: An Annual Biographical Dictionary (London, 1870–).

6. Memoirs, Autobiographies, etc.

ABERDEEN, Lord and Lady, We Twa, 2 vols. (London, 1925).

BALFOUR, A. J., Aspects of Home Rule (London, 1912).

BIRRELL, AUGUSTINE, Things Past Redress (London, 1937).

BLUNT, W. S., My Diaries (New York, 1923).

BODKIN, M. M., Recollections of an Irish Judge (New York, 1915).

DAVITT, MICHAEL, The Fall of Feudalism in Ireland (London and New York, 1904).

DUNRAVEN, Earl of, The Outlook in Ireland (Dublin, 1907).

——— Past Times and Pastimes, 2 vols. (London, 1922).

HEALY, T. M., Why Ireland Is Not Free: A Study of Twenty Years in Politics (Dublin, 1898).

——— Letters and Leaders of My Day, 2 vols. (London, 1928).

HUTCHINSON, HORACE G. (ed.) Private Diaries of Sir Algernon West (London, 1922).

LONG, WALTER, Memories (London, 1923).

LUCY, Sir HENRY W., A Diary of the Home Rule Parliament, 1892–5 (London, 1896).

——— A Diary of the Unionist Parliament, 1895–1900 (Bristol, 1901).

——— The Balfourian Parliament, 1900–1905 (London, 1906).

McCarthy, Justin, *Reminiscences*, 2 vols. (New York, 1899).
—— *An Irishman's Story* (New York, 1904).
McCarthy, Justin, and Mrs. Campbell Praed, *Our Book of Memories* (London, 1912).
MacNeil, J. G. Swift, *What I Have Seen and Heard* (London, 1925).
Morley, John, *Recollections*, 2 vols. (Toronto, 1917).
O'Brien, William, *Recollections* (London, 1905).
—— *An Olive Branch in Ireland and Its History* (London, 1910).
—— *Evening Memories* (Dublin and London, 1920).
O'Connor, T. P., *Memoirs of an Old Parliamentarian*, 2 vols. (New York, 1929).
Oxford and Asquith, Earl of, *Fifty Years of Parliament*, 2 vols. (London, 1926).
—— *Memories and Reflections, 1852–1927*, 2 vols. (London, 1928).

II. Secondary Works

1. General Histories

Ensor, R. C. K., *England, 1870–1914*, The Oxford History of England (Oxford, 1936).
Feiling, Keith, *A History of England* (London, 1950).
Halevy, E., *A History of the English People, Epilogue, 1895–1914*, 2 vols. (London, 1929 and 1934).
McCarthy, Justin, *A History of Our Own Times from 1880 to the Diamond Jubilee* (New York, 1897).
—— *A History of Our Own Times from the Diamond Jubilee to the Accession of Edward VII* (New York and London, 1905).
O'Connor, Sir James, *History of Ireland, 1798–1924*, 2 vols. (London, 1925).
O'Hegarty, P. S., *A History of Ireland under the Union, 1801–1922* (London, 1952).
Paul, Herbert, *A History of Modern England*, 5 vols. (London, 1904–6).
Trevelyan, G. M., *British History in the Nineteenth Century and After* (London, 1937).
Woodward, E. L., *The Age of Reform, 1815–1870*, The Oxford History of England (Oxford, 1938).

2. Special Subjects

BANKS, MARGARET A., "Edward Blake's Relations with Canada during his Irish Career, 1892–1907" (*Canadian Historical Review*, XXV, no. 1, 1954).

DRUS, ETHEL, "A Report on the Papers of Joseph Chamberlain relating to the Jameson Raid and the Inquiry" (*Bulletin of the Institute of Historical Research*, May, 1952).

HAMMOND, J. L., *Gladstone and the Irish Nation* (London, 1938).

KENNEDY, THOMAS, *A History of the Irish Protest against Over-Taxation from 1853 to 1897* (Dublin, 1897).

LYONS, F. S. L., *The Irish Parliamentary Party, 1890–1910* (London, 1951).

—— "The Irish Parliamentary Party and the General Election of 1895" (*Irish Historical Studies*, Sept., 1952).

—— "The Irish Parliamentary Party and the Liberals in Mid-Ulster, 1894" (*Irish Historical Studies*, March, 1951).

—— "The Irish Unionist Party and the Devolution Crisis of 1904–5" (*Irish Historical Studies*, March, 1948).

MACDONAGH, MICHAEL, *The Home Rule Movement* (Dublin, 1920).

MANSERGH, NICHOLAS, *Britain and Ireland* (London, 1946).

—— *Ireland in the Age of Reform and Revolution* (London, 1940).

O'DONNELL, F. H., *A History of the Irish Parliamentary Party, 1870–1890*, 2 vols. (London, 1910).

PLUNKETT, Sir HORACE, *Ireland in the New Century* (London, 1904).

POMFRET, JOHN E., *The Struggle for Land in Ireland, 1800–1923* (Princeton, 1930).

TANSILL, C. C., *Canadian-American Relations, 1875–1911* (New Haven, 1943).

VAN DER POEL, JEAN, *The Jameson Raid* (London, 1951).

3. Biographies

ANDERSON, R. A., *With Horace Plunkett in Ireland* (London, 1935).

BARTON, Sir D. P., *Timothy Healy, Memories and Anecdotes* (Dublin and Cork, 1933).

BIGGS-DAVISON, JOHN, *George Wyndham: A Study in Toryism* (London, 1951).
BLAKE, MARTIN J., *Blake Family Records*, 2 vols. (London, 1902 and 1905).
CHURCHILL, WINSTON S., *Lord Randolph Churchill*, 2 vols. (London, 1906).
CREWE, Marquess of, *Lord Rosebery*, 2 vols. (London, 1931).
DIGBY, MARGARET, *Horace Plunkett: An Anglo-American Irishman* (Oxford, 1949).
DUGDALE, BLANCHE E. C., *Arthur James Balfour*, 2 vols. (London, 1936).
ERVINE, ST. JOHN, *Parnell* (London, 1925).
FINCH, EDITH, *Wilfrid Scawen Blunt* (London, 1938).
FISHER, H. A. L., *James Bryce*, 2 vols. (New York, 1927).
FYFE, HAMILTON, *T. P. O'Connor* (London, 1934).
GARDINER, A. G., *The Life of Sir William Harcourt*, 2 vols. (London, 1923).
GARVIN, J. L., *The Life of Joseph Chamberlain*, 3 vols. (London, 1932–5).
GOOCH, G. P., *The Life of Lord Courtney* (London, 1920).
GWYNN, DENIS, *The Life of John Redmond* (London, 1932).
HAMMOND, J. L., *C. P. Scott of the Manchester Guardian* (New York, 1934).
HARRISON, HENRY, *Parnell Vindicated* (London, 1931).
LECKY, ELISABETH, *A Memoir of the Right Hon. William Edward Hartpole Lecky* (London, 1929).
MACDONAGH, MICHAEL, *The Life of William O'Brien* (London, 1928).
MCKAIL, J. W., and WYNDHAM, GUY, *Life and Letters of George Wyndham*, 2 vols. (London, 1925).
MORLEY, JOHN, *The Life of William Ewart Gladstone*, 3 vols. (London, 1903).
O'BRIEN, R. BARRY, *The Life of Charles Stewart Parnell*, 2 vols. (New York, 1898).
O'FLAHERTY, LIAM, *The Life of Tim Healy* (London, 1927).
O'HARA, M. M., *Chief and Tribune, Parnell and Davitt* (Dublin and London, 1919).

SKELTON, O. D., *The Life and Letters of Sir Wilfrid Laurier*, 2 vols. (Toronto, 1921).
SOMERVELL, D. C., *Disraeli and Gladstone* (New York, 1926).
SPENDER, J. A., *The Life of the Right Hon. Sir Henry Campbell-Bannerman, G.C.B.*, 2 vols. (London, 1923).
SPENDER, J. A., and ASQUITH, CYRIL, *Life of Henry Herbert Asquith, Lord Oxford and Asquith*, 2 vols. (London, 1932).
THOROLD, ALGAR, *The Life of Henry Labouchere* (London, 1913).
TREVELYAN, G. M., *Sir George Otto Trevelyan: A Memoir* (London, 1932).
WALLACE, W. S., *The Dictionary of Canadian Biography* (Toronto, 1926).
WILLIAMS, BASIL, *Cecil Rhodes* (London, 1921).

INDEX

ABERCORN, DUKE OF, 275
Aberdeen, Lord, 58, 193, 329
Abraham, William, 152, 236, 292n
Acland, A. H. D., 163
Act of Union, *see* Union
Advertiser (London, Ont.), reports Blake's Strathroy speech, 193–4
Agricultural and Technical Instruction, Department of, 318; founded, 198
Alaska boundary dispute, Blake as counsel for Canada in, 280–1, 286, 289, 303
All-Ireland Committee, 148, 150
Ancient Order of Hibernians, representation at Irish race convention, 170
Ancient Order of Hibernians (Board of Erin), representation at Irish race convention, 170
Anti-Parnellite party, *see* Irish parliamentary party
Asquith, H. H., 328
Australia: Davitt in, 134; Blake's visit to, 136–7; choice of delegates to Irish race convention, 170; gives financial aid to Irish party, 191; fund-raising for United Irish League in, 204; Commonwealth of, Constitution Bill, 250–2; Joseph Devlin in, 311

BALFOUR, ARTHUR J., 54, 149–50, 304
Balfour, Gerald, 198
Banks, Margaret A., 195n
Barbour, Sir David, 139–40, 142
Barrymore, Lord, 275
Birrell, Augustine: appointed Irish Chief Secretary, 316; and Irish Council Bill, 317, 319–20
Blake, Catherine Hume (mother of Edward), 13
Blake, Edward: invited to stand for British Parliament, 3, 10, 11; replies to invitation, 11; views on home rule, 11–12, 22–6, 30–1, 208, 334; career in Canada, 13–16; public opinion as to whether he should enter Irish politics, 16–20; sails for Ireland, 20–1; elected for South Longford, 28; elected to parliamentary committee of Irish party, 30; visits and fund-raising missions to Canada and United States, 34–5, 71–83, 92–8, 166, 177, 183, 185, 188–92, 219, 241n, 263–9, 302–8, 311, 316; views on Parnell and Parnellites, 36–8; rumours that he was to lead Irish party, 38–42; and Home Rule Bill (1893), 44–9, 52, 54–7, 60–3, 66–8; seeks to resign from party committee, 48, 64, 84–6, 124, 130; and Tweedmouth incident, 87–8, 92–101, 103–8; and Mayo convention, 112; and "Omagh scandal," 114–35; re-elected to party committee, 133–4; re-elected for South Longford, 136, 241n, 304; visits Australia and New Zealand, 136; suggested as chairman of Irish party, 136–7, 218–19; and financial relations question, 139, 141–2, 146–51, 153–60, 163–4, 198; and Irish race convention, 166–70, 172–5; and party resolutions (1897), 177–83; considers returning to service of Canada, 184, 186–7, 192–6, 305–6; and Privy Council work, 184, 302–3, 316, 343; advises Dillon to resign chairmanship of Irish party, 200–1, 204, 210; and United Irish League, 201–5, 217; and reunion of party, 205, 208–33; and relations between reunited

355

356 INDEX

party and United Irish League, 230–1, 234–7, 239–41; and inquiry into Jameson raid, 243–6, 248–9; attitude to Boer War, 247–8; and Queen's visit to Ireland, 249–50; and Commonwealth of Australia Constitution Bill, 251–2; and payment of members of Irish party (1901), 253–7, (1907), 257–9; speech on civil service estimates, 260–3; activities (1903–6), 274–5; and land conference (1902), 276–7; and Land Bill (1903), 280–90; and Alaska boundary dispute, 280–1, 286, 289, 303; and Irish university question, 290; and W. O'Brien's retirement, 291–2; and Cork writ, 292–302; and party resolution (1905), 303; and general election (1906), 304–5; and Irish Council Bill, 309, 311–19, 321–5; illness and retirement, 325–8; expressions of regret at retirement of, 328–32; summary and evaluation of Irish career of, 333–43
Blake, Edward Francis (son of Edward), 191, 281n, 303–4
Blake, Margaret (wife of Edward), 13, 86, 304, 325
Blake, Samuel Hume (brother of Edward), 13, 34
Blake, Samuel Verschoyle (son of Edward), 21, 86, 304
Blake, Verschoyle (grandson of Edward and son of Edward Francis), 13n, 21n, 343n
Blake, William Hume (father of Edward), 13
Boer War, 225, 227, 243, 246–7; attitude of British Liberals towards, 247; attitude of Irish Nationalists towards, 247–9; attitude of Canadians towards, 247–8, 266; attitude of Irish-Americans towards, 266
Boston Post, reports meeting addressed by Blake in Boston, 35

Boulogne negotiations, 9
Boyle, P., 17
Bradford Observer, comments on Blake's speech at Eighty Club, 32
Brampton-Gordon, Sir W., 329
British Daily Mail, 58n
Bryce, James, 30, 42n, 54; and Home Rule Bill (1893), 44–5, 339; and financial relations question, 163; and Cork writ, 295; and Irish Council Bill, 309–10, 312, 317; appointed British Ambassador at Washington, 316
Butt, Isaac, 3–4

CAMERON, JOHN, 58
Campbell-Bannerman, Sir Henry: and Home Rule Bill (1893), 44; and financial relations question, 163; and inquiry into Jameson raid, 243–5; becomes Prime Minister, 304; and "step by step" home rule policy, 307, 309; and Irish Council Bill, 310, 324; and Blake's retirement, 329–30
Canada: attitude to Irish demand for home rule, 12, 266–9; summary of Blake's career in, 13–16; home rule in, described by Blake, 30–1, 60–2, 251–2; Blake's visits and fund-raising missions to, 34–5, 71, 78–83, 92–6, 134, 166, 177, 183, 185, 188–92, 219, 241n, 263, 265–9, 302–8, 311, 316, 337–8; choice of delegates from, to Irish race convention, 170; remarks of Canadians at Irish race convention, 175; general election in (1896), 184; question of Blake's returning to service of, 184, 186–7, 192–6, 305–6; Supreme Court of, 187n, 306; chief justiceship of, 187n, 193; Dillon's visit to, cancelled, 265–6; Joseph Devlin's visit to, 266–7; Redmond's

visit to, 302; T. P. O'Connor's visit to, 308
Carnarvon, Lord, 6
Carson, Edward, 153–4
Castletown, Lord, 275
Chamberlain, Joseph: proposes local government for Ireland, 6; opposes Home Rule Bill (1886), 7; opposes Home Rule Bill (1893), 52–7; and Henry Labouchere, 58n; and Jameson raid, 244–6; and Commonwealth of Australia Constitution Bill, 250–1; withdraws from cabinet (1903), 273
Chicago World's Fair, 71–2
Childers, Hugh C. E., 139–40, 142
Chiltern Hundreds, 295n, 296, 308, 325ff
Churchill, Lord Randolph, 52
Clancy, J. J.: and financial relations question, 149–50, 153–6; and reunion of Irish party, 218
Clarke, Sir Edward, 51, 161
Cleary, Most Rev. J. V., Archbishop of Kingston, 79
Colonial Office, and Jameson raid, 245–6
Commons, House of (British): and Home Rule Bill (1893), 49–63, 66–8; and financial relations question, 149–50, 156–63; and Jameson raid, 246; and Redmond's speech on Boer War, 247; and Commonwealth of Australia Constitution Bill, 250–2; and civil service estimates, 260–3; and Land Bill (1903), 279–80, 288–9; and issue of Cork writ, 292–8; and Irish Council Bill, 320; and Committee of Selection, 325, 326
Congested Districts Board, 318
Connaught, Province of, and United Irish League, 205
Connors, Joseph, 248n
Conservatives: and general election (1880), 5; attitude towards home rule, 6; and general election (1892), 29; return to office (1895), 110; attitude towards issue of Cork writ, 295, 299; *see also* Unionists
Cork City: Blake's speech at, regarding "Omagh scandal," 116–18, 121ff; O'Brien's retirement as M.P. for, 274; issue of writ for, 292–302, 340
Costigan, John, 79, 80, 175
Courtney, Leonard, 57
Creighton, J. G. A., 17–18
Crewe, Lord, 69n
Crilly, Daniel, 111–12
Crimes Act (1887), 7; used against United Irish League, 259–60, 263; condemned by Blake and other Irish Nationalists, 261–3, 265
Croke, Most Rev. T. W., Archbishop of Cashel, 38, 40
Cronyn, Right Rev. Benjamin, Anglican Bishop of Huron (father-in-law of Blake), 14
Cronyn, Margaret, *see* Blake, Margaret
Crosbie, L. Talbot, 276
Curran, J. J., 82n
Curran, T. B., 152
Currie, Bertram W., 139, 142

Daily Nation (Dublin): reports speech by Lord Tweedmouth, 104–5; founded, 183; criticizes Blake and others, 211–12; reports November (1899) unity conference, 222–3; question of amalgamation with *Irish Independent*, 237; comments on national convention (June, 1900), 240
Daily News (London), 57n, 58n
Dane, Richard M., 163
Davitt, Michael, 11n, 40, 85, 191n, 338; inaugurates "New Departure" policy, 5; summary of career, 5n; and Blake's fundraising missions, 82, 192, 337–8;

and Tweedmouth incident, 95–6; re-elected to party committee, 133–4; and Irish race convention, 167; and party resolutions (1897), 178–9; and United Irish League, 201–4; and reunion of Irish party, 206–7, 211, 213n, 220; and chairmanship of reunited party, 233; visits United States as United Irish League delegate, 263–5, 268; attitude towards conciliation with Unionists, 272, 274; and land conference (1902), 277, 279; and Land Bill (1903), 287, 291; desires Irish independence, 335

Denmark, 335

Derry, see Londonderry

Devlin, Charles, 308

Devlin, Joseph, 303ff; visits United States and Canada, 266–7; and Irish Council Bill, 311, 323–4

Devolution proposals, 270–1, 309

Diamond, Charles, 102, 115, 122, 124

Dickson, Thomas, and "Omagh scandal," 114, 116–17, 119–26, 130–2

Dillon, Elizabeth (wife of John), 225n, 324, 338–9

Dillon, John, 11n, 30n, 36, 40, 81n, 84, 85n, 109n, 186, 249, 254, 290, 303, 328n, 338–9, 341; association with "Plan of Campaign," 7; summary of career, 7n; and Boulogne negotiations, 9; attitude towards Paris funds question, 33; and Home Rule Bill (1893), 46–8, 52n, 63; his views compared with Healy's, 69–71; and Tweedmouth incident, 88, 90, 94, 97, 100–1; and "Omagh scandal," 112–14, 117, 119–26, 128–9, 131–3; re-elected to party committee, 133–4; elected chairman of Irish party, 137; abolishes party committee, 137; and financial relations question, 148–56, 160n, 198; and Irish race convention, 165, 168–70; and party resolutions (1897), 177–8, 180, 182–3; and question of Blake's retiring from Irish politics, 184, 186–7, 193, 306; and Blake's visits to Canada and United States, 185, 188–92; and United Irish League, 199–206, 216–17; and question of resigning chairmanship of Irish party, 200–1, 204–5; and reunion of Irish party, 204–5, 207–8, 210, 211n, 213, 215–26, 228–30, 232–3, 339; resigns chairmanship of party, 210; and relations between reunited party and United Irish League, 230, 234–8, 240; and expulsion of Healy from Irish party, 242; and Queen's visit to Ireland, 250; and payment of members of Irish party (1907), 258; visits United States as United Irish League delegate, 263–6, 268; attitude towards conciliation with Unionists, 271–4; and land conference (1902), 277, 279; and Land Bill (1903), 290–1; and Cork writ, 294, 299–301; and Irish Council Bill, 310–11, 321–4

Dillonites, 234; and election of chairman of Irish party (1896), 136–7; and financial relations question, 148–9, 151–6, 160; and administration of party funds, 173–4; and party resolutions (1897), 177–83; and reunion of Irish party, 207, 213–31; and election of chairman of reunited party, 232–3; see also Irish parliamentary party

Donelan, Captain A., 133n, 134, 211–12, 231, 236

Down, South, 11, 20

Drus, Ethel, 245n

Duffy, Sir Charles Gavan, 216

Dunraven, Lord: and Irish university question, 270; and devolu-

tion proposals, 270–1, 274; and land conference (1902), 275–7
Durham, Lord, 60
Eastern Daily Press (Norwich), comments on Blake's speech at Eighty Club, 31
Education, 4, 171n; university, 4, 290; Irish University Bill (1873), 4; Lord Dunraven's university proposal, 270; and Irish Council Bill, 315, 318
Eighty Club (London), Blake's speech at, 30–1, 42n; press comments on, 31–2; Blake's comments on, 32
Elections: by-elections in Ireland (1871), 4; general election (1880), 5; general election (1886), 7; Kilkenny by-election, 8–9; general election in Ireland (1892), 10–11, 20, 22–9, 109–10, 128–9; general election (1892), results, 29; general election (1895) and dissension in Irish party, 109–36, 165; general election (1895), result, 125; South Kerry by-election, 168; general election in Ireland (1900), 241; general election (1906), 304–5, 306
Ellis, Thomas: and "Omagh scandal," 114, 118–20; and financial relations question, 163
Emmet, Dr. Thomas Addis, 35–6, 76, 78, 85n, 94
Esmonde, Sir Thomas, 78; and reunion of Irish party, 210–13, 215, 223, 231
Evening Echo, 39n
Evening Mail (Dublin), 39n, 41n
Evening News (London), 58n
Evening Telegram (Portland, Ore.), 39n
Everard, Colonel T. Nugent, 276
Evicted tenants: convention at Longford in support of, 36–8; and Paris funds, 38; administration of fund for, 74–5; attitude of Americans towards fund for, 75–6; campaign for funds for, 86–7; and Tweedmouth incident, 102–3
Express (probably) *Daily Express*, Dublin), 41n

FARRELL, J. P., 24
Farrer, Lord, 139, 142, 146
Fenians, *see* Irish Republican Brotherhood
Field, Admiral, 59–60
Finances of Irish parliamentary party: fund-raising in Canada and United States, 34–6, 71–3, 76, 77–83, 183, 185, 188–92, 337–8; fund-raising (general), 69, 76–7, 200ff; administration of party funds, 73–5, 83–5, 86, 177–83, 252–9; fund-raising in England (Tweedmouth incident), 88–108
Financial relations between Great Britain and Ireland, 3, 171n, 337; and Home Rule Bill (1893), 47, 51, 138–9; and Home Rule Bill (1886), 51–2, 68; history of inquiries into, 138–9; Longford meeting to consider question of, 198; and Irish Council Bill, 315–16, 318; *see also* Royal Commission on the Financial Relations between Great Britain and Ireland
Fisher, H. A. L., 54
Fitzpatrick, Rev. John, 216
Flannery, Rev. Dr. W., 175
Fox, Dr. J. F., 169
Foy, J. J., 185
Freeman's Journal (Dublin), 110n, 183, 333; changes sides in political controversy, 9; comments on Blake's speech at Eighty Club, 31; dispute regarding amalgamation with *National Press*, 32–3; reports convention, including Blake's speech, at Longford, 36–8; comments on Blake's speeches on Home Rule

Bill (1893), 57, 62–3; reports T. W. Russell's visit to Canada, 60; praises Blake's fund-raising in Canada, 82, 186, 192; and Tweedmouth incident, 89–90, 91, 95, 104n, 107; and "Omagh scandal," 115–16, 118, 124, 126–9, 135n; publishes reports of Financial Relations Commission, 140n; and financial relations conference, 151, 152n, 154n; reports and comments on Irish race convention, 171–5; publishes Blake's letter on party funds, 181–2; reports offer of Privy Council judgeship to Blake, 184; publishes statements of Blake and T. P. O'Connor, 211–12; publishes Patrick O'Brien's letter relating to party reunion, 216; publishes letters of Blake and William O'Brien on United Irish League, 217; publishes Blake's letter relating to party reunion, 226–8; reports conference resulting in party reunion, 229–31; reports party meetings, 233, 235, 257, 259; attitude towards Land Act (1903), 272; and issue of Cork writ, 298–302, 340; reports Irish national convention (1907), 324; publishes documents relating to Blake's retirement, 327; comments on Blake's retirement, 331

GAELIC ATHLETIC ASSOCIATION, 335
Gaelic Athletic Clubs, representation at Irish race convention, 169
Gaelic language, 171n
Gaelic League, 335
Garvin, J. L., 245n
Gazette (Giverton), 38n
Gladstone, Herbert, 163, 295, 299
Gladstone, William Ewart, 17–18, 27, 32–3, 58n, 72, 87, 266–7, 338; and Irish legislation (1869–73), 4; attitude to Joseph Chamberlain's local government scheme, 6; conversion to home rule, 6; seeks dissolution after defeat of Home Rule Bill (1886), 7; defeated in general election (1886), 7; and question of Parnell's leadership (1890), 8; becomes Prime Minister (1892), 29; and Blake, 30, 38–43, 72; and Home Rule Bill (1893), 44, 46–51, 59, 62n, 68; retires from premiership, 69; and Tweedmouth incident, 89–90, 92–7, 106; and financial relations question, 138–9
Glasgow: Dillon's speech at, 207; Blake's speech at, 208–9
Globe (Toronto), 16, 35n, 331n; comments on Blake's Irish invitation, 19; reports and comments on Blake's maiden speech in British House of Commons, 57–8; reports offer of Privy Council judgeship to Blake, 184; publishes Blake's letter on financial situation in Ireland, 189; reports Blake's speech at University of Toronto medical dinner, 195
Goschen, G. J., 138, 162–3
Grace, Morgan, 248n
Gwynn, Denis, 216n, 234n, 274n, 275n, 307n, 309n, 310n, 317n
Gwynn, Stephen, 328–9

HALIFAX, ARCHBISHOP OF, 80
Hamilton, Sir Robert, 139–40
Harcourt, Sir William, 57, 244–5, 248
Harrington, T. C.: and financial relations question, 152, 155; summary of career, 152n; and reunion of party, 207, 213–15, 220, 222–3, 225n, 226, 229–31; suggested as chairman of reunited party, 232–3; and relations between reunited party and United Irish League, 235–7; and expulsion of Healy from party, 242; and land conference (1902), 276–7

Harris, Rev. W. R., 175
Hayden, J. P., 225
Healy, Maurice, 241
Healy, Thomas J., 219, 224, 225n, 226n
Healy, Timothy Michael, 40, 42, 52, 75, 76, 172–3, 198; opposes Parnellites, 9; summary of career, 9n; and general election (1892), 11n, 27; and Paris funds question, 33, 65; and Tweedmouth incident, 89–90, 95–6, 98, 100, 101n, 103, 107; refuses to serve on party committee, 109; attitude towards Irish party's method of choosing candidates, 110–11; and Mayo convention, 112; and "Omagh scandal," 112–19, 121, 124–9, 131–3, 135; elected to party committee, 133–4; suggests Blake for chairmanship of Irish party, 137, 218–19; expelled from party committee, 137n, 168; and financial relations question, 151–2, 154–6; and Irish race convention, 165, 168–9, 176; expelled from Irish National League of Great Britain and Irish National Federation, 168; and organization of People's Rights Association, 176–7; and party resolutions (1897), 179–80; and reunion of Irish party, 206–9, 213–16, 218–20, 223–5, 228–33; and relations between reunited party and United Irish League, 234–7, 240; and general election (1900), 241; expelled from party, 242; and Queen's visit to Ireland, 249–50

Healyites, 71–3, 110–11; charges against committee of Irish party, 73–4, 83–6; and Tweedmouth incident, 89ff, 101; and "Omagh scandal," 114ff; and election of chairman of Irish party (1896), 136–7; and financial relations question, 148–9, 151–6; and Irish National Federation, 165, 168–9; and Irish race convention, 171ff; and administration of party funds, 173–4; found People's Rights Fund and Association, 176; resolutions against, 177–83; in South Longford, 187; and Longford meeting on financial relations, 198; and reunion of Irish party, 207–9, 211, 213–16, 218–20, 222–6, 228–31; and election of chairman of reunited party, 232–3; *see also* Irish parliamentary party

Hearn, Edward J., 302
Hemphill, Serjeant C. H., 113, 163
Herald (Chicago), 38n, 39n
Herschell, Lord, 44
Hicks-Beach, Sir Michael, 160–1, 244
Holland, 335
Home rule, 4, 8, 71, 171n, 185, 304, 308, 309, 314, 338; origin of movement for, 3; Blake's views on, 11–12, 22–3, 24–6, 30–1, 208, 334; attitude and comments of Canadians on, 12, 18–19, 34–5; Rosebery's attitude towards, 69, 338; slackening of interest in, 197; W. O'Brien's attitude towards (1898), 199; devolution proposals as modified form of, 270–1, 273–4; Campbell-Bannerman's attitude towards, 307
Home Rule Bill (1886), 6, 7, 12; provision for two orders in, 45; compared with Home Rule Bill (1893), 49–52
Home Rule Bill (1893), 29, 33, 40, 71, 315, 319, 334, 337, 339; preparation of, 44–9; provisions outlined by Gladstone, 49–51; compared with Home Rule Bill (1886), 49–52; Chamberlain's speech against, 52–3; Blake's speech on (first reading), 54–7; read first time in Commons, 59; debate on second reading begins, 59; T. W. Russell's speech against, 60, 61ff; Blake's speech

on (second reading), 60–2; second reading in Commons carried, 63; in committee stage, 63, 66–8; third reading in Commons carried, 68; defeated in Lords, 68, 69

Home Rule Bulletin (New York), 72n, 98n

Home Rule Union, 32

Hood, Acland, 295, 299

Howard, H. T., 21ff

Hunter, W. A., 139, 142

Hutcheson-Poe, Colonel W. H., 275–6

IMPERIAL PARLIAMENTARY FEDERATION, Blake's views on, 252

Independent Labour, representation in Parliament, 29

Irish Agricultural Organization Society, founding of, 198

Irish Catholic and Nation (Dublin), and Tweedmouth incident, 91

Irish Council Bill: drafts of, 309–11, 317–18, 319–20; attitude of Irish leaders to drafts of, 310, 311–16, 318–19; introduced in House of Commons, 320; proposed resolutions against, 320–4; rejected by Irish national convention, 324; dropped by government, 324

Irish Free State, 9n

Irish Independent (Dublin): becomes chief organ of Parnellite party, 9; comments on Blake's speech at Eighty Club, 32; comments on Blake's maiden speech in British House of Commons, 57; comments on Blake's fund-raising in Canada, 82; publishes Arthur O'Connor's letters, 83; and Tweedmouth incident, 90; and "Omagh scandal," 113–15, 121n, 131; and financial relations question, 151; comments on Irish race convention, 175–6; comments on Blake's resolution on party funds (1897), 180; publishes correspondence relating to suggestion for party reunion, 216; publishes Redmond's letter relating to conference on party reunion, 219; reports Parnellite meeting regarding party reunion, 225; reports joint meeting of Parnellite and anti-Parnellite committees, 226; question of amalgamation with *Daily Nation*, 237

Irish Independent and Nation (Dublin): reports party meetings, 257, 292; reports Redmond's speech at Cork regarding writ for that city, 301–2

Irish National Federation, 36, 75; founded, 9; Longford branch of, 24; Blake presides at meeting of, 40–1; and choosing candidates for election, 109–10; and "Omagh scandal," 114, 119–20, 133; and Healyites, 165, 168–9, 176, 178, 183; and Irish race convention, 169; decline of, 199–200, 202–3, 206, 234; replaced by United Irish League, 238, 263

Irish National Federation of America, 83, 94; Blake's meetings with officers of, 35–6, 73–6, 77–8, 81; Blake's meetings under auspices of, 35, 77, 81, 96–8; and representation at Irish race convention, 170; replaced by United Irish League of America, 263

Irish National Land League, 152n; founded, 5; suppressed by government, 9; replaced by Irish National League, 9

Irish National League, 152n; replaces Irish National Land League, 9; remains Parnellite after split, 9; and Paris funds, 33; replaced by United Irish League, 238

Irish National League of Great Britain, 35n, 102; London branches of, 88, 92, 102; Healy

INDEX 363

expelled from, 168; representation at Irish race convention, 170

Irish parliamentary party
the party before Parnell split of 1890: early history of, 3-4; attitude of, towards Land League, 5; attitude of, towards Land Act (1881), 6; and Parnell split, 8
the anti-Parnellite party, 1890-1900: invites Blake to join it, 3, 11; formed, 8; early history of, 8-10; and general election (1892), 10, 11, 20, 22-9, 109-10, 128-9; rumours regarding leadership of, 17, 38-42; and parliamentary committee of, 29-30, 35-6, 44, 46, 63-5, 73-5, 83-6, 109, 116ff, 130, 132-4, 137, 139; dissension within (general), 32-3, 69-71; and Paris funds, 33, 47, 65; Canadian attitude towards, 34-5; rumours of reunion with Parnellites, 38-9, 58; and Home Rule Bill (1893), 44-9, 51-2, 59, 63, 66; and O'Connor and O'Driscoll charges, 73-6, 83-6; and Tweedmouth incident, 86-108; and general election (1895), including "Omagh scandal," 109-136; McCarthy resigns chair of, 136; Dillon elected chairman of, 137; and financial relations question, 150, 151-2, 156-60, 163-4; and Irish race convention, 168-77; need for reunion and unity, 171-3, 177-83; attitude towards Local Government Bill (1898), 197; attitude towards recess conference (1895), 197; and question of Dillon's retirement from chair of, 200-5; and reunion with Parnellites, 200, 204-31, 339; Dillon resigns chairmanship of, 210-11; see also Dillonites, Healyites, Parnellites

the reunited party, 1900 and after: Redmond elected chairman of, 233; relations with United Irish League, 233-42; and general election (1900), 241; expulsion of Healy from, 241-2; attitude to Boer War, 247-9; condemns use of Crimes Act in Ireland, 261-3, 265; attitude towards conciliation with Unionists, 271-4; attitude towards land conference (1902) and Land Act (1903), 271-2, 276-7, 280-9; and W. O'Brien's resignation (1903), 291-2; and Cork writ, 292-302; and general election (1906), 304-5, 306; and Irish Council Bill, 309-25
and attitude towards British Empire, 334-5; summary of Blake's contributions to, 336-9; see also Finances of Irish parliamentary party

Irish People, comments on Blake's retirement, 331-2

Irish race convention: proposed by J. P. Ryan, 165-7; proposed by Archbishop Walsh, 167-8; attitude of Parnellites and Healyites towards, 170-1, 175-7; Bishop O'Donnell acts as chairman of, 171; resolutions of, 171; Blake's speeches at, 172-4; remarks of Canadians at, 174-5; results of, 176-7, 185, 188-90

Irish Reform Association: founded, 270; and devolution proposals, 270-1, 274

Irish Republican Brotherhood, 5

Irish Times (Dublin): comments on Blake's speech at Eighty Club, 31-2; comments on chairmanship of Irish party, 40; and Tweedmouth incident, 90, 98n; and "Omagh scandal," 113-15, 121n, 127n, 131; and financial relations question, 151

Irish Unionists, 110; attitude towards Home Rule Bill (1886), 6; and

Tweedmouth incident, 90; and "Omagh scandal," 114; and financial relations question, 147–55, 160–3; attitude towards recess conference (1895), 197–8; and Irish Council Bill, 321; *see also* Unionists

JAMESON, DR. L. S., 244–5
Jameson raid, 243–4; inquiry into, 244–6, 248–9
Jarvis, S. M., 13
Jordan, Jeremiah, 219, 223ff

KENNEDY, THOMAS, 139n, 140n, 150n
Kerry, South, 168
Kiely, G. W., 79
Kilkenny, 27; by-election in, 8, **9**
Knox, Vesey, 133–4, 183
Kruger, Paul, 246

LABOUCHERE, HENRY, 58, 245–6, 248
Labour: representation at Irish race convention, 169; resolution at race convention, 171n; party and general election (1906), 306; *see also* Independent Labour
Land, R. E. A., 248n
Land League, *see* Land question *and* Irish National Land League
Land question, 3, 171n, 268; Land Act (1870), 4; "New Departure" policy, 5; Irish National Land League, 5, 9, 152n; compensation for disturbance bill, 5; Land Act (1881), 6; "Plan of Campaign," 7; Land Act (1887), 7; Blake's views on, 25; and Home Rule Bill (1893), 47, 51; and Home Rule Bill (1886), 51; Land Act (1896), 197; Land Purchase Bill (1902), 270; land conference (1902), 270, 275–9; Land Act (1903), 270–2, 279–89, 339
Lash, Z., 18n
Laurier, Sir Wilfrid, 15, 32, 33, 175, 193; and question of Blake's returning to service of Canada, 184, 186, 305–6; and Alaska boundary dispute, 281, 289; evaluates Blake's character and ability, 341–2
Lea, Sir Thomas, 163
Lecky, W. E. H., 152, 154, 162–3
Leeds Mercury, comments on Blake's retirement, 330
Liberals: and general election (1880), 5; and Irish policy (1880–5), 5–6; attitude towards home rule, 6, 273, 307; attitude to Parnell's leadership (1890), 8; and general election (1892), 29; and contributions to Irish party funds (Tweedmouth incident), 89ff; government of, defeated in House of Commons (1895), 110; and "Omagh scandal," 114ff; defeated in election (1895), 125; and financial relations question, 162–3; attitude to Jameson raid, 245; attitude towards issue of Cork writ, 295, 299; form government (1905), 304; and general election (1906), 306; and House of Lords, 309
Liberal Unionists: attitude towards Home Rule Bill (1886), 7; and general election (1892), 29; support Conservatives (1895), 110
Limerick Board of Guardians, and reunion of Irish party, 207–9
Local government, 171n; Chamberlain's proposed scheme, 6; Local Government Act (1898), 197; Local Government Board, 318
Londonderry (City), Blake addresses meeting at, 22–3
Londonderry (County), disputes regarding seats, *see* "Omagh scandal"
Londonderry Sentinel, comments on Blake's speech at Londonderry, 23
Long, Thomas, 79

Longford (County), 21, 24, 27; financial relations meeting, 198
Longford (Town), 26–7, 28; Blake's speech at convention at, in support of evicted tenants, 36–8, 39n
Longford, North (constituency of), 27–8
Longford, South (constituency of), 29, 30; Blake to stand for, 20; Blake's election campaign in (1892), 21–8; Blake elected for, 28; Blake re-elected for, 136, 241n, 305; growing strength of Healyites in, 187; financial relations meeting in, 198; and general election (1906), 304–5; Blake's retirement as M.P. for, 325–8
Lords, House of, 309, 313, 321; rejects Home Rule Bill (1893), 68, 69
Louth, North, 27
Lucy, (Sir) Henry, 58–9, 329, 330–1
Lyons, F. S. L., 70n, 76n, 109n, 110n, 120n, 121n, 134n, 135n, 168n, 169n, 183n, 199n, 201n, 206n, 241n, 253n, 271n, 272n, 274n, 303n

McCartan, Canon M., 117
McCarthy, Justin, 12, 33, 35, 36, 69, 111, 338, 340, 341; elected chairman of anti-Parnellite party, 8; summary of career, 8n; and general election (1892), 11n, 22–3, 27–8; attitude towards Paris funds, 33; and Blake's fund-raising missions to Canada and United States, 34–5, 37, 73, 76–82; possible retirement of, 40–1; and Home Rule Bill (1893), 46–9, 66; and Blake's desire to resign from party committee, 48, 64–5, 84–6; and Tweedmouth incident, 87–97, 100–3, 104n; and "Omagh scandal," 115, 117–18, 121–31, 133, 135; resigns chairmanship of Irish party, 136; and Irish race convention, 165–6, 168; expresses regret at Blake's retirement, 328; attitude to British Empire, 334
MacDonnell, Sir Antony, 290, 312; and devolution proposals, 271, 309; and Land Bill (1903), 282–5, 339
MacDonnell, Dr. M. A., 137, 218, 271n; and Land Bill (1903), 282–4
McGuiness, F., 327n
McHugh, P. A., 231
McKean, John, 277n
McKenzie, Alexander, 14, 15
Mail and Empire (Toronto): condemns Blake's stand on Boer War, 248n; reports Toronto meeting attended by Redmond, 302; reports Toronto meeting attended by T. P. O'Connor, 308
Malloy, Bernard, 90
Marjoribanks, Edward, *see* Tweedmouth, Lord
Martin, C. E., 139, 142
May, Sir Erskine, 295
Mayo County: convention in, 111–12; and United Irish League, 198ff
Mayo, Lord, 275–6
Meath, Lord, 275
Millar, G. H., 28
Mills, David, 17, 20
Monahan, Peter, 28–9
Monck, Viscount, 13
Morley, John, 42n; elected for Newcastle, 32; and Home Rule Bill (1893), 44, 46–9, 62n, 66, 339; and financial relations question, 139, 162–3; attitude to Boer War, 247
Munster convention, and reunion of Irish party, 209–11
Murphy, John, 292n
Murphy, W. M., 116, 118, 128, 183n

Nation (weekly), Dublin: comments on Irish race convention, 176; comments on Blake's resolution on party funds, 180; bought by William Murphy, 183n

National Federation, *see* Irish National Federation

National League, *see* Irish National League

National Literary Society, representation at Irish race convention, 169

National Press (Dublin), 183; founded, 9; dispute regarding amalgamation with *Freeman's Journal*, 32–3

"New Departure," *see* Land question

New Zealand, 248; Blake's visit to, 136; choice of delegates to Irish race convention, 170

Newry Standard, 95

News (Toronto), condemns Blake's stand on Boer War, 247–8

Norris, William, 19n

O'BRIEN, J. F. X., 11n, 20n, 36n, 63, 77, 83, 85n, 119n, 253n; summary of career, 63n; and Tweedmouth incident, 88–9, 91–2, 96, 101–3; and "Omagh scandal," 120n, 121–3; and reunion of Irish party, 230; and relations between reunited party and United Irish League, 230, 236

O'Brien, K. E., 277n

O'Brien, Patrick: and financial relations question, 152; and reunion of Irish party, 210–13, 216, 222, 225, 231; and relations between reunited party and United Irish League, 236

O'Brien, William, 11n, 84, 86, 198n, 206–7, 250, 303, 338, 340; association with "Plan of Campaign," 7; summary of career, 7n; and Boulogne negotiations, 9; and Blake's desire to resign from party committee, 64–5, 85; and Tweedmouth incident, 97, 107; and Mayo convention, 112; and "Omagh scandal," 114, 117, 126, 128–9; and Blake's fund-raising missions to Canada and United States, 190n, 192; and United Irish League, 198–206, 208, 217–18; attitude to chairmanship of reunited party, 232–3; and relations between reunited party and United Irish League, 234–40; and general election (1900), 241; and expulsion of Healy from party, 242; and payment of members of party (1901), 256–7; attitude towards conciliation with Unionists, 272–3; retires from Parliament and National Directory of United Irish League, 272, 274, 291–2; and land conference (1902), 275n, 276; and Land Bill (1903), 282–3, 287–90, 339; and Cork writ, 293, 294, 296; re-elected for Cork City, 302; and Blake's retirement, 331

O'Callaghan, John, 263, 264n, 268, 307n, 311–12

O'Connell, Daniel, 28

O'Connor, Arthur: and Paris funds, 65; visit to United States and charges against Irish party committee, 71–5, 83–7, 122n, 126, 340; elected to party committee, 133–4; expelled from party committee, 137n, 168; and reunion of party, 212, 218

O'Connor, T. P., 52, 134–5, 291, 303, 312, 338; summary of career, 52n; and Tweedmouth incident, 88–9, 91, 94–7, 100; and "Omagh scandal," 117, 130; elected to party committee, 133–4; and financial relations question, 156; and reunion of Irish party, 211–12, 222, 228–9, 231, 339; and relations between reunited party and United Irish League, 238; attitude towards conciliation with Unionists, 272; and "step by step" home

rule policy, 307; visits United States and Canada, 308; and Irish Council Bill, 321; expresses regret at Blake's retirement, 328
O'Conor Don, the: and financial relations question, 139–42; and land conference (1902), 275
O'Donnell, Most Rev. Dr., Bishop of Raphoe, 171
O'Donnell, John, 277n
O'Driscoll, Florence, 71, 73–4, 83, 122n
O'Kelly, J. J., 213, 232
"Omagh scandal," 104n, 112–35, 340
Ontario, Province of, features of its legislature described by Blake, 45
O'Reilly, Frank, 191n
O'Shee, J., 277n

Pall Mall Gazette: comments on Blake's speech at Eighty Club, 31; comments on Blake's retirement, 330
Paris funds, 33, 38, 47, 65
Parnell, Charles Stewart, 10, 12, 17, 26, 30, 33, 37–9, 69, 72, 109, 232; elected chairman of Irish party, 4; elected President of Land League, 5; attitude towards Land Act (1881), 6; and divorce case, 8; and split in party, 8; and Kilkenny by-election, 8; opposition to, 9; death of, 9
Parnellites, 8–9; elect John Redmond leader, 10; and general election (1892), 10, 24, 26, 28–9, 172–3; Blake's attitude towards, 26, 37–8; and Paris funds, 33, 65; Canadian attitude towards, 34–5; American attitude towards, 35–6, 71–2, rumours of reunion with anti-Parnellites, 38–9, 58; and Tweedmouth incident, 90; and general election (1895), 110; and financial relations question, 147–56, 160, 163; and Irish race convention, 170–1, 175–7; attitude towards recess conference (1895), 198; and Longford meeting on financial relations, 198; and reunion with anti-Parnellites, 204–16, 218–20, 222–31; and election of chairman of reunited party, 232–3
People's Rights Association, 199; founded, 176; resolutions in opposition to, 177–83; replaced by United Irish League, 238; Healy refuses to disband, 240
People's Rights Fund: started, 176; resolutions in opposition to, 177–83
"Plan of Campaign," see Land question
Plunkett, Horace, 151–2, 163, 197–8
Political prisoners, amnesty for, 171n
Pomfret, John E., 280n
Power, P. J., 219, 223
Powerscourt, Lord, 275
Poyning's Act, 313, 317
Praed, Mrs. Campbell, 33, 46–9, 65
Preston, W. T. R., 16
Privy Council, Judicial Committee of, 187n, 318; Blake's practice before, 184, 343; suggested as judge on, 184; offered judgeship on, 186–7; question of Australian appeals to, 250–1; Blake gives up work for, 302–3; Blake seeks appointment to, 306; Blake accepts briefs in, 316
Protestant Episcopal Church in Ireland, disestablishment of, 4
Public Works, Department of, 318
Punch, publishes Lucy's comments on Blake's retirement, 330–1

QUEBEC, PROVINCE OF, 308; discussed in Home Rule Bill debate (1893), 60–2

REDMOND, JOHN, 290, 303, 304n, 305, 338, 341; elected leader of Parnellite party, 10; summary of career, 10n; and financial relations question, 138-9, 142, 151-3, 160; and Irish race convention, 170; and reunion of Irish party, 206-9, 213, 216, 218-20, 222, 224-5, 226n, 228-32; elected chairman of reunited party, 233; and relations between reunited party and United Irish League, 233-8, 240; and expulsion of Healy from party, 242; attitude to Boer War, 247; and Queen's visit to Ireland, 249-50; and payment of members of party (1901), 254-6, (1907), 257-9; speech on civil service estimates, 260; visits United States as United Irish League delegate, 263-6; attitude towards conciliation with Unionists, 272, 274; and land conference (1902), 275n, 276-7; and Land Bill (1903), 281-90, 339; and W. O'Brien's retirement, 291-2; and Cork writ, 294, 296-8, 300-2; visits Canada and United States, 302; and "step by step" home rule policy, 307; and Irish Council Bill, 309-14, 316-24; and Blake's retirement, 325-8; attitude to British Empire, 334

Rhodes, Cecil, 243-6
Rhodesia, 244
Robertson, T. E., 17n
Robinson, Sir Hercules, 244
Roche, Augustin, 294-5, 297
Roche, John, 112
Rosebery, Lord, 69, 126n, 247, 338
Ross, G. W., 18
Rowan, M., 18n
Royal Commission on the Financial Relations between Great Britain and Ireland: appointed, 139; members of, 139-40; terms of reference to, 140; work of, 140; majority report of, 140-2; separate reports of, 142; Sexton's report summarized, 142-6; Blake's memorandum summarized, 146-7; reaction in Ireland to report of, 147-9; attitude of government (proposed new commission), 149-50; conference to consider report of, 150-6; debate in Parliament on, 156-63

Russell, T. W.: visits Canada, 60; speech against Home Rule Bill (1893) refuted by Blake, 60-2; and land conference (1902), 276-7; and Land Bill (1903), 288
Ryan, Rev. Dr. Frank, 174-5, 189
Ryan, Hugh, 79, 185, 188-90
Ryan, Joseph P., 73n, 165-8

St. Stephen's Review, 38n
Salisbury, Lord, 29, 125, 138, 304
Saunderson, Colonel E. J., 151-5, 161, 163, 275
Scott, C. P., 329
Scottish Leader, 41n
Sexton, Thomas, 340; and Home Rule Bill (1893), 47-9, 63, 66; summary of career, 47n; and Tweedmouth incident, 97, 107n; and "Omagh scandal," 117, 121; re-elected to party committee, 133-4; refuses to be candidate for chairmanship of Irish party, 136; and financial relations question, 139, 141-8; and Irish race convention, 171; attitude towards conciliation with Unionists, 272; and Land Bill (1903), 291; and Irish Council Bill, 310-11; and Blake's retirement, 331
Shaw, William, 4n
Shawe-Taylor, Captain John, 275-6
Sheehy, David, 40-1
Skelton, O. D., 342n
Slattery, Henry F., 139, 142
Smith, Senator (later Sir) Frank, 34, 79, 188-90, 192
South Africa, 243; committee to inquire into Jameson raid, 244-6, 248-9; *see also* Boer War
Spencer, Lord, 44

Spender, J. A., 243n
Star (Toronto), 333n
Strathroy (Ont.), Blake's speech at, 193–5
Sullivan, Daniel P., 73n
Sullivan, James, 72n
Sullivan, T. D., 114, 117, 214
Sutherland, Sir Thomas, 139, 142

TANSILL, C. C., 281n
Thorold, Algar, 246n
Times, The (London): comments on Blake's speech at Eighty Club, 31; comments on Blake's maiden speech in British House of Commons, 59; and Tweedmouth incident, 102–5
Toronto World: reports opinions on Blake's Irish invitation, 17ff; reports Blake's trip to Ireland and election campaign there, 21–4, 26–8; reports comments on Blake's speech at Eighty Club, 31, 32
Transvaal, 243–4, 246–7
Tully, Jasper, and Cork writ, 292–9, 301–2
Tweedmouth incident, 86–108, 129
Tweedmouth, Lord, and contributions to Irish party funds, 87, 89–90, 92–9, 102–6, 108
Tyrone County: dispute regarding seats, see "Omagh scandal"

UITLANDERS, 243–4, 246
Ulster Unionists, see Irish Unionists
Union: dissatisfaction at, in Ireland, 3; Act of, 63; financial relations between Great Britain and Ireland under Act of, 138, 140–1, 143–5, 157ff
Unionists, 110, 335–6; and "Omagh scandal," 114; and financial relations question, 159–63; and policy of "killing home rule with kindness," 197; attitude to Jameson raid, 245; policy towards Ireland (1901–2), 259–63, 270; and Irish land policy (1902–3), 270, 279–85, 288–9, 339; attitude to devolution proposals, 270–1; dissension in ranks of, 273; defeat of government, 304; and general election (1906), 306; see also Irish Unionists
United Irish League, 7n, 256, 270ff, 324n; founded, 199; attitude of Irish leaders towards, 199–206, 217–18, 222–3, 227, 230–1, 234–40; spread of, 202–3, 205, 259; relations with reunited party, 230–1, 233–42; becomes national organization, 238; Redmond elected President of, 238; and general election (1900), 241; attitude of Unionist government towards, 259–60; sends delegates to convention in United States, 263; W. O'Brien resigns from National Directory of, 272; South Longford branch and Blake's retirement, 326–7
United Irish League of America, 311; holds national convention at Boston, 263–5; holds convention at Philadelphia, 307–8
United Irish League of Great Britain, 268n, 305, 326
United States of America, 209, 335n; Blake's visits and fund-raising missions to, 35, 71–6, 77–8, 81–2, 96–8, 263–5, 268–9, 337; choosing of delegates for Irish race convention, 170; no appeal for Irish cause in (1897), 191; and fund-raising for United Irish League, 204; Irish leaders visit, 263–5, 266, 268–9, 308; constitution of, 315
University education, see Education

VAN DER POEL, JEAN, 244n
Victoria, Queen, 249–50

WALSH, J. C., 328n
Walsh, Most Rev. John, Archbishop of Toronto, 79; and Irish race convention, 167–8, 185; and

fund-raising in Canada for Irish cause, 188–90; tribute to Blake by, 192
Waring, Colonel, 160–2
Webb, Alfred, 135, 141n, 163, 328, 340
Welby, Lord, 139–40, 142
Westminster Gazette, 57n; comments on Blake's retirement, 330
Westport (Co. Mayo), 198; United Irish League founded at, 199
Whitehall Review, comments on Blake's speech at Eighty Club, 32n
Whittaker, T. P., 160–1

Willison, J. S., 16, 163, 195
Wolff, G. W., 139, 142
Wolmer, Lord, 107
Wyndham, George: speech on civil service estimates, 260–1; and Land Purchase Bill (1902), 270; and devolution proposals, 271; resigns as Irish Chief Secretary, 273; and Land Bill (1903), 279, 282, 288, 339

YOUNG IRELAND SOCIETIES, representation at Irish race convention, 169
Young, James, 19n